Creative and Innovative Approaches to the Science of Management

Recent Titles in
The IC² Management and Management Science Series

Ordinal Time Series Analysis: Methodology and Applications in Management
Strategy and Policy
Timothy Ruefli, editor

Telecommunications Deregulation: Market Power and Cost Allocation Issues
John R. Allison, editor

Economic Logistics: The Optimization of Spatial and Sectoral Resource,
Production, and Distribution Systems
Sten Thore

Generating Creativity and Innovation in Large Bureaucracies
Robert Lawrence Kuhn, editor

Creative and Innovative Approaches to the Science of Management

Edited by
Yuji Ijiri

The IC² Management and Management Science Series, Number 5
W. Cooper and George Kozmetsky, Series Editors

Quorum Books
Westport, Connecticut • London

Library of Congress Cataloging-in-Publication Data

Creative and innovative approaches to the science of management /
   edited by Yuji Ijiri.
      p.   cm.—(The IC² management and management science series,
   ISSN 1058-5036 ; no. 5)
   Includes bibliographical references and index.
   ISBN 0-89930-642-X (alk. paper)
   1. Creative ability in business.   2. Industrial management.
I. Ijiri, Yuji.   II. Series.
HD53.C73   1993
658—dc20   91-44607

British Library Cataloguing in Publication Data is available.

Library of Congress Catalog Card Number: 91-44607
ISBN: 0-89930-642-X
ISSN: 1058-5036

First published in 1993

Quorum Books, 88 Post Road West, Westport, CT 06881
An imprint of Greenwood Publishing Group, Inc.

Printed in the United States of America

The paper used in this book complies with the
Permanent Paper Standard issued by the National
Information Standards Organization (Z39.48-1984).

10 9 8 7 6 5 4 3 2 1

Contents

Tables and Figures   ix

Preface   xv

Acknowledgments   xxiii

Part I: Accounting and Control

1   Variance Analysis and Triple-Entry
    Bookkeeping   3
        Yuji Ijiri

2   Accounting for Productivity Gains   27
        Rajiv D. Banker

3   On Assessing Internal Controls   43
        Ray G. Stephens

Part II: Computers and Decision Support

4   Qualitative and Causal Reasoning in
    Auditing   67
        Andrew D. Bailey, Jr.
        Yihwa Kiang
        Benjamin Kuipers
        Andrew B. Whinston

5   Implementation of Decision Support
Systems: An Empirical Study of Japanese
Production Control Systems   115
> Takehiko Matsuda
> Toshizumi Oota
> Toshiyuki Sueyoshi

6   Model Representation in Information
Resources Management   135
> Cheng Hsu
> William A. Wallace

Part III: Resource Management

7   Integrated Modeling Systems for Corporate
Human Resource Decisions   159
> Richard J. Niehaus

8   Tradeoffs between Efficiency and
Effectiveness in Management of Public
Services   177
> Arie P. Schinnar

9   Sensitivity of DEA to Models and Variable
Sets in a Hypothesis Test Setting: The
Efficiency of University Operations   191
> Taesik Ahn
> Lawrence M. Seiford

Part IV: Organization Design

10   The Optimal Size of a Law Firm and the
Contingency Fee Decision   211
> Ferdinand K. Levy
> Gerald L. Thompson

11   A Fractal Analysis of Capital Structure   233
> Bertil Näslund

12   Applying the Audit Risk Model to the
Organization Design of the Firm   249
> Arie Y. Lewin

Part V: Industry and Economy

13 Longitudinal Analysis of Industries: An
    Ordinal Time Series Approach   269
        Timothy W. Ruefli
        Ana R. Adaniya
        J. Armando Gallegos
        Seong-Joon Limb

14 An Analysis of the Financial
    Competitiveness of Defense Industry Firms   299
        William F. Bowlin

15 A Multiregional Model for India, 2000 A.D.   327
        Ranajit Dhar
        Sanjay Goel
        M. R. Rao

Part VI: Programming Models

16 Improved Linear and Integer Programming
    Models for Discriminant Analysis   365
        Fred Glover

17 Chance-Constrained Programming with
    Stochastic Processes as Parameters   397
        Raj Jagannathan

18 Single Machine Total Tardiness Problem
    Revisited   407
        Wlodzimierz Szwarc

Part VII: Methodological Issues

19 Multiple Criteria Decision Making and
    Negotiating: Some Observations   423
        Stanley Zionts

20 Bootstrapping: Implications for Decision
    Making   441
        Sheryl E. Kimes

21   Methodological Issues in Testing
      Contingency Theories: An Assessment of
      Alternative Approaches   453
         Anil K. Gupta
         Vijay Govindarajan

Bibliographical Essay   473

Author Index   479

Subject Index   489

About the Editor and Contributors   499

Tables and Figures

TABLES

1.1	Wealth Statement	4
1.2	Wealth-Income Statement	6
1.3	Income-Variance Statement	10
1.4	Income-Action Statement	15
1.5	Momentum-Impulse Statement	19
1.6	Momentum-Impulse Statement: Modified	21
1.7	Balance Sheets and Change Sheets	23
2.1	Estimation Results for Direct Labor	39
2.2	Estimation Results for Indirect Labor	40
5.1	Control Indices	126
5.2	Determining Factors by Factor Analysis	128
5.3	Information Systems and Control Indices	129
9.1	Experimental Design	199
9.2	Inputs: FacSal, PhyInv, OvhdExp; Outputs: UG-FTE, Grad-FTE	200
9.3	Inputs: FacSal, PhyInv, OvhdExp; Output: Total-FTE	201
9.4	Inputs: FacSal, PhyInv, OvhdExp, UG-FTE, Grad-FTE; Outputs: UG-Deg, Grad-Deg, Grants	202
9.5	Inputs: FacSal, PhyInv, OvhdExp, UG-FTE, Grad-FTE; Outputs: Total-Deg, Grants	203

10.1   Expected Profits, Optimal Hires, and Cost
       of Uncertainty Using a Normal
       Approximation to the Poisson Distribution
       for Different Billing Ratios and Various
       Means   216
10.2   Plantiff's Expected Gains and Maximum
       Costs from Litigation Expressed as a
       Percentage of the Most Likely Outcome   220
10.3   Expected Returns from Taking Cases on
       Contingency Fee Basis: $Y = 100$, $\alpha = 1/3$ 222
10.4   Expected Returns from Taking Cases on
       Contingency Fee Basis: $Y = 100$, $\alpha = 2/5$ 224
10.5   Minimum Values of p and p* for
       Contingency Fee Cases to Be Acceptable
       at Various Risk Levels   227
11.1   The Optimal Debt Ratio   242
12.1   Retrospective Summary of Inherent and
       Control Risk of the H.J. Heinz Company   252
12.2   Relationships among Environmental
       Uncertainty, Resource Dependency, and
       the Assessment of Combined Risk   255
14.1   Output and Input Variables   305
14.2   Financial Competitiveness Statistical
       Analysis—Aerospace Defense versus
       S&P 500   309
14.3   Financial Competitiveness Statistical
       Analysis—Aerospace Defense versus Dow
       Jones   311
15.1   Parameter Values   342
15.2   Transportation Costs (in Rs. per Rs. 1000
       of output transported) at 1984-85 Prices   343
15.3   Average Interregional Distance   344
15.4   Sectoral Post-Terminal/Maximum
       Specified Growth Rates of Output for Each
       Region and Gestation Lag (in years)   345
15.5   Sectoral Specified Per Capita
       Consumption Growth Rate for Each
       Region   346
15.6   Macro-Economic Balances (in Rs. Crores
       [10 million] at 1984-85 Prices)   347
15.7   Sectoral Gross Output for Each Region (in
       Rs. Crores [10 million] at 1984-85 Prices)   350
15.8   Sectoral Per Capita Consumption (in Rs. at
       1984-85 Prices)   351
15.9   Domestic Trade between Regions (in Rs.
       Crores [10 million] at 1984-85 Prices)   353

15.10   Changes in the Direction of Net Domestic
        Trade (in Rs. Crores [10 million] at 1984-
        85 Prices)   357
16.1   The Coordinates and the Penalties for
       Being Classified in the Wrong Group   371
19.1   The Discrete Points Used and Their
       Objective Function Values   426

FIGURES

4.1   Model-Based Reasoning in a Generate-
      and-Test Cycle   71
4.2   Abstraction from the Real-World System
      to Qualitative Models   73
4.3   Analytical Review Process   75
4.4 S^+ Function for $Y = S^+(X)$ $(x^1\,y^1)$ $(x^2\,y^2)$ 78
4.5   Cash-Flow Model   79
4.6   Complete Description of the Qualitative
      Structure of Cash Flow Model I   83
4.7   Cash-Flow Model I   85
4.8   Qualitative Graph of the Sequence of
      Qualitative Magnitudes of X   86
4.9   Propagating through the Cash-Flow
      Model   92
4.10   Complete Description of the Qualitative
       Structure of Cash-Flow Model II   100
4.11   Cash-Flow Model II   101
4.12   Complete Qualitative Description of Three
       Possible Initial States   105
5.1   Management Control Systems   124
5.2   Proposition Regarding DSS
      Implementation   125
5.3   Results of Chi-Square Test (Relationships
      among Computerized Control Indices,
      MCS Subsystems, and Performances)   130
6.1   Influence Diagram of the Response to the
      Exxon Valdez Oil Spill   139
6.2   SER Model for GIRD   145
6.3   Global Information Resources Dictionary
      (GIRD) OER   149
6.4   The Structured Modeling Approach to
      Model Representation   151
6.5   Model Resources Representation in GIRD   152
7.1   Integrated Human Resource Planning—
      Event Flow Approach   162
7.2   Integrated Human Resource Planning—
      Goal Programming Approach   163
7.3   Human Resource Planning Process   165

7.4   Microcomputer Optimization Model
      Operation   171
8.1   Outcome Effectiveness versus Resource
      Effectiveness   179
8.2   Cost Efficiency versus Effectiveness   180
8.3   Average Program Effectiveness by Level
      of Productivity and Efficiency   181
8.4   Relationship between Service Amount V
      and $\partial P/\partial V$, P Being Probability of
      Attaining Service Goals   187
8.5   Relationship between Service Amount V
      and Probability P of Attaining Service
      Goals   187
8.6   Relationship between Effectiveness and
      Efficiency   188
10.1 Expected Lawyer-Hour Demand Profile
      for a Case during the Planning Horizon   229
10.2 Total Cumulative Lawyer-Hour Demand
      Profile during the Planning Horizon   230
11.1 Construction of the Triadic Cantor Set   235
11.2 Grouping of Projects   235
11.3 Two Investments Forming a Group   237
11.4 The Relationship between p_n and p_{n-1} 239
11.5 An Organization with Three Lower
      Departments   245
12.1 Modeling the Design of Organizations   251
13.1 Transition Matrix (p_{ij} = The Frequency
      of Observed Transitions from Rank i to
      Rank j)   272
13.2 Partitioning of Total Uncertainty   274
13.3 Aluminum Industry Ordinal Behavior   276
13.4 Computer and Office Equipment Industry
      Ordinal Behavior   277
13.5 General Industrial Products Industry
      Ordinal Behavior   278
13.6 Petroleum Industry Ordinal Behavior   279
13.7 Pharmaceutical Industry Ordinal Behavior   280
13.8 Total Uncertainty for Entire Sample of
      Industries   281
13.9 Interindustry Risk for Sample of 101
      Industries   283
13.10 Hierarchical Context for Analysis   284
13.11 Petroleum Industry Total Uncertainty   286
13.12 Petroleum Industry Strategic Risk   287
13.13 Pharmaceutical Industry Total Uncertainty   288
13.14 Pharmaceutical Industry Strategic Risk   289
14.1 Procurement Policy Revisions   300
14.2 S&P 500 versus Aerospace Defense
      Financial Competitiveness Test Statistics   310

14.3 Dow Jones versus Aerospace Defense
      Financial Competitiveness Test Statistics   312
16.1 Group 1 and Group 2 Points with
      Misclassification Penalties   372
18.1 Adjacent Precedence Matrix of Example 1   412
18.2 Adjacent Precedence Matrix of Example 2   414
19.1 Discrete (a) and Continuous (b) Decision
      Variable Spaces   425
19.2 Discrete and Continuous Objective
      Function Spaces   427
19.3 Weight Space   429
19.4 Party Space   430
19.5 Party Weight Space   431
19.6 An Example of a Negotiation   432
19.7 An Edgeworth Box   434
19.8 A Convex Dominated Solution That Is
      Pareto Optimal   436
20.1 Bootstrapping Procedure   442
21.1 Alternative Contingency
      Conceptualizations   455
21.2 Complementary Representations of an
      Isomorphic Contingency Relationship   456
21.3 Alternative Representations of Non-
      Isomorphic Contingency Relationships   457
21.4 Multiplicative Interaction Approach:
      Mathematical Representation of
      Alternative Contingency Scenarios   464

To William W. Cooper

Our mentor and a founding father
of the Science of Management

Preface

This collection explores creative and innovative approaches to the science of management. All of the authors believe that research in management should be based on scientific grounds, in the sense of being general. However, such research must also exhibit a strong orientation toward applications with accompanying theoretical or methodological developments. All these chapters are creative in their own right, but, more importantly, they provide a rigorous foundation for further creativity and innovation in management practice and in management science. The following synopses make it clear that all of the chapters apply this approach to. a broad range of topics that are of interest to management.

The book is divided into seven parts. The first section, Accounting and Control, deals with creative and innovative approaches to accounting and control. The chapter by Ijiri, "Variance Analysis and Triple-Entry Bookkeeping," extends the conventional double-entry bookkeeping framework logically to a triple-entry systems. In the single-entry bookkeeping era, merchants could prepare balance sheets, but not income statements, in an integrated manner. Double-entry bookkeeping changed this state of affairs by requiring that every change in net assets resulting from operations be accounted for by income accounts, thereby linking "what happened," as reflected in changes on the balance sheet, with "explanations" in an income statement as to "why they occurred." This chapter focuses on an extension of double-entry bookkeeping to triple-entry bookkeeping by providing a systematic basis for the analysis of changes between two income statements, thus "explaining" why the changes occurred. The way in which this is accomplished can be regarded as a generalization of customary variance analyses in present-day cost accounting to the entire set of income statement accounts. These extensions to a triple-entry system are aided by introducing a new system of accounting concepts, which can be called "momentum accounting," in which all transactions are recorded not in dollar units, but in dollars per month. In this way the record keeping associated with momentum accounting can be said to deal with creation and dissipation of income momentum.

In the second chapter, "Accounting for Productivity Gains," Banker makes the. distinction between sustainable productivity gains due to process improvements and temporary efficiency fluctuations due to environmental variations. He accomplishes this by developing parametric and nonparametric models to separate sustainable productivity gains and temporary efficiency fluctuations. An interpretation is presented by means of accounting variances. The concepts in the chapter are demonstrated in terms of an actual application, using production data collected from a plant that employs a mature technology. The methodology developed by Banker, as reported in this chapter, contributes to the serious need of management to identify productivity gains for strategic, operational, and control decisions in such a way that gains are measured objectively with an accompanying theoretical and analytical basis, which makes the resulting measurements managerially meaningful.

In the third chapter, "On Assessing Internal Controls," Stephens provides an in-depth survey of accounting literature—academic as well as practitioner and official as well as unofficial—that is concerned with assessing the effectiveness of internal controls. Results from this survey are then compared to actions taken by the Securities and Exchange Commission with respect to requirements for public disclosures, which now take the form of a management report incorporated in the annual corporate report in order to disclose the results of such management assessments and the involvement of independent accountants with such assessments. Stephens documents the need for carefully developed criteria that management can use to assess internal control and goes on to evaluate the role of independent accountants and the benefits of such disclosures to users of the corporate reports. This is an important issue of public policy that is often debated—sometimes with confusion and generally without a proper theoretical foundation such as this chapter provides.

Part II of this book, Computers and Decision Support, starts with a chapter by Bailey, Kiang, Kuipers, and Whinston, entitled "Qualitative and Causal Reasoning in Auditing." This chapter explores the use of qualitative and causal reasoning in physical systems and provides a new way for auditors to strengthen their decisions in the analytical review portion of audit planning. The potential of this new technique, based on qualitative and causal approaches to predicting the dynamic behavior of physical systems, is illustrated in this chapter by means of a qualitative simulation model (QSIM) coupled with causal reasoning. The chapter compares this approach with currently popular "expert system" approaches to auditing and highlights the greater potential of this new technique.

In Chapter 5, "Implementation of Decision Support Systems: An Empirical Study of Japanese Production Control Systems," Matsuda, Oota, and Sueyoshi report the results of a survey of twenty-one Japanese manufacturing firms regarding the impact of implementing decision support systems in fifty-seven mainframe computer systems for production control. Specifically, the survey examined this impact on eight subsystems: (1) information, (2) responsibility, (3) goal-setting, (4) measurement, (5) evaluation, (6) incentive, (7) standard-setting, and (8) education. Two types of information systems (schedule control systems and man-hour control systems) were found to have influence over decision making for administrative control activities that was sufficient to affect the performance of subordinates.

In Chapter 6, "Model Representation in Information Resources Management," Hsu and Wallace work from a perspective in which formal models are regarded as an integral part of enterprise information resources and argue that these model resources should be represented and managed together with data resources and knowledge resources. This means that model structures should be defined at the same levels as data and knowledge and should include the interrelationships of these three types of resources. This leads to the development of a "metadatabase" as an organizationwide repository of all information resources. A representation of such a metadata structure, the global information resources dictionary (GIRD) model, is illustrated in the chapter.

Part III, Resource Management, examines resource management from human, economic, and financial perspectives. Chapter 7, "Integrated Modeling Systems for Corporate Human Resource Decisions," highlights the need for integrated modeling systems for human resource decisions in corporations and government agencies and Niehaus's experience with both civilian and military manpower planning for the U. S. Navy to demonstrate what can be accomplished by such an integrated modeling approach. The chapter also provides examples of integrated human resources modeling systems, such as the models developed at Mare Island Naval Shipyard. It then discusses the importance of the evolution of the information systems needed to carry out such integrated human resource modeling systems and emphasizes that with the development of microcomputer systems, integrated models for human resource management can be largely based at desktop workstation.

To properly manage any kind of resources, managers must have methods for evaluating efficiency and effectiveness, and Chapter 8, "Tradeoffs between Efficiency and Effectiveness in Management of Public Services," addresses this issue. In some studies, efficiency and effectiveness in the management of public services have been regarded as being negatively correlated. Schinnar provides a model that shows how this can occur, but at the same time he also shows situations where efficiency and effectiveness can be positively correlated. This provides not only insight for researchers, but also guidance for practitioners. Here efficiency is defined as a ratio of service activities to resources utilized, and effectiveness is defined in terms of outcomes relative to service activities. A simple model is formulated to show how, under quite reasonable conditions, the highest level of service effectiveness can be attained at moderate levels of efficiency. Beyond this level, efficiency and effectiveness are competitive, while below this level, the two are complementary.

Next is Ahn and Seiford's. "Sensitivity of DEA to Models and Variable Sets in a Hypothesis Test Setting: The Efficiency of University Operations," which focuses on issues of efficiency and effectiveness in comparing the performance of private and public universities. Conventional econometric approaches to estimating production functions involve a priori specification of a hypothesized parametric form, after which a set of parameter values is estimated. This choice of a functional form colors the analyses. Data envelopment analysis (DEA) offers a better alternative for studying these criteria because it does not require explicit specification of particular functional relationships between the inputs and the outputs. However, DEA could be modeled in several different ways—that is, ratio, additive, and multiplicative models—and this choice might affect the resulting evaluations along with the choice of alternate criteria. Using data from 153 universities, however, this study reports that the results are not sensitive to the choice of model—and thus are not affected by these choices—but the results are sensitive to the choice of variable set and hence to the criteria used. Of particular significance is the finding that public universities are more efficient than private universities when more highly visible output variables, which can be easily monitored, are used.

Part IV, Organization Design, opens with Levy and Thompson's "The Optimal Size of a Law Firm and the Contingency Fee Decision," which deals with the size decision for a law firm where a balance must be struck between unbilled hours, which result from having excess human resources, and lost billings, which could result from not having enough human resources. Using a simple form of statistical-probability distribution to represent the arrival of new clients or cases, Levy and Thompson first present a simple optimization case. They then complicate the situation in order to consider income from referral fees, which a firm may earn by referring excess demand to other firms. Finally, they cover conditions under which a law firm may be willing to accept a new client on a contingency fee basis. A general approach is thus provided for all of these possibilities, which evidently can bear on the issue of optimal size under varying policy constraints and possibilities.

Näslund's chapter, "A Fractal Analysis of Capital Structure," provides new insights into hierarchical organization structures. In this chapter, a firm is assumed to have a hierarchical financial structure. The relationship between a unit at level n and its subdivisions at level n + 1 is assumed to be the same for all n. Then, borrowing ideas from fractal geometry, the probability of bankruptcy for the firm as a whole is derived from the probability of bankruptcy at lower hierarchy levels of firms or subdivisions of a firm. This approach, via fractal geometry, also yields a precise value for the optimal debt ratio, which depends on (1) the risk and return of the individual projects of the firm and (2) the form of the hierarchical structure of the firm.

The chapter by Lewin, "Applying the Audit Risk Model to the Organization Design of the Firm," emphasizes the need for coordinating audit risk with the design of the organization to be audited. Using an actual case of improper accounting practices at a large corporation, the chapter identifies the audit risk associated with a given form of organization and discusses ways to improve organization design by considering it from the audit standpoint from the beginning of the design process. The chapter also proposes a new research agenda in light of the observed deficiency in the coordination between organization design and audit risk.

Part V, Industry and Economy, opens with a chapter by Ruefli, Adaniya, Gallegos, and Limb, entitled "Longitudinal Analysis of Industries: An Ordinal Time Series Approach." The chapter uses rank-order statistics for 101 industries over a twenty-year period. The rank-order statistics used are assets, employees, equity, net income, revenues, return on assets, return on equity, return on sales, and research and development (R&D). The aim is to study changes in ranks that can occur from period to period and to identify underlying patterns. For this purpose, the entropy statistic is used to identify (and quantify) the uncertainty levels associated with the year-to-year rank transitions. Using this statistic, R&D expenditures were found to have the lowest level of uncertainty, which means that the R&D rank of any industry remained highly stable over time. Intraindustry rank statistics were studied for two of the industries covered. It was noted that the intraindustry rank analysis resulted in patterns quite different from those observed in the interindustry rank analysis. This suggests that intraindustry behavior and interindustry behavior are governed by different mechanisms.

The title of the chapter by Bowlin, "An Analysis of the Financial Competitiveness of Defense Industry Firms," describes the topic that he addresses. Over twenty laws enacted since 1982 have impacted on the procurement policies and procedures of the Department of Defense. The widely held belief that this has adversely impacted on defense industry firms has been buttressed by certain defense-industry-sponsored studies, which have found this to be the case. Using data envelopment analysis Bowlin compares the financial performance of aerospace defense firms with the firms included in the Standard & Poor's (S&P 500) stock market index. The results of this DEA study fail to corroborate the defense industry's findings. The supposed adverse impact on defense industry firms during the period covered was found to be no worse than the deterioration found in other firms represented in the S&P 500 index.

In the next chapter, "A Multiregional Model for India, 2000 A.D.," Dhar, Goel, and Rao present their results from a multiregional and multisectional optimizing model that they constructed for the Indian economy. This study differs from earlier attempts to study this problem because this model deals with the availability of basic needs satisfactions in all regions simultaneously in order to reduce the existing inequalities among regions in terms of per capita aggregate household consumption levels. An appropriate consumption target is selected, and gross domestic product (GDP) or value added is maximized to achieve a more equitable distribution of income across the regions. Trading and transport implications of the results are also analyzed. The empirical analyses carried out in this study show, among many other things, that it is possible to reduce the regional disparity in income and consumption substantially while, at the same time, sustaining a growth rate in GDP of 5 5 to 6 percent a year.

Part VI moves more toward a focus on methodological contributions to a science of management, which we have grouped under the title Programming Models. It starts with a chapter by Glover entitled "Improved Linear and Integer Programming Models for Discriminant Analysis." In a departure from the common methodology of statistics, a series of research efforts have begun to appear that try to capture the goals of statistical discriminant analysis in a collection of linear programming (LP) formulations in order to make such analyses applicable to many types of problems. Glover demonstrates that the full power of the LP discriminant analysis models has not been achieved because a previously undetected distortion had attenuated the quality of the solutions generated. Glover also shows how to eliminate the distortion and develops special properties of the resulting models that provide links between continuous and discrete solutions. A postoptimizing procedure is introduced to exploit these properties for use with an integer programming objective directed to minimizing the number of misclassifications. These results open a door to new possibilities for model manipulation and simplifications, which include the use of a successive goal method to establish a series of conditional objectives for improved discrimination.

The next chapter, "Chance-Constrained Programming with Stochastic Processes as Parameters," also covers programming models and methods. Jagannathan extends the usual chance-constrained linear programming models in which the parameters are usually assumed to be random variables with known distributions. In this chapter, the right-side parameters of the model are allowed to be more general stochastic processes. The properties and solution methods of the chance-constrained programs are discussed first for the case of the finite index set and then for the case of the continuous index set. While Jagannathan's study is restricted to static model (zero-order) rules of chance-constrained programming, it is possible to generalize the results to the case of random left-side parameters along with more general multistage chance-constrained programming models.

Szwarc's chapter, "Single Machine Total Tardiness Problem Revisited," deals with the well-known single machine total tardiness model in which the problem is to schedule jobs for a single machine that can process only one job at a time. The objective is to minimize total overdue days—that is, the sum of overdue days associated with each job. It has been shown that the problem can be decomposed into smaller subproblems thereby reducing computational complexity. This chapter presents a theory of the total tardiness problem based on a precedence relation concept that determines the ordering between adjacent jobs. It then discusses the decomposability of the problem, which is shown to depend on the adjacent precedence relation matrix. The use of this theory demonstrates that further improvement is possible and that the decomposition result obtained in this chapter can be improved even further by reducing the number of possible partitions.

Part VII, Methodological Issues, opens with Zionts's "Multiple Criteria Decision Making and Negotiating: Some Observations." This chapter explores similarities and differences between two types of problems: one is the problem of making decisions subject to multiple conflicting objectives (which is known as the multiple criteria decision-making problem), and the other problem involves negotiations among parties with disparate objectives. Both problems involve multiple objectives: in the former they all reside in a single decision-making unit, while in the latter they are spread among multiple decision-making units. In particular, Zionts explores the relationship between concepts of nondominated solutions and Pareto-optimal outcomes, as well as the desirability of both, and also considers ways in which Pareto-optimal solutions can be achieved in negotiations.

In the next chapter, "Bootstrapping: Implications for Decision Making," Kimes shows how bootstrapping, a relatively new nonparametric, computer-intensive, statistical method, can be used to obtain information about sample distributions, error terms, and model validity. Advantages over traditional statistical methods are examined. The term "bootstrap" originated when one sample was used to give birth to many samples. It is a distribution-free method that depends on computer uses, rather than on the mathematically closed-form solutions that are characteristic of classical (precomputer) statistical approaches. This chapter examines three types of applications: (1) the determination of the true error of the estimate, (2) the determination of the true probability distribution underlying the data, and (3) whether information can be gleaned from a small sample. Cost and time requirements for bootstrapping are examined, as are tradeoffs between the cost and the value gained from bootstrapping.

This section concludes with Gupta and Govindarajan's "Methodological Issues in Testing Contingency Theories: An Assessment of Alternative Approaches." The contingency perspectives that have been widely adopted in organizational research generally make results conditional upon some environmental contingencies, or lack of them. Various approaches have been employed for testing contingency hypotheses that are bivariate in nature—namely, one context variable and one design variable have a predicted interactive impact on some performance variable. This chapter undertakes an assessment of such approaches in the form of (1) the split-sample approach, (2) the residual misfit approach, and (3) the multiplicative interaction approach. The chapter concludes that the multiplicative approach is significantly superior to the other approaches. The authors also note that with this approach the problem of multicollinearity is really a nonissue, at least for the interval-scaled data that are commonly employed in organization theory research.

This book concludes with a bibliographical essay to provide guidance to readers who are interested in background or additional reading materials to gain further insight into the problems and issues presented in this book.

Acknowledgments

This book, dedicated to Dr. William W. Cooper, was prepared from papers presented at the Conference held on October 23–24, 1989 at Carnegie Mellon University in honor of Dr. Cooper on the occasion of his 75th birthday. All chapters of the book are authored or coauthored by his former students or colleagues, reflecting the depth and the breadth of his influence. We wish to thank IC^2 Institute of The University of Texas at Austin and the RGK Foundation for their sponsorship of the Conference and of the publication of this book. We also wish to express our personal gratitude to Ronya and George Kozmetsky of RGK Foundation for their warm and generous support and encouragement. Special thanks are also due to Linda Teague of IC^2 Institute and Mark Kane of Greenwood Publishing Group, Inc. for their excellent work in the production of this book.

Part I

Accounting and Control

1

Variance Analysis and Triple-Entry Bookkeeping

Yuji Ijiri

A COMPARISON OF SINGLE- AND DOUBLE-ENTRY DATA

In July 1989, the American Accounting Association published the author's monograph titled *Momentum Accounting and Triple-Entry Bookkeeping: Exploring the Dynamic Structure of Accounting Measurements*. This monograph was dedicated to Professor William W. Cooper on the occasion of his seventy-fifth birthday. The present chapter is a follow-up of this monograph, illustrating the basic concepts and structure of momentum accounting and triple-entry bookkeeping as applied to a manufacturing concern.

Accounting for manufacturing concerns offers a useful base for such an illustration because the practice of analyzing *variances* has been well founded in this field of accounting. As we shall see shortly, variance analysis provides a stepping stone by which we extend the existing double-entry bookkeeping system to a triple-entry system.

A concrete example may be most helpful in elaborating the key concepts and the structure of the new system we wish to explore. Consider a small manufacturer that makes standardized glassware. Table 1.1 shows the balance sheet (called a wealth statement in order that the term "balance sheet" can be saved for more generic use) of the company at the end of March, April, and May, 19x1.

The company's wealth (assets and liabilities) consists of cash, materials, finished goods, equipment, and loans (negative wealth). All purchases and

Table 1.1. Wealth Statement

Wealth Accounts	Cash	Materials	Finished Goods	Equipment	Loans	Total = Owners' Equity
Balance 3/31	$120,000	$180,000	$300,000	$1,200,000	($300,000)	$1,500,000
Changes in April	$20,000	$0	$0	($20,000)	$30,000	$30,000
Balance 4/30	$140,000	$180,000	$300,000	$1,180,000	($270,000)	$1,530,000
Changes in May	($78,680)	$64,800	($30,00)	$30,000	$30,000	$16,200
Balance 5/31	$61,400	$244,800	$270,000	$1,210,000	($240,000)	$1,546,200

sales are assumed to be made in case, and all expenses are also assumed to be paid in cash to simplify the illustration. The production process are such that there are no work-in-process at the end of each day. The owners' equity account contains the original contributed capital of $1,200,000 and cumulative income of $300,000 up to and including income in March 19x1, with no dividends distributed in the past since the inception of the company.

Table 1.1, which consists of only the wealth accounts at the end of each month (along with the amounts of changes during the month filled in as plugs), reflects the records that were kept by a merchant during the single-entry bookkeeping period. Using Table 1.1, the company can still determine net income in each month (e.g., net income in April is $1,530,000 less $1,500,000, which is $30,000, and net income in May is $1,546,200 less $1,530,000, which is $16,200), taking into account the fact that there have been no contributions by the owners or distributions to them in the form of dividends after the company was established. (If there were any, the net income could be adjusted easily for such contributions and distributions.) However, what is missing from these single-entry data is an explanation of *why* and *how* income was earned.

Virtually all economic and business data reported regularly today are of the same kind—namely, they are single-entry data. Take the Dow Jones Industrial Average. It is reported daily, hourly, and in fact continuously as changes occur. We may consider the stock prices of the thirty companies included in the average to be analogous to the wealth items listed in Table 1.1. No matter how frequently they are reported, they are still single-entry data because they report only what happened, with no explanations of why and how they happened.

The heart of the evolution of the double-entry system lies in developing income accounts and interlocking them with wealth accounts. What characterizes the double-entry system in conventional accounting is income accounts that explain the reasons for increases or decreases in net wealth. Table 1.2, the Wealth-Income Statement, depicts the essence of the double-entry system by listing wealth accounts in columns and income accounts in rows. Changes in wealth accounts are classified by the nature of each change and reported under various income accounts. Some changes that do not affect net wealth (zero income transactions), such as loan refunding and equipment purchases, are also included in the table for the sake of completeness.

Therefore, in order to present the Dow Jones Industrial Average double-entry data, we must have a set of explanatory accounts that state the reasons for the net gain or loss on the average. Such explanations may be highly subjective initially, but may be made gradually more objective by means of the development of conventions that standardize our reasoning. This is

Table 1.2. Wealth-Income Statement

Wealth Accounts	Cash	Materials	Finished Goods	Equipment	Loans	Total = Owners' Equity
Balance 3/31	$120,000	$180,000	$300,000	$1,200,000	($300,000)	$1,500,000
Income Accounts: April						
Sales	$440,000					$440,000
Materials	($90,000)					($90,000)
Labor	($120,000)					($120,000)
Variable Overhead	($30,000)					($30,000)
Fixed Overhead	($40,000)			($20,000)		($60,000)
Fin Goods Net Chg			$0			$0
Var. Selling/Adm	($40,000)					($40,000)
Fixed Selling/Adm	($70,000)					($70,000)
Loan Refunding	($30,000)				$30,000	$0
Equipment Purchases	$0			$		$0
Net Income: April						$30,000
Balance 4/30	$140,000	$180,000	$300,000	$1,180,000	($270,000)	$1,530,000
Income Accounts: May						
Sales	$441,000					$441,000
Materials	($148,000)	$64,800				($83,200)
Labor	($93,600)					($93,600)
Variable Overhead	($26,400)					($26,400)
Fixed Overhead	($45,600)			($20,000)		($65,600)
Fin Goods Net Chg			($30,000)			($30,000)
Var. Selling/Adm	($45,000)					($45,000)
Fixed Selling/Adm	($81,000)					($81,000)
Loan Refunding	($30,000)				$30,000	$0
Equipment Purchases	($50,000)			$50,000		$0
Net Income: May						$16,200
Balance 5/31	$61,400	$244,800	$270,000	$1,210,000	($240,000)	$1,546,200

exactly what has happened in accounting since the inception of the double-entry bookkeeping system.

Comparing Tables 1.1 and 1.2, we can see the difference in data usefulness between single-data and double-entry data, both for planning and for control purposes. For planning, the single-entry data in Table 1.1 allow the users only some statistical time series analyses. The data show only by how much the owners' equity was increased or decreased; hence, there is no hint as to whether the increase or decrease will recur in the future or whether it is due to some one time events. Projections into the future based on such data are often unreliable because they lack the reasoning based on analyses of flow data. On the other hand, the data in Table 1.2 show not only how much was gained or lost, but also how such changes happened. Based on the data on income accounts, projections into the future can be made with a much higher degree of confidence since the recurring nature of events can be judged much more reliably when events are grouped based on their homogeneity.

For control purposes, too, there is an overwhelming difference in usefulness between the two types of data. Single-entry data show only the results of what happened with no explanations,; there is very little chance that one can learn from the past data in order to promote the recurrence of desirable events or to avoid the recurrence of undesirable events. Single-entry data can still be useful, but for those who wish to steer things toward a better state, they are far less useful than data that may indicate how the system may be steered toward a better state. Double-entry data are intended to satisfy such needs by showing the causal relationship between the event that happened and the reason why it happened.

Following the terminology of scientific explanation, we may call wealth accounts *explanandum* (things to be explained) and income accounts *explanans* (explanations). Thus, in double-entry bookkeeping we have two sets of interlocking accounts, explanadum and explanans. Hence, by interlocking we mean that there is not even a one-dollar gain or loss that is left unexplained because the bookkeeping system cannot balance without full and complete explanations.

It is an overstatement to say that during the single-entry bookkeeping era there were no explanations of events that resulted in gains and losses. Some ad hoc explanation must have been made from time to time. Furthermore, each individual wealth account, such as cash, receivables, and payables, had been kept in its own ledger with some descriptions of the events that resulted in increases or decreases in the account. What is missing is, however, a *system* that brings about comprehensive explanations across heterogeneous accounts on a regular and systematic basis.

Before we proceed further, it may be worthwhile to examine Table 1.2 and explain some specific matters in the income accounts. The income accounts are arranged in rows in the same sequence as we normally see them in an income statement—namely, starting with sales followed by expenses. To streamline the illustration, however, production accounts are all stated by the amount of resources consumed, followed by a one-line adjustment for the net change in the finished goods account. Thus, the amounts of materials, labor, and variable and fixed overhead are all entered in the owners' equity account column based on the amount of resources consumed. Due to the linkage with wealth accounts, all amounts are shown in such a way that a positive number is a gain and a negative number is a loss from the owners' standpoint.

"Materials" in the Cash column shows the amount of raw materials purchased. In April, the amount purchased and the amount consumed happened to be equal. In May, there was a substantial inventory buildup, as indicated by the $64,800 entry in the Materials column. Fixed overhead in April and in May includes the $20,000 per month depreciation, as shown in the Equipment column. There was no change in the finished goods inventory in April (production equaled sales). Hence, for April, both the cost of goods manufactured and the cost of goods sold are $300,000 (which equals the sum of materials, labor, and variable and fixed overhead shown in the Owners' Equity column.) There was a drawdown of finished goods inventory in May. Hence, the cost of goods manufactured in May was $268,800, while the cost of goods sold in May was $298,900. Interest on loans is included in fixed selling and administrative expenses for simplicity. Loans are refunded at the rate of $30,000 per month. In May there was a cash purchase of equipment amounting to $50,000. Both loan refunding and equipment purchases yield zero income, but such zero-income accounts are also treated as a degenerated case of income accounts so that these accounts can be collectively called income accounts for the sake of simplicity.

INCOME-VARIANCE STATEMENT: A PRELIMINARY STEP

We are now ready to extend our system to triple-entry bookkeeping. Since the double-entry system was created from the single-entry system by joining and interlocking the income accounts with the wealth accounts, we may consider making income accounts explanadum—namely, things to be explained. We may then look for a set of accounts that explain the reasons for changes in income from one period to the next. Table 1.3 illustrates this by means of the income-variance statement, which offers a preliminary step toward developing what is called the income-action statement, which will be examined in the next section.

First, let us examine the format of the income-variance statement. Setting aside the first three columns, the table contains each of the eight income accounts in columns, but omits the two zero-income accounts—namely, loan refunding and equipment purchases—since they do not affect the net income, which we now wish to explain. The amounts shown in the row labeled "Income Statement: April" are all taken from the Owners' Equity Column of Table 1.2 for the month of April. Likewise, the amounts shown in the row labeled "Income Statement: May" are all taken from the same table for the month of May. In between are the explanations of why and how changes in the respective income account have occurred between the month of April and the month of May.

Such explanations are classified into a set of accounts called action accounts in later tables. In Table 1.3, however, they are all classified and measured by means of variances that have been traditionally developed in cost accounting. Such variance accounts offer a convenient base from which we can construct action accounts. At least for now, then, we may regard Table 1.3 as a first step toward a full-fledged income-action statement.

The company uses a standard cost system, under which all variances are closed to income of the month. For ease of illustration, we assume that operations in the month of April were used in determining the standards so that in this month's operation there were no variances between the actual and the standard. Such standards are shown in detail in the lower part of the table and are reflected in the rows titled "Sales Data: April" and "Production Data: April." To review such standards, note that the standard sales and production volumes are both 1,000 units per month. Standard selling price is $440 per unit, and standard cost is $300 per unit consisting of the following items:

Materials (10 pounds at $9/pound)	$90
Labor (5 hours at $24/hour)	$120
Variable Overhead ($30/unit)	$30
Fixed Overhead	
($60/unit = $60,000/1,000 production volume)	$60
Standard Production Cost per Unit	$300

Standard fixed overhead is $60,000 per month, and since the standard production volume is 1,000 units per month, allocated fixed overhead per unit is $60. The total of these production cost items yields the standard production cost of $300 per unit. In addition, standard variable selling and administrative cost is $40 per unit of sales and standard fixed selling and administrative cost is $70,000 per month or $70 per unit of sales at the standard sales volume of 1,000 units per month.

As shown in the row for "Income Statement: April," if everything were at standard, the company would have earned $30,000 for the month of May.

Table 1.3. Income-Variance Statement

	Units: Sales Volume	Units: Prod Volume	Sales	COGS: Materials	COGS: Labor	COGS: Variable Overhead	COGS: Fixed Overhead	COGS: Finished Goods Net Change	S&A: Variable Selling/Adm	S&A: Fixed Selling/Adm	TOTAL: Net Income
Sales Data: April	1000		$440.00	($90.00)	($120.00)	($30.00)	($60.00)	($300.00)	($40.00)	($70.00)	$30.00
Production Data: April		1000						$300.00			
Income Statement: April	1000	1000	$440,000	($90,000)	($120,000)	($30,000)	($60,000)	$0	($40,000)	($70,000)	$30,000
VARIANCES											
1. Selling Price Var			$45,000								$45,000
2. Sales Volume Var	-100		($44,000)					$30,000	$4,000		($10,000)
3. Var S&A Rate Var									($9,000)		($9,000)
4. Fixed S&A Exp Var										($11,000)	($11,000)
5. Prod Volume Var		-200		$18,000	$24,000	$6,000		($60,000)			($12,000)
6. Material Price Var				($14,800)							($14,800)
7. Material Usage Var				$3,600							$3,600
8. Labor Rate Var					($7,200)						($7,200)
9. Labor Usage Var					$9,600						$9,600
10. Var. Overhead Var						($2,400)					($2,400)
11. Fixed Overhead Var							($5,600)				($5,600)
NET VARIANCES	-100	-200	$1,000	$6,800	$26,400	$3,600	($5,600)	($30,000)	($5,000)	($11,000)	($13,800)
Income Statement: May	900	800	$441,000	($83,200)	($93,600)	($26,400)	($65,600)	($30,000)	($45,000)	($81,000)	$16,200
Sales Data: May	900		$490.00	($104.00)	($117.00)	($33.00)	($82.00)	($332.00)	($50.00)	($90.00)	$18.00
Production Data: May		800						$336.00			

10

	Units		Sales	Cost of Goods Sold					Selling & Adm Exp		TOTAL
	Sales Volume	Prod Volume	Sales	Materials	Labor	Variable Overhead	Fixed Overhead	Finished Goods Net Change	Variable Selling/Adm	Fixed Selling/Adm	Net Income
ACTUAL: May											
Q: Quantity Purchased (Material Only)				14,800lbs							
Q: Quantity Sold or Used			900	7,600lbs	3,600hrs	800	800		900	900	
U: Unit Price or (Cost)			$490.00	($10.00)	($26.00)	($33.00)	($82.00)		($50.00)	($90.00)	
T: Total Revenue or (Cost)			$441,000	($76,000)	($93,000)	($26,400)	($65,600)		($45,000)	($81,000)	
STANDARD: April Output =				800	800						
N*: Std Input Qty/Unit of Output				10lbs/unit	5hr/unit						
Q*: Quantity Sold or Used			1,000	8,000lbs	4,000hrs	800	1,000		1,000	1,000	
U*: Unit Price or (Cost)			$440.00	$9.00	$24.00	($30.00)	($60.00)		($40.00)	($70.00)	
T*: Total Revenue or (Cost)			$440,000	($72,000)	($96,000)	($24,000)	($60,000)		($40,000)	($70,000)	
VARIANCES: May over April											
PV: Price Variance = (U-U*)xQ or Q'			$45,000	($14,800)	($7,200)	($2,400)	($17,600)		($9,000)	($18,000)	
QV: Quantity Variance = (Q-Q*)xU*			($44,000)	$3,600	$9,600	$0	$12,000		$4,000	$7,000	
TV: Total Variance = PV + QV			$1,000	($11,200)	$2,400	($2,400)	($5,600)		($5,000)	($11,000)	

It turned out that actual income for May was only $16,200, a 46 percent loss in income compared with April or a standard month. Naturally, management asks, "What happened?"

Unfortunately, just as merchants in the single-entry era could not get a systematic explanation as to why their net wealth went up or down, present-day management in the double-entry era cannot get a systematic explanation as to why their income went up or down. To generate such explanations systematically as a part of the ongoing bookkeeping mechanism, we must have a triple-entry bookkeeping system. Table 1.3 is in fact a rudimentary form of a statement that could be generated if we had such a system aimed at explaining the reasons for income changes. In the absence of such a system, the best we can do is to construct a statement that might be obtained if we already had a full-fledged bookkeeping system based on triple-entry bookkeeping. Table 1.3 is one such result.

Let us consider how we might "account for" this significant decline in income. There may be numerous ways of doing this, but let us start with sales. The detailed data for the month indicate that at the beginning of May the selling price of the product was raised from $440 per unit in April to $490 per unit. Naturally, this had a negative impact on sales volume, resulting in a 10 percent decline from 1,000 units to 900 units. Thus, the sales revenue ended up showing a slight increase as a result of the price increase; namely, the May sales of $490 x 900 = $441,000 was higher than the April sales of $440 x 1,000 = $440,000 by $1,000. Since a reduction in volume should bring a reduction in cost of production, the decision to raise price seems to have been a success. To be more specific, the 100-unit reduction in sales volume brought about savings of $30,000 in cost of goods sold at the standard unit cost of $300 and $4,000 in variable selling and administrative cost. All in all, the price increase resulted in a contribution of $35,000 in income ($45,000 in price variance and -$10,000 in sales volume variance).

Unfortunately, $20,000 out of the $35,000 income contribution by the price increase was neglected by the increased variable and fixed selling and administrative expenses ($9,000 in variable expense rate change and $11,000 in fixed expense increase). Still the selling and administrative side alone would have produced a net profit contribution of $15,000.

There is, however, one more item to consider that may be indirectly related to the decision to increase the price. That is the production volume variance, which reduced income by an additional $12,000, making the net contribution merely $3,000 ($15,000 − $12,000). This production volume variance was caused by the 200-unit reduction in production volume in anticipation of the adverse volume impact of the price increase. Since the company must pay the $60,000 per month fixed overhead regardless of the actual production volume, a reduction in production volume from 1,000 to

800 means that there is $12,000 (20% of $60,000) underabsorbed overhead that must be charged to the income in May. This is the production volume variance.

Still, the company would have had a $3,000 increase in income were it not for some unfavorable rate and usage variances which collectively amounted to a $16,800 adverse impact on income. The net of the two items, $3,000 favorable and $16,800 unfavorable variances, accounts for the $13,800 income decline ($16,200 in May versus $30,000 in April).

In examining production variances, we note that material and labor usages were actually better than the standard, contributing $3,600 and $9,600, respectively, to income for the total of $13,200. It was all the other rate-related factors that collectively resulted in an income decline of $30,000. Of this, variable overhead ($2,400) and fixed overhead ($5,600) account for $8,000, and labor rate accounts for another $7,200. But the largest item was caused by the material purchase price variance ($14,800), which requires a closer analysis.

The price of the raw materials had been on the rise and the company decided to increase its stock in anticipation of the higher price in the future. The company bought 14,800 pounds of raw materials at $10 a pound. Only 7,600 pounds were consumed in production in May and the remaining 7,200 pounds were added to the inventory. Since the standard price for the raw materials is $9 a pound, the purchase of 14,800 pounds resulted in an unfavorable purchase price variance of $14,800—namely, ($10 – $9) times 14,800. We may regard $7,600 of this variance as the normal price variance associated with the purchase to replace raw materials used and the remaining $7,200 as resulting from the decision to purchase the extra volume in anticipation of the future price increase.

Some of these explanations are not directly tied to the underlying economic events, but are needed to reconcile the income effects of a particular accounting treatment that the company decided to use. For example, the production volume variance would not have arisen had the company been using direct costing. The raw material price variance for extra purchases would not be charged to this month's income had the company not segregated material price variance at the point of purchase. Nevertheless, what makes a statement like Table 1.3 useful is its completeness—every dollar change in income from one period to the next or between actual and standard must be accounted for. Hence, it is true that there may be some explanations that belong to accounting technicalities. Those who support comprehensive recording, however, favor full and complete explanations even though some of them are purely technical in nature. They fear that without the requirement of complete explanations the statement may No longer force people to look into the hard-to-explain discrepancies.

INCOME-ACTION STATEMENT: A MEANS-END ANALYSIS

We may not proceed from the income-variance statement to the income-action statement by regrouping the explanations so that they are more action-oriented. Table 1.4 shows the result of such a regrouping. Table 1.4 is exactly the same as Table 1.3, except for the middle portion that accounts for the income change.

The reasons for the $13,800 decline are divided into six actions, the first four being internal actions and the remaining two being actions by external forces. The internal actions are

A. **Selling Price Increase**: Management took actions to increase the product price.

B. **Production Volume Reduction:** Management decided to reduce the production volume, which turned out to be more than the actual reduction in sales due to the price increase.

C. **Production Efficiency:** Management took action to reduce materials and labor usage per unit of output.

D. **Material Excess Purchases:** Management decided to purchase raw materials that are not immediately needed because of the anticipated price increase.

The external actions are:

E.   **Factor Unit Cost Increase:** The unit costs of variable input factors increased due to the inflationary force in the market.

F.   **Factor Fixed Cost Increase:** The total cost of fixed input factors inceased due to the inflationary force in the market.

Having selected these six elements as explanatory items, we resolve some of the interactions among them by reasoning that may go as follows. First, we decide to split the production volume variance of $12,000 into the portions that would and would not have occurred if the company had made a perfect forecast of the demand under the new price and had tried to maintain the inventory volume at the same level as in the beginning. In this case, the production volume would have been set at 900 units, still a reduction of 100 units compared with the standard of 1,000 units observed in April. Since the production volume variance of $12,000 was caused by a 200 unit reduction, the variance should be split evenly between the two actions, A and B.

Action A, "Selling Price Increase," will be presented together with its impact of volume. Although it is debatable whether or not the actual reduction of 100 units is due solely to the price increase, we proceed on the assumption that it is. Then, this action receives credits: a gain of $1,000 in sales (net of volume reduction), a gain of $9,000 in materials (1,000 units times $9), a

Table 1.4. Income-Action Statement

	Units		Sales	Cost of Goods Sold					Selling & Adm Exp		TOTAL
	Sales Volume	Prod Volume	Sales	Materials	Labor	Variable Overhead	Fixed Overhead	Finished Goods Net Change	Variable Selling/Adm	Fixed Selling/Adm	Net Income
Sales Data: April	1000										
Production Data: April		1000	$440.00	($90.00)	($120.00)	($30.00)	($60.00)	($300.00) $300.00	($40.00)	($70.00)	$30.00
Income Statement: April	1000	1000	$440,000	($90,000)	($120,000)	($30,000)	($60,000)	$0	($40,000)	($70,000)	$30,000
ACTIONS											
A. Selling Price Increase	-100	-100	$1,000						$4,000		$29,000
B. Prod Volume Reduction		-100		$9,000	$12,000	$3,000		($30,000)			($6,000)
C. Production Efficiency				$9,000	$12,000	$3,000					$13,200
D. Material Excess Purchase				$3,600	$9,600						($7,200)
E. Factor Unit Cost Increase				($7,200)	($7,200)	($2,400)					($26,200)
F. Factor Unit Cost Increase				($7,600)			($5,600)		($9,000)	($11,000)	($16,600)
NET ACTIONS	-100	-200	$1,000	$6,800	$26,400	$3,600	($5,600)	($30,000)	($5,000)	($11,000)	($13,800)
Income Statement: May	900	800	$441,000	($83,200)	($93,600)	($26,400)	($65,600)	($30,000)	($45,000)	($81,000)	$16,200
Sales Data: May	900		$490.00								
Production Data: May		800		($104.00)	($117.00)	($33.00)	($82.00)	($332.00) $336.00	($50.00)	($90.00)	$18.00
ACTUAL: May											
Q': Quantity Purchased (Material Only)				14,800lbs							
Q: Quantity Sold or Used			900	7,600lbs	3,600hrs	800	800		900	900	
U: Unit Price or (Cost)			$490.00	($10.00)	($26.00)	($33.00)	($82.00)		($50.00)	($90.00)	
T: Total Revenue or (Cost)			$441,000	($76,000)	($93,000)	($26,400)	($65,600)		($45,000)	($81,000)	
STANDARD: April Output =				800	800						
N*: Std Input Qty/Unit of Output				10lbs/unit	5hr/unit						
Q*: Quantity Sold or Used			1,000	8,000lbs	4,000hrs	800	1,000		1,000	1,000	
U*: Unit Price or (Cost)			$440.00	($9.00)	($24.00)	($30.00)	($60.00)		($40.00)	($70,000)	
T*: Total Revenue or (Cost)			$440,000	($72,000)	($96,000)	($24,000)	($60,000)		($40,000)	($70,000)	
VARIANCES: May over April											
PV: Price Variance = (U-U*) xQ or Q'			$45,000	($14,800)	($7,200)	($2,400)	($17,600)		($9,000)	($18,000)	
QV: Quantity Variance = (Q-Q*)xU*			($44,000)	$3,600	$9,600	$0	$12,000		$4,000	$7,000	
TV: Total Variance = PV + QV			$1,000	($11,200)	$2,400	($2,400)	($5,600)		($5,000)	($11,000)	

gain of $12,000 in labor (500 hours times $24), a gain of $3,000 in variable overhead (100 units times $30), and a gain of $4,000 in variable selling and administrative expenses (100 units times $40), for the total gain of $29,000. This result may be reconciled with variances shown in Table 1.3 by taking the selling price variance ($45,000), the sales volume variance (-$10,000), and half of the production volume variance (-$12,000 times 0.5).

Action B, "Production Volume Reduction," shows a loss of $6,000, half of the production volume variance. Responsibility for this action must be analyzed further in order to properly attribute the loss to the right person or the division. It may very well be that the loss is beyond management's control and hence should be attributed to an external action.

Action C, "Production Efficiency," is one of the clear cases since it generally reflects the efforts by management and the workers to reduce waste and improve yield. The total is a gain of $13,200.

Action D, "Material Excess Purchases," is a result of the conscious action by management to stockpile raw materials. Whether this loss of $7,200, relative to the standard price, can save more money in the future is yet to be seen. At least this could be viewed as an investment that awaits the final settlement in a future month.

Action E, "Factor Unit Cost Increase," covers the price effects of all variable input factors. They are segregated from increases in fixed costs because of different cost behavior. The total loss is $26,200.

Action F, "Factor Fixed Cost Increase," covers the increase in all fixed costs, both the manufacturing and the selling and administrative costs. The total loss is $16,600.

Without these explanations by means of action accounts, management may be left in the dark as to whether this income decline is a tentative event or a symptom of a trend to be continued in the future. These explanations seem to point out the fact that the income decline was caused largely by the increase in price in the factor market. While management took action to compensate for it by increasing the product price, succeeding in increasing net contributions to income, this was not enough to overcome the cost increase.

Explanations such as the one stated in the previous paragraph are commonly observed in monthly or quarterly management reports presented to the boards of directors. They are invariably partial explanations, as against complete explanations, such as those demonstrated in Table 1.4. Using Table 1.4, we may still summarize narratively by highlighting major items in the income-action statement. This is, however, quite different from being satisfied with partial explanations from the beginning without a sound backup like Table 1.4.

Table 1.4 was prepared retrospectively after observing the income data over two periods. Additional data, such as price and quantity of input factors consumed, were obtained from various production and cost records. This is analogous to merchants in the single-entry era trying to construct something that resembles an income statement by means of bits and pieces of supplemental data after the beginning and ending balance sheets have been determined. Under the double-entry system, we have a systematic and continuous record of income accounts, and at the end of the period all we need to do is to take care of some end-of-period adjustments. What would be a counterpart of such a systematic and continuous recording for action accounts?

When we compare the income-action statement in Table 1.4 with the wealth-income statement in Table 1.2, we notice that they are not exactly comparable. This is because in the wealth-income statement *explanadum*—namely, wealth—is a set of stock variables, while in the income-action statement, explanadum (income) is a set of flow variables. Wealth can be specified at a single point in time, but income cannot be specified without fixing two points in time, the beginning and the ending of a period in which the flow took place.

Thus, changes in wealth can be accounted for by means of income accounts on a continuous basis, but changes in income cannot be accounted for before the two periods being compared are completed. This point gives rise to a new insight into the triple-entry bookkeeping system. If the conventional double-entry system was created by linking stock accounts called wealth with flow accounts called income as explanations for wealth change, would it not be possible to create stock accounts out of income?

It is certainly possible to take the time derivative of the income flow, obtaining not the income earned in a period, but the rate at which income is being earned at a single point in time—not the distance traveled by an automobile in a time period, but its speed at a given point in time, so to speak. We call such time derivatives of income elements *income momenta* or *momenta* for short. We call this new accounting system, focused on momenta, *momentum accounting*. In this accounting system, all events are recorded and reported not in a monetary unit, such as dollars, but in a monetary unit per unit of time, such as dollars per month. Then changes in net momenta are matched, under a double-entry framework, with *impulses*, which are considered to be the reasons for the momentum changes. We shall in the next section examine a momentum-impulse statement that links the two sets of accounts.

MOMENTUM-IMPULSE STATEMENT:
A DOUBLE-ENTRY SYSTEM FOR TIME DERIVATIVES

Let us examine a new statement shown in Table 1.5. It looks very much like Table 1.4; in fact, all figures in both tables are the same, but their measurement units are not. In Table 1.5 amounts per unit of product are all stated in dollars, but all other amounts are stated not in dollars, but in dollars per month (denoted by $/mo). Furthermore, the line titled "Income Statement: April" in Table 1.4 has been changed to "Momentum Statement: 4/30" in Table 1.5. A similar change has been made in the ending line titled "Income Statement: May," which is now "Momentum Statement: 5/31." Namely, what were flow amounts during a month in Table 1.4 have now been changed to stock amounts at the end of a month in Table 1.5. The same alteration is also observed in the variance details at the bottom of the table with respect to the time reference (instead of ACTUAL: May, STANDARD: April, and VARIANCES: May over April, we have ACTUAL: 5/31, STANDARD: 4/30, and VARIANCES: 5/31 over 4/30).

While the numbers may be the same, Table 1.5 focuses on a different dimension of the operations of the company, compared to Table 1.4. Let us interpret it step by step. The line "Momentum Statement: 4/30" states the rate at which income is being earned as of April 30. As of this date, the company was selling products at the rate of $440,000/mo. It was incurring costs (classified into six different types) at the total rate of $410,000/mo. These yield an income rate of $30,000/mo. Hence, if this state had been maintained throughout the month of May, the company would have earned $30,000 ($30,000/mo x 1 mo) for May. However, this momentum-impulse statement tells us that this was not the case.

The impulse section of the statement states that six different factors contributed to the changes in the revenue and expense momenta. They all occurred on 5/1, an important piece of information. (Later we examine a situation where this is not the case.) These impulses collectively changed net momenta from $30,000/mo to $16,200/mo, a reduction of $13,800/mo. No further changes in momenta occurred during the month of May; hence, the net momenta on 5/31 are $16,200/mo, the details of which are shown in the line called "Momentum Statement: 5/31."

Since the net momenta were $16,200/mo throughout the month of May, the income for the month of May was $16,200/mo x 1 mo = $16,200, as shown in all earlier tables. Similarly, the net momenta in April were maintained at the rate of $30,000/mo throughout the month of April (a fact that may be shown in the momentum-impulse statement for the month of April, which is omitted here); hence, the net income in April was $30,000, as shown in all earlier tables.

Table 1.5. Momentum-Impulse Statement

	Units		Sales	Cost of Goods Sold					Selling & Adm Exp		TOTAL
	Sales Volume	Prod Volume	Sales	Materials	Labor	Variable Overhead	Fixed Overhead	Finished Goods Net Change	Variable Selling/Adm	Fixed Selling/Adm	Net Income
Sales Data: 4/30	1000		$440.00	($90.00)	($120.00)	($30.00)	($60.00)	($300.00)	($40.00)	($70.00)	$30.00
Production Data: 4/30		1000						$300.00			
Momentum Stmt: 4/30	1000	1000	$440,000/mo	($90,000/mo)	($120,000/mo)	($30,000/mo)	($60,000/mo)	$0/mo	($40,000/mo)	($70,000/mo)	$30,000/mo
IMPLUSES: (All occurred on 5/1)	-100										
A. Selling Price Increase	-100		$1,000/mo						$4,000/mo		$29,000/mo
B. Prod Volume Reduction		-1000						($30,000/mo)			($6,000/mo)
C. Production Efficiency				$9,000/mo	$12,000/mo	$3,000/mo					$13,200/mo
D. Material Excess Purchase				$9,000/mo	$12,000/mo	$3,000/mo					($7,200/mo)
E. Factor Unit Cost Increase				$3,600/mo ($7,600/mo)	$9,600/mo ($7,200/mo)	($2,400/mo)			$9,000/mo		($26,200/mo)
F. Factor Fixed Cost Increase							($5,600/mo)			($11,000/mo)	($16,600/mo)
NET IMPLUSES	-200		$1,000/mo	$6,800/mo	$26,400/mo	$3,600/mo	($5,600/mo)	($30,000/mo)	($5,000/mo)	($11,000/mo)	($13,800/mo)
Momentum Stmt: 5/31	900	800	$441,000/mo	($83,200/mo)	($93,600/mo)	($26,400/mo)	($65,600/mo)	($30,000/mo)	($45,000/mo)	($81,000/mo)	$16,200/mo
Sales Data: 5/31	900		$490.00	($104.00)	($117.00)	($33.00)	($82.00)	($332.00)	($50.00)	($90.00)	$18.00
Production Data: 5/31		800						$336.00			

ACTUAL: 5/31

	Sales	Materials	Labor	Variable Overhead	Fixed Overhead	Variable Selling/Adm	Fixed Selling/Adm
Q: Quantity Purchased (Material Only)		14,800lbs/mo					
Q: Quantity Sold or Used	900/mo	7,600lbs/mo	3,600hrs/mo	800/mo	800/mo	800/mo	1,000/mo
U: Unit Price or (Cost)	$490.00	($10.00)	($26.00)	($33.00)	($82.00)	($50.00)	($90.00)
T: Total Revenue or (Cost)	$441,000/mo	($76,000/mo)	($93,600/mo)	($26,400/mo)	($65,600/mo)	($45,000/mo)	($81,000/mo)

STANDARD: 4/30   Output = 800/mo

	Sales	Materials	Labor	Variable Overhead	Fixed Overhead	Variable Selling/Adm	Fixed Selling/Adm
N*: Std Input Qty/Unit of Output	800/mo	10lbs/unit	5hr/unit	800/mo	800/mo	800/mo	1,000/mo
Q*: Quantity Sold or Used	1,000/mo	8,000lbs/mo	4,000hrs/mo	800/mo	800/mo	1,000/mo	1,000/mo
U*: Unit Price or (Cost)	$440.00	($9.00)	($24.00)	($30.00)	($60.00)	($40.00)	($70.00)
T*: Total Revenue or (Cost)	$440,000/mo	($72,000/mo)	($96,000/mo)	($24,000/mo)	($60,000/mo)	($40,000/mo)	($70,000/mo)

VARIANCES: 5/31 over 4/30

	Sales	Materials	Labor	Variable Overhead	Fixed Overhead	Variable Selling/Adm	Fixed Selling/Adm
PV: Price Variance = $(U-U^*) \times Q$ or Q^*	$45,000/mo	($14,800/mo)	($7,200/mo)	($2,400/mo)	($17,600/mo)	($9,000/mo)	($18,000/mo)
QV: Quantity Variance = $(Q-Q^*) \times U^*$	($44,000/mo)	$3,600/mo	$9,600/mo	$0/mo	$12,000/mo	$4,000/mo	$7,000/mo
TV: Total Variance = $PV + QV$	$1,000/mo	($11,200/mo)	$2,400/mo	($2,400/mo)	($5,600/mo)	($5,000/mo)	($11,000/mo)

Table 1.5 shows that as of 5/31 the company is earning income at the rate of $16,200/mo. This does *not* mean that the income in June will be $16,200; what it means is that *in the absence of any new impulses* the company will keep earning income at that rate and in that event the income for June will be $16,200. This is the base line, or status quo. If the actual outcomes turn out to be differences from this base line, we must account for the difference by making proper journal entries in momentum accounting.

Note the difference between conventional "wealth" accounting and this new "momentum" accounting. In wealth accounting, the status quo is zero income. Even if the net momenta stay at $16,200/mo throughout the month of June, $16,200 of income will be earned in June; hence, journal entries must be made to account for the departure from the base line and management performance in the amount of $16,200 will be recognized. This is not the case in momentum accounting. The $16,200 income earned in June is nothing but a realization (by the passage of time) of momenta created in earlier periods (possibly by the previous management) and is not viewed as a contribution made during the month of June, which occurs only if net momenta are changed.

This change in the perspective on performance is somewhat analogous to the change in perspective introduced by Newton's first law of motion. Before the introduction of this law, people regarded that "stillness" as the status quo and a moving object as moving only as long as a force is applied continuously. The first law of motion introduced a totally different way of viewing the motion—namely, that in the absence of force a moving object continues its linear motion with constant velocity. Previously, people had to look for reasons (forces) whenever they saw an object moving; now they do not necessarily look for reasons (forces) just because an object is moving.

With this in mind, we now look at Table 1.6, which is a momentum-impulse statement with some modifications from Table 1.5. Unlike Table 1.5, in which all impulses occurred at the beginning of May, we assume that the first three impulses occurred on 5/1 and the last three impulses occurred on 5/16. To be more precise, on 5/1 the company initiated the product price increase, cut the production rate, and introduced a program that improved production efficiency (impulses A, B, and C). On 5/16, all of the factor cost increases occurred, pushing the cost of materials from $9/pound to $11/pound, wages from $24/hour to $28/hour and so on as shown in the lower part of Table 1.6. The company, anticipating the factor price increase, started to stockpile materials. While this action started on 5/1, during the first half of the month it did not produce any changes in momenta since the material price was still $9/pound during the first half of the month. Hence, the effective date of the impulse D, "Material excess purchases," is shown as

Table 1.6. Momentum-Impulse Statement: Modified

	Units		Sales	Cost of Goods Sold					Selling & Adm Exp		TOTAL
	Sales Volume	Prod Volume	Sales	Materials	Labor	Variable Overhead	Fixed Overhead	Finished Goods Net Change	Variable Selling/Adm	Fixed Selling/Adm	Net Income
Sales Data: 4/30	1000		$440.00	($90.00)	($120.00)	($30.00)	($60.00)	($300.00)	($40.00)	($70.00)	$30.00
Production Data: 4/30		1000						$300.00			
Momentum Stmt: 4/30		1000	$440,000/mo	($90,000/mo)	($120,000/mo)	($30,000/mo)	($60,000/mo)	$0/mo	($40,000/mo)	($70,000/mo)	$30,000/mo
IMPULSES: (effective date)											
A. Selling Price Increase (5/1)	-100	-100	$1,000/mo	$9,000/mo	$12,000/mo	$3,000/mo			$4,000/mo		$29,000/mo
B. Prod Volume Reduction (5/1)		-100		$9,000/mo	$12,000/mo	$3,000/mo		($30,000/mo)			($6,000/mo)
C. Production Efficiency (5/1)				$3,600/mo	$9,600/mo						$13,200/mo
D. Material Excess Purchase (5/16)				($14,400/mo)							($14,400/mo)
E. Factor Unit Cost Increase (5/16)				($15,200/mo)	($14,400/mo)	($4,800/mo)			($18,000/mo)		($52,400/mo)
F. Factor Fixed Cost Increase (5/16)							($11,200/mo)			($22,000/mo)	($33,200/mo)
NET IMPULSES	-100	-200	$1,000/mo	($8,000/mo)	$19,200/mo	$1,200/mo	($11,200/mo)	($30,000/mo)	($14,000/mo)	($22,000/mo)	($63,800/mo)
Income Statement: May	900	800	$441,000/mo	($98,000/mo)	($100,800/mo)	($28,800/mo)	($71,200/mo)	($30,000/mo)	($54,000/mo)	($92,000/mo)	($33,800/mo)
Sales Data: 5/31	900		$490.00	($122.50)	($126.00)	($36.00)	($89.00)	($365.33)	($60.00)	($102.22)	($37.56)
Production Data: 5/31		800						$373.50			

ACTUAL: 5/31

	Sales	Materials	Labor	Variable Overhead	Fixed Overhead	Variable Selling/Adm	Fixed Selling/Adm
Q: Quantity Purchased (Material Only)		14,800lbs/mo					
Q: Quantity Sold or Used	900/mo	7,600lbs/mo	3,600hrs/mo	800/mo	800/mo	900/mo	900/mo
U: Unit Price or (Cost)	$490.00	($11.00)	($28.00)	($36.00)	($89.00)	($60.00)	($102.22)
T: Total Revenue or (Cost)	$441,000/mo	($83,600/mo)	($100,800/mo)	($28,800/mo)	($71,200/mo)	($54,000/mo)	($92,000/mo)
STANDARD: 4/30 Output =		800/mo					
N*: Std Input Qty/Unit of Output		10lbs/unit	5hr/unit				
Q*: Quantity Sold or Used	1,000/mo	8,000lbs/mo	4,000hrs/mo	800/mo	1,000/mo	1,000/mo	1,000/mo
U*: Unit Price or (Cost)	$440.00	($9.00)	($24.00)	($30.00)	($60.00)	($40.00)	($70.00)
T*: Total Revenue or (Cost)	$440,000/mo	($72,000/mo)	($96,000/mo)	($24,000/mo)	($60,000/mo)	($40,000/mo)	($70,000/mo)
VARIANCES: 5/31 over 4/30							
PV: Price Variance = (U-U*)xQ or Q'	$45,000/mo	($29,600/mo)	($14,400/mo)	($4,800/mo)	($23,200/mo)	($18,000/mo)	($29,000/mo)
QV: Quantity Variance = (Q-Q*)xU*	($44,000/mo)	$3,600/mo	$9,600/mo	$0/mo	$12,000/mo	$4,000/mo	$7,000/mo
TV: Total Variance = PV + QV	$1,000/mo	($26,000/mo)	($4,800/mo)	($4,800/mo)	($11,200/mo)	($14,000/mo)	($22,000/mo)

5/16, rather than 5/1 since the impact on momenta started on 5/16. The effective date of the two remaining impulses (E and F) is, of course, 5/16.

We can now look at the entire picture which is summarized in Table 1.7. On the left-hand side, the table shows the balance sheet (wealth statement) and the change sheet (income statement), both being statements prepared in wealth accounting. On the right-hand side, the table shows the balance sheet (momentum statement) and the change sheet (impulse statement), both being statements prepared in momentum accounting. Each of the two accounting systems follows its own double-entry bookkeeping system; yet, the two systems interlock rigidly, as indicated in the reconciliation of $16,200 in income for May with momenta and their changes in May shown in the lower part of Table 1.7.

Here, we see that the company had a terrific first half of the month, but a miserable second half. During the first half, the net momenta were $30,000/mo carried over from April, plus the impact of the three impulses A, B, and C totaling $36,200/mo, the two summing to $66,200/mo. This means that after 0.5 month the company earned $66,200/mo x 0.5 mo = $33,100. In the second half, however, these momenta of $66,200/mo carried over from the first half were drastically reduced by the three impulses D, E, and F, all coming from the factor cost increases, totalling a $100,000/mo reduction. The net momenta in the second half were thus -$33,800. This resulted in the second half income of -$33,800 x 0.5 mo = -$16,900. Combined with the first half income of $33,100 the income for the month of May became $16,200, as shown in all earlier tables.

By comparing the left-hand and the right-hand sides of Table 1.7, we note that momentum accounting provides much more timely data for planning purposes by giving management earlier warnings and much more action-oriented data for control purposes by relating data closely to managerial actions. For example, a comparison of the income statements for April and May indicates a decline of income from $30,000 to $16,200, a loss of $13,800. Should this trend continues linearly, the June income may be estimated to be merely $2,400 ($16,200 - $13,800). The momentum statement, on the other hand, shows a much more serious turn of events. In fact, in the absence of new events, the net momenta of 5/31 tell us that the company should expect a loss of $33,800. The reason for this discrepancy is that only half of the impact of the factor cost increase ($100,000/mo) was included in the May income. Thus, an additional loss of $50,000 must be anticipated in the June, causing a net loss of $33,800 ($16,200 – $50,000). Clearly, the momentum statement shows the urgency of the matter in a way that is not observable in the income statement.

Table 1.7. Balance Sheets and Change Sheets

Wealth Accounting

(Balance Sheet)
Wealth Statement as of 4/30/19x1

Cash	$140,000
Materials	$180,000
Finished Goods	$300,000
Equipment	$1,180,000
Loans	($270,000)
Owners' Equity	$1,530,000

(Change Sheet)
Income Statement for May 19x1

Sales	$441,000
Materials	($83,200)
Labor	($93,600)
Variable Overhead	($26,400)
Fixed Overhead	($65,600)
Finished Goods Net Change	($30,000)
Variable Selling and Adm Expenses	($45,000)
Fixed Selling and Adm Expenses	($81,000)
Net Income	$16,200

(Balance Sheet)
Wealth Statement as of 5/31/19x1

Cash	$61,400
Materials	$244,800
Finished Goods	$270,000
Equipment	$1,210,000
Loans	($240,000)
Owners' Equity	$1,546,200

Momentum Accounting

(Balance Sheet)
Momentum Statement as of 4/30/19x1

Sales	$440,000/mo
Materials	($90,000/mo)
Labor	($120,000/mo)
Variable Overhead	($30,000/mo)
Fixed Overhead	($60,000/mo)
Finished Goods Net Change	$0/mo
Var Selling & Adm Exp	($40,000/mo)
Fix Selling & Adm Exp	($70,000/mo)
Net Momenta	$30,000/mo

(Change Sheet)
Impulse Statement for May 19x1

A. Selling Price Increase	$29,000/mo
B. Production Volume Reduction	($6,000/mo)
C. Production Efficiency	$13,200/mo
Effective 5/1	$36,200/mo
D. Material Excess Purchases	($14,400/mo)
E. Factor Unit Cost Increase	($52,400/mo)
F. Factor Fix Cost Inc	($33,200/mo)
Effective 5/16	($100,000/mo)
Net Impulses	($63,800/mo)

(Balance Sheet)
Momentum Statement as of 5/31/19x1

Sales	$441,000/mo
Materials	($98,000/mo)
Labor	($100,800/mo)
Variable Overhead	($28,800/mo)
Fixed Overhead	($71,200/mo)
Finish Goods Net Chan	($30,000/mo)
Var Selling & Adm Exp	($54,000/mo)
Fix Selling & Adm Exp	($92,000/mo)
Net Momenta	($33,800/mo)

Reconciliation

	First Half	Second Half
Momenta as of 4/30	$30,000/mo	$30,000/mo
Impulses Effective 5/1	$36,200/mo	$36,200/mo
Impulses Effective 5/16		($100,000/mo)
Net Momenta for the Half	$66,200/mo	($33,800/mo)
Income for the Half (x0.5)	$33,100	+ ($16,900) = $16,200 Net Income for May

CONCLUSION

We started out with a series of balance sheets in Table 1.1, which were the primary source of financial data in the single-entry era. The double-entry bookkeeping system improved the nature of financial data drastically by requiring that every event change in wealth be accounted for by means of income accounts, as demonstrated in Table 1.2. As a step toward triple-entry bookkeeping, we examined in Table 1.3 an income-variance statement, incorporating variance analysis data. Using it as a stepping stone, we regrouped the data in Table 1.4 to obtain an income-action statement, which accounts for every net change in income by means of managerial or external actions that are judged to be responsible for the gains or losses. Thus, we show a system in which actions explain net changes in income, and, in turn, income explains net changes in wealth.

Based on Table 1.4, we created a momentum-impulse statement in Table 1.5 by changing the measurement units, while leaving the figures unchanged. Managerial interpretations of the resulting statement were shown to be quite different from those of the income-action statement because in Table 1.5 everything is stated in the time rate of income rather than the amount of income earned. In this table, all impulses that affected momenta were assumed to have occurred at the beginning of the month. In Table 1.6, this situation was modified so that half of the six impulses were assumed to have occurred in mid-month. The result, a drastically worsening performance, was shown on the momentum-impulse statement, but was not observable in the income-action statement. This point was highlighted further in Table 1.7, which summarized all four key statements; wealth, income, momentum, and impulse statements.

The logical step of evolution from double-entry bookkeeping to triple-entry bookkeeping lies in the development of a mechanism by which income changes are accounted for. In this chapter, we took advantage of variance analysis that has been developed in cost accounting. However, the basic factors in variance analysis are limited to price and quantity. Explanations for income changes strictly based on price and quantity factors are rather limited, and many more varieties of explanations, such as statistical and econometric reasoning, should be introduced to enhance our explanations. At least, however, this chapter demonstrates how a new system of explanations may be developed based on a continuous recording system (as against ad hoc studies) and based on a complete and interlocking system (as against a system for partial explanations).

REFERENCE

Ijiri, Yuji, *Momentum Accounting and Triple-Entry Bookkeeping: Exploring the Dynamic Structure of Accounting Measurements*, Studies in Accounting Research Volume 31, American Accounting Association, 1989.

2

Accounting for Productivity Gains

Rajiv D. Banker

Increasing competitive pressures in the 1980s led many firms to identify productivity improvements as a principal competitive objective (McComas, 1985). Firms in mature industries needed to control costs in order to maintain their profitability, as they were unable to pass on price increases to customers. Continuous productivity improvements thus became an important means to obtaining a competitive advantage that could translate into higher profitability. In 1990s, productivity improvement continues to remain prominent on the agenda of business executives.

What is important for sustained competitive advantage is productivity gain that is sustained from period to period, and not just a transitory improvement in performance in a particular period that cannot be replicated in subsequent periods. Distinguishing between sustained productivity gains and transitory efficiency fluctuations is the focus of this chapter.

Firms can obtain sustained productivity gains by investing in new capital equipment for improved technology. In industries with mature technologies, however, only limited opportunities for productivity improvements are afforded by new capital investments. Many firms have looked to better manufacturing practices to reduce labor costs. While improvements in direct labor productivity are often difficult to make, smoother production flows and more efficient support services management present possibilities for reducing in overall labor costs. Many firms have introduced gain sharing and other incentive programs involving all (direct and indirect) workers to motivate them to come up with new ideas for increasing labor productivity.

Such firms are extremely interested in monitoring their production performance over time in order to identify the extent of productivity gains. Analytically, this requires estimation of the extent to which the production frontier has been shifted outward, and such production frontier shifts need to be distinguished from efficiency deviations from the production frontier. The emphasis must be on permanent shifts, rather than simply temporary variations. The conventional accounting variance reports, in contrast, focus on fluctuations from fixed standards, rather than on sustainable gains.

In this chapter, we present an analytical framework for estimating production frontier shifts and period-specific efficiency variations. We also present a method to incorporate estimates of productivity gains and efficiency variations in an accounting variance analysis framework. We illustrate our model with reference to actual production data collected for a period of twenty-four weeks before and twenty-four weeks after a gain sharing program was introduced in a plant employing a mature production technology.

This chapter has the following structure. The first section develops the basic model that articulates the distinction between productivity gains and efficiency variations and links these ideas with accounting variance analysis. The next section presents parametric and nonparametric approaches for estimating the model. The third section discusses the data and empirical results.

THE CONCEPTUAL MODEL

We begin by defining the two basic concepts of productivity and efficiency:

- *Productivity* gains are permanent or sustainable shifts in the production frontier due to technology or process improvements. Such gains persist in periods following the period in which the improvements are instituted.

- *Efficiency* fluctuations are positive or negative deviations from the production frontier due to managerial or environmental factors that are not sustained period after period, but that have effects that may linger on for the period immediately following.

The concepts developed here are applicable to any general production technology, but for specificity, we will impose additional structure to reflect the condition at our research site. Given the technology in place at a plant, we assume a production technology separable in input requirements represented by Leontief-type production functions. In particular, we write the base period (period $t = 1$) production frontier relation for the labor input as

$$z_1 = g(y_1) \tag{1}$$

where y_1 is the vector of actual output quantities, z_1 is the number of labor hours, and $g(\cdot)$ is the production function. Let y_t and z_t be the observed levels of output and labor input in periods $t = 1,...T$.

In the $t = 2$ period, the actual labor consumption z_2 may differ from that predicted on the basis of the production frontier in the preceding period $(t = 1)$. We represent the extent of any shift in the production frontier effected by process improvements in period 2 by $\psi_2 \geq 0$. We now write the difference as

$$g(y_2) - z_2 = \psi_2 + \phi_2 \tag{2}$$

where ϕ_2 is the efficiency fluctuation in period 2. Efficiency fluctuations can be positive or negative. If $\phi_2 > 0$, then there is a favorable labor efficiency variance in period 2, and if $\phi_2 < 0$, then there is an unfavorable variance.

In the $t = 3$ period, the level of labor input required that was predicted on the basis of the production frontier at the end of the preceding (second) period is given by $g(y_3) - \psi_2$ because the production frontier has shifted in the preceding period by ψ_2. We now write the difference between the previous production frontier and actual labor consumption as follows:

$$g(y_3) - \psi_2 - z_3 = \psi_3 + \phi_3 \tag{3}$$

where, as before, ψ_3 is the further shift in the production frontier and ϕ_3 is the efficiency fluctuation in period 3. Writing $\xi_3 = \psi_2 + \psi_3$ and rearranging the terms in equation (3), we obtain

$$z_3 = g(y_3) - \xi_3 - \phi_3 \tag{4}$$

More generally, we write

$$z_t = g(y_t) - \xi_t - \phi_t \tag{5}$$

where

$$\xi_t = \sum_{k=1}^{t} \psi_k \tag{6}$$

represents the *cumulative* productivity gain over all periods from period 2 to period t relative to the base period ($t = 1$) benchmark ϕ_t and is the efficiency fluctuation in period t.

We will consider the estimation of these variables in the next section; but first we examine the question of variance analysis. Let w_B and w_t be the budgeted and actual labor wage rates, respectively, (for a period t). Let the standard labor costs be based on the base period production frontier $g(\cdot)$.[1] Then the expected labor cost for a budgeted output y_B in a period t is given by the following:

$$\text{Budgeted labor cost} = g(y_B)w_B \tag{7}$$

Since the actual output and labor input are y_t and z_t, the flexible budget target for labor consumption is given by

$$\text{Flexible budget target cost} = g(y_t)w_B \tag{8}$$

Therefore, the total variance between the original budget and the actual labor cost is given by

$$\text{Total variance} = g(y_B)w_B - z_t w_t \tag{9}$$

The total variance is analyzed further into

$$\text{Activity variance} = [g(\underline{y}_B) - g(\underline{y}_t)]w_B \tag{10}$$

and

$$\text{Flexible budget variance} = g(\underline{y}_t)w_B - z_t w_t. \tag{11}$$

The former is simply the difference between equations (7) and (8). The latter, in turn, is analyzed into

$$\text{Productivity gain variance} = \psi_t w_B \tag{12}$$

$$\text{Efficiency variance} = \phi_t w_B \tag{13}$$

$$\text{Cumulative past productivity gains} \\ \text{variance} = \xi_{t-1} w_B \tag{14}$$

and

$$\text{Wage rate variance} = z_t(w_B - w_t). \tag{15}$$

It is easy to verify that equations (12), (13), (14), and (15) add up to equation (11), and that equations (10) and (11) add up to the total variance in equation (9). The key difference from conventional variance analysis is that what is usually reported as an aggregate labor quantity variance ($[\xi_t + \phi_t]w_B$) is analyzed further into productivity gain, efficiency, and cumulative past productivity gain variances in order to emphasize the sustainable gains from a shift in the production frontier due to process improvements.

THE ESTIMATION MODELS

We will first consider a parametric approach to the estimation of sustained productivity gains. For this purpose, we assume that ψ_t are independently and identically distributed and that ϕ_t follows an AR (1) process such that

$$\phi_t = \phi_{t-1} + \eta_t \tag{16}$$

where η_t are independently and identically distributed (i.i.d.), and also distributed independent of ψ_t. First differencing then yields

$$z_t - z_{t-1} = g(y_t) - g(y_{t-1}) - \varepsilon_t \tag{17}$$

where

$$\varepsilon_t = \psi_t + \eta_t \tag{18}$$

and the distribution of ε_t is the convolution of the distributions of ψ_t and ϕ_t. Let $\underline{\varepsilon} = (\varepsilon_1, \ldots, \varepsilon_T)$ and let $L(\underline{\varepsilon})$, be the likelihood function. Then the estimation problem can be written as

$$\text{Maximize } L(\varepsilon) \tag{19}$$

subject to

$$\varepsilon_t = [g(y_t) - g(y_{t-1})] - [z_t - z_{t-1}] \, for \, t = 2, \ldots, T \tag{19.1}$$

The model in equation (19) resembles the stochastic production frontier model of Aigner, Lovell, and Schmidt (1977), except that equation (19) is specified in the first difference form. But this similarity allows us to access the estimation methods developed in the stochastic production frontier literature. Accordingly, we specify a parametric form for the production function $g(y; \underline{\beta})$, where $\underline{\beta}$ is the vector of parameters characterizing the production function and $g(\bullet)$ is linear in $\underline{\beta}$. For example, if $g(\bullet)$ is also assumed to be linear in $\underline{y}$, then it can be expressed as

$$g(\underline{y};\underline{\beta}) = \beta_0 + \sum_{j=1}^{J} \beta_j y_j$$

where j indexes the J outputs.

In addition, we assume that the non-negative productivity gains, ψ_t, follow a half-normal distribution, $\psi_t \sim \mid N(0,\sigma_\psi) \mid$, and that efficiency variations, η_t, are normally distributed, $\eta_t \sim N(0,\sigma_\eta)$. These assumptions make it possible to derive the distribution of the convolution ε_t (see Aigner, Lovell, and Schmidt, 1977). The estimation model in equation (19) can now be represented as the following maximum likelihood problem:

$$\text{Maximize} \ln \mathcal{L} (\underline{\varepsilon}; \underline{\beta}, \sigma_\psi, \sigma_\eta) \qquad (20)$$
$$\underline{\beta}, \sigma_\psi, \sigma_\eta$$

where

$$\varepsilon_t = [g(\underline{y}_t; \beta) - g(\underline{y}_{t-1}; \beta)] - [z_t - z_{t-1}]$$

$$\text{for } t = 2, \ldots, T \qquad (20.1)$$

Specifically, for the case when $g(\bullet)$ is linear in $\underline{y}$ and β, we can write ε_t as

$$\varepsilon_t = \sum_{j=1}^{J} \beta_j(y_{jt} - y_{j,t-1}) - (z_t - z_{t-1})$$

$$\text{for } t = 2, \ldots, T \qquad (20.1')$$

Once the parameters $\underline{\beta}$, σ_ψ and σ_η , and hence the residuals ε_t are thus estimated, we can employ the method suggested by Jondrow, Lovell, Materov, and Schmidt (1982) to obtain maximum likelihood estimates of ψ_τ and η_t, conditional on the estimated $\hat{\varepsilon}_t$. Accordingly, we have

$$\psi_1 = 054 \qquad \text{for } \hat{\varepsilon}_t \leq 0$$

$$= \hat{\varepsilon}_t \, \hat{\sigma}_\psi^2 / \hat{\sigma}_\varepsilon^2 \qquad \text{for } \hat{\varepsilon}_t \geq 0 \qquad (21)$$

Next we address the question of nonparametric estimation of production frontier shifts by drawing on data envelopment analysis (DEA) models introduced by Charnes, Cooper, and Rhodes (1978). Accordingly, instead of specifying a possibly restrictive parametric form for the production function $g(\bullet)$, we impose minimal structure in terms of desirable regularity conditions of monotonicity and convexity for the production function (Caves and Christensen, 1980; Banker and Maindiratta, 1988).

Following the stochastic DEA model introduced by Banker (1988), we can represent a general monotone increasing and convex function in terms of inequality constraints on its gradient. Maintaining the same distributional assumptions for ψ_t and η_t as in the parametric model in equation (20), we can now write the maximum likelihood problem as follows:

$$\text{Maximize } L\,(\varepsilon;\, \sigma_\psi,\, \sigma_\eta)$$
$$z^* \, \gamma^*,\, \sigma_\psi,\, \sigma_\eta \qquad (22)$$

subject to

$$\varepsilon_t = [z^*_t - z^*_{t-1}] - [z_t - z_{t-1}] \quad \text{for all } t = 2, \ldots, T \qquad (22.1)$$

$$z^*_t - z^*_k \leq \gamma^*_t \, (y_t - y_k) \qquad \begin{array}{l} \text{for all } t,k = 1, \ldots, T; \\ t \neq k \end{array} \qquad (22.2)$$

$$z^*_t,\, \gamma^*_t \geq 0 \qquad \text{for all } t = 1, \ldots, T \qquad (22.3)$$

$$\sigma_\psi,\, \sigma_\eta \geq 0 \qquad (22.4)$$

and where

$$z^*_t = g(y_t) \text{ for all } t = 1, \ldots, T.$$

The optimization problem in equation (22) has a nonlinear objective function and $T(T-1)$ linear inequality constraints. While this formulation has the advantage of direct comparison with the stochastic frontier formulation in equation (20), it is not convenient to solve the large nonlinear programming problem. Instead, we recommend the following linear programming formulation based on the stochastic DEA model of Banker (1988):

Minimize
$$\sum_{t=2}^{T} \psi_t + \eta^+_t + \eta^-_t$$

$$z^*, \gamma^*, \psi_t, \eta^+_t, \eta^-_t \tag{23}$$

subject to

$$\psi_t + \eta^+_t - \eta^-_t = [z^*_t - z^*_{t-1}] - [z_t - z_{t-1}]$$

for all $t = 2, \ldots, T$ \hfill (23.1)

$$z^*_t - z^*_k \geq \gamma^*_t (y_t - y_k)$$

for all $t,k = 1, \ldots, T; \ t \neq k$ \hfill (23.2)

$$\psi_t, \eta^+_t, \eta^-_t, z^*_t, \tau^*_t \geq 0$$

for all $t = 1, \ldots, T$ \hfill (23.3)

Recent Monte Carlo studies by Banker, Gadh and Gorr (1989) indicate that the linear programming formulation in equation (23) performs as well as or better than the parametric formulation in equation (20).

In many applications, there is considerable interest in determining whether there were significant productivity gains in some time periods, such as after a management change or after the implementation of a new incentive program. Consider a partition of the T time periods into $\Omega_1 \equiv \{1 \ldots, T_1\}$ and $\Omega_2 \equiv \{T_1 + 1, \ldots, T\}$. Let $T_2 = T - T_1$. We maintain the following assumptions

a. $\eta_t = 0$ for all $t = 2, \ldots, T$

b. ψ_t are *i.i.d.* half normal with

   b.1 $\psi_t \sim |N(0, \sigma_{\psi 1})$ for $t \varepsilon \Omega_1$

   b.2. $\psi_t \sim |N(0, \sigma_{\psi 2})$ for $t \varepsilon \Omega_2$

where the sustained productivity gains in Ω_2 are greater, on average, than the gains in the earlier periods in Ω_1. The null hypotheses is specified as

$$H_0: \sigma_{\psi 1} = \sigma_{\psi 2}$$

and the alternate hypothesis as

$$H_1: \sigma_{\psi 1} < \sigma_{\psi 2}$$

The rejection of the null hypothesis (and the acceptance of the alternate hypothesis) indicates that the estimated distribution of sustained productivity gains in Ω_2 stochastically dominates the estimated distribution of sustained productivity gains in Ω_1. While an exact test cannot be devised in this case unless a specific distribution is assumed for η_t, we can employ as a heuristic the test statistic given by

$$\frac{\sum_{t \varepsilon T_1} \hat{\psi}_t^2 / T_1}{\sum_{t \varepsilon T_2} \hat{\psi}_t^2 / T_2} \tag{24}$$

which follows the F-distribution with (T_1, T_2) degrees of freedom if all $\eta_t = 0$ (see Banker, 1990). Here the estimated values $\hat{\psi}_t$ are derived as below. This model modifies equation (23) by setting $\eta^+_t = \eta^-_t = 0$ for all t. It also represents an extension of the usual DEA-BCC (Banker, Charnes, Cooper) efficiency evaluation model (see Banker, Charnes, and Cooper, 1984) in that the "efficiency score" in a later period is restricted to be greater than or equal to the "efficiency score" in an earlier period because of the impact of sustained productivity gains. Thus, for the model to estimate $\hat{\psi}_t$ for the test statistic in equation (24), we have

$$\text{Minimize} \quad \sum_{t=1}^{T} \hat{\psi}_t \tag{25}$$

subject to

$$\sum_{k=1}^{t} \hat{\psi}_t \geq \gamma^*_t - z_t \qquad \text{for all } t = 1, \ldots, T \tag{25.1}$$

$$z^*_t - z^*_k \leq \gamma^*_t (y_t - y_k)$$

$$\text{for all } t, k = 1, \ldots, T; \ t \neq k \tag{25.2}$$

$$\hat{\psi}_t, z^*_t, \tau^*_t \geq 0 \qquad \text{for all } t = 1, \ldots, T \tag{25.3}$$

Unlike equation (23), however, we estimate the $\hat{\psi}_1$ value here. It is interpreted as the base period productivity relative to which subsequent productivity gains are measured. The DEA "efficiency frontier" here corresponds to the final period $(t = T)$ production frontier given by

$$g(y) - \sum_{k=1}^{t} \hat{\psi}_k$$

ILLUSTRATIVE APPLICATION

We illustrate the application of some of the models developed in this chapter with reference to actual production data collected for a period of about two years from a plant manufacturing a fairly mature product.[2] There were no new additions to the existing capacity or replacement of existing equipment. At about the middle of our data period a gain sharing program was implemented at the plant to motivate the workers to find ways to improve labor productivity. The employee newsletter at the plant reported on the activities of many task forces constituted by the workers to suggest improvements in the manufacturing process and methods.

An analysis of the cost structure at the plant revealed that direct materials comprised only about 30 percent of the total costs. Material costs per unit output were monitored closely for each of the four principal products manufactured at the plant. The principal means for such monitoring were the weekly materials variance reports, which detailed the deviations between actual and standard materials consumption. The materials standards were developed for each product based on past engineering experience. We found the materials variances to be extremely small—less than half a percent—for the two-year period for which we analyzed the plant data. No significant materials productivity gains were considered possible because of the mature technology that had optimized materials consumption over several years. Tight quality standards were required by the customers, and, consequently, inspection checks instituted at the plant ensured that labor productivity could not be enhanced by substituting lower materials productivity or lower production quality.

Direct labor also comprised about 30 percent of the total production costs. For cost accounting purposes, direct labor was tracked directly with the output levels for each of four products, and variances of actual direct labor consumption from the standard requirements for each product were monitored closely via weekly reports. The weekly direct labor variances were less than 1.2% percent over a two-year period. No significant productivity gains were expected in direct labor for the same reasons as those recounted for direct materials.

Indirect labor was considered to have the greatest potential for productivity gains. It included labor for material handling, set-ups, supervision, inspection, janitorial services, security and staff services ranging from accounting to production scheduling. Indirect labor costs comprised almost 35 percent of the total production costs. The emphasis in the productivity improvement program was on reducing indirect labor costs.

We collected data on direct and indirect labor consumption for each of four products from weekly labor reports for twenty-four weeks preceding the implementation of the gain sharing program and for the twenty-four corresponding calendar weeks subsequent to the implementation of the program. We also collected data from weekly plant production reports on actual output levels for the four products.

We estimated four stochastic production frontiers for the direct labor for each of the four products using the package LIMDEP. We specified models as in equation (20), with the change in output level for each product being the single independent variable. We also estimated a similar stochastic production frontier for indirect labor, with the change in total production, aggregated over the four products, as the single independent variable. The estimation results are reported in Tables 2.1 and 2.2. We also checked for cross-correlation between the residuals across the five estimated equations. Correlation coefficients were all below 0.12, suggesting that efficiency gains from estimating the five equations together as a system with a general covariance specification are likely to be small.

Table 2.1. Estimation Results for Direct Labor

	Product 1	Product 2	Product 3	Product 4
Intercept	−19.6	−2.0	0.05	0.15
	(.9948)	(.6855)	(.9999)	(.9254)
Product i	1.321	1.265	1.634	1.099
	(.0000)	(.0000)	(.0000)	(.0000)
$\lambda = \sigma_\psi/\sigma_\eta$	0.021	0.000	0.045	0.000
	(.9999)		(.9999)	
σ^2_ε	66.4	33.2	16.7	11.5
	(.9663)		(.9407)	

The results indicate that no sustained productivity gains were achieved for any of the four direct labor categories. For products 2 and 4, σ_ψ was estimated to be zero and model estimation was then equivalent to ordinary least squares estimation in the first differenced variables. This implied that $\hat{\psi}_t = 0$ for the two equations, and, therefore, no sustained productivity gains were detected. For products 1 and 3, some ψ_t were estimated to be greater than zero, but $\hat{\lambda} = \sigma_\psi / \sigma_\eta$ was very small in both cases and not significantly different from zero.

Table 2.2. Estimation Results for Indirect Labor

Intercept	−137.8
	(.5608)
$\sum\limits_i$ Product i	1.258
	(.0092)
$\lambda = \sigma_\psi / \sigma_\eta$	1.839
	(.0653)
σ^2_ε	283.8
	(.1220)

The results for indirect labor were different. Several of the $\hat{\psi}_t$ were estimated to be positive, especially in the period subsequent to the implementation of the gain-sharing program.[3] The estimate for σ_ψ was, in fact, greater than that for σ_η, suggesting that sustained productivity gains in indirect labor were likely to be achieved during the period under consideration.

These results were corroborated by the DEA-based test of Banker (1990), although it maintains somewhat different assumptions. The test statistic specified in equation (22) was not significant for any of the four direct labor categories. The test-statistic in the indirect labor case was 1.593, which is significant at the 1 percent level for the F-distribution with (24,24) degrees of freedom.

CONCLUSION

The distinction between sustainable productivity gains and transient efficiency fluctuations is important in many applications, especially in firms that have instituted productivity improvement programs. Significant competitive advantage from productivity improvements can be obtained only if productivity gains are sustained over time. When competitive strategy dictates that productivity be continually improved, it becomes important to have means to monitor the extent of productivity gains attained and sustained over time. In this chapter we have taken a step in this direction by developing models to estimate sustained productivity gains and relatively transient efficiency variations and to distinguish one from the other.

The illustrative application of our models to actual production data collected from a manufacturing plant employing a mature technology provided some interesting insights. No sustained productivity gains were achieved in direct labor, as direct labor requirements are dictated by the technology, and the potential for improvement is minimal when the technology is mature. The situation is very different in relation to indirect labor costs, which have been growing for many manufacturing industries and now constitute a significant portion of the total production costs. Improvements in manufacturing process and better process flow management present the possibility of considerable improvements in overall labor productivity. Indeed, we find significant sustained productivity gains in indirect labor for our illustrative application.

NOTES

1. The variance analysis presented here can be modified easily to accommodate shifting standard costs so that budgeted labor cost is given by $[g(\bar{y}_B) - \xi_{t-1}]w_B$.

2. The data have been scaled to disguise competitively sensitive information.

3. A shortcoming of the use of the stochastic frontier estimation model in this application is that the serial correlation in ψ_t is ignored.

REFERENCES

Aigner, D. J., C. A. K. Lovell, and P. J. Schmidt. "Formulation and estimation of stochastic frontier production function models," *Journal of Econometrics* (July 1977): 21-37.

Banker, R. D. "Maximum likelihood consistency and data envelopment analysis: A statistical foundation," working paper, Minneapolis, MN: University of Minnesota, 1989.

Banker, R. D. "Stochastic data envelopment analysis," mimeo (1988).

Banker, R. D., A. Charnes, and W. W. Cooper. "Models for the estimation of technical and scale inefficiencies in data envelopment analysis," *Management Science* (September 1984): 1078–1092.

Banker, R. D., V. Gadh, and W. Gorr. "A Monte Carlo comparison of stochastic frontier estimation methods," mimeo (1989).

Banker, R. D., and A. Maindiratta. "Nonparametric analysis of technical and allocative efficiencies in production," *Econometrica* (November 1988): 1315–1332.

Caves, D. W., and L. R. Christensen. "Global properties of flexible functional forms," *American Economic Review* (1980): 422–432.

Charnes, A., W. W. Cooper, and E. Rhodes, "Measuring the efficiency of decision making units," *European Journal of Operations Research* 2 (1978): 429–444.

Jondrow J., C. A. K. Lovell, I. S. Materov, and P. Schmidt. "On the estimation of technical in efficiencies in the stochastic frontier production function models," *Journal of Econometrics* 19, no. 2 (August 1982): 233–238.

McComas, M. "Atop the Fortune 500: A survey of the CEOs," *Fortune* (April 28, 1986).

3

On Assessing
Internal Controls

Ray G. Stephens

Assessing the effectiveness of internal controls periodically has received significant amounts of attention from managers and accountants, both practitioners and academics. The two most recent periods of attention have largely resulted from a focusing of public attention on the failure of internal controls to prevent members of organizations from taking actions deemed contrary to the public interest.

This chapter surveys the legal and accounting literature, both academic and practitioner, assessing the effectiveness of internal controls. The survey reveals that assessing the effectiveness of internal controls, while receiving substantial attention, currently specifies a judgment process to be undertaken consistent with an externally specified criterion. The specific tradeoffs from implementing one set of internal controls in contrast to another set of internal controls are left to the subjective judgment of those responsible for making the assessments.

The results of the literature survey are then compared to the current Securities and Exchange Commission (SEC) proposal for management report that publicly discloses the results of management's assessment and the involvement of independent accountants with such an assessment. The comparison reveals that consideration of the SEC proposal requires careful understanding of what criterion is to be used by management when making such an assessment, of the role of independent accountants, and of what can be gained by users of the disclosure.

HISTORICAL PERSPECTIVE

Management has long recognized the need to implement controls in organizations.[1] Accountants, because of their expertise in the collection and distribution of information in organizations, have long been involved in the implementation and operation of controls.[2] For business enterprises subject to the federal securities laws, a legal requirement for implementation of controls is specified in the Foreign Corrupt Practices Act (FCPA) of 1977, as amended.[3]

Kohler's Dictionary for Accountants defines control as the

> Ability to influence behavior in desired amounts and directions, with the degree of conformance providing a measure of the state of control. For accounting and auditing, control may be further formalized as the process by which the *activities* of an *organization* are conformed to a desired plan of action and the plan is conformed to the organization's activities.[4]

This broad definition includes the need for processes by which the activities of an organization are conformed to many items. Only the responsibilities to maintain the controls required by regulation or proposed regulation will be discussed in this chapter. In some instances, this has been previously defined as internal accounting control to distinguish it from other types of controls covered in the definition of control above, the modifier "internal" noting that these controls are within the organization as opposed to other controls external to the organization. Note that the definition above, in the domain of accounting and auditing, specifies only internal control.

Public awareness in the 1970s of payments to foreign government officials, illegal under U.S. law, led to the passage of the FCPA. Some of its provisions require that enterprises subject to the registration requirements of the Securities Exchange Act of 1934 devise and maintain a system of internal accounting control sufficient to provide reasonable assurances that:

(i)   transactions are executed in accordance with management's general or specific authorization;

(ii) transactions are recorded as necessary (a) to permit preparation of financial statements in conformity with generally accepted accounting principles or any other criteria applicable to such statements, and (b) to maintain accountability for assets;

(iii) access to assets is permitted only in accordance with management's general or specific authorization; and

    (iv) the recorded accountability for assets is compared with the existing assets at reasonable intervals and appropriate action is taken with respect to any differences.[5]

The FCPA also specifies a "books and records" requirement,[6] and both the "books and records" requirement and the lack of internal accounting controls have often been the subject of SEC enforcement actions.[7]

The SEC's original interpretation was that internal accounting control does not have to conform to a standard of absolute exactitude; there was a *de minimus* exemption in the term "reasonable assurance."[8] Reasonable assurance requires consideration of the chance an event will occur and the significance of the impact of that occurrence. Reasonable assurance also requires consideration of the cost of internal controls in terms of the benefits, reduction in chance, or significance of impact to be obtained.[9] Recently, Congress defined reasonable assurance as the level of assurance that would satisfy prudent officials in the conduct of their affairs.[10]

The SEC proposed, in response to the FCPA, that management make public disclosure of its assessment of the effectiveness of internal accounting control through a statement by management on internal accounting controls (SMIAC) in annual reports and annual filings with the SEC on Form 10-K. This statement would have been audited by a registrant's independent accountants.[11] The SEC SMIAC proposal was consistent with the conclusion of the Commission on Auditors' Responsibilities (generally referred to as the Cohen Commission) that users of financial information are interested in whether controls are adequate to reduce the risk of asset loss and to produce reliable financial information.[12] The SEC withdrew its SMIAC proposal in response to private sector initiatives, while noting the continued importance of adequate internal accounting control and encouraging experimentation by registrants and auditors concerning statements on internal accounting control.[13]

A series of fraudulent financial reporting situations during the 1980s led to the formation of the Commission on Fraudulent Financial Reporting (generally, and hereafter, referred to as the Treadway Commission). One recommendation of the Treadway Commission follows:

> All public companies should be required by SEC rule to include in their annual reports to stockholders management reports signed by the chief executive officer and the chief accounting officer and/or the chief financial officer. The management report should acknowledge management's responsibilities for the financial statements and internal control, discuss how these responsibilities were fulfilled, and provide management's assessment of the effectiveness of the company's internal controls.[14]

The Treadway Commission focused only on financial disclosures, as opposed to other violations of law, and noted that the process for generating reliable financial statements involves efforts by management, independent accountants, the SEC, and other authorities.[15] The independent accountant would be involved, in some fashion, in the management report under Statement of Auditing Standards (SAS) No. 8[16] since this statement would be other information in documents which contains an audited financial statement.

THE PRESENT STATE OF GUIDANCE ON ASSESSING INTERNAL ACCOUNTING CONTROLS

A large body of literature exists, professional and academic, concerning assessment of the effectiveness of internal controls. The following bodies of literature will be discussed: (1) official professional auditing literature, (2) unofficial professional auditing literature, (3) empirical research in publications by professional groups and in professional journals, and (4) theoretical work in publications by academics.[17]

After the discussion of the literature, the internal controls in the SMIAC proposal will be compared with those in the 1988 management report proposal. Some summary comments offer guidance in assessing the effectiveness of internal controls.

Official Professional Literature

The official professional literature of the Auditing Standards Board provides two separate standards relating to assessment of internal accounting control. The first standard is SAS No. 30, *Reporting on Internal Accounting Control* (July 1980). This SAS provides guidance for auditors when expressing an opinion on the internal accounting control of a registrant.[18] It would seem that a pronouncement that covers an examination leading to an opinion on an entity's internal accounting control at a specific date must provide guidance on assessment.

SAS No. 30, while specifically issued by the Auditing Standards Board to provide guidance to auditors for expressing an opinion on internal accounting control, contains within it an overall system for assessing internal control.[19]

In order for an auditor to express an opinion, a system of internal accounting control should provide reasonable, but not absolute, assurance that assets are safeguarded from unauthorized use or disposition and that financial records are reliable to permit the preparation of financial statements. The definition [taken from AU 320.27] also sets forth the following operative objectives that are necessary to achieve the broad objectives:

a. Transactions are executed in accordance with management's general or specific authorizations.

b. Transactions are recorded as necessary (1) to permit preparation of financial statements in conformity with generally accepted accounting principles or any other criteria applicable to such statements and (2) to maintain accountability for assets.

c. Access to assets is permitted only in accordance with management's authorization.

d. The recorded accountability for assets is compared with the existing assets at reasonable intervals and appropriate action is taken with respect to any differences.[20]

An inherent limitation of any evaluation is noted: "any projection of a current evaluation of internal accounting control to future periods is subject to the risk that the procedures may become inadequate because of changes in conditions and that the degree of compliance with prescribed procedures may deteriorate."[21]

Additional official professional guidance on assessment is available in SAS No. 55, *Consideration of the Internal Control Structure in a Financial Statement Audit* (April 1988), which provides guidance to auditors who intend to rely on the internal control structure [22] in order to reduce substantive testing during an audit. SAS No. 55 distinguishes between (a) whether an internal control structure policy or procedure has been placed in operation and (b) its operating effectiveness (paragraph 17). While SAS No. 55 leaves the final decision concerning reliance to the auditor's judgment, it provides some guidance concerning an assessment of internal controls.

SAS No. 60, *Communication of Internal Control Structure Related Matters Noted in an Audit* (April 1988), does not deal with assessment. It deals only with the communication of "reportable conditions" noted during an audit.

Unofficial Professional Guidance

The official professional guidance has been supplemented by more detailed unofficial professional guidance. The American Institute of Certified Public Accountants (AICPA) established a Special Advisory Committee on

Internal Accounting Control which issued its unofficial professional guidance in this area, the *Report of the Special Advisory Committee on Internal Accounting Control* (generally, and herein, referred to as the Minahan Report.[23] The Minahan Report focused on internal controls for authorization, accounting,[24] and safeguarding.[25]

The Minahan Report intended to flesh out the guidance for internal controls broadly defined in the existing official professional literature by providing guidance for a process and factors to be used in evaluating[26] internal controls.

The process should consist of procedures related to

a. A reexamination of the accounting control procedures in place and the ongoing process of evaluating them.

b. The need for more explicit documentation of these control procedures and the process of evaluating them.[27]

The Minahan Report then discusses several specifics of internal control: organizational structure, personnel, delegation, budgets and financial reports, organizational checks and balances (including financial control functions and internal auditing), and EDP considerations.[28]

The Minahan Report lists several factors to be considered *leading to* undertaking an evaluation:[29]

• Changes in the control environment (philosophy of operations, organizational structure, accounting system, and personnel practices),[30]

• Lack of formalization of important corporate or accounting policies,

• Limitations on internal audit or supervisory review

• Knowledge of weaknesses in internal control,[31]

• Unexplained variances or trends, and

• Changes in line of business, number of locations, or materiality of assets at risk.

The Minahan Report also lists several factors to be considered *when making* the evaluation of internal controls—that is, the addition or deletion of a control procedure or technique to meet a specific control objective:[32]

• Size of company,

• Control environment,

• Nature of business and industry,[33]

• Types of transactions, and

• Cost-benefit considerations.[34]

The Minahan Report also includes a detailed example applying its guidance to a manufacturing company.

The Minahan Report increases the level of detailed guidance for making evaluations of internal control in meeting authorization, accounting, and safeguarding objectives. It provides a process,[35] detailed explanations of factors affecting internal control, factors to be considered in undertaking an evaluation, and factors to be considered in making an evaluation. The differences in companies are so great that application of this process, using the process and factors included in the Minahan Report, requires complex, subjective judgments. Persons making these judgments must have both knowledge and experience. The report notes the lack of empirical knowledge about existing implementation of internal control procedures at the time of the report.

In addition, even more detailed unofficial professional guidance has been provided by all eight of the then "Big Eight" accounting firms—Arthur Andersen,[36] Arthur Young,[37] Coopers and Lybrand,[38] Deloitte, Haskins & Sells,[39] Ernst & Whinney,[40] Price Waterhouse,[41] Peat Marwick,[42] and Touche Ross[43]—by personnel associated with these firms,[44] his guidance is primarily concerned with documenting and evaluating internal controls for specific control objectives, giving much more detailed guidance than the Minahan Report.[45] This literature provides little help in aggregating the judgments at the detail level or making the cost-benefit tradeoffs more concrete or objective. Johnson and Jaenicke, however, support evaluating management's process for making these decisions if auditors are involved in examining internal controls.[46]

In addition to the Big Eight accounting firms, others have been cocnerned aobut the assessment of internal controls. Wallace has written a handbook in this area,[47] and Burns and his colleagues[48] have developed both computerized and microcomputerized assessment models.[49] In the electronic data processing (EDP) area, the National Bureau of Standards, Department of Commerce, has developed several standards that could be utilized.[50] At least five expert systems have been developed in the area of EDP control evaluation.[51]

Empirical Research in Assessing Internal Controls

Empirical researchers have begun to provide knowledge that can be of assistance in assessing internal control. The empirical research consists of two different types. The first type of research provides information about internal control usage and documentation in the United States. The information was obtained as the result of a large scale study of U.S.

corporations, which included a survey, a set of interviews, and a set of evaluations performed by team members of internal control policies and procedures. The second type conducted primarily by academic researchers, provides information about the judgment process used in evaluating internal control.

The Financial Executives Research Foundation funded an extensive study of internal controls.[52] This study contains a large amount of empirical data in the following areas:

1. It provides quantitative information about the use of a large number of frequently recommended internal control practices. This constitutes a description of the state of the art in the most practical and understandable terms possible.

2. It reports the ratings by a large number of corporate executives of their own internal control systems, thus offering one measure of the quality of internal control practices in U.S. companies.

3. A number of questions were designed to test the existence of general agreement on the scope and meaning of terms such as "internal control" and "internal accounting control." The results provide some illuminating answers.

4. The same questions also tested the existence of a consensus on what constitutes a "material weakness" in internal control.[53]

The study also includes data on internal controls use by company size and by industry.

In their summary evaluation, Mautz et al note two cautions about the results of their study: (1) corporate executives tend to overrate the quality of their internal control systems, at least from the standpoint of a disinterested observer, and unintentionally exaggerate the employment of control practices since they view questions about internal control quality as if they were directed at their own personal competence; and (2) no single internal control practice is indispensable, regardless of how widely used, since an appropriate combination of other practices, operating relationships, or situational peculiarities can mitigate its nonuse.[54]

Mautz et al. note tremendous diversity in practice concerning documentation of internal controls. Their evaluation, based upon team members' examination of company documentation and consideration of factors known about the company, is that documentation, like use of a specific internal control practice, is very "situation-specific, reflecting the company's business strategy, its corporate structure, the nature and location of operations, and, equally important, its management philosophy and style."[55] Their empirical findings, based upon expert judgments in many different situations, provide some guidance on documentation requirements that were not provided by the Minahan Report. Note, however, that the amount and type of documentation should vary, based upon analysis of the researchers' empirical evidence, as a result of the same factors that affect the evaluation of internal controls, or the implementation of controls, in the Minahan Report.

Academic researchers have conducted several studies of the analytical abilities of auditors in making judgments about internal controls. The results of this empirical research indicate that experience is the only way to obtain consistency in these judgments because of their complexity.[56] This is consistent with the research that shows tremendous diversity in the use of controls in practice[57] and with SEC releases.[58]

The academic research compares favorably with the intuition about a situation where no unique set of controls is applicable in any given circumstance because of the different configurations that will yield cost-beneficial control in any given set of facts and circumstances.[59] Experience is the only way to learn the ability to make the complex judgments in non-unique situations.[60] This body of academic research tells us that experienced managers will be necessary in order to make the tradeoffs necessary to assess the effectiveness of internal controls.[61]

Theoretical Models of Internal Control Evaluation

Academic researchers have developed four different theoretical models for evaluating internal control systems based upon statistics, Bayesian statistics, chance-constrained programming, and expert systems. The stochastic system uses an output orientation to develop an assessment model. Within this model, effectiveness of a control is based upon whether it reduces the overall amount of error.[62] The Bayesian statistical model develops a belief about the effectiveness of the controls, which is updated by information about effectiveness. The development of the model allows for joint consideration of individual controls in making an overall assessment, which is usually not available in pure stochastic models.[63] The chance-constrained programming model allows for interaction and the existence or absence of a control.[64] It provides information about the effectiveness of adding a control, but does not provide as an output an overall assessment of effectiveness. However, one measure of overall effectiveness is to take the average marginal increment of additional control provided by adding specific controls as a measure of benefit.[65] An expert system has been developed as a theoretical model for internal control systems development and evaluation. This attempts to put into computer processing form, without the limits of a single mathematical form, the expert judgments that auditors make.[66]

Comparison of Two Proposed Statements

There are tremendous differences between an assessment that might be required under the proposed 1979 Statement by Management on Internal Accounting Control and an assessment that might be required under the proposed 1988 report. The assessment in the SMIAC proposal was an assessment, by management, of whether the system of internal controls provides reasonable assurance that transactions are authorized and appropriately reflected in the books and records, that financial statements are in conformity with generally accepted accounting principles (GAAP), and that assets are safeguarded. The assessment in the management report proposal would be an assessment, by management, of whether the system of internal controls provides reasonable assurance as to the integrity and reliability of financial reporting.

The first difference between the two proposals lies in the scope of the internal controls for which an assessment is required. The management report does not consider controls concerning authorization and appropriate reflection in the books and records or the safeguarding of assets contained in the SMIAC proposal, except to the extent that these controls affect the integrity and reliability of financial reporting.

The second difference is the criterion that the internal controls must meet concerning financial statements. The management report proposal does not just permit financial statements in conformity with GAAP, as under the SMIAC proposal, but rather requires that financial statements in conformity with GAAP must be effected and properly disclosed.

The third difference also concerns the scope of internal controls. The internal controls under the management report are not limited to financial statements, as they are in the SMIAC proposal. The management report proposal goes to all financial reporting. The focus on financial reporting does bring another criterion to bear, that of materiality, which does not exist in the SMIAC proposal. Thus, in the management report proposal, the scope is both increased by requiring disclosures beyond the financial statements and decreased by adding the criterion of materiality for financial statement items, when compared with the SMIAC proposal.

The new materiality criterion deserves special attention. The proposing release uses the definition in Securities Exchange Act Rule 12b-2:

> The term "material," when used to qualify a requirement for the
> furnishing of information as to any subject, limits the information

required to those matters to which there is substantial likelihood that a reasonable investor would attach importance in determining whether to buy or sell securities.[67]

This materiality related to "determining whether to buy or sell securities" differs from other available definitions, such as "deciding how to vote"[68] or "the magnitude of the item is such that the judgment of a reasonable person relying upon the report would have been changed or influenced."[69] The materiality concept has importance for an assessment of the effectiveness of internal control to the extent that items of information for public disclosure required under one definition are not required under another definition. Thus, the definition of materiality is an important factor in determining the scope of internal controls whose effectiveness must be assessed beyond simply reducing certain quantitative or qualitative information to be disclosed in the financial statements.

SUMMARY OF GUIDANCE ON ASSESSMENT OF INTERNAL CONTROL

There is a lot of private sector guidance on assessment of the effectiveness of internal controls at several different levels, as illustrated above.[70] At one level, the guidance is very general, such as that contained in SAS No. 30, SAS No. 55, and the academic theoretical models. This broad guidance sets objectives for the assessment process and lists factors to be considered in making tradeoffs. At another level, the guidance is very detailed, such as the guidance on documentation and assessment of specific control objectives in some of the unofficial professional literature. The process structure and the factors to be considered in the Minahan Report and the recommendations by Mautz and his colleagues, authors of the empirical study on the use of internal controls, provide some guidance on how to integrate the general and detailed guidance in other literature through, respectively, discussion of the evaluation process and use of internal controls in practice.

On applying guidance, management must consider the costs and benefits of the controls, especially since implementation of all the controls contained in the detailed guidance would be too costly for any enterprise. Since both costs and benefits are extremely difficult to measure, subjectivity will be involved in making the judgments. Subjective judgments seem to be better and to be more consistently made, regardless of the criterion of better, by experienced individuals according to the empirical research. Materiality needs to be explicitly noted as a criterion to be considered.

The available guidance does not prescribe a set of controls in a given set of circumstances. Rather, it means that any evaluator will have to consider whether a set of controls is effective, given the need to provide reasonable assurance as to the integrity and reliability of financial reporting.[71] Any way you say it, it comes out to be consistent with the usual interpretation of reasonable assurance—providing assurance, but not absolute assurance.

The private sector guidance seems to allow four different approaches for management to use when translating the broad objectives into specific control objectives in undertaking an assessment of internal controls:

1.   a cycle approach—considering controls in relation to groups of similar transactions,

2.   a transaction approach—considering controls in relation to types of transactions,

3.   an organizational approach—considering controls in relation to organization units, and

4.   an asset approach—considering controls in relation to assets (and liabilities) and changes thereto.

Note that the guidance in SAS No. 30 (AU 624) or SAS No. 55 could apply to any of these approaches since these pronouncements specifying the broad objectives, even though the internal controls they are considering are different. In general, the unofficial professional guidance seems to prefer either a cycle approach (Minahan Report) or a transaction approach (some Big Eight accounting firm literature, such as Johnson and Jaenicke). The empirical literature does not ascertain the type of approach used, in either the study of use of controls in practice or the research into judgments. The academic theoretical models seem to be consistent with any of the four approaches since the tradeoffs contemplated are at a very abstract level. It should be noted that the fourth approach does not encompass the scope of internal controls contemplated in the management report proposal.

The point-in-time assessment of the proposed rule on management reports would be consistent with the process for examing of internal accounting controls by independent accountants in SAS No. 30 and different from an auditor reliance on the internal control structure for reducing the amount of substantive testing in SAS No. 55. This difference is due to the operating effectiveness required by the auditor in examining the internal control system in order to rely upon the internal control to reduce substantive testing, which extends to a period of time rather than a point in time. The point-in-time assessment would therefore seem to require management to assess whether the controls placed in operation at the date of assessment were effectively designed, and (1) if placed in operation for a reasonable period prior to the point-in-time assessment, were operating effectively, or (2) if placed in operation for less than a reasonable period prior to the point-in-time assessment, would be effective if operated as designed.[72] It would not be possible to test whether an internal control is operating as designed unless it has been placed in operation for some time period. The definition of operating effectiveness in SAS No. 55 is also different because it goes only to preventing material misstatements in the financial statements, not to providing reasonable assurance as to the integrity and reliability of financial reporting.

Even though SAS No. 55 is different from the management report proposal, it does provide some guidance on the process for making assessments because of its discussion of the difference between operating effectiveness for the period and for the point in time when the evaluator is aware of the difference between reasonable assurance and material misstatements. Further, the definition of reportable conditions in SAS No. 60 seems to recognize the difference between guidance for the assessment in the proposed rule on management reports and SAS No. 55. SAS No. 60 is only limited because it does not require auditors to search for reportable conditions that are not material weaknesses.[73]

The assessment of internal control would have to consider risk aggregation regardless of which of the approaches—cycle, transactional, organizational, or asset/liability—was utilized for developing and documenting specific control objectives. The aggregation of risk (of unauthorized transactions, transactions not reflected in the books and records, unauthorized use and/or disposition of assets, and material misstatements in financial statements) could be performed in any reasonable manner deemed appropriate by management. Use of any reasonable approach to developing specific control objectives and aggregation of risk would meet the requirements of the proposed rule on management reports. Effectively, present guidance is voluminous and management must choose from the guidance to meet their responsibilities.

One difficulty with the present guidance is the number of sources that management would have to consult. The more comprehensive private sector sources (the Minahan Report and the published guidance by Big Eight public accounting firms) are becoming dated. Almost all professional guidance, except the new SASs recently promulgated as part of the expectations gap project, was published between 1979 and 1981 in direct response to congressional and SEC actions. After the SEC determined not to proceed with requiring a SMIAC, very little has been undertaken by the private sector in this regard. The results of the empirical guidance have not been integrated, except those included in SAS No. 55. The SAS No. 55 guidance is both high level and limited in this regard because of its focus on the materiality of financial statements and the ability of auditors not to rely on internal control

(assess control risk at the maximum) in an audit. In particular, the guidance that might be obtained from consideration of specific controls, the role of EDP, and SEC enforcement actions has not been integrated. This indicates a need for updated, integrated professional guidance. However, the updated, integrated professional guidance would not be expected to change the guidance, only to allow more efficient consideration by management. Further, the undertaking of a project or projects to provide the updated, integrated private sector guidance will probably not be undertaken absent some pressing need, such as SEC action, if history is used as precedent.[74]

NOTES

1. See, for example, F. J. Rothlisberger's 1936 article, "Understanding: A Prerequisite of Leadership," in *Man in Organization: Essays of F.J. Rothlisberger* (Belknap Press of Harvard University Press, 1968): 20–34.

2. See, for example, R.N. Anthony, *Management Accounting: Text and Cases* (Richard D. Irwin, 1956).

3. Title I of Pub. L. 95-213.

4. W. W. Cooper and Yuji Ijiri (eds.), *Kohler's Dictionary for Accountants* (Prentice-Hall, 1983), p. 123, (emphasis in the original).

5. Codified in § 13(b)(2)(B) of the Securities and Exchange Act of 1934, 15 U.S.C.§ 78m(b)(2)(B).

6. The books and records provisions of the FCPA requires subject registrants to "make and keep books, records and accounts which in reasonable detail, accurately and fairly reflect the transactions and dispositions of the assets." See codification in § 15 U.S.C. 78m(b)(2)(A).

7. See footnote 6 to SEC Release No. 34-25925, *Report of Management's Responsibilities* (July 19, 1988) (53 Fed. Reg. 28,009) for some examples of these actions.

8. See SEC Release No. 34-17500 (January 29, 1981) (46 Fed. Reg. 11,544).

9. See Securities Act Release No. 15772 (April 30, 1979) (44 Fed. Reg. 26,702).

10. The amendments to 15 U.S.C. § 78m were enacted on August 23, 1988, as part of the Omnibus Trade and Competitiveness Act of 1988, Pub. L. No. 100-418, § 5002, 102 Stat. 1107 (1988). H.R. Rep. No. 576, 100th Cong., 2d Sess. 917 (1988) (the Conference Report) indicates that the Conference Committee adopted the prudent man qualification "in order to clarify that the standard does not connote an unrealistic degree of exactitude or precision. The concept of reasonableness of necessity contemplates the weighing of a number of factors, including the costs of compliance."

11. SEC Release No. 34-15772 (April 30, 1979) (44 Fed. Reg. 26,702).

12. Commission on Auditors' Responsibilities, *Report, Conclusions, and Recommendations* (AICPA, 1978), p. 55. Similar comments are made in M. V. Brown, "Auditor's and Internal Controls: An Analysts View," *CPA Journal* (September 1977): 27-31.

13. Accounting Series Release No. 278 (June 6, 1980) (45 Fed. Reg. 40,134).

14. National Commission on Fraudulent Financial Reporting (NCFFR), *Report of the National Commission on Fraudulent Financial Reporting* (1987), p. 11.

15. NCFFR, p. 2.

16. SAS No. 8, *Other Information in Documents Containing Audited Financial Statements* (December 1975).

17. The organization of the literature generally follows the hierarchy for professional guidance established in SAS No. 52. SAS No. 52 is not precisely relevant since it refers to a hierarchy of sources of generally accepted accounting principles. The hierarchy of literature for internal controls is, however, consistent with that pronouncement, which refers to a hierarchy of sources as follows: senior technical committees, pronouncements of bodies of expert accountants that follow a due process procedure, practices widely recognized, and other literature.

18. This statement was not the first issued in this area. SAS No. 30 superseded Statement on Auditing Procedures (SAP) No. 49, *Reports on Internal Control* (issued in November 1971 and codified in SAS No. 1, Section 640) and SAP No. 52, *Reports on Internal Control Based on Criteria Established by Governmental Agencies* (issued in October 1972 and codified in SAS No. 1, Section 641).

19. "Internal accounting control" in SAS No. 30 (and in SMIAC) is not the same as "internal control" as used in the proposed rule on management reports. See the final section of this chapter, comparing SMIAC with management report proposal.

20. Criteria were utilized in the Foreign Corrupt Practices Act (FCPA) of 1977 (Title I of Pub. L. 95-213) codified as Section 13(b)(2) of the Securities Exchange Act [15 U.S.C. § 78m(b)(2)]. Thus, these criteria comprise legal requirements in addition to being official professional auditing standards. However, it should be noted that the books and records requirement of the FCPA [Section 13(b)(2) of the Securities Exchange Act] is not explicitly contained in the official professional auditing guidance.

21. AU 642.08, quoting from AU 320.25.

22. SAS No. 55, in its discussion, uses the term "internal control structure.," which is equivalent to "internal control" as used in the proposed rule on management reports, except for the scope of controls to be considered. The

new terminology was utilized in SAS No. 55 to distinguish it from the more limited context of internal accounting controls which was developing in accounting practice, and to separate the terminology from the FCPA.

23. American Institute of Certified Public Accountants (AICPA), *Report of the Special Advisory Committee on Internal Accounting Control* (AICPA, 1979).

24. The Special Advisory Committee believed that this objective should be extended to include information in the management discussion and analysis and the president's letter in addition to the financial statements and supplemental information. See AICPA, p. 11. It should be noted that the materiality criterion for public disclosures (see the discussion below) could probably be interpreted consistent with the Special Advisory Committee's belief since both the management discussion and analysis and the president's letter are public disclosures.

25. See AICPA, p. 1. These represent the Special Advisory Committee's terminology and classification for the objectives defined in greater detail in the FCPA, adopted from the official professional literature and currently contained in SAS No. 30. It should be noted that, just as in SAS No. 30, the Minahan Report does not explicitly contain or address the books and records requirement of the FCPA [Section 13(b)(2) of the Securities Exchange Act].

26. The Minahan Report uses "evaluating" to mean "assessing the effectiveness of."

27. AICPA, p. 3. It should be noted, however, that the Minahan Report contains no specific further guidance on documentation. SEC Release No. 34-15772 (April 30, 1979) (44 Fed Reg. 26,702) states the following:

> Very few, if any, registrants could perform an effective review of their systems of internal accounting control without documenting their specific control objectives and the control procedures in place which should contribute to achieving these objectives. Documentation of tests of controls in effect is necessary to determine that the tests were appropriately planned and performed and that the results of the tests were appropriately considered. Because of the subjective aspects which may be important to cost-benefit analyses, a record of the bases for management's conclusions with respect to reasonable assurance considerations may be particularly important.

Similar wording is contained in Accounting Series Release (ASR) 278 (June 6, 1980).

28. The discussion of organizational checks and balances and EDP considerations contains lists of many specific control objectives, procedures, and techniques. It should be noted that one member of the Special Advisory

Committee, Roger N. Carlson of Northwest Bancorporation, assented with qualification to the report because he objected to separation of EDP considerations as an "influencing characteristic" since he believed that it is integral to consideration of internal control (AICPA, p.28).

29. Since the Minahan Report was written in response to the FCPA (even though it was published prior to final passage and the text denies that the FCPA was a motivating factor), it was intended to assist with compliance—that is, presuming that this was the first (formal) evaluation. I have reclassified the factors presuming an ongoing evaluation process, to provide factors that cause an evaluation to be undertaken. See AICPA, pp. 22-23, for more description of the specific factors whose summary salient characteristics are summarized.

30. The Treadway Commission (AICPA, 1987, p. 11) further refined this area by noting that the "tone at the top" set by management is of great importance in preventing fraudulent financial reporting because of the strong influence of top management on the corporate environment.

31. This would include management-obtained knowledge in addition to recommendations by experts, such as internal auditors or independent accountants.

32. See AICPA, pp. 23-24.

33. Separated from control environment (where it was included in the Minahan Report) to be consistent with factors leading to making an evaluation (where it was separate in the Minahan Report).

34. One member of the Special Advisory Committee, Donald R. Wood of Touche Ross & Co., qualified his assent since materiality was never mentioned in the report, although he noted that it might be included as part of the cost-benefit considerations. However, the term "materiality" was never defined by him and thus may not relate to the current situation where materiality refers only to public disclosures. This was supported by John Leslie Livingstone and Richard M. Steinberg, "SEC's Proposed Internal Control Reporting Rules," *Journal of Accountancy* (December 1979): 39–43. Livingstone and Steinberg say that materiality is inherent in any concept of reasonable assurance and in cost/benefit tradeoffs. Note that the accounting definition of materiality, used for financial statements (public disclosures), was never contemplated in relation to the "reasonable assurance" of internal controls which had a higher standard, allowing only ade minimis exemption. See SEC Release No. 34-17500 (April 29, 1981) (46 Fed. Reg. 11,544).

35. A process for evaluating internal control is also contained in SEC Release No. 34-15772 (April 30, 1979) (44 Fed. Reg. 26,702) and repeated in ASR 278 (June 6, 1980). A five-step general process is contained in these releases: (1) evaluate the overall control environment, (2) translate broad objectives into specific control objectives, (3) consider specific control procedures and individual control environment factors contributing to the

achievement of specific control objectives, (4) monitor the control procedures and their effectiveness, and (5) consider the costs and benefits of additional or alternative control procedures.

36. Arthur Andersen & Co., *A Guide to the Study and Evaluation of Internal Control* (AA & Co., 1978).

37. Arthur Young, *Evaluating Accounting Controls: A Systematic Approach* (1980).

38. Kenneth P. Johnson and Henry R. Jaenicke, *Evaluating Internal Control: Concepts, Guidelines, Procedures, Documentation* (John Wiley and Sons, 1980).

39. Deloitte, Haskins & Sells, *Internal Accounting Control: An Overview of the DH&S Study and Evaluation Technique* (1979).

40. Ernst & Whinney, *Evaluating Internal Controls: A Guide for Management and Directors* (1979).

41. Price Waterhouse issued Joseph Connor's *Guide to Accounting Controls* in 1979 in pamphlet form. The first of these was entitled "Establishing, Evaluating and Monitoring Internal Control Systems." Supplements were issued in 1981 through 1985, for a total of eight pamphlets, according to David Parker, partner with Price Waterhouse.

42. Item #175 P, issued in 1979, in the AICPA Library.

43. Touche Ross & Co., *Accounting Control Evaluation: Controlling Assets and Transactions—How to Review and Improve Internal Accounting Control.* Also see James K. Loebbecke and George R. Zuber, *"Evaluating Internal Control," Journal of Accountancy* (February 1980): 49-56.

44. Other CPA firms may have issued detailed guidance. This listing was obtained from the *Accountant's Index*, available in most libraries, and from conversations with accounting academics familiar with the area of internal control.

45. In effect, this guidance fits into the process in SEC Release No. 34-15772 by providing detailed guidance for documenting specific control objectives and the current or proposed control procedures to meet these objectives.

46. Johnson and Jaenicke, p. 59.

47. Wanda A. Wallace, *Handbook of Internal Accounting Controls* (Prentice Hall; 1984).

48. See David Burns et al., "The BSA: Internal Control System Design, Documentation, and Evaluation," *Internal Auditing* (Summer 1986): 3–23; David C. Burns et al., "Risk Assessment and Evaluation: Bank Field Tests of the BSA," *Internal Auditing* (Winter 1987): 19–35; David C. Burns et al., "Riskbuster: A Microcomputer Software Package to Support Compliance with SAS No. 47," *EDP Auditor* (1987): 4–34); James Cashell and David C. Burns,

"Evaluating Internal Control Concerns in Systems Acquisition Proposals," *Internal Auditing* (Winter 1989): 40–65.

49. Because these assessment models go beyond internal accounting controls, they generally are termed risk assessment or risk analysis models. However, the concepts and techniques developed therein are just as applicable when used in the more limited evaluation.

50. See, for example, FIPS Publication 65, *Guideline for Automatic Data Processing Risk Analysis*, which states the following as its purpose: "[Risk analysis] looks at an organization's ability to perform its mission and tasks correctly and in a timely manner under conditions which can affect physical environment, personnel, equipment, content of files, and processing capability in conjunction with the chances for such conditions to take place... The aim of risk analysis is to help ADP management strike an economic balance between the impact of risks and the cost of protective measures" p.5.

51. See Andrew W. Bailey and Varghese Jacob, "Expert Systems in Auditing: A Network Approach," unpublished working paper, The Ohio State University, for a listing of these systems.

52. Robert K. Mautz, Walter G. Kell, Michael W. Maher, Alan G. Merten, Raymond R. Reilly, Dennis G. Severance, and Bernard J. White, *Internal Control in U.S. Corporations* (Financial Executives Research Foundation, 1980).

53. Mautz et al., p. 15.

54. This is consistent with the SEC's conclusion in SEC Release No. 34-17500 (April 29, 1981) (46 Fed. Reg. 11,544): "This means that the issuer need not always select the best or the most effective control measure. However, the one selected must be reasonable under the circumstances. . . [T]here is an almost infinite variety of control devices which could be utilized in a particular business environment."

55. Mautz et al., p. 105.

56. To be precise, some researchers found inconsistency in judgments about internal control. Other researchers found the same inconsistencies, but found that the amount of inconsistency declined as the subjects became more experienced. See, for example, Philip M.J. Reckers and Martin E. Taylor, "Consistency in Auditors' Evaluations of Internal Control," *Journal of Accounting, Auditing, and Finance* (Fall 1979): 42-55; Philip M.J. Reckers and Martin E. Taylor, "Under the Microscope: Evaluating Internal Accounting Controls," *Internal Auditor* (October 1980): 27-32; American Institute of Certified Public Accountants, A Case Study on the Extent of Audit Samples, New York: American Institute of Certified Public Accountants (A/A 1955); J.C. Corless, "Assessing Prior Distributions for Applying Bayesian Statistics in Auditing," *The Accounting Review* (July 1972): 556-566; R. Weber, "Auditor Decision Making in Overall System Reliability: Accuracy, Consensus, and the

Usefulness of a Decision Aid," *Journal of Accounting Research* (Autumn 1978): 368-388; and Robert H. Ashton, "An Experimental Study of Internal Control Judgments," *Journal of Accounting Research* (Spring 1974): 143–157.

57. See Mautz et al., and Stanford Research Institute, *Systems Auditability and Control Study* (Stanford Research Institute, 1977).

58. See, for example, SEC Release No. 34-15772 that states "Therefore, many decisions on reasonable assurance will necessarily depend in part on estimates and informed judgments by management."

59. Another way of saying this is that there are controls which are substitutes for other controls and, further, that substitution does not have to occur on a one-to-one basis.

60. The finding that experience aids in making judgments in complex situations is not all that unusual. See Ray G. Stephens, *Uses of Financial Information by Bank Lending Officers* (UMI Research Press, 1979). When large amounts of information which cannot be easily aggregated in mathematical form, or when the mathematical form in which it should be aggregated is unknown, and when time is not limited, experience seems to be the only way to learn to process the information reasonably, making the tradeoffs.

61. The academic research also says something about the experience of both internal auditors and independent accountants in making recommendations about internal accounting control.

62. See S. Yu and J. Neter, "A Stochastic Model of the Internal Control System," *Journal of Accounting Research* (Autumn 1973): 273-295.

63. See Barry E. Cushing, "A Mathematical Approach to the Analysis and Design of Internal Control Systems," *Accounting Review* (January 1974): 24-41. See also A. Ishikawa, "A Mathematical Approach to the Analysis and Design of Internal Control Systems: A Brief Comment," *Accounting Review* (January 1975): 148-150 and Barry E. Cushing, "A Further Note on the Mathematical Approach to Internal Control," *Accounting Review* (January 1975): 151-154.

64. Existence or absence, effect or no effect, is difficult to model in the mathematics of stochastic processes or Bayesian statistical processes. The tradeoff is that an overall assessment is unavailable in chance-constrained programming without an independent, externally derived tradeoff algorithm. The overall assessment is internally derived in stochastic processes or Bayesian statistics due to the nature of the mathematics.

65. See Susan S. Hamlen, "A Chance-Constrained Mixed Integer Programming Model for Internal Control Design," *Accounting Review* (October 1980): 578-593.

66. See Andrew D. Bailey, Jr., Gordon L. Duke, James H. Gerlach, Chen-en Ko, Raymond D. Meservy, and Andrew B. Whinston, "TICOM and the Analysis of Internal Controls," *Accounting Review* (April 1985): 186-201

67. 17 CFR § 240.12b-2.

68. TSC Industries v. Northway, 426 U.S. 438, 449 (1976).

69. *Statement of Financial Accounting Concepts No. 2, Qualitative Characteristics of Accounting Information* (FASB, May 1980), para. 132.

70. In addition, there is a fair amount of guidance in law (the Foreign Corrupt Practices Act and amendments thereto) and in SEC releases, consistent with this private sector guidance, that provides additional guidance: (a) the proposal for a management report assessing internal controls and examination of that report by independent accountants, Securities Act Release No. 15772 (April 30, 1979) (44 Fed. Reg. 26,702); (b) ASR No. 278, *Statement of Management on Internal Accounting Control* (45 Fed. Reg. 40,134); SEC Release 17500 (46 Fed. Reg. 11,544); and ASR No. 305, *Statement of Management on Internal Accounting Control* (SEC Release No. 34-18451). There is also a fair amount of guidance from various SEC enforcement actions.

71. Livingstone and Steinberg (pp. 39–43) express the belief that prescriptive guidance at a detailed level should be avoided because of the differences in facts and circumstances. While this recommendation was primarily directed at the SEC, it seems to apply to private sector guidance as well. The development of guidance to handle all facts and circumstances would, if possible, be a very long process.

72. SAS No. 55 also distinguishes between effectiveness of design and operation. Note that effectiveness of design involves an analysis of the ability to control only irregularities and errors explicitly recognized in the design. Effectiveness of operation requires analysis of performance with design characteristics. In some rare cases, effectiveness of design automatically ensures effectiveness of operation, as with some EDP controls.

73. The Auditing Standards Board (ASB) seems to recognize that the auditor must identify conditions for reportable "material weakness" as part of the understanding of internal control for planning purposes under SAS No. 55. At the January 1989 meeting of the ASB, an auditing interpretation allowing auditors to send a letter concerning a negative finding of material weaknesses was approved. SAS No. 55 prohibits sending a communication that says there were no reportable conditions because the audit standards do not require performance of procedures searching for reportable conditions, only reporting those that came to the auditor's attention as the result of performing audit procedures.

74. There is also a need for more research designed to provide guidance about the judgment process in evaluating internal controls. This type of research, except for development of an expert systems models, has also been limited. John Rapp, in "Developing Criteria for Internal Control Systems Review," *CPA Journal* (June 1979): 86-87, suggested academic involvement with management advisory services engagements. Since SAS No. 30, similar

statements could be made concerning these engagements. No projects have been published to date. If advances have been made in this area, it is proprietary information not in the public domain.

Part II

Computers and Decision Support

4

Qualitative and Causal Reasoning in Auditing

Andrew D. Bailey, Jr.
Yihwa Kiang
Benjamin Kuipers
Andrew B. Whinston

Many decision-making problems require choices based on incomplete information. Incomplete knowledge about causal relationships is one aspect of the decision maker's problem and an important fact of life in reasoning about accounting and auditing systems. Recent work in qualitative and causal reasoning, while it has focused on predicting the dynamic behavior of continuous physical systems, offers an opportunity to extend the capability of current auditing decision support software systems. Qualitative simulation of behavior from structure (causal understanding) is a valuable method for reasoning about partially known systems. We believe that the introduction of qualitative and causal reasoning based on an understanding of the business and accounting environment will strengthen existing audit decision support.

This chapter introduces auditors and accountants to a new form of modeling that specifically addresses the issue of incomplete knowledge of causal relations. We illustrate the potential of this technique, qualitative and causal reasoning, in an analytical review setting and compare the technique to the currently popular expert systems applications in auditing.

Expert systems have been the subject of numerous auditing research and application studies in recent years. A number of these systems [e.g. Peat Marwick's Loan Probe System, Coopers & Lybrand's Expertax, and Arthur Young's Decision Support System] (Jacob and Bailey, 1989) are being used in the auditing environment. Although the current expert systems may perform impressively, experience and analysis indicate that an inference method based almost solely on empirical association between observable findings and hypotheses has serious limitations. Moreover, these limitations are unlikely to be overcome within the current theoretic context of expert systems.

This chapter will extend the potential of expert systems in auditing. We illustrate the potential of qualitative and causal reasoning concepts in the application of these methods to an analytical review setting. Analytical procedures have recently gained in prominence as an audit technique. Statement of Auditing Standards (SAS) No. 56 requires the use of analytical procedures in virtually all audits during the planning and overall review phases of the audit American Institute of Certified Public Accounts (AICPA, 1988). In addition, SAS No. 56 permits the use of analytical procedures as a substitute for other substantive tests. Whatever one's current belief about the power and potential of analytical procedures as an efficient and effective audit tool, strengthening the potential effectiveness of this family of tools would appear to be of importance to the practicing auditor.

Analytical procedures "consist of evaluations of financial information made by a study of plausible relationships" (American Institute of Certified Public Accountants, 1988, paragraph 2)" and presume the relatively stable existence of predictable relationships among financial and nonfinancial data. The methods of performing analytical review vary, but have largely relied on auditor judgment and expert knowledge in evaluating information related to the firm and its environment. A common technique involves computing computation of financial statement ratios and assessing the relationships among the ratios based on the auditor's knowledge of the firm, its business policies, and its specific and general business conditions (Kinney and Felix, 1980; Kinney and Salamon, 1982). More advanced methods use statistical techniques, such as regression-based model building (Wallace and Akresh, 1980). The efficacy of these techniques has been brought into question by recent research results (Kinney, 1987; Loebbecke and Steinbart, 1987).

Except where the analytical review procedure relies rather directly on the auditor's judgment, a fundamental limitation of these techniques is their inability to incorporate causal relationships in the analysis. Even the advanced approaches relying on regression techniques include causal aspects in only a very indirect manner. It does seem likely that audit experts do consider causal relationships in performing analytical reviews—their individual explanations of unexpected results often include explanations of causal linkages among ratios and other observed data. However, the well-known limitations of human information processing suggest that formal modeling efforts intended to support the auditor in this effort are likely to improve these judgments.

Recent work in qualitative and causal reasoning, while it has focused on predicting the dynamic behavior of continuous physical systems, offers an opportunity to extend the capability of current auditing decision support software systems. Qualitative simulation of behavior from structure (causal understanding) is a valuable method for reasoning about partially known systems. We believe that the introduction of qualitative and causal reasoning based on an understanding of the business and accounting environment will strengthen existing audit decision support.

The recommendation that causal models be used as the basis for analytical review is not completely new. However, previous recommendations were based on models that required a substantially more precise understanding of the firm than do qualitative and causal reasoning models. For example, Kaplan (1979) proposed a similar approach based on the use of linear programming as the means of modeling the reporting process. In the late sixties and even into the seventies, operations research techniques of this nature were expected to make substantial contributions to accounting and auditing. As with the parallel developments in the area of artificial intelligence, the promise was more than could be delivered and the techniques, while still in use, settled into relative obscurity.

The use of statistical models, particularly regression techniques, grew during the seventies and eighties and continues as the most common modeling methodology in analytical review. These models only implicitly incorporate causal knowledge and encounter data and breadth problems in application (Wallace and Akresh, 1980). During the last several years, more advanced, but still largely association-based modeling techniques in the form of expert systems have swept the field. While the power of these techniques can be impressive, they are, as noted above and elsewhere in this chapter, limited in theory and application. The emergence of qualitative and causal modeling is, in principle, a return to the operations research style of modeling efforts previously proposed. The significant advantage of qualitative and causal modeling lies in the reduced modeling requirements vis-à-vis an understanding of the firm and data demands. The ability to obtain useful predictions from qualitative and causal models is based on technology developments in computer software (Kuipers, 1986) and is the topic of this chapter.

In this chapter we explain the basic concepts of model-based reasoning and contrast these concepts with the more traditional rule-based expert systems approaches and discuss the development of a prototype analytical review model based on these qualitative and causal modeling concepts. We also explain and demonstrate the solution processes and potential of qualitative and causal modeling. We conclude with some observations concerning the potential of qualitative and causal reasoning in the auditing area.

RULE-BASED VERSUS MODEL-BASED REASONING

Whether frame-, script-, or rule-based, expert systems are largely a collection of associations of the if-then form. These associations are generally heuristic rather than causal, capturing what experts are observed to do, though they are not necessarily able to explain why experts acted as they did (Quinlan, 1979). As the ability to explain their reasoning is one of the objectives of the expert system applications of artificial intelligence (AI), this is clearly a significant limitation in concept and application. The inability to explain the reasoning behind an unexpected set of financial relationships during an analytical review would be particularly problematic because analytical review is intended to direct the auditor's attention toward areas likely to require investigation. Current techniques rely on the auditor to provide the logical and causal links and thus bridge the gap to the particular accounts or transaction flows that warrant additional attention. Our proposal will attempt to incorporate as many of these linkages as possible directly in the analysis and thus permit the model to provide some part of the causal reasoning for observed deviations from expectations.

Where no well-defined causal theories exist, expert systems are a useful way of systematically accumulating large numbers of fragmentary rules of thumb. However, one important consequence of this kind of knowledge is its brittleness. Current expert systems may provide impressive results on the narrowly defined tasks for which they were designed; however, if the nature of the task is altered, sometimes even slightly, the performance deteriorates significantly or fails completely (Bell, 1985). It is possible that the expert system user will not recognize the failure until it has led to significant negative consequences.

The major difficulty is that current expert systems are not built upon a basic causal theory; therefore, they cannot reason about system changes that are not already encoded in their if-then rules (Kuipers, 1989). Humans can handle changes that are well outside of their immediate experiences because they often have a general understanding of the workings of the system even though they do not understand the system in great detail. For example, an auditor who observes a significant increase in inventories may readily consider alternative explanations based upon his/her understanding of accounting and the business environment even though the auditor has never encountered many of the scenario explanations. Thus, while the auditor may not have a previously encoded set of detailed rules to rely on in a specialized situation, the auditor's qualitative/causal model of the environment still supports a significant and powerful reasoning potential.

The qualitative and causal reasoning approach developed in this chapter is based on deep reasoning models. These models incorporate a structural description of the system, which captures the underlying causal relationship between each component in the system and allows us to predict the behavior of the system over time. By contrast, expert systems incorporating only shallow reasoning models make decisions directly from observed features of the presented situations without an understanding of the underlying structure (Kuipers, 1987).

The current research effort is a part of a larger effort by the artificial intelligence research community. It is an attempt to develop and add substance to the framework of Figure 4.1 by extending the power of qualitative model-based reasoning methods and developing an appropriate style of interaction between rule-based and model-based reasoning methods. It is an attempt not to replace existing support systems, but to substantially increase their reasoning powers and thus expand the inherent range of their domains.

Figure 4.1
Model-Based Reasoning in a Generate-and-Test Cycle

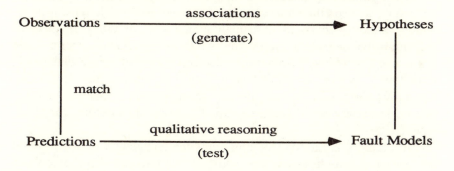

QUANTITATIVE VERSUS QUALITATIVE REASONING

Managers encounter two major classes of decision problems in their business life. One class of problems can be characterized by well-understood means/ends conditions and are often called structured decision problems. The effectiveness of decisions for this class of problems is heavily dependent upon accurate and reliable data. Most of the decisions in this class are routine and subject to programming and hence are matters for lower-level managers (Jaedicke et al., 1966). Many of these structured decisions, like the inventory reorder decision, can be quantified because the underlying descriptive models are sufficiently precise in the specification of causality.

Unfortunately, most of the important decisions made by higher-level managers relate to planning, controlling, and evaluating tasks for which the means/ends conditions are not well understood. This class of decision problem is referred to as unstructured or semistructured decisions. These decisions are most frequently made from highly summarized data and are generally not sensitive to minor fluctuations in data accuracy or completeness. "Analytical procedures used in planning the audit generally use data aggregated at a high level" (American Institute of Certified Public Accountants, 1988, paragraph 7). While the better the management's understanding of the environment is the better the decision is likely to be, there is a qualitative difference in the information needs of a decision maker in this setting. A qualitative model will support decisions in this context.

A qualitative model or description is one that captures certain distinctions that make an important, qualitative difference and ignores others (Kuipers, 1984). An accounting and auditing example will serve to illustrate this point. The valuation of accounts receivable is an important aspect in any audit. However, perfect accuracy is not required; measurement to materiality limit is sufficient. Any over– or understatement (recorded error) within materiality limits is regarded as qualitatively insignificant. The point at which the account receivable exceeds the materiality limit is a qualitatively important point, which would be included in a qualitative model of the audit process. Deviations below the materiality limit would be aggregated under a single qualitative description, "insignificant." A qualitative model of the audit would not allow or support quantification or analysis of actions for all valuation deviations. However, it would permit the qualitative distinction between actions necessary for material deviations and those necessary for lessor deviations.

In Figure 4.2, the top row represents the complexity of a real-world accounting and auditing system, while the bottom row represents finite descriptions of that system. The lower part of Figure 4.2 would include only qualitatively significant relationships (Kuipers, 1986). Qualitative description makes fewer distinctions than are actually present in the real system. If the qualitative model is sufficiently simple, it may be computationally feasible to simulate the accounting and/or auditing process using the qualitative model.

If the qualitative model accurately describes the structure of the accounting and/or auditing system, the behavior predicted by the solution to the qualitative model will accurately describe the actual behavior of the accounting and/or auditing system. Note, however, that the predictions will not have the numeric precision of an Economic Order Quantity (EOQ) model.

Figure 4.2
Abstraction from the Real-World System to Qualitative Models

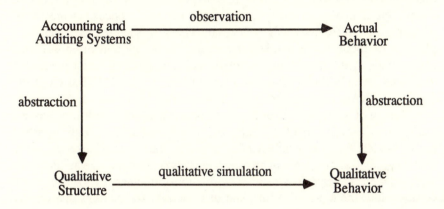

In this chapter, we focus on auditing and accounting issues where knowledge of the causal relations is limited—insufficient to permit quantitative or analytic modeling, but sufficient to permit qualitative and causal modeling. Several areas in the audit recommend themselves as candidates for a qualitative and causal reasoning approach (e.g., analytical review, internal control evaluation, and inherent risk assessment). In each case, the auditor has some, albeit incomplete, concept of the causal model underlying the analysis. This seems particularly appealing with respect to internal control systems where the flow of information is clearly understood and the underlying double-entry system of accounting is operating. The analytical review area, as previously discussed, is based on the presumption of a set of stable underlying causal chains relating the firm's results to its activities through the accounting system and therefore also appears to be a good candidate. Inherent risk assessments is a less well understood area, but still seems to suggest some underlying causal operators. There are, no doubt, other areas of potential as well. We have chosen to consider analytical review in this chapter.

CURRENT EXPERT SYSTEMS AND MODELING APPROACHES IN AUDITING

In the natural sciences there is a long tradition of numeric and analytical models based on differential equations. Social scientists have attempted to emulate this model of science, but have had difficulty in applying it in management environments, due to the general lack of explicit causal knowledge available in many areas of the natural sciences. In the social sciences, the limited knowledge of causal mechanisms has tended to lead to a plethora of theories and models involving competing and often complex assumptions. Although recent developments in computer science have lead to improved tractability in complex situations [e.g., TICOM (Bailey et al., 1985) and FAAM (Han 1989)], the achievements are still limited.

The use of analytic or quantitative models in auditing is still very limited, and often informal. One of the more well developed areas in auditing is the use of models for analytical review. Currently, four approaches are used in analytical review. To carry out an effective analytical review, the auditor must estimate what the expected balance or relationship under review should be, compare it to the reported results and then identify fluctuations that require investigation. Figure 4.3 illustrates the fundamental requirements of any analytical review process (i.e., prediction model, reported results, comparison, and auditor response). Four methods of currently arriving at these expectations and identifying fluctuations requiring investigation are outlined below (Kinney and Salamon, 1982).

1. Results of prior years—rules of thumb
2. Experienced prediction
3. Trend extrapolation
4. Statistical techniques

In practice, methods one, two and three can often be used together and can be categorized as "judgmental" or "nonstatistical." Method four, which also includes judgmental elements, can be categorized as "statistical."

The problem with these techniques is that all of them rely heavily on implicit knowledge and auditor expertise for data capture, processing, analysis, and interpretation. The difficulty with this is the informality of the approaches and thus their lack of rigor. The more recent quantitative techniques, such as linear regression, contribute to supporting the auditor with more explicit judgmental requirements, but still rely heavily on implicit knowledge of the underlying relationships (Wallace and Akresh, 1980).

Recently, articles about the use of expert systems in audit areas, such as analytical review, have begun to appear in the auditing literature (Bailey,

1987). A good expert system reaches the same conclusions as the expert would reach if faced with a comparable problem. The scarcity of expertise in the ever increasingly complex auditing environment makes expert systems an attractive productivity tool despite their previously noted limitations. However, prior research efforts have had only limited success (Messier and Hansen, 1987).

Figure 4.3
Analytical Review Process

Analytical Review Process

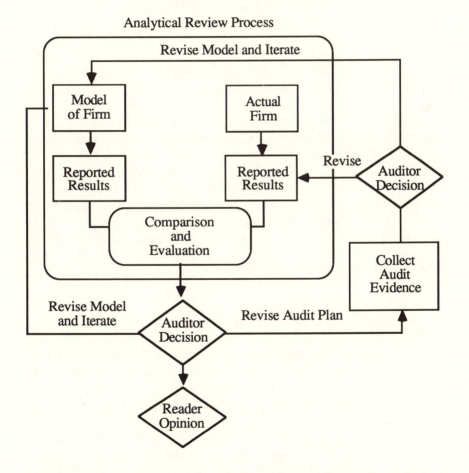

The past research efforts were either too narrowly defined with respect to the ability to reason about the system [e.g., TICOM (Bailey et al., 1985)] or limited by the use of primarily heuristic knowledge of the auditor evaluation process [e.g., ARISC (Meservy et al., 1986)]. Nevertheless, each of the prior projects relied, to some extent, on a sometimes explicit, but more often implicit, qualitative/causal model of accounting. Unfortunately, neither TICOM nor ARISC took full advantage of the underlying qualitative/causal model of accounting.

The challenge we wish to address is the development of computer-compatible accounting system representations that support qualitative/causal reasoning. While the objectives are the same as those specified by current expert systems researchers, our approach differs from the expert systems approach in significant ways. We want to reason from a basic understanding of the system (i.e., from a causal theory of economics and accounting), rather than from empirical relations alone.

CONCEPTS OF QUALITATIVE REASONING AND QUALITATIVE SIMULATION

The study of qualitative reasoning for problem solving originated in the AI research work on qualitative physics. It focuses on using common sense or incomplete knowledge to reason about the everyday physical world. The motivation for this approach is the observed human ability to reason about common physical processes through intuition, rather than through intensive mathematical calculations. There is evidence that the states of incomplete knowledge, the reasoning from structure to behavior, and the algorithm for local propagation of implications within components all correspond well with the human reasoning mechanism and its representations (deKleer and Brown, 1984; Kuipers and Kassirer, 1984).

Incomplete Knowledge

Both common sense and expert knowledge are always incomplete. No one understands down to the last detail how any mechanism actually works. Even if it were possible to construct a model of something as simple as an oil furnace, down to the level of quantum electrodynamics, the model would be absurdly, uselessly large. What is needed is a model that is "good enough" for its purposes (Kuipers, 1988a). In an auditing context, we do not need a model that explains every aspect of internal control, but only one that is good enough for the auditor to identify the critical strengths and weaknesses. Similarly, analytical review models do not have to be complete to the level of individual customer accounts.

Certainly the ability to focus on the important distinctions and ignore the unimportant ones is an excellent way to cope with incomplete knowledge. But how do we formalize this insight? A qualitative simulation program, called QSIM, makes it possible to solve qualitative/causal models (i.e., models that are incomplete and deal with only important distinctions) by computer (Kuipers, 1984).. In the following sections, we use a simple bathtub-like example in the accounting domain to illustrate how QSIM works.

Building Qualitative Models

QSIM is useful as a tool in building qualitative causal models, but is particularly important for representing and reasoning with incomplete knowledge. The primary tool QSIM provides for model building is a language of qualitative constraints and landmarks. The qualitative model is basically an abstraction of the quantitative model in which each time-dependent parameter is represented by the relationship of its magnitude to certain landmark values and the sign of its first derivative.

A QSIM model consists of parameters and constraints. Each parameter in QSIM represents a real-valued function of time, but its range of values is modeled symbolically by a quantity space—a finite, totally ordered set of landmark values. Landmark values correspond to real values, which are important or critical to the parameter, but only ordinal properties of quantities are involved; therefore, actual addition and multiplication for landmark values are not meaningful. At any time, each parameter has a unique qualitative value in its quantity space, either at a landmark value or in the interval between two adjacent landmarks. This value is called a qualitative magnitude. In addition, each parameter has a qualitative direction, indicating whether the parameter is increasing, steady, or decreasing.

Each constraint is between two or more parameters in the model and limits the simultaneous combinations of values that can be taken by those parameters. Constraints in QSIM include the familiar mathematical operators (e.g., +, *, and d/dt) and some special-purpose functional relationships (e.g., M^+, M^-, S^+, S^-). Qualitative addition and multiplication are not functions, but relations that represent the actual mathematical relations of addition and multiplication.

If two variables, X and Y, have the relationship of $Y = f(X)$, where f is a monotonically increasing function, then we can use the M^+ function to model the relation of X and Y in QSIM as $Y = M^+(X)$. The term M^+ refers to an unspecified member of the class of monotonically increasing functions. By the same token, an unspecified monotonically decreasing function can represented by the term M^-. The exact relationship between such accounts as sales and cash is not specified either because the exact form of that function is not known with certainty or because the information about the exact form of that function is not needed for the type of analysis that we plan to carry out.

Function $Y = S^+(X)$ is used to model the relationship of X and Y where Y is monotonically increasing over a certain interval [e.g. (x^{1*}, x^{2*})] with X, and will remain constant when the value of X is below x^{1*} or above x^{2*}. The S^- constraint is handled similarly. Figure 4.4 shows the shape of the S^+ function between variables X and Y $[Y = S(X)]$ and the format of the function in QSIM.

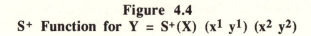

Figure 4.4
S^+ Function for $Y = S^+(X)$ $(x^1\ y^1)$ $(x^2\ y^2)$

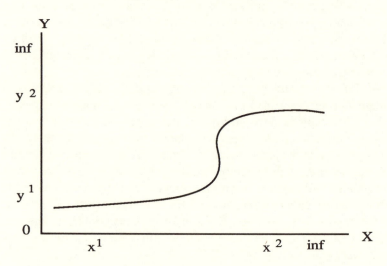

The concept of "time" has special characteristics in QSIM. QSIM models time as an alternating sequence of time points and open time intervals, and the initial state always begins at time instant t^0. The change from that point in time puts us into an open interval on the time line, (t^0, t^1), during which the qualitative description remains fixed until we reach another distinguished time-point where a qualitative change can take place. Thus, the second state description applies not to a single instant in time, but to every time point in the interval (t^0, t^1). The purpose of modeling time in this way is to simplify the simulation; hence, we can always direct our attention only to the time points where distinctive qualitative changes occurred and ignore the states of time intervals.

Given a parameter with its qualitative magnitude and directions of change at a certain time point, implicit continuity constraints restrict the possible changes it can take in the following open time interval. For instance, it is possible for a parameter to jump from one landmark (e.g. 0) to another (e.g. inf) without passing through the intermediate state (e.g. 0, inf). And it is not possible to convert the directions of change from decreasing to increasing or from increasing to decreasing without passing the intermediate state, "steady." In addition, it is also impossible for the qualitative description of a parameter to alter from an open interval to a landmark value while moving from a time instant (e.g. t^0) to a time interval (e.g., t^0, t^1), but it is allowed when moving from a time interval toward a time instant. The reason is that it would require a finite amount of time to reach the boundary (landmark) of its interval, but it can always move off a landmark value instantaneously. Even though the qualitative descriptions are not allowed to change during a time interval, in the following example, several parameters are actually changing. As long as the changes do not cross any qualitative boundary [e.g., changing within the range of (0, inf)], the qualitative description of the changing system remains constant during that time interval.

In the following sections, a number of the important concepts of qualitative simulation are explored through a simple, one-tank fluid-flow system: cash-flow management. In order to build a qualitative/causal model for this system, the first step is to understand the structure and behavior of the system. To understand how the cash-flow system operates we begin with its most basic constituents: the cash inflow (inlet of the tank), the cash outflow (drain of the tank), and the total cash on hand (the amount of water (cash) in the tank). Figure 4.5 shows the analogy between the bathtub and cash-flow system.

Figure 4.5
Cash-Flow Model

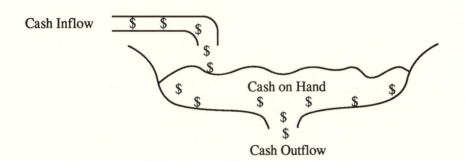

The cash-flow management system can help to regulate the amount of cash held by a company. In this example and the rest of this chapter, the term "cash flow" is used broadly to represent funds provided by operations. The structure of the system is as follows. When the system is at equilibrium, the amount of cash inflow should be equal to the amount of cash outflow, and the cash netflow (difference between cash inflow and cash outflow) is zero. In this simple system the sales are at a certain level and stable (this can, in this simple setting, be inferred from the constant cash inflow condition) as are the total cash on hand and current liabilities. In this basic example, with stable cash on hand, the level of current assets will remain unchanged. Both stable current assets and current liabilities implies that the current ratio is steady, so are the health and cash payment rate, i.e. the system would be in equilibrium.

Cash, credit and inventory are three main elements of current assets. Reasoning qualitatively, and not knowing the exact rate of increase of current assets to cash on hand, this state of incomplete knowledge can be expressed more exactly, but still in a qualitative way, as some unspecified, but monotonically increasing function relating cash on hand to current assets. The reader may find it worthwhile to reference Figure 4.6 as the development of this example continues.

$$\text{Current-assets} = \text{M}+ \text{(Cash)} \tag{1}$$

The values which Cash and Current-assets can take are also qualitative instead of quantitative. The quantity space of a parameter shows all the possible qualitative values, also known as landmark values, which the parameter can take. Landmark values are the values which can make an important or relevant distinction when reasoning about different states of the system. The quantity spaces for Cash and Current-assets are:

Cash	0...c*...inf	(a)
Current-assets	0...ca*...inf	(b)

The landmarks minf and inf [Figure 4.6, quantity space (e)] represent negative infinity and positive infinity, respectively. Along with landmark 0, these landmark values have known properties and can be used in any quantity space. Other landmarks are symbols that have meanings specific to the particular quantity space and that are defined only by their relationships with other landmarks. Therefore, the landmark ca* represents the present level (normal level) of current assets—a level somewhere in the interval of (0 inf), but otherwise unspecified. We will frequently use a superscript such as "*" to generate a distinct symbolic name for a landmark value of a parameter. Finally, since the amounts of current assets and cash are necessarily non-negative, the lower bounds of the quantity spaces are both 0.

If we have additional knowledge about the monotonic function that relates parameters, we can describe those relationships as corresponding values for that constraint, thereby defining specific points that the function passes through. In the case of current assets and cash, the value of cash must be zero when the amount of current assets is zero. This relationship can be written as (0 0) under the corresponding value of that constraint [Figure 4.6, constraint (1)]. In addition, the corresponding value (inf inf) can also be asserted for that constraint, which has the effect of preventing the function Current-assets = M^+(Cash) from having a horizontal or vertical asymptote.

Current-ratio is equal to Current-assets/Current-liabilities and can be viewed as a surrogate measure of firm health, where Health is positive only when the Current-ratio is greater than 2. The level of the cash payment rate is in turn determined by the health of the firm. In our example, we use an S^+ function to model the relationship between Health and Cash-payment-rate [Cash-payment-rate = S^+ (Health)], where Cash-payment-rate = 0 for Health < 0 and Cash-payment-rate = M^+(Health) for Health > 0. In this scenario the firm will not make cash payments when Health < 0 (Current-ratio < 2).

Equilibrium in the cash-flow system can come about only when cash inflow is equal to cash outflow. There is also a monotonically increasing function relating Cash-payment-rate to Cash-outflow. We use functions (2), (3), (4), and (5) to represent these relationships.

Current-assets = Current-ratio * Current-liabilities   (2)

Health = M^+ (Current-ratio)   (3)

Cash-payment-rate = S^+ (Health)   (4)

Cash-outflow = M^+ (Cash-payment-rate)   (5)

The ratio of current assets to current liabilities, is one of the ratios frequently used in analyzing the level of the cash payment rate. An oft-quoted standard for this ratio is that it should be held at a value not less than 2:1. A declining trend in this ratio indicates that the company is becoming short of cash relative to its current liability payment requirements and may have difficulty in meeting its current obligations. In order to avoid a zero cash balance, it is necessary to reduce the level of the cash payment rate. Constraints (2), (3), (4), and (5) accomplish this end and represent a specific cash management policy for the firm being modeled. These constraints represent a policy that does not permit cash to be overdrawn (i.e., no negative cash balances are allowed in this model). Further, the rate at which cash is used to pay liabilities is constrained by the level of liabilities and by management's policy concerning maintenance of a satisfactory current ratio. In the context of this firm's model (i.e., this example), the current ratio policy may be viewed as management's surrogate measure of firm health. Alternatively, it could be an imposed condition necessary to satisfy a debt covenant. The important point here is that this is only one of many cash management policies that could be modeled even within the context of this simple example. Future extensions of this model might include consideration of long-term credit options. Such a consideration would introduce new constraints and allow for a more elaborate cash management policy that incorporates borrowing. The introduction of long-term assets and liabilities would permit a more complex set of relationships and expectations. There is also no reason why existing statistical modeling measures of firm health cannot be incorporated in the qualitative and causal models. For example, Altman's (1982) z-score and similar firm failure or distress models might be incorporated. The firm may view a z-score as a serious health measure for internal management control purposes or as simply a means to avoid flagging their firm as distressed during an analytical review. A variety of other options of this type present themselves for consideration: for example the use of Lev's (1969) observation that firm financial ratios appear to regress toward an industry mean could be explicitly incorporated in a model.

The multiplier in the constraint (2) and the addition in constraint (6) in Figure 4.6 represent the actual mathematical relationships of multiplication and addition, but only applied to qualitative descriptions of quantities. For instance, if the amount of current assets is zero, then the level of current ratio is also equal to zero. If the amount of current liabilities is constant at some positive value (cl*), then the constraint will behave like the Current-ratio = M^+ (Cash) relationships. This all means that the amount of cash on hand has a direct influence on the level of Current-ratio. Constraint (5) means that the amount of Cash-outflow is directly dependent on the level of Cash-payment-rate. Hence, when the level of Cash-payment-rate changes, the amount of Cash-outflow will also vary with the direction of the cash payment rate changes.

Since the landmark values defined for each parameter are meaningful only in their own quantity spaces, this amounts to using different measurements to describe the quantity space for different variables. Therefore, we cannot do the actual addition or multiplication of two landmark values from different quantity spaces; we can only use the ordinal relationship between them to filter out the impossible combinatorial state(s) of the system. The quantity spaces of Current-liabilities, Current-Ratio, Health, Cash-payment-rate, and Cash-outflow are as follows:

Current-liabilities	0...cl*...inf	(c)
Current-ratio	0...2...cr*...inf	(d)
Health	minf...0...h*...inf	(e)
Cash-payment-rate	0...cpr*...inf	(f)
Cash-outflow	0...co*...inf	(g)

Figure 4.6
Complete Description of the Qualitative Structure of
Cash Flow Model I

Model: Cash-Flow Management
Quantity Spaces:

Cash	0...c*...inf	(a)
Current-assets	0...ca*...inf	(b)
Current-liabilities	0...cl*...inf	(c)
Current-ratio	0...2...cr*...inf	(d)
Health	minf...0...h*...inf	(e)
Cash-payment-rate	0...cpr*...inf	(f)
Cash-outflow	0...co*...inf	(g)
Cash-inflow	0...ci*...inf	(h)
Cash-netflow	minf...0...inf	(i)
Sales	0...s*...inf	(j)

Constraints and Corresponding Values

Current assets = M+ (Cash)	(0 0), (ca* c*), (inf inf)	(1)
Current-assets = Current-ratio * Current-liabilities		(2)
Health = M+ (Current-ratio)	(0 minf), (2 0), (inf inf)	(3)
Cash-payment-rate = S+ (Health)	(0 0), (inf inf), (h* cr*)	(4)
Cash-outflow = M+ (Cash-payment-rate)	(0 0), (cpr* co*), (inf inf)	(5)
Cash-inflow = Cash-outflow + Cash-netflow		(6)
Cash-netflow = d/dt (Cash)		(7)
Cash-inflow = M+ (Sales)	(0 0), (ci* s*), (inf inf)	(8)
Current-liabilities = M+ (Sales)	(0 0), (s* cl*), (inf inf)	(9)

The difference between cash inflow and cash outflow is called cash netflow. An "excessive" amount of cash inflow (positive cash netflow) in the cash-flow system tends to raise the amount of total cash on hand, while the total amount of cash on hand will decline when cash outflow is greater than cash inflow. The value of cash netflow represents the rate of change of total cash on hand. These two facts can be represented by two functions.

$$\text{Cash-inflow} = \text{Cash-outflow} + \text{Cash-netflow} \tag{6}$$

$$\text{Cash-netflow} = d/dt \ (\text{Cash}) \tag{7}$$

In qualitative and causal reasoning, the factor in which we are most interested are not the exact values of each parameter in the constraints, but rather, the relationship between parameters. Thus, constraint (7) can be interpreted as representing the direction of change of total cash on hand. The quantity spaces of Cash-inflow and Cash-netflow are shown below:

Cash-inflow	0...ci*...inf	(h)
Cash-netflow	minf...0...inf	(i)

Finally, increases in the amount of total sales can be associated with increases in the amount of cash inflow and the level of current liabilities. Increasing Sales will generate Cash-inflow and an increasing rate of acquisition for raw material and inventory, resulting in increasing Current-liabilities.

$$\text{Cash-inflow} = M^+ \ (\text{Sales}) \tag{8}$$

$$\text{Current-liabilities} = M^+ \ (\text{Sales}) \tag{9}$$

Constraints (8) and (9) indicate that when the amount of total sales increases, the amount of cash we can collect from sales will also increase, as will the obligation for payment (current liabilities). The quantity space of Sales is as follows:

Sales	0...s*...inf	(j)

By combining all these qualitative constraints (1-9), along with their corresponding values and the quantity space of each parameter (a-j), we can derive the complete description of the qualitative structure of the cash-flow management system shown in Figure 4.6. Figure 4.7 is the graphical representation of the cash-flow system. The model is, of course, a highly simplified account of how any cash flow system actually operates. For our present purpose, however, a simplified sketch is sufficient to give us a general idea about how useful qualitative reasoning may be in accounting and auditing.

Qualitative Knowledge of State. Relying on only the qualitative structure of the cash-flow management system, it is not possible to

Figure 4.7
Cash-Flow Model I

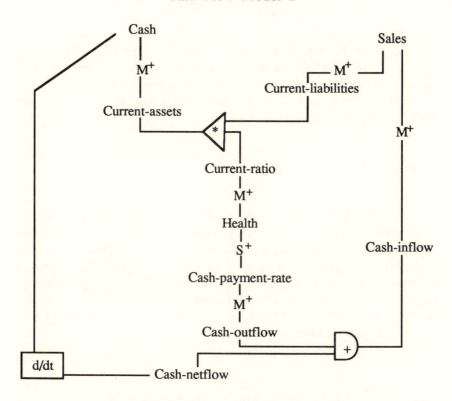

understand exact system functions. Therefore, the next step is to describe the dynamic behavior of the system—the sequences of qualitative states the system may pass through as it changes with time.

Assume that X(t) has this quantity space: 0...xl...inf. If X is increasing, the sequence of qualitative magnitudes of the parameter will be

$$X(t): \ 0 \dashrightarrow (0, x^l) \dashrightarrow x^l$$

meaning that after the time that X(t) = 0 and until X(t) = xl the value of X(t) is somewhere in the open internal (0, x^l).

In addition to qualitative magnitude in the quantity space, we also need to know the direction of change of each parameter in order to determine the transitions from one qualitative state to another. Thus, for each parameter, we describe its qualitative state in terms of its magnitude (in the quantity space) and its direction of change: increasing (inc), decreasing (dec), or steady (std), depending on the derivative of that parameter at that particular time point. Some researchers use +, -, and 0, or $\downarrow$, + and θ for this dexcription, instead of inc, dec and std (deKleer and Brown, 1984). The direction of change—inc, dec, and std—corresponds to a derivative of positive, negative, and zero. Therefore, a parameter with a positive derivative means that the direction of change of that parameter at that instant is increasing. We can rewrite the above sequence of changes of X as follows

$$X(t): <0, inc> \text{-->} <(0, x^l), inc> \text{-->} <x^l, inc>$$

A qualitative graph can help us to convey more clearly and understandably the complete description of the behavior of an individual parameter. In a qualitative graph, the only values the vertical axis can take are the landmark values in the quantity space of that parameter. The horizontal axis represents the distinguished time points. Figure 4.8 shows the qualitative graph of the behavior of $X(t)$ as the amount of X is increasing. Qualitative values are plotted at, or midway between, landmark points, and the symbol plotted represents the direction of change.

Figure 4.8
Qualitative Graph of the Sequence of
Qualitative Magnitudes of X

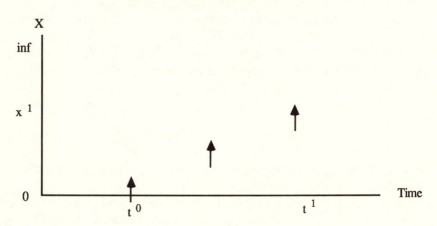

Predicting Behavior from Initial Conditions. A qualitative simulation problem usually starts with a description of the system in terms of the quantity space for each parameter, the constraint set and their corresponding values. Then an initial state (i.e., the initial values for the parameters) is given. QSIM uses this information to derive all the possible behaviors of that system.

In an analytical review context, the results of QSIM represent the potential expected relationships among the accounts (see Figure 4.3). These expectations are fundamental to the analytical review effort in that observed deviations from these expectations represent areas of potential interest for extended evidence collection during the audit. More traditional regression models (Wallace and Akresh, 1980) also provide expected values against which the auditor can compare observed results. Qualitative and causal models go a step beyond the provision of an expected result because of the causal linkages incorporated in the model. These linkages will permit a form of model reasoning about expectations not available in strictly associational approaches.

OSIM has two categories of variables, dependent and independent variables. Independent variables are the variables that must have values given in the initial state description and are assumed to remain constant throughout the whole simulation process. The value and directions of change of the dependent variables may change over time during the QSIM simulation and do not need to be provided at the beginning of the processes. The items of audit interest should be specified as dependent variables. In our example, the dependent variables are Cash, Current-assets, Cash-payment-rate, etc., and the independent variable is Sales.

Suppose that before the simualtion process started, the system was at an equilibrium state where the amount of total Cash (on hand) was equal to c^*, total Sales were s^*, and all the other parameters were stable. Observing a substantial decrease in the amount of sales results in the following initial conditions:

$$t = t^0 ==> \quad \text{Sales} = <(0, s^*), \text{std}>$$

$$\text{Cash} = <c^*, ?>$$

Sales are between 0 and the immediate preceding landmarks s^*. By specifying std, we mean that Sales declined to a new steady state. Cash will change, but the direction of change is unknown and thus is represented by "?". A complete qualitative state description is needed to start the simulation process. This means that we need to know the qualitative magnitude and direction of change for each parameter in the model before we can start the QSIM simulation. Thus, the next step is to derive the complete initial state description by propagating the above information across the constraint set in Figure 4.6.

Starting with information we had about the amount of sales $(0, s*)$, and constraint (8), Cash-inflow = M^+(Sales) with corresponding value $(0\ 0)$ and $(ci*\ s*)$, we can infer that the amount of Cash-inflow should be somewhat less than $ci*$, but greater than 0. This is necessary because of the M^+ relation and corresponding values between the two parameters.

$$\text{Sales} = (0, s*) ==> \qquad \text{Cash-inflow} = (0, ci*)$$

Because of the absence of additional landmarks, this is the best available description for the value of Cash-inflow expressible in its quantity space. We can employ the same method to obtain the magnitudes of both current-assets and Current-liabilities.

$$\text{Sales} = (0, s*) ==> \qquad \text{Current-liabilities} = (0, cl*)$$

$$\text{Cash} = c* ==> \qquad \text{Current-assets} = ca*$$

The same propagation algorithm is applied to the multiplication relation in constraint (2). Given Current-assets = Current-ratio * Current-liabilities and the corresponding values $(ca*\ cr*\ cl*)$, we can assert that the level of Current-ratio should be somewhere in between $cr*$ and inf $(cr*, \text{inf})$.

$$\text{Current-assets} = ca* \quad \text{and} \quad \text{Current-liabilities} = (0, cl*)$$

$$==> \quad \text{Current-ratio} = (cr*, \text{inf})$$

Again, by using the same mechanism, we can obtain the level of Health from the M^+ function, modeling the relationship between Current-ratio and Health.

Current-ratio = (cr*, inf)

==>   Health = (h*, inf)

From constraint (4), we know that when the value of Health is within teh interval of (0, inf), the relationship between Health and Cash-payment-rate is the same as a monotonically increasing function, with the corresponding value at (h* cpr*) and (inf inf). We derive the level of Cash-payment-rate as follows:

Health = (h*, inf)

==>   Cash-payment-rate = (cpr*, inf)

Because of the corresponding values at (cpr* co*) and (inf inf) of constraint (5), Cash-outflow = M^+ (Cash-payment-rate), we can conclude that:

Cash-payment-rate = (cpr*, inf)

==>   Cash-outflow = (co*, inf)

The addition in constraint (6), Cash-inflow = Cash-outflow + Cash-netflow, has corresponding value at (ci* co* 0). We also know from the argument above that Cash-inflow = (0, ci*) and Cash-outflow = (co*, inf). Therefore, the magnitude of Cash-netflow must be somewhat less than 0, but greater than minf.

Cash-inflow = (0, ci*)   and   Cash-outflow = (co*, inf)

==>   Cash-netflow = (minf, 0)

The derivative constraint (7) can now be used to determine the direction of change of cash on hand. The notation qdir(X) is used to represent the qualitative direction of X, and qmag(X) denotes the qualitative magnitude of X.

$$qmag(\text{Cash-netflow}) = (minf, 0) \quad ==> \quad qdir(\text{Cash}) = dec$$

The directions of change can be propagated through the monotonic functions as follows:

$$qdir(\text{Cash}) = dec ==> \qquad qdir(\text{Current-assets}) = dec$$

$$qdir(\text{Sales}) = std ==> \qquad qdir(\text{Current-liabilities}) = std$$

$$qdir(\text{Sales}) = std ==> \qquad qdir(\text{Cash-inflow}) = std$$

Directions of change also propagate through the multiplication constraint:

$$qdir(\text{Current-assets}) = dec \ \text{ and } \ qdir(\text{Current-liabilities}) = std$$

$$==> \quad qdir(\text{Current-ratio}) = dec$$

And the following completes the initial state description:

$$qdir(\text{Current-ratio}) = dec$$

$$==> \quad qdir(\text{Health}) = dec$$

$$qdir(\text{Health}) = dec \ \text{ and } \ qmag(\text{Health}) > 0$$

$$==> \quad qdir(\text{Cash-payment-rate}) = dec$$

$$qdir(\text{Cash-payment-rate}) = dec$$

$$==> \quad qdir(\text{Cash-outflow}) = dec$$

$$qdir(\text{Cash-outflow}) = dec \ \text{ and } \ qdir(\text{Cash-inflow}) = std$$

==>   qdir(Cash-netflow) = inc

The final result of this propagation is a complete, qualitative description of the cash-flow management model at the initial instant, t^0. The QSIM algorithm performs these steps automatically. Figure 4.9 illustrates the propagation process by working through the graphical representation of cash-flow model.

Our presentations so far only consider a means of deriving the complete initial state description with partial knowledge (observations) at a particular time point. We accomplish this derivation by local propagation around the network of constraints. Very little has been presented concerning changes taking place over time. With a complete initial state description of the model, we can start the QSIM simulation process. While the above qualitative state description indicates that several of the parameters are changing from their initial state, we next predict the evolution of the system over time by looking at the nature of the possible qualitative changes.

Predicting the Next State. Since each parameter changes continuously with time, it is relatively easy to predict the successors to a given state. If, at the initial instant t^0, the amount of cash on hand is equal to $c*$ and decreasing, then, in the next qualitative state at time (t^0, t^1), the amount of cash on hand will be less than $c*$ and decreasing [i.e. Cash = < (0, $c*$), dec>]. Applying the same scenario to Current-assets, we obtain Current-assets = <(0, $ca*$), dec>. The amount of total Sales, <(0, $s*$), std>, is given as an independent variable (constant) and will not change during the whole simulation. Consequently, the amount of Current-liabilities, <(0, $cl*$), std>, and the amount of Cash-inflow, <(0, $ci*$), std>, will also remain unchanged throughout the entire simulation. The values of Current-ratio, Health, Cash-payment-rate, Cash-outflow and Cash-netflow can be derived by QSIM through similar methods, resulting in

Current-assets (t0, t1) = <(0, $ca*$), dec>

and Current-liabilities (t0, t1) = <(0, $cl*$), std>

==> Current-ratio (t0, t1) =<($cr*$, inf), dec>

Current-ratio (t^0, t^1) = <($cr*$, inf), dec>

==> Health (t^0, t^1) = <($h*$, inf), dec>

Figure 4.9
Propagating through the Cash-Flow Model

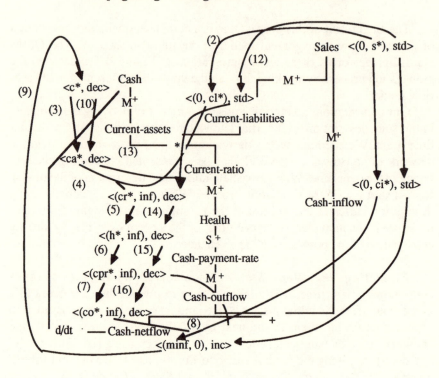

Health (t^0, t^1) = <(h*, inf), dec>

   ==> Cash-payment-rate (t^0, t^1) = <(cpr*, inf), dec>

Cash-payment-rate (t^0, t^1) = <(cpr*, inf), dec>

   ==> Cash-outflow (t^0, t^1) = <(co*, inf), dec>

Cash-outflow (t^0, t^1) = <(co*, inf), dec>

   and Cash-inflow (t^0, t^1) = <(0, ci*), std>

   ==> Cash-netflow (t^0, t^1) = <(minf, 0), inc>

Thus, we get the complete qualitative description of the next system state as follows:

	Cash	= <(0, c*), dec>
	Current-assets	= <(0, ca*), dec>
	Current-liabilities	= <(0, cl*), std>
	Current-ratio	= <(cr*, inf), dec>
	Health	= <(h*, inf), dec>
$t = (t^0, t^1)$	Cash-payment-rate	= <(cpr*, inf), dec>
	Cash-outflow	= <(co*, inf), dec>
	Cash-inflow	= <(0, ci*), std>
	Cash-netflow	= <(minf, 0), inc>
	Sales	= <(0, s*), std>

An auditor might apply the following interpretation to this state description. The declining Cash balance and Current-assets condition can be sustained over some period of time. However, the inevitable consequence of extending this condition into the future is a decline in the Current-ratio and Health of the firm, which, unless remedied, could cause the firm to fail to meet the Cash needs of Current-liabilities. Such an interpretation would potentially raise concerns in the auditor's mind about the going-concern viability of the firm in a "next state" analysis. Although we speak of the "next state," the underlying process we are describing is continuous, and there is, strictly speaking, no next state. However, the sequence of distinct qualitative state descriptions is a discrete sequence, so the "next state" of a mechanism refers to the next distinct qualitative description in that sequence. Therefore, the meaning of time in qualitative and causal reasoning is different from the meaning of calendar time. The length of each time interval depends solely on how fast the system is changing from one distinct qualitative state to another. Extending the above auditor's interpretation of the resulting state description, given this interpretation of time, may lead the auditor to conclude that the firm's "next state" condition with respect to Cash, Current-assets, Health and Cash-payment-rate is more than one annual reporting period in the continuous time future. Thus, the going-concern assumption with respect to the current reporting period can be sustained. The following simulation will show which event determines the time point t^1 that terminates this interval. This form of analysis may be useful in refining the auditor's interpretations.

Limit Analysis. The previous qualitative state description applied to all time points in a time interval $t = (t^0, t^1)$. We now need to determine the qualitative change that defines the time $t = t^1$ that terminates this interval. A parameter that is not steady over an open time interval may either reach its next landmark value, or stay in the same interval, and it may keep moving in the same direction or change or become steady at the succeeding time point. Therefore, several kinds of qualitative changes are possible:

1. Changes in qualitative magnitude (qmag):
    a. moving from an open interval toward a landmark value—
        for example, $X(t^0, t^1) = <(0, x^*), dec> ==> X(t^1) = <0, dec>$
    b. staying in the same open interval (no change in qmag)—
        for example, $X(t^0, t^1) = <(0, x^*), inc> ==> X(t^1) = <(0,x^*), inc>$
2. Changes in direction of change (qdir):
    a. changing from moving (increasing or decreasing) to steady—
        for example, $X(t^0,t^1) = <(0, x^*), inc> ==> X(t^1) = <(0, x^*), std>$
    b. keeping the same direction of change (no change in qdir)—
        for example, $X(t^0,t^1) = <(0, x^*), dec> ==> X(t^1) = <(0, x^*) dec>$

When several parameters are reaching their landmarks at the same time, the number of possible next states depends on the number of different combinations of both the possible qualitative magnitude (qmag) and the direction of change (qdir) of those parameters. The process of determining which limits (landmarks) may or may not be reached in the next qualitatively distinct state is known as limit analysis. In our example, seven parameters are moving toward various limits, for a theoretical maximum of $4^7 = 16,384$ possible combinations of qualitative changes. The corresponding values on the multiplication, addition, and monotonic function constraints, however, greatly reduce this set. In the end, we are left with only a single possible behavior at $t = t^1$:

	Cash	$= <(0, c^*), std>$
	Current-assets	$= <(0, ca^*), std>$
	Current-liabilities	$= <(0, cl^*), std>$
	Current-ratio	$= <(2, cr^*), std>$
	Health	$= <(0, h^*), std>$
$t = t^1$	Cash-payment-rate	$= <(0, cpr^*), std>$
	Cash-outflow	$= <(0, co^*), std>$
	Cash-inflow	$= <(0, ci^*), std>$
	Cash-netflow	$= <0, std>$
	Sales	$= <(0, s^*), std>$

Simulation stops when all branches of the solution tree reach equilibrium for all possible initial states (there is only one in our example). Each limb of the solution represents one possible behavior of the system. The final result of this simulation is given in Appendix A. Again extending the above auditor's interpretation, does the resulting equilibrium contribute to the auditor's concern for the firm's continuity?

Creating New Landmark Values. At time t^1, the cash-flow system reaches equilibrium while the amount of cash on hand is still in the open interval $(0, c*)$, and its qualitative state is described as

$$Cash(t^1) = <(0, c*), std>$$

Since the value of cash when $t = t^1$ is a critical value of the function Cash(t) (i.e. its derivative is 0), where the system reached equilibrium, it may be convenient for us to place a name in the quantity space so that it can be referred to later in other contexts.

From the outcome of the simulation, $Cash(t^1)$ lies strictly between the two existing landmarks, $(0, c*)$. We can give this point a name (e.g., newc*) and insert it as a new landmark in the quantity space for cash:

Cash   0...newc*...c*...inf

In Appendix A, newc* is cash-107. Following this strategy for the other parameters that reach critical values between landmarks, we augment the quantity spaces for the cash-flow management system for the first initial condition as follows:

Quantity Spaces:

Cash	0...newc*...c*...inf
Current-assets	0...newca*...ca*...inf
Current-liabilities	0...newcl*...cl*...inf
Current-ratio	0...newcr*...2...cr*...inf
Health	minf...0...newh*...h*...inf
Cash-payment-rate	0...newcpr*...cpr*...inf
Cash-outflow	0...newco*...co*...inf
Cash-inflow	0...newci*...ci*...inf
Cash-netflow	minf...0...inf
Sales	0...news*...s*...inf

Several of the constraints can now define new corresponding values based on the new landmark values as follows:

Constraints	New corresponding values
Current-assets = M$^+$(Cash)	(0 0), (newca* newc*), (ca* c*), (inf inf)
Current-assets = Current-ratio * Current-liabilities	(newca*, newcr*, newcl*), (ca* cr* cl*)
Health = M$^+$(Current-ratio)	(0 minf), (2 0), (newcr* newh*), (cr* h*), (inf inf)
Cash-payment-rate = S$^+$(Health)	(0 0) (inf inf) (newh* newcpr*), (h* cpr*)
Cash-outflow = M$^+$(Cash-payment-rate)	(0 0), (newco* newcpr*), (co* cpr*), (inf inf)
Cash-inflow = Cash-outflow + Cash-netflow	
Cash-inflow = M$^+$(Sales)	(0 0), (newci* news*), (ci* s*), (inf inf)
Current-liabilities = M$^+$(Sales)	(0 0), (newcl* news*), (cl* s*), (inf inf)

Cash-netflow = d/dt(Cash)

The final equilibrium state of the system can now be described concisely in terms of the new landmarks (see Appendix A);

Cash	<newc*, std>	<cash-107, std>
Current-assets	<newca*, std>	<current-assets-107, std>
Curremt-liabilities	<newcl*, std>	<current-liability-1, std>
Current-ratio	<newcr*, std>	<current-ratio-320, std>
Health	<newh*, std>	<health-324, std>
Cash-payment-rate	<newcpr*, std>	<cash-payment-rate-202, std>
Cash-outflow	<newco*, std>	<cash-outflow-202, std>
Cash-inflow	<newci*, std>	<cash-inflow-122, std>
Cash-netflow	<0, std>	<0, std>
Sales	<newci*, std>	<sales-122, std>

The representation and inference process discussed above is embodied in QSIM, a very efficient constraint-filtering algorithm (Kuipers, 1985). Given the structure of the system in terms of its constraints, corresponding values and quantity spaces of its parameters, QSIM will generate the state tree of all possible behaviors. The graphical representations of the behavior derived from QSIM are provided in Appendix A. The result shows that the management's cash management policy does sustain a Current-ratio of 2:1 in the new equilibrium. The firm arrives at a new and apparently sustainable equilibrium, which is somewhere lower than the original equilibrium point cr*, but higher than 2, thus eliminating the auditor's concerns in the scenario above. Other scenarios might be envisioned by the auditor. The above has been offered as merely one example.

Using the Results of Qualitative Simulation. Although there are many different kinds of qualitative and causal reasoning, one of the key operations in qualitative simulation is to predict the set of qualitatively possible behaviors of a mechanism given a qualitative description of its structure and its initial state.

In this example, we started with a system at equilibrium where Cash-inflow (ci*) is equal to Cash-outflow (co*), and all the other parameters are stable. By changing the value of Sales we were able to predict all the possible behaviors of the other parameters when the amount of Cash-inflow changed.

In this simple example, we observe that there is only one analytical review conclusion that might be reached from the simulation outcome; that is, when the level of sales is decreased, it drives all the other accounts in the system down to a lower equilibrium level. An observed pattern consistent with this result would be consistent with expectations. An observed pattern different from the simulated outcome would suggest the need for investigation. Assuming a more complete model of the cash-flow management system, such a pattern would be unexpected and require explanation. Of course, in our simple example many possible explanations exist because of model limitations. However, added specificity, based on firm-specific knowledge of constraints and/or parameter and landmark values, could reduce the variety of explanations and thus better focus an investigation. Model extension offers obvious advantages as well. It is our intent to investigate each of these possibilities in our future efforts.

Quasi-Static Equilibrium Reasoning

QSIM in one of two major approaches to qualitative simulation. QSIM is a dynamic simulation. It predicts both equilibrium and nonequilibrium states of the system and describes how the system passes through nonequilibrium states, possibly eventually reaching equilibrium (Kuipers, 1984). The other simulation method is called the quasi-static approximation approach. This alternative approach assumes that the system is always at, or infinitely close to, equilibrium and predicts the result of a perturbation to the system (deKleer and Brown, 1984).

The model used in quasi-static equilibrium reasoning rests on the assumption that the quasi-equilibrium state is realistic. Where the assumption of quasi-equilibrium does not hold, we must be skeptical of the benefits of this approach. Inventory control problems where the level of inventory on hand may at times fluctuate rapidly with demand may be a case in point. However, when the quasi-equilibrium assumption is valid, the quasi-static equilibrium reasoning is computationally more efficient than dynamic simulation. In addition it avoids ambiguity which may be encountered in the transient states of a dynamic simulation.

While we will give further consideration to the appropriateness of quasi-equilibrium analysis, this chapter will continue to emphasize dynamic simulation. The use of both approaches within differing audit contexts may be appropriate.

Building Qualitative Models

The major processes in qualitative reasoning are model building and qualitative simulation. We posited a simple example model and used it to discuss qualitative simulation. For the sake of discussion we assumed that the abstraction was a sufficient representation of the structure of the underlying system. Model building is a more open-ended problem than the simulation process itself (Forbus, 1984).

Although there are a number of methods for building qualitative models, the area of qualitative model building technology is still not well developed. Future research is suggested in the developing effective approaches to the model-building problem in qualitative reasoning.

QUALITATIVE AND CAUSAL REASONING IN AUDITING

In this section, an extended version of the cash-flow management model is developed and implemented. This is followed by a discussion of the perceived advantages and difficulties in using qualitative and causal reasoning for accounting and/or auditing purposes.

Model Building

The model used in this section is a revised version of the earlier cash-flow model. The main difference between these two models is the level of detail used in specifying the qualitative structure of the system. In general, a greater level of detail improves the ability to determine the underlying relationship.

The most significant change in the revised model is our attempt to account for the costs of acquiring salable inventory separately from other liabilities. In this way, the relationship between sales changes and inventory acquisition rates can be made explicit in the model. As the increase/decrease in cash outflows for salable inventory is likely to be more directly affected by increases/decreases in sales than are other liabilities, this separation allows for a more precise process description.

Variables (a)-(f) and (j) remain the same as in the previous model; so do constraints (1)-(4) and (9) (see Figure 4.6). Some of the variables' names are changed (see Figures 4.6 and 4.10): Cash-outflow (g) is changed to AcquisitionRate, Cash-inflow (h) is changed to CashInRate, and Cash-netflow (i) is changed to dCash in order to coincide with the newly inserted variables [e.g. dLiab (k), which represents the differences between AcquisitionRate and CashPmtRate, or the net change Current-liabilities]. Constraints (5)-(7), and (9) (see Figure 4.10) are actually the same as in the previous model; only some of their variables' names are changed, as we described above. Constraint (8) [AcquisitionRate = CashPmtRate + dLiab] and constraint (10) [dLiab = d/dt(Current-liabilities)] are added to model how the costs of acquiring of salable inventory will affect the amount of current-liabilities.

Figure 4.10 indicates the various quantity spaces, constraints and corresponding values, while Figure 4.11 is a graphical illustration of the model.

Since modification of the model is relatively simple in QSIM, auditors can easily extend or simplify the existing model whenever necessary.

**Predicting Behavior from
Structure—Qualitative Simulation**

Simulation of the revised model is somewhat different from that of the previous simple model. A different method for determining the initial equilibrium value is used. In the previous example, we manually assigned landmark values for the initial equilibrium values of the system (i.e. Cash = c*). This time we let QSIM create the initial equilibrium values for each parameter (e.g., Cash = normal). For our example, the system is initially at equilibrium where the amount of sales, cash, liabilities, etc., are all stable at "normal" rates. The simulation process then determines what happens when the amount of sales is increased from the normal state to a certain specified level.

Figure 4.10
Complete Description of the Qualitative Structure
of Cash-Flow Model II

Model: Cash-Flow Management
Quantity Spaces

Cash	0...inf	(a)
Current-assets	0...inf	(b)
Current-liabilities	0...inf	(c)
Current-ratio	0...2...inf	(d)
Health	minf...0...inf	(e)
CashPmtRate	0...inf	(f)
CashInRate	0...inf	(g)
AcquisitionRate	0...inf	(h)
dCash	minf...0...ing	(i)
Sales	0...inf	(j)
dLiab	minf...0...inf	(k)

Constraints and Corresponding Values:

Current-assets = M+ (Cash)	(0 0), (inf inf)	(1)
Current-assets = Current-ratio * Current-liabilities		(2)
Health = M+ (Current-ratio)	(0 minf), (2 0), (inf inf)	(3)
CashPmtRate = S+ (Health)	(0 0), (inf inf)	(4)
CashInRate = M+ (Sales)	(0 0), (inf inf)	(5)
AcquisitionRate = M+ (Sales)	(0 0), (inf inf)	(6)
CashInRate = CashPmtRate + dCash		(7)
AcquisitionRate = CashPmtRate + dLiab		(8)
dCash = d/dt (Cash)		(9)
dLiab = d/dt (Current-liabilities)		(10)

Figure 4.11
Cash-Flow Model II

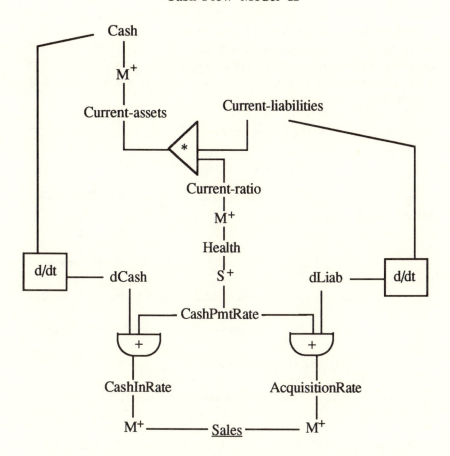

Given the following information about the value of sales, cash, and liabilities and the direction of sales change, we can apply the same propagation algorithm as we did for the previous model to derive all the possible complete initial states following the given incomplete knowledge about the system.

$t = t^0$ Given: Sales = <(normal, inf), std>

Cash = <normal, ?>

Current-liabilities = <normal, ?>

Current-ratio = <normal, ?>

Starting with qmag(Sales) = (normal, inf) and constraint (5) [CashInRate = M⁺(Sales)] with corresponding values (normal normal) and (inf inf), we can infer that the amount of CashInRate should be somewhat less than inf, but greater than normal. This is necessary because of the M^+ relation and corresponding values between the two parameters.

qmag(Sales) = (normal, inf)

==>   qmag(CashInRate) = (normal, inf)

We can employ the same method to obtain the magnitudes of Current-assets and Current-liabilities.

qmag(Cash) = normal ==> qmag(Current-assets) = normal

qmag(Current-ratio) = normal ==> qmag(Health) = normal

qmag(Health) = normal ==> qmag(CashPmtRate) = normal

qmag(Sales) = (normal, inf)

==>   qmag(AcquisitionRate) = (normal, inf)

The same propagation algorithm is applied to the addition relation in constraints (7) and (8). Given CashInRate = CashPmtRate + dCash, we can assert that the level of dCash should be somewhere in between zero and inf, (0, inf); and same propagation algorithm can be applied to obtain the magnitude of dLiab.

qmag(CashInRate) = (normal, inf)

and qmag(CashPmtRate) = normal

==>   qmag(dCash) = (0, inf)

qmag(AcquisitionRate) = (normal, inf)

and qmag(CashPmtRate) = normal

==>   qmag(dLiab) = (0, inf)

The derivative constraints, (9) and (10), can now be used to determine the direction of change of cash on hand and current liabilities.

qmag(dCash) = (0, inf) ==> qdir(Cash) = inc

qmag(dLiab) = (0, inf) ==> qdir(Current-liabilities) = inc

The direction of change can be propagated through the monotonic function s as follows:

qdir(Cash) = inc ==>   qdir(Current-assets) = inc

qdir(Sales) = std ==>   qdir(CashInRate) = std

qdir(Sales) = std ==>   qdir(AcquisitionRate) = std

From the argument above we know that in the multiplication relation in constraint (2), Current-assets = Current-ratio * Current-liabilities, both qdir(Current-assets) and qdir(Current-liabilities) are increasing. But there is still not enough information for us to determine the exact direction of change of Current-ratio. This is because we cannot decide based on the above information whether the rate of increase of Current-assets is greater than, less than, or equal to the rate of increase of Current-liabilities. Since there are no remaining constraints to help resolve this ambiguity, our prediction for the initial state must branch nondeterministically.

A nondeterministic prediction simply means that the qualitative description of the system does not contain enough information to specify its state uniquely. A unique specification might be possible if more causal knowledge was available and included in the model. The three possible initial statea at time t^0 are listed below:

1.   The rate of increase of Current-assets is less than the increase of Current-liabilities, and the direction of change of Current-ratio is

decreasing, qdir(Current-ratio) = dec. The cost-to-revenue relationship implied will not sustain operations indefinitely. If this condition were thought to be one that would persist, this analytical review result might suggest consideration of the firm's ability to operate as a going concern. Such a conclusion would have a significant impact on the audit planning process.

2.   The rate of increase of Current-assets is equal to the increase of Current-liabilities, and qdir(Current-ratio) = std. The result of this branch represents a possible behavior where the increase in total sales does not contribe to the firm's net income; in other words, the contribution margin for the extra units sold is zero. Knowledge of the result provides insights into the possible riskiness of certain courses of actions.

3.   The rate of increase of Current-assets is greater than the increase of Current-liabilities; therefore, the direction of change of Current-ratio is increasing, qdir(Current-ratio) = inc, a clearly preferred alternative.

Reasoning intuitively, we can confirm that all three of these possible states are perfectly legitimate. The actual monotonic functions involved and the relative magnitudes of Current-assets and Current-liabilities determine the unique behavior the system will take. The monotonic functions in the model are equivalent to the market conditions and cash management strategies the firm has adopted. Differing conditions and strategies will produce differing results.

This type of nondeterministic prediction is an important feature of qualitative simulation. A specific cash management strategy is a deterministic mechanism and cannot choose arbitrarily which alternate behavior to take. In this case, our qualitative description of the firm is sufficiently incomplete that it cannot determine which behavior to expect. Many different cash management strategies satisfy the same specified qualitative description. A better qualitative description either involves provides more specificity with respect to the monotonic functions, constraints, and parameter values and/or an extended model on all fronts.

Extension of the model will occur at a later date. At this time, we will finish describing the QSIM modeling process. For purposes of illustration, we concentrate on the discussion of the third initial state; that is, the increase of Current-assets is greater than the increase of Current-liabilities resulting in the increasing of Current-ratio. The simulation of the other two possible initial states can be derived later using the same mechanism.

Directions of change propagate through the multiplication constraint:

qdir(Current-assets) = inc   and   qdir(Current-liabilities) = inc

==>   qdir(Current-ratio) = inc

And the following completes the initial state description:

qdir(Current-ratio) = inc   ==>   qdir(Health) = inc

qdir(Health) = inc   and   qmag(Health) > 0

==>   qdir(CashPmtRate) = inc

The final result of this propagation is a complete qualitative description of the cash-flow management model at the initial instant, t^0. The QSIM algorithm performs these steps automatically. Figure 4.12 shows the complete qualitative description of all three initial states. The results of the simulation based on the above information are presented in the behavior graphs found in Appendix B.

Figure 4.12
Complete Qualitative Description of Three Possible Initial States

t = t0	1	2	3
Cash	<normal, inc>	<normal, inc>	<normal, inc>
Current-assets	<normal, inc>	<normal, inc>	<normal, inc>
Current-liabilities	<normal, inc>	<normal, inc>	<normal, inc>
Current-ratio	<normal, inc>	<normal, inc>	<normal, inc>
Health	<normal, dec>	<normal, std>	<normal, inf>
Cash-payment-rate	<normal, dec>	<normal, std>	<normal, inc>
CashInRate	<(normal, inc), std>	<(normal, inc), std>	<(normal, inc), std>
AcquisitionRate	<(normal, inc), std>	<(normal, inc), std>	<(normal, inc), std>
dCash	<(0, inf), inc>	<(0, inf), std>	<(0, inf), dec>
dLiab	<(0, inf), inc>	<(0, inf), std>	<(0, inf), dec>
Sales	<(normal, inf), std>	<(normal, inf), std>	<(normal, inf), std>

Although QSIM is guaranteed to predict all possible behaviors, it may also predict spurious behaviors, which, if uncontrolled, can lead to an intractably branching tree of behaviors. Prediction of spurious behaviors can be caused by the actual behavior of the system or by inadequacies in either the description of the qualitative constraints or the filters available to the qualitative simulation algorithm. The result is that QSIM obtains too many possible successors (i.e., too many alternatives survive the pruning process). The revised cash-flow management model produces an intractable number of possible "solutions"; only one of the solutions is presented in Appendix B. This may be a common problem for accounting-style models.

While intractable solutions may turn out to be a common problem in dynamic accounting models, in some cases extensions of the model can remove most or all of the competing "solutions." We tried a number of additional constraints based on an analysis of the three initial state conditions. Assuming that information exogenous to the model suggests that the third initial state condition is most appropriate to the analysis of a going concern, we added the following constraint:

$$Current\text{-}ratio = M^+(Current\text{-}assets)$$

This constraint is less than an ideal representation of the empirical relationship present in most business contexts. In general ,the relationship is not as simple as suggested by the above constraint. In that sense, this particular choice of constraint limits our results to a narrow domain of possible settings. However, it will suffice to demonstrate the most direct mechanism by which intractable solutions can be eliminated. Future model developments will hopefully produce better descriptive representations.

After this new constraint is added, our cash-flow model is rerun and only one possible behavior remains as presented in Appendix C. The auditor would next compare this unique simulation result to the reported account values. If the simulated and reported values are not materially different, the auditor will conclude that the analysis has provided no new evidence suggesting specific concerns requiring a change in the audit plan. If the simulated and reported values differ materially for one (or more) account(s), the auditor will focus additional evidence collection efforts on these accounts. This additional effort may take one of a number of forms. First, the auditor may attempt to elicit an explanation from management. Such explanations may suggest changes in the QSIM constraints, functions, landmarks, or other aspects of the model. In this case, the simulation could be rerun after model revision (see Figure 4.3). If the explanations prove to be internally consistent and result in a model prediction consistent with the reported values, the auditor may conclude that no special attention need be given the accounts in question. Second, if differences continue to persist, the auditor will revise the nature, extent, and/or timing of subsequent audit tests of controls, transactions, and balances. Because these tests tend to be more expensive than analytical review procedures, the total cost of the audit will increase in order to provide acceptable assurance that material errors in the account are not present after the completion of all audit procedures.

LIMITATIONS AND FURTHER RESEARCH

Qualitative and causal reasoning technology has proven useful in solving relatively simple models. As favorable empirical evidence accumulates and as the models described herein become accepted, future research will focus on scaling this technology up to handle realistic models. In order to apply qualitative and causal reasoning methods to more complex problems, several important areas of future research are suggested:

1. Incorporating more powerful mathematical methods in both model-building and qualitative simulation processes to give better descriptions of the qualitative model and to filter out spurious and/or inconsistent predictions (Chiu, 1988). The curvature constraint inserted in cash-flow management model II is an example of one of these methods. In this case it eliminated intractable branching.

2. Hierarchically decomposing a complex model into a set of simpler models so that the proper relationships between components in different modules are still retained (Kuipers, 1988b). Several decomposition methods have been developed to date. One, called time-scale abstraction, isolates widely differing time scales into several simple processes, each on its own time-scale. Another method is to isolate weakly interacting components of a system into several small systems. This philosophy is reflected in practice and in the prior research efforts of two of the authors (Bailey et al., 1985). In that work, internal control systems were reduced to a set of subsystems with strong internal linkages and well-specified "weak" interactions with other subsystems. A similar approach can be used in building analytical review models.

3. Using incomplete quantitative knowledge in qualitative reasoning to refine the results of qualitative simulation and

eliminate contradicting behaviors (Kuipers and Berleant, 1988). By inserting additional knowledge about the ranges each parameter could take in the cash-flow model, we will be able to prune some of the branches that are inconsistent with this more quantified description of the model.

4. Narrowing the possible state outcomes for monitoring and control purposes by introducing additional constraint conditions based on specific contextual knowledge. This again results in a somewhat more quantified model. For instance, integrating human factors (e.g., preferences) into the model will eliminate states with lower preferences from the simulation (Bridgeland, 1989). In the current cash flow models, the manager always prefers a current ratio that is greater than or equal to 2:1; we thus eliminate all the possible behaviors where the resulting ratio is less than 2:1.

Each of the techniques offers some promise that future efforts will result in realistic models capable of interesting solutions by techniques such as QSIM.

REFERENCES

Altman, E. I., "Accounting Implications of Failure Prediction Models," *Journal of Accounting, Auditing and Finance* (Autumn 1982), 4-19.

American Institute of Certified Public Accountants, *Statement on Auditing Standards,* No. 56, New York, AICPA, April 1988.

Bailey, A.D., Jr., ed., "Auditor Productivity in the Year 2000," *Proceedings of the Arthur Young Professors' Roundtable,* 1987.

Bailey, A. D., Jr., G. Duke, J. Gerlach, C. Ko, R. Meservey, and A.B. Whinston, "TICOM and the Analysis of Internal Controls," *Accounting Review* 60, no. 2 (April 1985): 186-201.

Bell, M. A., "Why Expert Systems Fail," *Journal of the Operational Research Society* 36 (1985): 613-619.

Bridgeland, D. M., "Qualitative Simulation Extensions to Support Economics Models," unpublished thesis, University of Texas-Austin, 1989.

Chiu, C., "Higher Order Derivative Constraints and a QSIM-based Total Simulation Scheme," Technical Report AITR 88-65, 1988.

deKleer, J., and J. S. Brown, "A Qualitative Physics Based on Confluences," *Artificial Intelligence* 24 (1984): 7-83.

Forbus, K. D., "Qualitative Process Theory," *Artificial Intelligence* 24 (1984): 85-168.

Han, K. S., "A Formal Algorithmic Model Compatible with Accounting Information Systems," unpublished dissertation, Purdue University, 1989.

Jacob, V., and A. D. Bailey, Jr., "A Decision Process Approach to Expert Systems in Auditing," 2nd International Workshop on Artificial Intelligence in Economics and Management, Singapore, January 1989, North-Holland.

Jaedicke, R. K., Y. Ijiri, and Oswald Nielsen, *Research in Accounting Measurement, AAA Collected Papers,* Sarasota, FL.: American Accounting Association, 1966.

Kaplan, R. S., "Developing a Financial Planning Model for Analytical Review: A Feasibility Study," in *Symposium on Auditing Research III*, Urbana, IL.: University of Illinois, 1979.

Kinney, W. R., Jr., "Attention-Directing Analytical Review Using Accounting Ratios: A Case Study," *Auditing: A Journal of Practice & Theory* 6 (Spring 1987): 59-73.

Kinney, W. R., Jr., and W. L. Felix, Jr., "Analytical Review Procedures," *Journal of Accountancy* 150, no. 4 (October 1980): 98-103.

Kinney, W. R., Jr., and G. L. Salamon, "Regression Analysis in Auditing: A Comparison of Alternative Investigation Rules," *Journal of Accounting Research* 20, no. 2 (Autumn, 1982): 350-366.

Kuipers, B. J., "Commonsense Reasoning about Causality: Deriving Behavior from Structure," *Artificial Intelligence* 24 (1984): 169-204.

Kuipers, B. J., "Qualitative Simulation," *Artificial Intelligence* 29 (1986): 289-338.

Kuipers, B. J.,"Qualitative Simulation as Causal Explanation," *IEEE Transactions on Systems, Man, and Cybernetics (SMC-17),* no. 3 (1987): 32-444.

Kuipers, B. J., *Qualitative and Causal Reasoning,* text manuscript, 1988a.

Kuipers, B. J., "Qualitative Simulation Using Time-scale Abstraction," *Artificial Intelligence in Engineering* 3, no. 4 (1988b).

Kuipers, B. J., "Qualitative Reasoning: Modeling and Simulation with Incomplete Knowledge," *Automatica* 25, no. 4 (July 1989): 571-585.

Kuipers, B. J., and D. Breleant, "Using Incomplete Quantitative Knowledge in Qualitative Reasoning," *AAAI* (1988): 324-329.

Kuipers, B. J., and C. Chiu, "Taming Intractible Branching in Qualitative Simulation," *Proceedings of the Tenth International Joint Conference on Artificial Intelligence* (IJCAI-87). Los Altos, CA: Morgan Kaufman Publishers (1987): 1079–1085.

Kuipers, B. J., and J. P. Kassirer, "Causal Reasoning in Medicine: Analysis of a Protocol," *Cognitive Science* 8 (1984): 363-385.

Lev, B., "Industry Averages as Targets for Financial Ratios," *Journal of Accounting Research* 7 (1969): 290-299.

Loebbecke, J. K. and P. J. Steinbart, "An Investigation of the Use of

Preliminary Analytical Review to Provide Substantive Audit Evidence,"
Auditing: A Journal of Practice & Theory (Spring 1987): 74-89.

Meservy, R. D., A. D. Bailey, Jr., and P. E. Johnson, "Internal Control
Evaluation: A Computational Model of the Review Process, *"Auditing: A
Journal of Practice & Theory* 6 (Fall 1986): 44-74.

Messier, W. R. Jr., and J. V. Hansen, "Expert Systems in Auditing: The
Stage of the Art," *Auditing: A Journal of Practice & Theory* 7, no. 1 (Fall
1987): 94–105.

Quinlan, J. R., "Discovering Rules By Induction from Large Collections of
Examples," *Expert Systems in the Micro Electronic Age,* Ed. D. Michie,
Edinburgh University Press: Edinburgh (1979).

Wallace, W., and A. Akresh, "The Application of Regression Analysis for
Limited Review and Audit Planning," Fourth Symposium in Auditing Research,
University of Illinois, November 1980.

APPENDIX A

Structure: Equilibrium of cash inflow and cash outflow,
Initialization: sales amount deceased [S-1416]
Behavior 1 of 1: [S-1416 S-1417 S-1419 S-1420 S-1422.
Final state: [QUIESCENT], NIL, NIL.

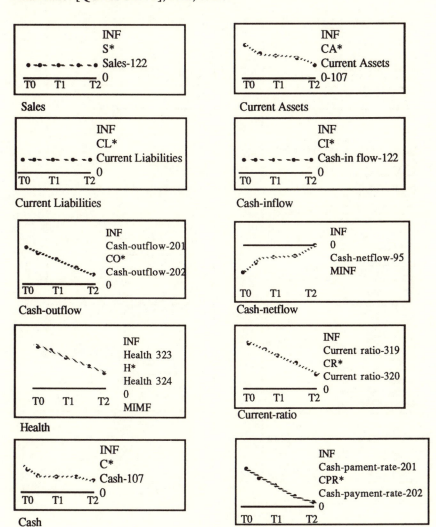

Sales

Current Assets

Current Liabilities

Cash-inflow

Cash-outflow

Cash-netflow

Health

Current-ratio

Cash

Cash-payment-rate

APPENDIX B

Structure: Cash and liabilities
Initialization: [ONE OF SEVERAL-COMPLETIONS-OF S-1074] [S-1075]
Behavior 6 of 16: [S-1075 S-1081 S-1088]
Final state: [QUIESCENT], NIL, NIL.

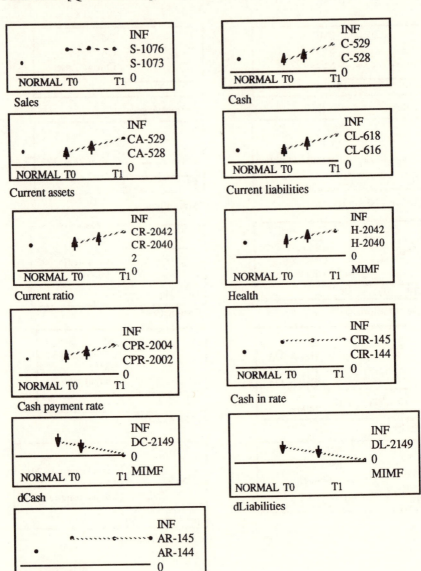

APPENDIX C

Structure: Cash and liabilities
Initialization: [INITIALIZED-WITH ((TIME . (t0 inc)) (CASH . (c-533 nil))
(CURRENT-ASSETS . (CA-533 nil)) (CURRENT-LIABILITIES . (cl-621
nil))
Behavior 1 of 1: [S-1115 S-1117 S-1119]
Final state: [QUIESCENT], NIL, NIL.

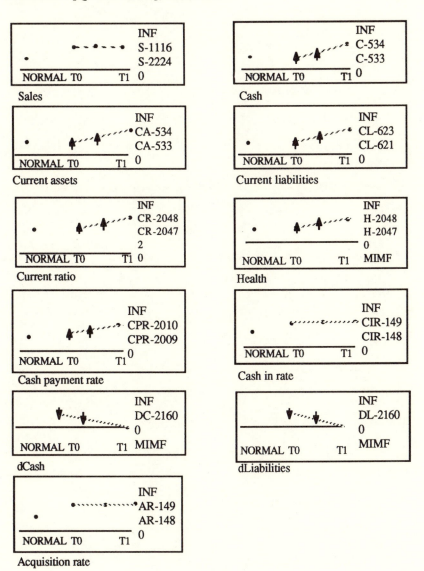

Sales

Cash

Current assets

Current liabilities

Current ratio

Health

Cash payment rate

Cash in rate

dCash

dLiabilities

Acquisition rate

5

Implementation of Decision Support Systems: An Empirical Study of Japanese Production Control Systems

Takehiko Matsuda
Toshizumi Oota
Toshiyuki Sueyoshi

Computer-based information systems have come to be recognized as essential to the efficiency and effectiveness of modern management decision-making processes. In modern private and public management, the information provided by computer systems is expected to be linked to the processes by which managers arrive at decisions. Unfortunately, this expectation has not be fulfilled, and we observe many computer systems that are used only to collect, manipulate, and distribute information in various organizations without having very much effect on the decision making.

Extensive research has been conducted in recent years on problems associated with computer-based management. The interaction between computer systems and decision-making processes is sometimes referred to as management information systems (MISs), which extends to decision support systems (DSSs) intended to enhance management decision-making capabilities.

The purpose of this chapter is to investigate DSS implementation issues based upon an exploration of both organization control activities and DSS as they interact in decision making. We classify the research works on DSS into the following three sets of topics: (1) implementation consideration, (2) organization and information design, and (3) use in management decisions.

First, the DSS designer and researcher must deal with problems concerning implementation and utilization of computer systems. Keen and Scott-Morton (1978) have argued that the issues of DSS design and implementation are inseparable for DSS success. Issues of implementation are not new. Operations researchers and management scientists are aware of how critical implementation issues are to model development and its related process. Much research has been conducted on implementation and its inherent problems. [See, e.g., Bean et al. (1975), Doktor and Hamilton (1973), Ginzberg (1975), Harvey (1970) and Huysmans (1970). In particular, Schultz and Slevin (1975) have discussed important factors that determine implementation success and failure, and have suggested alternative strategies for implementation of Operations Research/Management Science (OR/MS) models.]

Alavi and Henderson (1981) argued that these concepts and techniques for OR/MS implementation might also be applied to DSS. Many studies, accompanied by the rapid evolution of modern computers and related needs for DSS implementation, have been conducted to explore the issues of DSS implementation as a natural extension of OR/MS implementation. [See, e.g., Henderson and Schilling (1985), Robey and Farrow (1982), Kim and Lee (1986), Schonberger (1980), Doll (1985), Ference and Uretsky (1976), and Saunders and Courtney (1985).]

OR/MS implementation focuses on situational factors such as top managment support, the relationship between users and model developers, client-felt need, characterization of models, clear definition of objectives, clear problem statement, and organization support of the OR/MS group. To some extent, these factors may be associated with successful DSS implementation and may suggest a set of necessary conditions for implementation. On the other hand, the DSS implementation study also needs to view implementation issues as part of a process of social/organizational change. The change included the interactions between organization and information system design as they relate to managerial decision making. [See Keen and Scott-Morton (1978) and Alavi and Henderson (1981).]

The feature of DSS implementation brings us to the second class of research activities that need to be examined. The interaction between organization structure and decision making process must be investigated along with DSS design since these factors are influenced by information produced through computer systems and, further, the changes of these factors influence the success or failure of DSS. To explore the relationship between DSS and organization structure, organization scientists have recast their own formulations in order to view organizations as information processing systems as in Tushman and Nadler (1978). This has enabled them to examine the determinants of effectiveness of DSS using the conceptual framework of organizational communication. (See Huber, 1982.)

Pioneering work along these lines was conducted by Galbraith (1974, 1977), who focused on interpreting organization designs in terms of information systems. For this perspective, Galbraith employed an internal information processing view of organization design in which specific design variations were proposed as determinants of desirable outcomes. The outcomes were thus to be utilized as a standard for measuring the success of DSS implementation. Furthermore, the introduction of DSS as a strategy of organization design may be viewed in terms of an increase in information processing capability to respond to uncertainty/turbulence in the post industrial environment envisioned by Huber (1982). The success or failure of DSS implementation may thus be viewed within the framework of an organization design/information processing paradigm. [The term "paradigm" is used to refer to conceptual frameworks or elaborations of perspectives on a field (e.g., organization) that provides a point of view from which problems are discussed and results are assessed.] Kmetz (1984) has investigated DSS implementation along the paradigm.

Finally, besides the two research perspectives, a number of articles have argued another perspective in which DSS design is to be regarded from the standpoint of whether it is compatible with the structures and processes of the organization in which the computer systems resides. These articles provide guidelines for DSS design and implementation processes based upon the nature of relationships among human decision making, information processes, and computer systems.

This brings us to the third part of the literature in terms of how DSS and organization design relationships relate to decision making. The classic article by Ackoff (1967) on "Management Misinformation Systems" appears to be the first to argue the importance of understanding MIS developments that fit organization decision making processes and control systems. [See, e.g., Dearden (1978), King and Clelland (1975), Markus (1984), Huber et al. (1978), Huber (1984) and Carter (1984), which have used this perspective in their studies.]

An important research strategy for approaching DSS issues, which complements the organization-DSS design approach, was proposed by Huber and McDaniel (1986). Paying attention to cognitive aspects of a decision maker, Huber and McDaniel expressed the need for integration between organization design and decision making as well as the need for compatibility between DSS and organization design. Thus, various issues regarding DSS implementation are related not only to situational factors explored in the conventional implementation studies, but also to the organization design issues.

Taking off from the three benchmarks, this chapter sets forth and tries to formalize another paradigm that provides a linkage between the information processing/organization design paradigm and the decision-making paradigm. The objective is to provide a theoretical explanation of why DSS implementations may end with success or failure. For this purpose we propose a new conceptual model for the study of DSS implementations based on so-called "management control systems." While retaining the link to the preceding work on organization design and decision making, this study moves from organization decision making to decision making/control processes. The change to a control focus will add a major factor that influences the implementation process.

The remainder of this chapter is organized as follows. In the first section we elaborate upon the nature of management control systems by describing some of their major elements and discussing these relationships to parameters that are presently found in the DSS literature regarding organization design and decision-making processes. The second section discusses the significance of administrative control as part of the framework that needs to be represented in studying the success or failure of DSS implementation. The results of this discussion are formulated as a hypothesis that can be examined in an empirical study for DSS implementation to validate the proposed control paradigm. Some empirical findings related to the hypothesis are presented in the next section. We conclude with a discussion of the implications of this study and future directions for research and uses of the proposed paradigm.

MANAGEMENT CONTROL SYSTEMS

This section presents management control systems (MCSs) and subsystems as well as examining relationships between MCS and conventional research on organizations. Perhaps the earliest approach to organizational control may be found in the classical organization and management theory that is still widely used in current studies regarding organization. Weber (1947) emphasized the importance of control as a design consideration by reference to knowing who is accountable for fulfilling which responsibility among members in an organization.

Given the authority structure, leaders attempt to control their subordinates to keep satisfying their accountability and responsibility requirements. In classical organization and management theory, important concepts are represented by identifying principles of management (e.g., span of control and unity of control). [See, e.g., Urwick (1944) and Mooney (1947).] The classical approach has not been emphasized in modern organization studies because the authors of these studies believe that the classical approach fails to explain the political and technical complexity of organizational structures. (See, e.g., Huber and McDaniel (1986).) Moreover, the classical theory of organization does not formally identify organization information processes within its framework.

This study, however, adds an important dimension to the classical theory by connecting it to the DSS implementation issue. This extension to the classical theory distinguishes two types of decision making processes. First, superior and subordinate comprise the relationship of decisions that are explicitly linked in the form of the control activity. Next, a formal framework is provided by connecting the organization design and the two decision-making processes. That is, an organization structure consists of power/authority (role) positions, and, hence, organization control activities originate from the organization structure as part of the formal organization decision-making process. The resulting theory (hereafter referred to as management control) may be used as a basis for guiding or studying DSS implementation in a way that maintains contact with not only classical, but also modern organization design considerations, as in Galbraith (1977), and decision making processes, as in Cyert and March (1963), March and Simon (1958), Pettigrew (1973), Huber (1982), and Huber and McDaniel (1986).

Itami (1978) studied control activities and organization information systems and thereby proposed a paradigm called the MCS. Itami discussed control activities in an article (in Japanese) that provides a collection of definitions, concepts, and propositions in this area. This chapter attempts to extend Itami's framework into a more elaborate one so that we can discuss a DSS implementation issue within the resulting paradigm. Itami defined management control activities in terms of a superior's decision making, which controls and influences his subordinate's decision-making process. Itami's MCS has eight subsystems: (1) information, (2) responsibility, (3) goal-setting, (4) measurement, (5) evaluation, (6) incentive, (7) standard-setting, and (8) education. Here, each system is defined in terms of the information transformation that a superior uses to exercise administrative control over subordinate activities.

Before attempting to extend Itami's MCS, we elaborate on these concepts.

First, the information system to be considered is an organization information processing function through which administrators acquire and internally disseminate the information needed to carry out the critical decision making and control activities. The information indicates that the function (system) deals with not only computer-based information, but also other message transformation devices, such as telephone conversations, written documentation, and face-to-face conversations. The information system may also be considered as a network that conveys various messages to all individuals in the organization. In many cases, a large amount of information processing capability is required in order to convey these messages. This may cause an overload of cognitive/logical capabilities of individuals and work groups in which it becomes necessary to search for an efficient information process device to convey the requisite messages. Computer systems may be considered as one of the more efficient techniques to perform the organization information processing function. Messages that are collected, transformed, and conveyed by computer systems have considerable advantages in time lines and in such other attributes as relevance, accuracy, and record keeping. The greater uncertainty of the environment gives rise to a need for ensuring decision-making control processes that are more accurate, faster, and more frequent. The information system thus performs an important ignition function that can be used to start other MCS subsystems functioning.

Second, the uses of computerized information systems can result in drastic changes to the organization. Consider, for instance, the responsibility system. This is the organization function that assigns responsibilities to individuals and small groups. In Weberian terms, it is the system that determines who is accountable for fulfilling which responsibilities and allocates authority sufficient to enable them to carry out these responsibilities. Computerization and networking of information process may evidently change these arrangements.

The responsibility/accountability relationships are tied to organization structure. We therefore next consider centralized and decentralized structures as well as their responsibility systems. Centralization concerns the dispersion of responsibility/authority in the organization. If responsibility accumulates with a high-level administrator, the organization is said to be centralized; conversely, if it is diffused, the organization is considered to be decentralized. In many contexts, if the top-level managers can access information regarding their subordinates' decision making and their results with accuracy and timeliness (Lorsch, 1976; Galbraith, 1977)), and if they seek power or have little trust in their subordinates' decision-making ability or prediction, then they will delegate very little responsibility/authority. [See, e.g., Vroom and Yetton (1973).] A centralized organization structure will then be a preferred design.

In contrast, if an administrator wants to maximize job satisfaction of subordinates through job enrichment, as in Szilagyi and Wallace (1983), and if the administrator has difficulty in accessing information regarding his subordinates' decision making and their performance, then he will delegate responsibility/authority, and a decentralized structure will emerge.

The responsibility system of MCS may, hence, be determined by the two factors: organization structure and organizational information processing capability. Evidently, the utilization of DSS may influence these two factors with changes that will impact the responsibility/authority system.

The organizational activities or functions that satisfy goals of individuals and small work groups in a certain time period can be referred to as the goal-setting system. Within the framework of the responsibility system, the goal-setting system determines one or more objectives/tasks concerning responsibility/accountability. In such a goal-setting system, individual responsibilities are transformed into so-called "control indices" that accord measurable form to responsibility/accountability. Based upon these indices, an administrator may allocate goals to subordinates in the form of expected performance levels and evaluate performances of subordinates.

Such control indices can consist of quantitative and qualitative variables. For instance, the number of defectives and the inventory cost constitute quantitative indices. Motivations and/or willingness to cooperate with other members to achieve group goals represents qualitative variables. The latter are usually difficult to measure so that, in many cases, superiors substitute other attributes known as substitute variables, for the qualitative ones. As examples of such substitute variables, managers may use absenteeism of subordinates as a measure of their motivation in achieving prescribed goals, and they may use the number of friends of a subordinate as a measure of his social cooperativeness. The messages concerning these quantitative and substitute variables can then provide the information needed for administrative control activities/decision making processes.

This brings us to the fourth subsystem—that is, the measurement system, by which we indicate the organization function that provides measures of subordinate perofrmance levels to be used to compare with predetermined goals in the goal-setting system. Putting goals and performances together provides a set of control indices for use in a monitoring function and thereby provides a feedback loop process. (See, e.g., Ashby, 1963.) Such a feedback process is a very important component in the MCS's information system. Information regarding the control indices can be used in decisions of a superior regarding job improvement. For instance, an inventory control manager can use the standard cost for purchased items as a qualitative index, and the standard cost can then be compared with the actual cost for the items. In fact, the information can be forwarded to the manager in this control form to enable him to take the necessary steps in order to ensure that the future purchase costs do not deviate significantly from the standard cost.

This aspect now brings us to another consideration in terms of the information system. If the information concerning the standard costs is out of date, the measurement system may be irrelevant to or perhaps even misleading in identifying inefficiency in the inventory contol operation.

Hence, an important feature to consider in this part of the information system is adjustment/renewal of the standard cost as part of a control index, and this aspect needs to be considered in a computer-based information system.

Fifth, the evaluation system is the part of the organization function that evaluates individual achievement by comparing the actual and expected performance levels provided by the control system. The function may be related to the cognitive and perceptual processes of an administrator in which information on subordinate's performance is transformed into rewards and/or recognition. Which variables are used in the administrator's checklist depends both on his cognitive processes and on the organization information processing capability of the information system. For instance, if the measurement system cannot send numerical messages on subordinate job performance sufficiently, the administrator tends to use qualitative variables, based on his subjective judgment, in order to evaluate subordinates' achievements. Furthermore, if the administrator has cognitive and perceptual limitations that bias him against quantitative and substitute variables, he will then have a tendency to distort the numerical messages even if these are sufficient. Therefore, this study concludes, as do Huber and McDaniel (1986), that computer systems must be designed to fit the cognitive processes of administrators if the information produced by computers is to influence the evaluation process in a correct manner.

Sixth, by the incentive system, we shall indicate the organization activities that determine the rewards for organization participants in accord with the superior's evaluation of their performances. For instance, salary and promotion are explicit rewards, and social status associated with a job is an implicit reward. In addition to various rewards, the incentive system might also include incentive identification processes. The latter processes are needed to match the rewards offered with what employees want and need.

Seventh, the standard setting system refers to activities that simplify, standardize and routinize job contents and procedures so that organizations can reduce the complexity of decision making. The system is needed not only to improve decision making, but also to enhance its control functions. The function is exhibited more clearly when the organization needs to directly influence the employee's decision-making processes via prescribed job procedures. For instance, documentation, in which standard/routine working procedures are fully described as in a cookbook, may provide employees with an efficient way to perform their tasks. The most common application of this function is at the operational level of manufacturing or clerical operations, rather than at the level of strategic decision making where maximum flexibility in processes as well as outcomes may be disirable.

Finally, the education system is the organizational function that provides formal and informal education, such as job training (formal), self-enlightenment (informal), and personal associations (informal) inside/outside the organization. Employee abilities and skills are critical in securing better results/performances in addition to his morale. The education system is designed to influence each employee's ability by providing various types of job-related knowledge. For instance, a group study provides an opportunity to share valuable and essential information (e.g., new technology, such as computers and industrial robotics) among the group participants so that they can adjust themselves to the new complexity related to their jobs.

PROPOSITION AND METHOD FOR EMPIRICAL STUDY

Proposition

Given these eight MCS subsystems described by Itami (1978), this study now discusses how they relate to success or failure of DSS implementation. Figure 5.1 visually describes three important factors that influence DSS implementation: (1) organization structure, (2) MCS (decision making of an administrator), and (3) decision making of employees. The subfactors of these three are linked by arrows in accord with the causal relationships that are assumed on the basis of the conventional literature concerning organization discussed above. The importance of Figure 5.1 is that it incorporates the decision-making processes of an administrator in the form of the MCS. The MCS provides a series of links between organization structures and the decision-making processes of subordinates. It is already well known that computers maintain considerable advantages in many aspects, such as timeliness, accuracy and relevancy of information. The use of computers is therefore expected to yield changes in administrative control activities and organization decision-making processes. Our research interest can be summarized by the following proposition:

Proposition: The use of computer systems as part of an organization information system will change other parts of the MCS. The change in these subsytems will affect the decision-making processes of subordinates. These changes may influence the success or failure of DSS implementation.

The proposition is graphically expressed in Figure 5.2. The proposition emphasizes the need for simultaneous consideration of administrative control activities and technologically supported information systems in order to achieve successful implementation of DSS.

Figure 5.1
Management Control Systems

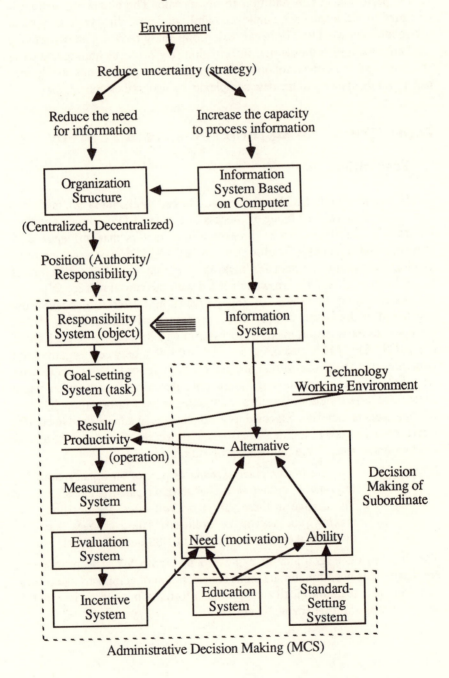

Environment

Reduce uncertainty (strategy)

Reduce the need for information

Increase the capacity to process information

Organization Structure

Information System Based on Computer

(Centralized, Decentralized)

Position (Authority/ Responsibility)

Responsibility System (object)

Information System

Goal-setting System (task)

Technology Working Environment

Result/ Productivity (operation)

Alternative

Decision Making of Subordinate

Measurement System

Evaluation System

Need (motivation)

Ability

Incentive System

Education System

Standard- Setting System

Administrative Decision Making (MCS)

Figure 5.2
Proposition Regarding DSS Implementation

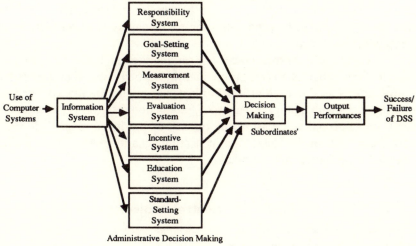

Administrative Decision Making

As discussed before, the information for administrative control activities is referrred to as control indices. Such control indices make it possible for administrators to use their control activities and authority to fulfill their responsibility. The content of the control indices to be considered, of course, depends upon the type of jobs and the levels of the organizational hierarchy that are involved in the proposed DSS. For instance, operational managers may use real time information in the form of such control indices as the hours worked on a job and the number of defective units produced. On the other hand, administrators at the strategic level may depend much less upon real time information and may refer instead to such measures as the profitabilities of plants and products that are generated only periodically, rather than in real time.

Method

For empirical content this chapter reports on an investigation of the current status of DSS implementation in Japanese manufacturing firms. In particular, the above proposition was used to guide our interview survey conducted in the field followed by a questionnaire. We first conducted the interview survey in order to pre-screen respondents for the questionnaire and to identify the control indices used by production managers at operational levels. Based on the interviews and conventional literature on computer-based production control system (e.g., Namiki (1959)), this empirical study was formulated around six groups of twenty-nine production control indices: (1) quality, (2) cost, (3) time, (4) quantity, (5) morale, and (6) efficiency; these were found to be used by production control managers as major features of their production control activities.

The groups and control indices are summarized in Table 5.1. The first column of the table lists each group, and the second column describes the control indices used in each group. For instance, paying attention to the five control indices with quality in Table 5.1, production managers at operational levels are expected to measure the quality of products, to provide their subordinates with useful suggestions concerning quality improvement, and to measure the performance of workers.

Table 5.1. Control Indices

Group	Control Indices
Quality	Percentage of In-Process Defects, Percentage of Defects at Shipping, Number of Defects Due to Careless Mistakes, Customer Claims, Quality Characteristics.
Cost	Material Cost, Labor Cost, Sampling Cost, Total Inventory Cost, Inventory Cost for Parts, In-Process Inventory Cost, Managerial Cost.
Time	Lead Time, Due Days, Man-Hours, Cycle Time, Overwork Time, Total Work Hours.
Quantity	Outputs, Quantity of Parts Inventory, Sales Quantity, Work In-Process, Quantity of Defects.
Morale	Number of Accidents, Absentees.
Efficiency	Yield, Labor Productivity, Utilization Rate, Rate of Machine Breakdown.

A data set for this study was drawn from the questionnaire that was sent to operational-level managers who controled assembly line production. The survey covered twenty-one firms and fifty-seven mainframe computer systems for production control. All the firms surveyed in this study belonged to a manufacturing (assembly) industry.

The questionnaire used for this empirical study was comprised of three groups of subquestionnaires. The first one was designed to identify the names of computer systems and control indices used in the information system of the MCS. These names helped to clarify the purpose for which each computer system was to be used and the functional area for which each respondent (manager) was responsible. The second questionnaire was designed to measure the kind of computer-based indices used for control activities by superiors and to investigate which subsystems of the MCS were significantly influenced by the utilization of the computer sytems. The third questionnaire inquired into the improvements, if any, in subordinate job performances due to the use of computer-based information systems. The second and third questionnaires were measured on a five point Likert-type scale. The three types of questionnaires were thus designed to investigate empirically our proposition presented before.

RESULTS

Result of Factor Analysis

Factor analysis was used in order to identify what these twenty-nine control indices have in common. The technique is a multivariable method that has as its aim the explanation of relationships among many difficult-to-interpret, correlated variables (e.g., the control indices in this study) in terms of a few conceptually meaningful, relatively independent factors (e.g., the names of computer systems). The result of the analysis could explore the relationship between the names of computer systems that indicated the purposes of these systems and the control indices that were incorporated in the computer systems for production control. [See, e.g., Kleinbaum and Kupper (1978) for a detailed description of factor analysis.]

Table 5.2 presents the results of the factor analysis applied to our data set. By the factor analysis, twenty-nine control indices were reduced to more manageable six dimensions (i.e., principal axes) that are presented in the second column and the first row of Table 5.2. All the numbers in Table 5.2 (except the last row) indicate factor-loading scores that describe the correlations between the factors emerging from the factor analysis and the control indices used in the construction of the six factors. The primary use of such factor-loading scores was to pinpoint control indices that were highly correlated (i.e., "load high") with a given factor, so that the factor could be interpreted by the use (name) of computer systems. For instance, total work hours (0.904), man-hours (0.839), overwork time (0.738), labor productivity (0.731), utilization rate (0.629), cycle time (0.597) and absentees (0. 453) have maintained high scores with the first factor. These seven control indices could be considered to possess a common unique feature that was characterized by the names of the computer systems in this study. Since these control indices were often found to be incorporated in the computer systems for the use of man-hour control, we referred to the factor as "information system for man-hour control."

Table 5.2. Determining Factors by Factor Analysis

Seq.	Axis	Control Index	1	2	3	4	5	6
1	1	Total work hours	0.904*	0.010	-0.022	0.101	0.084	-0.004
2	1	Man-hours	0.839*	-0.109	-0.056	0.028	0.032	0.203
3	1	Overwork time	0.738*	-0.035	0.007	-0.049	0.228	-0.184
4	1	Labor productivity	0.731*	0.070	0.120	0.138	0.376	-0.259
5	1	Utilization rate	0.629*	0.135	0.009	0.311	0.220	-0.010
6	1	Cycle time	0.597*	-0.114	-0.017	0.143	0.071	0.468*
7	1	Absentees	0.453*	0.090	0.019	0.041	0.383	-0.502*
8	2	Inventory cost for parts	-0.029	0.852*	-0.076	-0.063	0.252	-0.201
9	2	Total inventory cost	-0.044	0.801*	0.071	-0.009	0.180	0.321
10	2	Quantity of parts inventory	-0.073	0.527*	-0.187	0.436*	-0.036	-0.038
11	2	In-process inventory cost	-0.219	0.517*	0.065	0.088	0.666*	0.051
12	3	Number of defects due to careless mistakes	-0.154	-0.084	0.892*	0.035	-0.144	0.020
13	3	Percentage of defects at shipping	-0.121	-0.038	0.842*	-0.119	-0.146	0.001
14	3	Percentage of in-process defects	0.177	-0.082	0.742*	0.151	0.229	0.128
15	3	Quality characteristics	0.063	-0.034	0.528*	0.116	0.112	0.018
16	3	Customer claims	0.025	-0.011	0.485*	-0.277	-0.023	-0.102
17	4	Quantity of defects	0.079	0.065	0.053	0.713*	0.051	-0.025
18	4	Work in-process	0.176	0.336	0.004	0.696*	0.111	-0.092
19	4	Outputs	0.133	-0.183	0.002	0.619*	0.121	-0.035
20	5	Managerial cost	0.336	0.131	0.095	0.223	0.746*	0.038
21	5	Labor cost	0.299	-0.018	0.002	-0.123	0.743*	-0.185
22	5	Material cost	0.041	0.203	-0.082	0.221	0.620*	-0.169
23	6	Sales quantity	0.006	0.096	-0.070	0.165	0.110	-0.493*
24	6	Yield	0.096	0.332	-0.045	0.263	0.112	-0.443*
25	6	Due days	-0.025	-0.201	-0.306	0.347	-0.076	0.457*
Variance of principal component			5.82	3.34	2.72	1.88	1.01	0.365
Proportion of total variance explained by principal component			36.2%	20.72%	16.90%	11.68%	6.27%	5.34%

Observing control indices grouped by the factor analysis and the names of the computer systems that computerized these indices, this study has determined the names of factors which are summarized in Table 5.3. Six names were assigned to six factors that included the control indices listed in the third column of Table 5.3.

Table 5.3. Information Systems and Control Indices

Axis	Name of Factor	Control Indices
1	Information Systems for Man-Hour Control	Total Work Hours, Man-Hours, Overwork Time, Labor Productivity, Utilization Rate, Cycle Time, Absentees
2	Information Systems for Inventory Cost	Inventory Cost for Parts, Total Inventory Cost, Quantity of Parts Inventory, In-Process Inventory Cost
3	Information Systems for Quality Control	Number of Defects Due to Careless Mistakes, Percentage of Defects at Shipping, Percentage of In-Process Defects, Quality Characteristics, Customer Claims
4	Information Systems for Inventory Quantity Control	Quantity of Defects, Work In-Process, Outputs
5	Information Systems for Cost Computation	Managerial Cost, Labor Cost, Material Cost
6	Information Systems for Scheduling Control	Sales Quantity, Yield, Due Days

Result of Chi-Square Test

After characterizing common features of control indices by the names of the computer systems, this study used the chi-square test of a contingency table in order to empirically examine the proposition presented above. Our proposition was separated into the following two hypotheses:

H_0: the use of computer systems for production control does not influence the subsystem of the MCS which was examined by responses to the second questionnaire, and

H_1: the changes to these MCS subsystems do not improve the job performances of subordinates

which was measured by responses to the third questionnaire. Each of the two questionnaires had two different criteria (changes in the MCS and job improvements of subordinates before and after the use of computer systems). Each criterion was measured on a five-point Likert-type scale. Hence, the data set (i.e., observed frequency) was summarized in the form of a contingency table.

Since we are interested in testing our proposition (i.e., the two linked hypotheses), we present here only results in which the two null hypotheses are rejected so that a path between the first and second hypotheses is confirmed by the chi-square test. Figure 5.3 depicts such results. The numbers in this figure indicate the highly significant chi-square values where "highly" indicates statistical significance at five or ten percent. The table omits results that do not show below 10 percent in the test.

Figure 5.3
Results of Chi-Square Test (Relationships among Computerized Control Indices, MCS Subsystems, and Performances)

"Due Days" in "Schedule Control System"	4.44* ------>	Change of "Evaluation System"	4.20* ------>	Reduce Delays of Due Days
"Labor Productivity" in "Man-Hour Control System"	4.44* ------>	Change of "Evaluation System"	2.86+ ------>	Improve Labor Productivity
"Cycle Time" in "Man-Hour Control System"	3.04* ------>	Change of "Responsibility System	4.85* ------>	Reduce Length of Cycle Time
"Cycle Time" in "Man-Hour Control System"	5.45* ------>	Change of "Standard-Setting System"	5.69* ------>	Reduce Length of Cycle Time

Note: + --- 10% significance and * --- 5% significance

Figure 5.3 presents the following DSS implementation process. First, "due days" (a control index) was computerized in the information sytems for schedule control; then superiors for schedule control started using quantitative information regarding "due days" to evaluate their subordinates. As a result, the change in their evaluation system might reduce the delays of "due days." This produced an administrative benefit by computerization. Second, "labor productivity" (a control index) was computerized in the information systems for man-hour control; then superiors tended to use quantitative information concerning "labor productivity" to evaluate their subordinates. As a consequence, the change in their evaluation system improved the labor productivity of subordinates. Third, "cycle time" (a control index) was computerized in man-hour control systems; then superiors started using numerical information on man-hours to determine the responsibility of their subordinates. As a result, the change in the responsibility system might reduce the length of cycle time. Finally, computerization of the cycle time also produced the change in the standard-setting system. That is, information on the cycle time was also used to simplify subordinates' job contents by computerization. Further, the change might reduce cycle time.

The chi-square test could not statistically explore the changes in MCS subsystems due to the computerization of four production control activities—inventory cost control, quality control, inventory quantity control, and cost computation. However, this study found that information, for instance, for quality control was computerized in manufacturing firms, and then that the computerization influenced the improvement of product quality only because of the timeliness and accuracy of computer-based information systems. However, the information systems for quality control did not affect administrative control activities. That is, the computer systems were used as an instrument of organizational information processing systems, but they could not be a basis of administrative decision making. This implies that the status of computerization in Japanese manufacturing firms needed to be improved for better decision making.

CONCLUSION

This chapter investigated DSS implementation issues based on the conceptual framework of the MCS. The framework we proposed in this study may provide a link among organization structure, decision making process, and administrative control activities, whichare all essential for DSS design/implementation. The MCS has eight subsystems: information, responsibility, goal-setting, measurement, evaluation, incentive, standard-setting, and education. We focused on this proposition: the use of computer systems as part of an organization information processing system changes other parts of the MCS. Changes in these subsystems affect the decision making processes of subordinates. Therefore, these changes may influence the success of DSS implementation.

Based on this proposition, this study empirically examined current computerization and DSS implementation processes in Japanese manufacturing firms. We found that two information systems (i.e., the schedule control system and the man-hour control system) influenced decision making for administrative control activities and also affected subordinates' performances. Other information systems that were detected in this research did not show the same results as these two.

The chapter focused on the.DSS implementation process at the operational level of manufacturing firms (in particular, assembly firms). As a future extension, we may easily apply the framework discussed to other areas (e.g., marketing, sales, R&D, personnel, accounting, and others) and to other organization decision-making levels (e.g., strategic and tactical levels) to investigate DSS implementation process.

REFERENCES

Ackoff, R. L., "Management Misinformation Systems," *Management Science* 14, no. 4 (1967):147–156.

Alavi, M., and J. C. Henderson, "An Evolutionary Strategy for Implementing a Decision Support System," *Management Science* 27, no. 11 (1981): 1309–1323.

Ashby, A. S., *Introduction to Cybernetics,* John Wiley, New York, 1963.

Bean, A. S., N. M. Radnor, and D. A. Tansik, "Structural and Behavioral Correlates of Implementation in U.S. Business Organizations," in *Implementing Operations Research/Management Science,* R. L. Schultz and D. P. Sleuth, eds., American Elsevier, New York, 1975, 77-132.

Carter, N. M., "Computerization as a Predominate Technology: Its Influence on the Structure of Newspaper Organizations," *Academic Management Journal* 27, no. 2 (1984): 247-270.

Cyert, R. M., and R. G. March, *A Behavior Theory of the Firm,* Prentice-Hall, Englewood Cliffs, N.J., 1963.

Dearden, J., "MIS is a Mirage," *Harvard Business Review* 50, no. 1 (1978): 466–492.

Doktor, R. H., and W. F. Hamilton, "Cognitive Style and the Acceptance of Management Science Recommendations," *Management Science* 19, no. 8 (1973): 884-894.

Doll, W. J., "Avenues for Top Management Involvement in Successful MIS Development," *MIS Quarterly* 9, no. 1 (1985): 17–35.

Ference, T. P. and M. Uretsky, "Computers in Management: Some Insights into the State of the Revolution," *Management Datamatics* 5, no. 2 (1976): 55-63.

Galbraith, J. R., "Organization Design: An Information Processing View," *Interfaces* 4, no. 3 (May 1974): 28–36.

Galbraith, J. R., *Organizational Design,* Addison-Wesley, Reading, Mass., 1977.

Ginzberg, M. J., "A Process Approach to Management Science Implementation," Ph.D. dissertation, M.I.T., 1975.

Harvey, A., "Factors Making for Implementation Success and Failure," *Management Science* 16, no. 6 (1970): 312-321.

Henderson, J. C. and D. A. Schilling, "Design and Implementation of Decision Support Systems in the Public Sector, *MIS Quarterly* 9, no. 2 (1985): 157–169.

Huber, G. P., "Organizational Information Systems: Determinants of Their Performance and Behavior," *Management Science* 28, no. 2 (1982): 138-155.

Huber, G. P., "The Nature of Design of Post-Industrial Organizations," *Management Science* 30, no. 8 (1984): 928–951.

Huber, G. P. and R. R. McDaniel, "Decision-Making Paradigm of Organizational Design," *Management Science* 32, no. 5 (1986): 572–589.

Huber, G. P., J. Ullman, and R. Leiferm, "Optimum Organization Design," *Academic Management Review* 4, no. 4 (1979): 567-578.

Huysmans, J.H.B.M., "The Effectiveness of the Cognitive Style Constraint in Implementing Operations Research Proposals," *Management Science* 17, no. 1 (1970): 92-104.

Itami, H., "Management Control" (in Japanese), Working Paper (Schgaku Kenku), Hitotsubashi University, 1978.

Keen, P. G. W., and M. S. Scott-Morton, *Decision Support Systems: An Organizational Perspective,* Addison-Wesley, Reading, Mass., 1978.

Kim, E., and J. Lee, "An Exploratory Contingency Model of User Participaiton and MIS Use," *Information and Management* 11 (1986): 87-97.

King, W. R., and D. I. Clelland, "The Design of Management Information Systems: An Information Analysis Approach," *Management Science* 22, no. 3 (1975): 286–297.

Kleinbaum, D. G. and L. Kupper, *Applied Regression Analysis and Other Multivariable Methods,* Duxbury Press, North Scituate, Mass., 1978.

Kmetz, J. L., "An Information-Processing Study of a Complex Workflow in Aircraft Electronics Repair," *Administrative Science Quarterly* 29 (1984): 255–280.

Lorsch, J. W., "Contingency Theory and Organization Design: A Personal Odyssey," in *The Management of Organizational Design,* R. H. Kilman, L. R. Pondy, and D. P. Slevin, eds., North-Holland, New York, 1976, chap. 8.

March, J. G., and H. A. Simon, *Organizations*, John Wiley & Sons, New York, 1958.

Markus, M. L., *Systems in Organizations: Rugs and Features*, Pitman Publishing, Marshfield, Mass., 1984.

Mooney, J. D., *The Principles of Organizations*, Harper & Row, New York, 1947.

Namiki, T., *Production Control Handbook* (in Japanese), Nikankoguo Shinbunsha, Tokyo, 1959.

Pettigrew, A. M., *The Politics of Organizational Decision-Making*, Tavistoch, London, 1973.

Robey, D., and D. Farrow, "User Involvement in Information System Development," *Management Science* 28, no. 1 (1982): 73-85.

Saunders, G. L., and J. F. Courtney, "A Field Study of Organizational Factors Influencing DSS Success," *MIS Quarterly* 9, no. 1 (1985): 7793.

Schonberger, R. J., "MIS Design: A Contingency Approach," *MIS Quarterly* 4, no. 1 (1980): 13–20.

Schultz, R. L., and D. P. Slevin, eds., *Implementing Operations Research/Management Science*, American Elsevier, New York, 1975.

Szilagyi, A. D., and M. J. Wallace, *Organizational Behavior and Performance*, Scott, Foresman and Company, Glenview, Ill,. 1983, chap. 5.

Tushman, M., and D. A. Nadler, "An Information Processing Approach to Organizational Design," *Academy Management Review* 3, no. 3 (1978): 613–624.

Tushman, M., and T. J. Schnlan, "Boundary Spanning Individuals: Their Role in Information Transfer and Their Antecedents," *Academy. Management Journal* 24, no. 2 (1981): 289–305.

Urwich, L., *The Elements of Administration*, Harper & Row, New York, 1944.

Vroom, V. H., and P. W. Yetton, *Leadership and Decision Making*, University of Pittsburg Press, Pittsburgh, 1973.

Weber, M., *The Theory of Social and Economic Organization*, translated by A. M. Henderson and Talcott Parson, Oxford University Press, New York, 1947.

6

Model Representation in Information Resources Management

Cheng Hsu
William A. Wallace

Modeling as a science involves the creation of new representations of reality and their formalization into a structure suitable for use by computer technology. It requires an investigation of the process of modeling, the model structure, and model resources management. Following the tradition established in early-day management science (e.g., by Charnes and Cooper, 1961), recent major efforts include structured modeling (Geoffrion, 1987) and the notion of model bases in decision support systems (Bonczek, et al., 1981). In this chapter, *models are considered as an integral part of enterprise information resources* (i.e., community model resources to be shared throughout the enterprise). We contend further that these model resources should be represented and managed together with other types of enterprise information resources, particularly data resources (as in databases) and knowledge (as in knowledge-based systems). Accordingly, the model structures (and, to a certain extent, the process itself) have to be defined at the same levels as data and knowledge, encompassing the *interrelationships* of all three types. Toward this end a unified representation method for model resources integrated with data resources and knowledge is presented. The process of modeling is reviewed, focusing on two new techniques: (1) visualization of modeling and (2) combination of symbolic with numeric computing for matching problems with models.

Modeling is at the heart of management science. A great tradition of this discipline is the research paradigm that conceptualizes and articulates management problems with analytical models permitting scientific results (see Charnes and Cooper, 1961). In addition to developing new types of fundamental models, the tradition always calls for modeling application problems using existing models as basic building blocks. These dimensions of modeling lead to a paradigm of metamodels: model structure, modeling process, and model resource management. The concept of "model type" and model approximation (i.e., approximating one model by another model) developed in Charnes and Cooper (1961) is a milestone for such a paradigm. Recent developments in structured modeling (Geoffrion, 1987) and the notion of model bases in decision support systems (see, e.g., Bonczek et al., 1981) further formalized this topic as a research area.

These recent developments have utilized results from computer and information sciences, most notably database theory. The concept of database is really an *integrated* repository of enterprise data resources. Thus, it entails models—models of an enterprise's functions from the perspective of data processing and data resources management. To implement this concept, the field has obtained extensive results on data models, modeling methodologies, and, above all, rigorous database architecture that support the sharing of data resources among differing applications across the enterprise in a unified design. Although less extensive, both the vision and the techniques of structured modeling and model bases research are clearly following the same spirit, but still treat analytical models as an entirely independent subject.

It is our belief, however, that models, data, and knowledge, as in knowledge-based systems, are fundamentally overlapped, with models being a class of application-level representations of data and knowledge. Thus, when models are stored and managed with data and knowledge, all three must be integrated into an enterprise information resources management framework. A unified representation for data, model, and knowledge is central to accomplishing the integration.

A basic reason for this is simply the information content of analytical models: a model prescribes and describes data resources (model parameters and variables), represents operating knowledge (in the form of mathematical functions) and, when implemented, embodies computing algorithms and routines. To truly analyze for modeling primitives or achieve model sharing among applications, the notion of model resources has to be fully developed to the level of data resources, knowledge (base) resources, and their representation methods. A case in point is a recent effort by Dolk (1988), which proposed a model management scheme for structured modeling, thereby extending the latter into the context of enterprise information resources management. This scheme, however, would be confusing in practice unless it could be mapped to and reconciled with other information resources—that is, data and knowledge (this is discussed further below). Finally, from the perspective of databases and knowledge-based systems, analytical models are both end-users (i.e., application programs using databases or knowledge bases) and internal processing tools (e.g., search algorithms used for query optimization in databases or inference in knowledge-based systems).

Besides logical synergies that can be achieved through information resources management, there are practical needs driving this integration. In a computerized environment, information and decision systems are on-line and connected. All three types of information resources are indifferentiable in implementation. The management problem and its process have to be dealt with as a whole. Again, the requirement is clear: there is only one world for all enterprise information resources and they have to be modeled and managed together in a unified way. In the next section we review the process of modeling, in the spirit of metamodels. From Charnes and Cooper (1961) to Geoffrion (1987), and then to model resources management is a logical course of development. A discussion of model bases in the context of model resources management is presented in the second section. We propose an information model, two-stage-entity-relationship, as the basis for unified information resources representation in the third section. Next, the representation method itself, the global information resources dictionary, is presented, along with some comparisons with the structured modeling method.

THE PROCESS OF MODELING

The process of modeling is not a well-understood phenomenon since it involves cognitive processes of which we have very limited knowledge. However, two generalizations about cognitions have been used (perhaps not by design) in modeling science: (1) we create visualizations or "mental models" of the reality we wish to represent, and (2) we reason by analogy about this representation in attempting to formalize it. Recent research in model structuring that employs graphical displays and the coupling of numeric and symbolic computing are two examples.

Concerning the first example, recent research has sought to develop mathematical formalisms that facilitate the structuring process involved in modeling [see Geoffrion (1987) and Howard (1989) as examples, while Smith, 1988 provides an extensive discussion]. Inherent in this work is the desire to provide visualizations to help decision makers define the problem and elicit knowledge from experts in the problem domain. In some cases, these graphical techniques are just that—ways of gaining agreement on a problem definition similar to flip charts or blackboard drawings (Eden et al., 1984). We are concerned here with structuring, or the formalization phase of modeling (Willemain, 1989), using "a formal mathematical framework, computer-based environment" (Geoffrion, 1987, p. 547).

We would like to illustrate model structuring by applying one such technique, influence diagrams, to the immediate response to the Exxon Valdez accident (Harrald et al., forthcoming). We selected this example because of Professor Cooper's past research in developing models to provide guidance to the U.S. Coast Guard in managing their resources devoted to marine environmental protection (Charnes et al., 1979).

As defined by Shachter (1988), an influence diagram is a network representation of probabilistic and deterministic variables, decisions, and an objective. The stochastic variables are represented by single ovals, the deterministic variables by double ovals, and decisions by rectangles. Arrows represent the direction of influence. An influence diagram not only shows relationships between variables and decisions, but also implies the information requirements for decision making. Howard and Matheson (1984), Owen (1984), and Shachter (1986) show how the influence diagram can be used to model complex decision processes. Shachter (1988) shows that if a diagram's structure is determined and if the outcomes and distributions of key variables are specified, then the diagram may be solved in a manner similar to a decision tree. Figure 6.1 represents the use of influence diagrams to structure the emergent stage of the response to the Exxon Valdez oil spill.

A useful interpretation of the influence diagram of the Exxon Valdex response can be made using Simon's (1960) model of the decision-making process. In his information processing view of cognition, the decision-making process starts with an intelligence-gathering phase, which leads to the development of alternatives, or design phase. Once alternatives are generated, the decision maker is able to compare alternatives and make a choice. The final state is implementation.

In Figure 6.1, the upper level of the influence diagram represents the stochastic and deterministic variables that must be known in order for the decision maker to make informed strategic choices. This corresponds to the diagnosis, or intelligence gathering, stage of decision making. In the Exxon Valdez incident, for example, the alternate captain of the port was actually sent out to board the vessel to ascertain the extent of the damage, the stability of the vessel, and the rate of cargo loss.

The next level of the diagram represents a series of strategic choices, the validity of which depends heavily on the quality of information available.

Figure 6.1
Influence Diagram of the Response to the Exxon Valdez Oil Spill

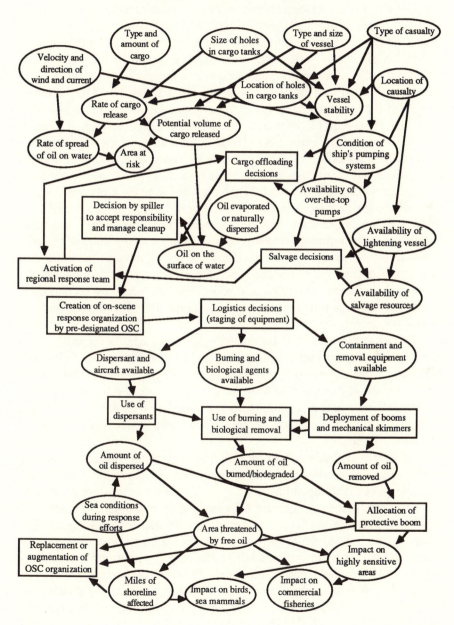

These decisions include the decisions to offload the vessel, to initiate salvage measures, to activate the regional response team, to initiate the staging of response resources, to activate the predesignated on-scene coordinator organization, and to accept Exxon's responsibility for cleanup.

The outputs of these decisions were the organizational structures and resources (equipment and people) that were available to combat the spill in the early days. These deterministic variables acted as constraints for the round of tactical decisions that made up the next round of decision making: the use of dispersants, the allocation of containment and removal equipment, and the use of biological and burning agents to combat the oil. The variables describing the results of these decisions represent the amount of oil removed, dispersed, burned, or biodegraded. Since this was a relatively small amount, the final round of decision making in the initial stage of the spill response involved the allocation of booms to protect vulnerable resources and the replacement and augmentation of on-scene resources.

The output variables describing the completion of the emergent stage of the spill response are variables describing the miles of beach affected, including the impact on fisheries and on bird and marine mammal populations. The influence diagram does not show the evolution of the spill response into a massive beach-cleaning operation and media event. The diagram also does not show the goal of the decision process during the Exxon Valdez incident (which would be indicated by a rounded rectangle). It is not clear from the initial analysis that decision makers had a consistent and clear set of goals.

This example illustrates the modeling process using a formalism. We might also mention that through visualization of a decision process, a hierarchy of decision models needed at various stages is implied. The model for the overall problem is characterized in terms of these submodels and the "dynamic" knowledge pertaining to the process. Charnes et al. (1986) provide a similar formulation without visualization, that is, the notion of "decision regimes."

Another recent advance in modeling science is the capacity to couple symbolic and numeric computing (Kitzmiller and Kowalik, 1987). This technology was developed initially to provide guidance to users in order to solve numeric problems. The users understood their problem, but were not able to employ the sophisticated algorithms needed for its solution. The ability to match the problem with the appropriate solution procedure (i.e., the current model), was in the past left to the user (or intermediary). "User-friendly" software helped, but still could not ensure the proper matching of problem and model. Symbolic techniques employing qualitative reasoning are being investigated to help users "navigate" and find the appropriate numeric procedures (Talukdar et al., 1986). Heuristics have been employed in the past to help solve large-scale mathematical programming problems. Such heuristics can now be coded symbolically and integrated with numeric procedures.

These coupled systems may also be of value in the modeling process itself. Many analysis and design problems contain components that are not sufficiently understood to be expressed in a way that is conducive to traditional numeric solution procedures.

An example is the controlling of a fully autonomic robot (Kowalik et al., 1986). Many of the tasks of the robot can be controlled by traditional techniques employing numeric procedures. However, the more human like tasks may require the incorporation of judgment and knowledge obtained from human counterparts. This integration (as opposed to coupling) will enable the modeler to provide a system that more closely matches his representation of the reality being modeled.

We are engaged in a research program in high-temperature materials processing, which requires new approaches to integrate data with knowledge as well as to combine symbolic with numeric computing. The objective is to integrate models of physical phenomena with the judgment of engineers. The models used by the researchers are, in reality, sets of complex hypotheses. "Good" models are those that embody significant theories from, for example, heat transfer, and that upon exercising, provide results useful for design and production engineering. When dealing with complex systems, however, heuristics or "rules-of-thumb" are often used (1) in creating the model itself, (2) in interpreting the output of the model, and (3) in converting the output into a form useful in engineering development and practice.

As an example, consider a system designed to reason about the domain of networks of heat exchanges. The system could call on its heuristic knowledge to set the variables in a numerical simulation, using finite difference equations that describe the physical process of heat exchange. The system could then compare the output of the simulation to field data and assess various design or manufacturing conditions.

In addition to the descriptive models, "optimization" models are also needed to find the best schedule or production process. Again, however, the judgment of experts—in this case, design and manufacturing engineers—must be incorporated into the model. Their heuristics can guide the optimization routines or modify the output to meet current production capabilities.

In order to make full use of the technologies being developed to support the modelling process, we need an integrated environment. The users of a structured modeling technique must be able to incorporate the results into the enterprise information resources, as well as be able to use enterprise data in the modeling process. Helping users build models by analogy requires a database format that facilitates matching their problem with the appropriate model.

In summary, the process of modeling calls for modeling constructs that both define and specify the process and its results—models. This leads naturally to a common architecture for models sharing the same characterizations. Thus, from the logic and structural perspective, the notion of model base is in order; but the model base no doubt owes its actual origin to the influence of database theory in computer science through the development of decision support systems (see, e.g., Elam et al., 1980 and Bonczek et al., 1981).

MODEL BASES AND MODEL RESOURCES MANAGEMENT

Based on an analogy to databases, the concept of model base entails a repository of model resources that are (1) consolidated from differing application models, (2) managed at a community level to allow model sharing by all users, and (3) structured to support the model-structuring process and form new as well as pro forma models for various decision problems upon users' requests. The first requirement points to the concept of model resources primitives and model base design—a metamodel similar to the relational model or object-oriented paradigm in data and knowledge systems. The second requirement leads to the incorporation of model resources into an overall framework of enterprise information resources management, structurally alongside data resources and knowledge bases. The third requirement is squarely at the heart of model base implementation: namely, the representation (and manipulation) of model resources as persistent computing objects or abstract data.

Most previous research on model bases or model management does not consider models as an integral part of enterprise information resources. Many of these researchers do not even formulate the problem at a model resources level, but consider models as individual, unique structures that are designated for particular applications, users, or systems. A commonly used approach in analyzing model structures is to categorize a model's components in the light of the original management problem (e.g., Dolk and Konsynski, 1984). Thus, the resultant structures tend to be problem-dependent (e.g., "constraint" is peculiar to mathematical programming models). Structured modeling is perhaps the only result that contains primitives (e.g., primary entity and compound entity) transcending the context of models and model types. Still, it is unclear whether or not these primitives are appropriate for sharing model resources. As mentioned before, the structure employed in structured modeling is seemingly compatible with the basic concept of model base structures; however, the research has focused on the process of modeling only from the perspective of individual endeavors.

There are, of course, considerable efforts in the literature that investigate model resources primitives and decompose end-user application models into common resources for consolidation into the model base. Almost invariably these efforts use some "unit models," determined more or less on an ad hoc basis such as subroutines, to constitute the model base (see, e.g., Dutta and Basu, 1984). Certain standard database technology is applied to designing the model base (e.g., Blanning, 1985). Some knowledge-based techniques have also been employed for model manipulation in several cases (e.g., Remus and Kotteman, 1986). But models themselves are not treated as encompassing databases or knowledge bases.

A recent work by Dolk (1988) is perhaps one of the most notable efforts on model resources representation and management. This work explicitly recognizes model management as an information resources management problem and extends the scope of structured modeling into this domain. The information resources dictionary system (IRDS) that the National Bureau of Standards developed for conventional data dictionary systems in the database area is also adopted in the work to represent and manage the model resources generated from Structured Modeling.

Our hope for this IRDS-based framework is that the model resources representation will be integrated with IRDS's standard data representation. That is, if an information system uses both model bases and databases, then there will be only one unified IRDS representation for both, rather than having one IRDS for data resources and another for model resources. The basic reason for this requirement is simply this: even using the same construct, logically identical or shared data and procedures between model bases and databases will probably not result in the same form if they are analyzed and designed separately. To ensure the integrity of these common data and procedures, model resources need to be calibrated to data resources from the perspective of information processing in order to provide a baseline for the decomposition of models into "basic sub-routines" or model resources primitives. The recursive structure of models can be fully recognized only when such a baseline exists.

Finally, to reap the complete benefits of a shared, community model base, it is necessary to establish a clear separation of application models and persistent model resources (similar to end-user views versus community base relations in a relational database). Strictly speaking, all model base efforts mentioned above do not provide a definitive framework for this separation, due, we believe, to the lack of integration with data resources.

As a matter of fact, model resources should calibrate to both data resources and knowledge bases since models not only embody data but also represent and encompass knowledge. More specifically, the recursive structure of models can and should be captured with the same data model primitives and knowledge representation primitives as in the rest of enterprise information resources management. As such, models are merely high-level views or configurations of data and knowledge primitives.

We next present a method for enterprise information resources management from the perspective of databases and knowledge-based systems. The method was developed to integrate data resources with knowledge bases using a particular information model. The resultant repository of information resources was termed *metadatabase*. Before extending this method to incorporate model resources, its basic concepts are discussed below.

A METHOD FOR INFORMATION RESOURCES MANAGEMENT

The Metadatabase Approach

Essentially, a metadatabase is an organizationwide repository from which users can obtain information in a timely manner without having to rely on inexact personal communication and without knowing where information resides or how to access it. The metadatabase provides an enterprise view and local views of the information contained in the individual subsystems, thereby supporting decision-making activities of those who are not users of specific subsystems. This view consolidation is a type of integration that facilitates systemwide information sharing. While the metadatabase does describe such activities, it will not interfere with routine data transfers between subsystems or with self-contained subsystem operation. The repository also facilitates the development of computer-aided software engineering (CASE) applications: since the metadatabase contains information about application data structures, production rules, and the databases accessed by application programs, the job of application maintenance and development can be eased and, in some cases, automated.

Scope of Metadata. It is worth emphasizing, however, that the scope of the metadatabase goes beyond the conventional notion of data dictionary or repository and includes the organization's operating knowledge. Specifically, metadata describes data, views, structures, knowledge, decision logic, and communication and control protocols. The need to include operating knowledge with data models can be explained as follows. The various knowledge-based systems in a complex organization should have a global repository. The repetitive or predetermined decision logic should be modeled with respect to its data content to facilitate computerization; similarly, communications and control procedures that are automated should also be related to the data resources they affect.

Metadata Representation: The GIRD Model. Because of the nature and complex structure of metadata, are presentation method is needed to organize the contents, and a modeling methodology is needed to obtain the metadata. The global information resources dictionary (GIRD) model has been developed as a representation method. The GIRD model represents the four major classes of metadata: enterprise functions, functional models, structural models, and users and resources. Note that each class of metadata (shown by the rectangles in Figure 6.2) reflects the perspective with which a certain group of users understands the enterprise as a whole.

Figure 6.2
SER Model for GIRD

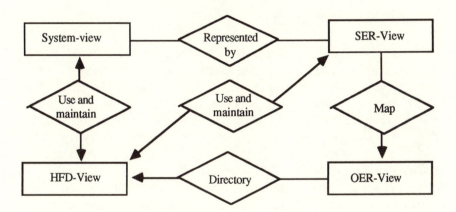

Enterprise functions are the highest-level descriptions of the basic organization subsystems. This view reflects an executive-level understanding of the subsystems and how they interact with each other. The functional models (semantic data models, data flow models, and high-level CASE models) are more detailed in scope and describe the major modules and the decision logic contained in each subsystem. A functional model reflects the enterprise view of the mid-level managers, who see their enterprise as a series of logically related processes. Structural models (data models and rule bases) refer to data-structure and rule-structure translations of the higher-level functional models. This class of metadata describes the underlying schemata of databases and knowledge bases and reflects the enterprise as viewed by information systems people. Thus, by reflecting the different orientations that enterprise members use in describing the organization, these first three classes of metadata provide the information normally required for decision making.

Finally, the users and resources class of metadata describes the individuals as well as the hardware, files, and documents of the organization. This class of metadata reflects information implementation, control, and security in the enterprise. The various relationships among these four views are depicted by the diamonds in Figure 6.2.

The GIRD representation employs a modeling methodology called the two-stage entity-relationship (TSER) approach, which provides one set of constructs for functional modeling and another set for data- and rule-structure modeling. (Figure 6.2 is an example of a TSER functional model.) It also includes algorithms that automatically generate the structural models from the functional models task of the metadatabase approach.

Modeling Methodology

The two-stage entity-relationship (TSER) model (Hsu, 1985) was first developed to integrate some tasks of system analysis with database design; it was later expanded to include knowledge representation. The TSER entails two levels of modeling constructs devised, respectively, for semantics-oriented abstractions (SER) and cardinality-oriented representations (OER) of data and production rules. The constructs allow for top-down system design, as well as for bottom-up or reverse engineering of existing applications or software packages into the TSER constructs. Rigorous TSER algorithms that map from semantic to structural models ensure that the resulting structures are in at least third normal form. TSER algorithms also integrate views, thus allowing systematic consolidation of any number of data models. The integrity constraints built into the TSER constructs are used to facilitate the management and control of the metadatabase. The three parts of TSER are summarized as follows:

1. The Modeling Construct.

Functional Constructs: Used for system analysis and information requirements representation; referred to in the TSER model as the SER mode.

    a.   Subject (SE): Contains data items, functional dependencies, intrasubject rules, and class hierarchy information. Subjects generally represent functional units of information, such as user views, application systems, and decision models and are analogous to a frame or object. A clas hierarchy generalizes and aggregates subjects

b. Context (SR): Contains intersubject control knowledge, such as production rules, operating rules, algorithms, and procedures in the form of decision rules, data conversion rules, model formation or solution rules, and communication rules. An analogous construct is processing logic.

Structural Constructs: Used as a neutral structural representation of data semantics and production rules from the SER model for logical database design; referred to in the TSER approach as the OER model. There are four basic constructs.

a. Operational Entity (OE): Objects identified by a singular primary key, and (optional) alternative keys and nonprime attributes.

b. Plural Relationship (PR): Association of entities characterized by a composite primary key and signifying a many-to-many and independent association.

c. Functional Relationship (FR): A many-to-one association that signifies characteristic or inheritance relationships. FRs represent a referential integrity constraint implied by the existence of a foreign key,

d. Mandatory Relationship (MR): A one-to-many fixed association of OEs. MRs represent the existence-dependency constraint.

2. The Mapping Algorithms. There are three basic classes of mapping algorithms.

a. Modeling Procedures: These algorithms link the SER and OER, generate and decompose views, and identify relations and data structure diagrams.

b. Validation Procedures: These algorithms are used to verify the OER model itself when users create or modify one, as well as to produce integrity constraints for schema design.

c. Interface Procedures: These algorithms include high-level system functions, such as communication with other types of system analysis and functional modeling methods, and modeling interfaces for the users.

3. **The Knowledge Base.** There are three basic categories.

a. Application-Specific Knowledge: These constructs contain the contents of user-supplied operating rules and architectural knowledge forming the context within which the organization operates. The notions of events and sequencing are handled with this type of knowledge.

b. Design-Specific Knowledge: This category includes information model and system definitional knowledge, data equivalence and related knowledge such as naming conventions and domain definitions, interapplication knowledge, and mapping knowledge.

c. Modeling Knowledge: This category contains generic heuristics and decision/semantic rules for data modeling (e.g., view integration around the TSER construct).

The first two categories of knowledge are represented with context and, to a lesser extent, subject; they constitute the metadata that go beyond the traditional data models. The third category is internal to the TSER system and will not be output to the metadatabase. [This section is based on a paper by Hsu, et al. (1990).]

MODEL RESOURCES REPRESENTATION IN GIRD

The results of TSER modeling give rise to a metadatabase, or a repository of enterprise information resources. The contents of the metadatabase are again structured using the TSER constructs—in particular, the OER model. Therefore, two layers of TSER application are involved: the first layer is the information model itself (i.e., metadata) in terms of SER and OER; the second is an OER representation of these metadata themselves. This type of recursive structuring is considered self-descriptive in software engineering. For clarity, we refer to the second layer of OER structure as meta-entities and metarelationships. In essence, these meta-entities and metarelationships represent the basic types of metadata from the perspective of model structure and hence are generic.

This generic, standard structure is the basic GIRD model for enterprise information resources representation. Figure 6.3 depicts the GIRD model. All constructs in the model follow precisely the same definitions and conventions of the OER model. Thus, all meta-entities are characterized with singular primary keys and all meta-PRs represent many-to-many associations among meta-entities. Meta-MRs and meta-FRs also imply, respectively, fixed and functional dependencies between meta-entities. For example, the meta-PR associating subject with context, called *relates*, has a binary-relation type of structure containing the subject name and the context name for each pair of associated subject and context in the metadata (the first layer). The fact that certain subjects are associated (e.g., forming an application model) according to some definitive operating rules—which are defined in a context—is represented through the tuples (pairs) in relates that contain this context name. Similarly, all rules contained in all contexts and subjects are consolidated and represented into three meta-entities: rules, condition, and action, where rules contain only the rule-type and rule name data, with the contents of rules consolidated into condition (the left-hand side of rule) and Action (the right-hand side). This way the same rules will be stored only once, but shared by as many contexts or subjects as called for by the applications. The details of this GIRD model, including its derivation and data structures, are given in Hsu et al., (1989); some of the details that are most pertinent to model resources representation are given below.

Figure 6.3
Global Information Resources Dictionary (GIRD) OER

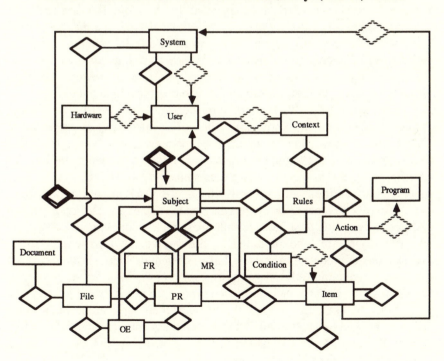

The basic idea of developing via the TSER a unified representation for analytical model resources, data resources, and knowledge resources is based on two arguments:

1. For computerization and information resources management, a "largest common denominator" needs to be identified and developed for generic model base, database, and knowledge base constructs. The TSER provides an approach toward this end.

2. All basic model elements recognized in the literature of model management can be further simplified into more fundamental representations of data and knowledge. (After all, analytical models are but another form of data and knowledge.)

To illustrate the second point, we consider below the basic elements employed in structured modeling. Figure 6.4 summarizes the major modeling elements and their representation using the MBS's IRDS design. One might wonder how these primary entities and compound entities can be structurally related to the "regular" IRDS entities and relationships. Similarly, the separation of attribute from variable attribute, and that of both attributes from entities and function, is significant to model formulation per se, but is not necessarily meaningful to data management. Furthermore, function and these structural types all embody a mathematical/logical form that may be unified with a production rule type of representation. In other words, the differentiation among these three structure types as well as between them and the model, may be replaced with a recursive structure, thereby avoiding possible excessive arbitrariness in model resources development.

Moving toward a "largest common denominator" that unifies model resources with data and knowledge, the GIRD alternative is presented in Figure 6.5. As shown an application-level model will simply be represented as a subject, using the regular construct defined in the previous section. All data items, based on their standard data semantic constraints, will be later mapped into entities and relationships in the OER model and thereby consolidated with other OER models derived for databases. The interpretation and operation of the data items within the model, along with all constraints and functions, are also included in the subject as intrasubject rules. Associations of models for the overall management problem are characterized as contexts, containing the structural rules and operations. Solution logic or algorithms are similarly included either within the pertinent subjects or as a part of the context, depending on the scope of their application. These rules will then be consolidated through TSER into meta-entities Rules, Condition, Action, File and Program as mentioned above for Figure 6.3. Some detailed examples are given in Hsu and Dong (1989).

Figure 6.4
The Structured Modeling Approach to Model Representation

Structured Modeling Construct (Geoffrion, 1987):

- Six element types:
  PE   (primary entity)
  CE   (compound entity)
  ATT   (attribute)
  VA   (variable attribute)
  TEST   (test
  FCN   (function)

- Three structure types:
  Elemental, Generic and Modular structure

Structured Modeling Representation in IRDS (Dolk, 1988):

- Extended IRDS entity types for structured modeling:
  PE   CE   ATT   VA   TEST   FCN   MODEL

- Generic structural representation:
  CALLS (ce, pe)   CALLS (va, pe)   CALLS (test, test)
  CALLS (att, pe)   CALLS (va, ce)   CALLS (test, fcn)
  CALLS (att, ce)   CALLS (test, va)   CALLS (fcn fcn)
  CALLS (test, att)   CALLS (fcn, va)   CALLS (fcn, test)
  CALLS (fcn, att)

- Modular structural representation:
  CONTAINS (module, module)   CONTAINS (model, module)
  CONTAINS (module, pe)   CONTAINS (model, pe)
  CONTAINS (module, ce)   CONTAINS (model, ce)
  CONTAINS (module, att)   CONTAINS (model, att)
  CONTAINS (module, va)   CONTAINS (model, va)
  CONTAINS (module, test)   CONTAINS (model, test)
  CONTAINS (module, fcn)   CONTAINS (model, fcn)

It is worth noting that this approach does not entail a hierarchy of models or modules as many of the previous results do. The interwoven associations of models in decision systems are simply represented through the hierarchy of subjects. That is, the hierarchy is considered an integral part of the ad hoc application, rather than some a priori or generic characterization of models. This emphasis on decoupling model resources from applications is essential to incorporating model management into enterprise information resources management.

Figure 6.5
Model Resources Representation in GIRD

Modeling Construct:

System	(overall management problem/decision systems)
Subject	(application/model)
Context	(associations between models)
Item	(parameter and decision variable)
Rule	(model structural rules, solution logic/procedure and operation/assertion)
Condition	(constraint, function, and mathematical/logical statement)
Action	(feasibility, optimality, and mathematical/logical statement)
File	(input, output, and other interfaces)
Program	(executable algorithm/code)

Model Resources Representation:
- Meta-Entities

System	(Systname, descript, addedby, dateadded, uname)
Subject	(Sname, descript, addedby, dateadded, uname)
Context	(Cname, descript, addedby, dateadded, uname)
Item	(ItemCode, iname, represent, length, domain, descript, defvalue, addedby, dateadded)
Rule	(Rname, rtype, descript, addedby, dateadded)
Condition	(Condid, iname, operator, value)
Action	(Actid, acctype, exemode, actcont)
OE	(OEname, PKey, AKey, descript, addedby, dateadded)
PR	(PRname, PKey, AKey, descript, addedby, dateadded)
MR	(MRname, PKey, AKey, descript, addedby, dateadded)
FR	(FRname, Dant, Ded, descript, addedby, dateadded)
File	(Fname, ftype, accessmode, descript, addedby, dateadded)
Document	(Dname, doctype, numpages, author, addedby, dateadded, descript)
Hardware	(Hname, htype, location, comnet, addedby, dateadded, descript)
User	(Uname, usagename, position, phone, office, address)
Program	(Progname, descript, language, addedby, dateadded)

- Metarelationships: mostly binary relations associating meta-entities

Relates	(Cname, Sname)	CondOf	(Condid, Rname)
Describes	(Iname, Sname)	Actof	(Actid, Rname)
Contains	(Cname, Rname)	Applies	(Sname, Rname) etc.

CONCLUSIONS

Modeling science is clearly the theoretical underpinning to information and decision systems in computerized enterprises. Compared to models in database and knowledge-based paradigms, analytical models in management science have a much longer tradition, but a less rigorous development in metamodel theory, including the process of modeling, model structure, and model resources management. Nonetheless, there has always been such a dimension of metamodels in management science. This tradition has an origin in such founders as Charnes and Cooper (1961) and has achieved prominence since the emergence of decision support systems in late 1970s. However, previous research largely concentrated on studying analytical models per se without also considering their structural overlaps with other information technology.

We, on the other hand, consider analytical models as a special class of data and knowledge representation that can be constructed from certain generic data and knowledge modeling primitives. The GIRD model is proposed for this purpose, resulting in a unified structure not only for data resources and knowledge, but also for model resources. As such, model base, database, and knowledge base are treated as application-oriented subsets of a common information base under an integrated enterprise information resources management. Therefore, analytical models are no longer just application programs, but become a resource that can be shared by the entire user community across an enterprise.

This chapter focused on the representation of model resources. Nevertheless, the GIRD model, as interpreted this way, also amounts to model structural primitives that can be employed to structure the process of modeling and to support both visualization and modeling by analogy. Another direction for further study is the actual implementation of the proposed structure. A prototype metadatabase is currently under construction using a relational database management system (Rdb) coupled with a LISP environment for its platform. This prototype is being extended to support model management at Rensselaer Polytechnic Institute.

NOTE

We wish to express our appreciation to Professor William W. Cooper. As a master modeler, he created abstract structures that contributed toward our understanding of the world around us, he helped us improve our modeling skills by example and techniques, and he gave us models with rigor and elegance, and with relevance to societal needs.

REFERENCES

Blanning, R. W., "A Relational Framework for Model Management in DSS," *Decision Support Systems* 1, no. 1 (January 1985): 69–81.

Bonczek, R., Holsapple, C. W., and Whinston, A. B., *Foundations of Decision Support Systems*, New York: Academic Press, 1981.

Charnes, A., and Cooper, W. W., *Management Models and Industrial Applications of Linear Programming*, New York: John Wiley & Sons, 1961.

Charnes, A. and Cooper, W. W., *Creative and Innovative Management: Essays in Honor of George Kozmetsky*, Cambridge Mass.: Ballinger, 1984.

Charnes, A., Cooper, W. W., Gorr, W. L., Hsu, C., and von Rabenau, B., "Decision Models and Methods for Emergency Government Interventions: Case Study of Natural Gas Shortages," *Management Science* 32, no. 10 (1986): 1242-1258.

Charnes, A., Cooper, W. W., Karwan, K., and Wallace, W. A, "A Chance Constrained Goal Programming Model to Evaluate Response Resources for Marine Pollution Disasters," *Journal of Environmental Economics and Management* 6 (1979): 244-274.

Dolk, D. R., "Model Management and Structured Modeling: The Role of an Information Resources Management System," *Communications of the ACM* 31, no. 6 (1988): 704-718.

Dolk, D. and Konsynski, B., "Knowledge Representation for Model Management System," *IEEE Transaction on Software Engineering,* SE-10, no. 6 (1984): 619-628.

Dutta, A., and Basu, A., "An Artificial Intelligence Approach to Model Management in Decision Support Systems," *IEEE Computer* 17, no. 9 (1984): 89-97.

Eden, C., Jones, S., and Sims, D., *Messing About in Problems*, New York: Pergamon Press, 1984.

Elam, J., Henderson, J., and Miller, L., "Model Management System: An Approach to Decision Support in Complex Organizations," *Proceedings of the First International Conference on Information Systems,* Philadelphia, PA (1980): 98–110.

Evans, J. R., "A Review and Synthesis of OR/MS and Creative Problem Solving: Part 1—Creativity and Problem Solving," Working Paper No. QA-1988-04, Department of Quantitative Analysis and Information Systems, College of Business Administration, University of Cincinnati, Cincinnati, Ohio, 1988.

Geoffrion, A. M., "An Introduction to Structured Modeling," *Management Science* 33, no. 5 (1987): 547-588.

Harrald, J., Marcus, H., and Wallace, W. A. "A Rapid Assessment of the Immediate Response to the Exxon Valdez Accident: Management and

Engineering Systems Considerations," Report to the National Science Foundation, Decision Sciences and Engineering Systems, Rensselaer Polytechnic Institute, Troy, New York.

Howard, R. A., and Matheson, J. E., "Influence Diagrams," *The Principles and Applications of Decision Analysis* Vol. 2, R. A. Howard, and J. E. Matheson, eds., Strategic Decision Group, Menlo Park, CA, 1984, 719-762.

Hsu, C., "Structured Database Systems Analysis and Design Through Entity-Relationship Approach", Proceedings 4th International Conference on Entity-Relationship Approach, IEEE Computer Society (1985): 56-63.

Hsu, C., Bouziane, M., Cheung, W. C., Nogus, J., Rattner, L., and Yee, L., "A Metadata System for Information Modeling and Integration," Proceedings International Conference on Systems Integration 1990, IEEE Computer Society, 1990.

Hsu, C., Bouziane, M. Rattner, L. and Yee, L., "A Meta database Architecture for Heterogeneous, Distributed Environments: Global Information Resources Dictionary (GIRD)," Working Paper 37-88-157, Rensselaer Polytechnic Institute, Troy, N.Y. 12180, April 1989.

Hsu, C., and C. Dong, "Model Resources Representation and Management," Working Paper 37-89-217, Troy, N. Y.: Rensselaer Polytechnic Institute, 12180, October 1989.

Kitzmiller, C.T., and Kowalik, J.S., "Coupling Symbolic and Numeric Computing in Knowledge-Based Systems," *AI Magazine* 8, no. 2 (Summer 1987): 85-90.

Kowalik, J.S., Chalfan, K.M., Marcus, R.I., and Skillman, T.L., "Composite Software Systems", Technical Report, Seattle, Wash.: Boeing Computer Services, 1986.

Owen, D.T., "The Use of Influence Diagrams in the Structuring of Complex Decision Problems," in *The Principals and Applications of Decision Analysis*, R. A. Howard, and J. E. Matheson, eds., Strategic Decisions Group, Menlo Park, CA, 1984, pp. 763-772.

Remus, W. E., Kotteman, J., "Toward Intelligent Decision Support System: An Artificial Intelligent Statistician," *MIS Quarterly* 10, no. 4 (1986): 403-418.

Schachter, R.D., "Evaluating Influence Diagrams," *Operations Research* 34, no. 6 (1986): 871–882.

Schachter, R.D., "Probalistic Inference and Influence Diagrams," Operations Research 36, no. 4 (1988): 589-604.

Simon, H. A., *The New Science of Management Decision*, New York: Harper and Brothers, 1960.

Smith, G. F., "Toward a Heuristic Theory of Problem Structuring," *Management Science* 34, no. 12 (1988): 1489-1506.

Talukdar, S. N., E., Carbozo, E., L. Leào, R. Banares, and A. Joobbavz, "A System for Distributed Problem Solving," in *Coupling Symbolic and Numerical*

Computing in Expert Systems, ed. J. S. Kowalik, 59-68, Amsterdam, The Netherlands: North Holland, 1986, 59–67.

Willemain, T., *Exploring The Process of Model Formulation*, Proposal to the National Science Foundation, Decision Sciences and Engineering Systems, Rensselaer Polytechnic Institute, Troy, New York, 1989.

Part III

Resource Management

Integrated Modeling Systems for Corporate Human Resource Decisions

Richard J. Niehaus

Modeling capabilities have been used for human resource planning for many years. Much of the current technology had its inception in the late 1960s, with subsequent intensive development in the 1970s. This chapter is dedicated to William W. Cooper, who is a major contributor to this development (along with Charnes, Niehaus, and others). In addition to the seminal technological contributions, this work, from its beginning, focused on issues requiring integration of complex organizational functions. This chapter discusses such integrated human resource modeling issues as they relate to corporate- or headquarters-level decision making. In human resource terms, this translates into issues having long-term or large-scale systemic impacts, such as:

1. Training requirements implied by long-term workload projections.

2. Conformance with across-the-board policy issues such as EEO/AA.

3. Career development assignments (rotation) to fit within the organization's overall workload distribution.

Tactical decisions—that is, short-term skills balancing or individual assignment planning—will be discussed briefly.

A comprehensive review of the human resource or manpower modeling work of Charnes, Cooper, and Niehaus (1968, 1971, 1972a, 1972b, 1974,

1975, 1978) was completed recently (Niehaus and Bres, 1987). In-depth discussions, particularly concerning implementation issues, can be found in Niehaus (1979, 1988). In this chapter, the earlier work will be summarized in a condensed form. Since this chapter was written to honor Bill Cooper, the bibliography contains a listing of the papers developed in conjunction with the U.S. Navy's support of joint research with Charnes, Cooper, Niehaus, and others.

This chapter will focus on the issues from a managerial perspective. First, the relationship of modeling to policy decisions as learned through using human resource planning models is discussed. Examples of several integrated modeling systems will be provided, followed by discussion of the wider issue of how these fit within their supporting information systems. A discussion of expected technology trends leads into the summary and conclusions of this chapter.

RELATIONSHIP OF MODELING TO POLICY DECISIONS

The development of analytic tools for assisting in policy decisions has been the subject of many management science publications. In this instance, policy decisions refer to those questions affecting the strategic direction or influencing large segments of an organization. One person's policy decision may be another person's operational decision. The ability to use analytical tools may be dependant upon the perception of the decision maker. Further, the structure of the models themselves may overspecify the data requirements and overconstrain the results to a level unattainable or undesirable in practice. Perhaps the most difficult part of the problem is the uncertainty with which the forecasted events will occur, with a related issue being the accuracy of the data upon which the forecasts are based. This quickly shifting fluid environment is the norm for much policy decision making in the human resources area.

The use of analytical tools has to be approached from the point of view that the outputs should be a natural part of the process by which the decisions are being made. There may be complex modeling processes going on to develop these outputs. On the other hand, the outputs may look relatively simple, such as a set of bar graphs, etc. The person making the decision may have little interest in the fact that the latest mathematical programming or profit-logit econometric model was used to develop the answers. The question becomes what assistance modeling can provide to human resource policy making and how the analyst should approach the issue to ensure that the value added by the models is recognized and used to advantage.

In human resource policy analysis, among the most useful products is the provision of consistency, both across related functional or business issues and over time. If multiple organizational tiers or levels of detail are involved, the need for agreement also exists. The model outputs tend to be used to evaluate conformance with standards, predict order of magnitude conditions at major milestones, or predict turning points. Developing more precise data may require a second level of analysis, using another set of models or analytical techniques. The idea is to use the models to test alternative views of the world or even the structure of the decision-making process itself. This could then be followed by downstream linking with more complex models in order to set the standards and controls for the follow-on operational decision making.

An important use of modeling during policy analysis is to check the usefulness and interrelatedness of a complex set of ideas or processes. In this case, the model may never be used beyond the initial numerical example phase. The model's usefulness depends upon providing an analytical check of a planned set of related policies to determine their consistency and effects upon one another. A small hypothetical numerical example may be enough to seek the revision of the policies before their issuance. The follow-on information support system may be limited to a simplified reporting system.

Human resource models have been used to determine the weight to be given to policy decisions that may have to be considered. In this case, alternative examples are computed with and without the additional policies. Depending on the results, the decision maker has a much better idea of how to negotiate for the desired outcome. The preferred decision may be suboptimal as viewed from the modeling results, but fit better with judgmental considerations outside the scope of the model. Such modeling has been particularly effective in budgetary negotiations where relatively small changes may lead to a much broader acceptance of the overall program required at the time.

Structurally, integrated systems can take many forms. One such form is the integrated sequential process shown in Figure 7.1. In this case, each process or subsystem provides data to the subsequent process in a linear, interactive fashion. The value of such an event flow approach is that it is easy to understand and maintain, providing needed consistency throughout the process. This approach is particularly useful when a quick answer is needed for a rapidly emerging policy question. A possible risk in the approach is that the results may be of a satisfying rather than an optimal nature, leading to a less efficient resolution of the underlying issues.

Another integrated approach is the highly centralized approach, typified by goal programming methods, illustrated in Figure 7.2. In this case, the various data are input into an integrated goal programming model. This approach provides consistency and simultaneous consideration of all the factors within an optimization solution process. One disadvantage of the goal programming approach is that it is normally highly data intensive, possibly overconstraining the recommended courses of action.

Figure 7.1. Integrated Human Resource Planning—Event Flow Approach

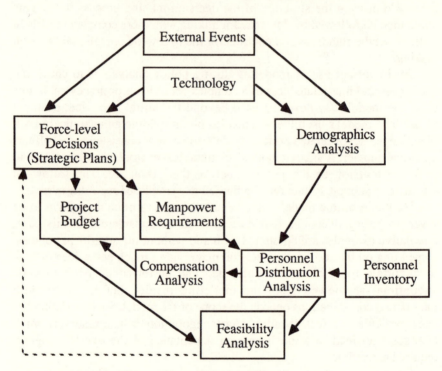

In actual practice, a hybrid approach may be best. The goal programming model is used after parts of the data input are developed in some form of integrated sequential system. The final management reports may also bring in additional comparisons not included in the goal programming model. This approach permits the development of less complex models, which are much easier to maintain. User acceptance may be higher since there is less need to rely on experts to verify that the results are technically sound.

Experience indicates that many model builders become too enamored of a complicated model formulation, which may be more complex than is needed during the initial and final stages of policy analysis. Simplification of the modeling approaches and outputs, particularly during the early and final phases of analysis, is central to success in dealing with the underlying business problem. In between, all the complexities of elegant modeling applications may be needed.

Figure 7.2. Integrated Human Resource Planning—Goal Programming Approach

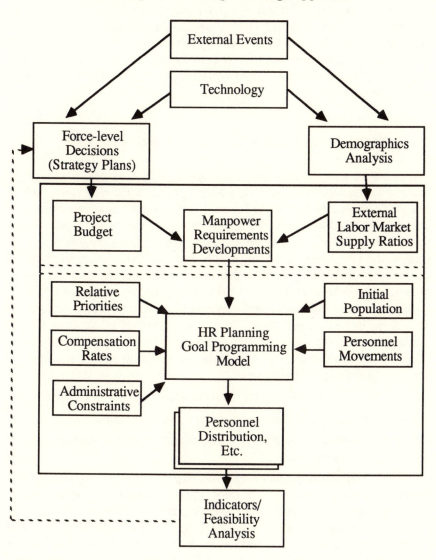

It is at the highest organizational levels that the need for integration becomes most important to adequately support policy decisions. In the human resources area, this integration may require that all elements of the personnel process be considered. For example, it may go beyond plans to move staffing distributions to meet manpower requirements in order to consider the training needed to develop the required skills in available personnel. The integration may take the form of relating the outside labor market with the internal workforce or so-called supply-demand models. It may also take the form of multitiered concerns. A system of macro policy development models may be linked with more detailed control models for specific functions or suborganizations. Such designs normally arise as a hybrid system of model technologies, computer support requirements, etc. Examples of such approaches to several human resource planning problems will be illustrated in the next section.

EXAMPLES OF INTEGRATED MODELING SYSTEMS

From its inception in 1967, the research of Charnes, Cooper, and Niehaus into manpower modeling or human resource planning issues took an integrated approach. As seen in Figure 7.3, the initial business problem was stated as the need to minimize differences among manpower requirements, staffing distributions, and individual assignments. Goal programming was used as the integrating technology with state-of-the-art improvements that consisted of embedding Markov decision models into the underlying goal program. Over the next few years the initial model was improved, both by increasing computational capabilities and by adding needed functions not considered in the original design. Prototype versions of information support systems were also developed, tested, and used to assist in many policy issues of major concern at that time. Among the early management issues added to complete to the original model were

1. Explicitly accounting for expected retirements.
2. Evaluation of the impact of average grade constraints.
3. Integration of training as a natural part of the human resource planning process.

Goal programming technology was exploited further to directly link versions of input-output support-on-support models for weapons system planning with the human resource planning models. Examples of military-civilian personnel mix models were developed to improve understanding of the relationships of the components of the total force. Uncertainty considerations were also examined through the extension of the models into a chance-constrained configuration. Many of these more advanced capabilities were used to focus on what was required for the models to support ongoing civilian personnel management issues. Over the years, the information support system has been simplified with a balance between models addressing the impact of the external world and models concerned with internal staffing issues.

Figure 7.3
Human Resource Planning Process

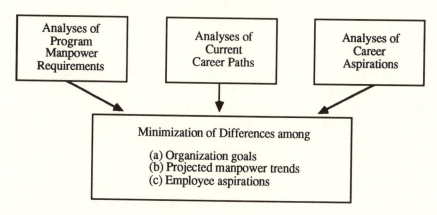

As mentioned, a triple-track approach was used in developing goal programming models for human resource planning. Parallel, reinforcing efforts were undertaken to address the business reasons for the models, technical development of the models, and development of computational and information support systems. The original model structures, while portraying the business issues, was computationally inefficient. A continuing series of structural innovations were made with orders-of-magnitude improvements in computational efficiency. Eventually, new model structures, such as goal-arc distribution models, were substituted for some modeling issues. Conversely, in recent applications, ideas from the goal-arc models were introduced into models that were best solved using generalized linear programming methods. A condensed review of many modeling applications follows. These will principally cover recent developments to illustrate the contexts in which the models are currently being used.

Shipyard Studies

The continuing series of studies to support the Naval Sea Systems Command (NAVSEA), as well as one of the public shipyards, illustrates many of the models designed to assist in civilian personnel resource and skills planning (see Bres, Niehaus, Sharkey, and Weber, 1987,1988; and Aguilar, Bres, Niehaus, and Sharkey, 1990). The original support was needed in a matter of days to provide backup material for congressional hearings concerning major reductions planned for the eight public shipyards. The workforce was to be reduced from 80,000 to 72,000 work years. As a result of the data provided from the models and other sources, eventually only fifty-eight people were terminated reach the required staff reduction of 8,000 work years.

Subsequent modeling studies at the Mare Island Naval Shipyard addressed ways to understand and manage occupational structure issues constrained by total workload requirements. One of the issues dealt with was how to maintain the skilled workforce needed for long term workload in the face of an intermediate 30 percent dip in requirements. The most recent models concerned the determination of required inputs to the in-house apprentice training program, which has provided 40 to 50 percent of the journeymen in the skilled trades.

Rather than using technical modeling terms to describe the models, more general terms understandable to the average manager are used. For example, "Forced Fit Model" is used to describe a simple Markov process. "Best Fit Model" is used for a goal programming model using linear programming. and "Flexible Flow Model" is used to describe a goal-arc distribution model. In the most complex case, "Best Fit Flex Model" is used for the model that combines features of the goal-arc model with a goal programming model solved using linear programming methods.

EEO/AA Planning

Integrated information support capabilities are essential for assistance in developing equal employment opportunity/affirmative action (EEO/AA) plans. In this case, extensive modeling research was conducted to examine not only the internal workforce dynamics, but the external labor markets as well. The original modeling work concerning the internal workforce (Charnes, Cooper, Lewis, and Niehaus, 1976, 1978; Lewis, 1977; Charnes, Cooper, Nelson, and Niehaus 1982) was aimed at understanding the management and social issues surrounding EEO/AA planning. In parallel, research was conducted on econometric modeling to improve understanding of the external labor force (Atwater, Niehaus, and Sheridan, 1980). The resulting information support system relies on simplified decision rules combined with available labor force data by race, national origin, and sex to provide an integrated set of reports for all echelons of the Department of Navy (Niehaus and Nitterhouse, 1980). This information support system is still in use today. The latest improvements are initial software modifications to accommodate the 1990 Census update of available labor force data.

The modeling research has yielded a rich harvest of new methods and techniques, which have found use in many other applications, in addition to providing the intellectual underpinnings used to develop the EEO/AA planning system. For example, flexible flow models were needed, which, in turn, were used in both military and civilian personnel applications. The external labor market models were generalized and used for many policy analysis studies outside of EEO/AA.

Supply-Demand Models

Supply-demand models are among the most integrated applications of human resource policy analysis models. A system of models was developed to examine the Navy's requirements for civilian engineering technicians in an increasingly competitive labor market (Atwater, Bres, Niehaus, and Sheridan, 1982). This linked a series of econometric models to a constrained regression model in order to project hiring requirements. The results showed the impact of increasing relative wage differentials on the ability of the Navy to hire and retain personnel in this critical occupation.

Another important use of the supply-demand models was an evaluation of the impact on the Navy's civilian workforce of different versions of legislation proposed to change the Federal Civil Service Retirement System. The results were used in the Department of the Navy's input, which was provided to the relevant congressional committees. The final legislation was close to what appeared to be the best alternative as determined from the modeling study.

Military Personnel Applications

In the early 1970s, assistance was requested to develop models for the military manpower and personnel areas. For example, an integrated system of models was developed to support forecasts of officer needs, including their distribution to individual units (Cass, Charnes, Cooper, and Niehaus, 1973, 1974; Eubanks and Thompson, 1977). Another model was developed to examine the best mix of sources for acquiring and training naval officers (Bres, Burns, Charnes, and Cooper, 1980).

Later work examined across-the-board issues for enlisted personnel. A noteworthy study involved a goal programming system need to plan the sea-shore rotation of enlisted personnel (Charnes, Cooper, Golany et al., 1985). In this case, models developed for one application (civilian EEO/AA planning) formed the theoretical basis for models to support another (Navy enlisted personnel sea-shore rotation policies).

A workbench approach continues to be used in developing more recent versions of the human resource planning models. There is a wealth of existing modeling capabilities and ideas. Much of the work lies in fitting these capabilities to the issue at hand, rather than crafting another model from scratch. Equally important is information engineering, which should provide the necessary computer support capabilities with the least effort. The next section discusses these concerns.

INTEGRATION WITH CORPORATE INFORMATION SYSTEMS

Modeling is only one part of a corporate policy support information system. Such decision support systems (DSSs) and related management information systems (MISs) use a variety of corporate databases. In large organizations, a hierarchy of support capabilities may be needed, starting at the operational field level.

In the human resources area, integration becomes difficult because each subfunction (staffing, training, compensation, etc.) has unique information and decision support requirements. In many cases, human resource modeling is needed more in functions outside the human resource or personnel organization. For example, the workload planning or resource planning organization may have more need for analyses using integrated approaches. The difficulty is that development responsibilities need to cut across the various organizations. At this point, ownership of the final system may be much harder to determine and maintain.

Another problem, particularly in the current era of movement toward large databases, is the emphasis on building the databases, rather than on developing the applications themselves. The information systems organization may assume that once the relational databases are constructed with appropriate retrieval software, most of the needed support will be in place. For decision support systems, relational databases are of less value. The needed database structures generally are constrained by the modeling processes themselves so that relational database methodologies are of little assistance. This is particularly true in human resource models involving multiple time series comparisons and projections.

Complex integrated human resource models may have ten or more different data sources. The models tend to use those data elements that record change rather than those that record one-time events, such as gaining some sort of status. These change data files, in many cases, are best kept as sequential files with as few data elements as possible to facilitate sorting. Also, models many times use computed values, such as retention rates or pay tables. Specialized files using well-defined planning categories might need to be constructed to speed processing. For example, some econometric models for human resource policy analysis use specially constructed cross-sectional time series (CSTS) files that map multiple time periods into the same file. In addition to the aforementioned databases, a variety of needed current status information may be obtained from the MIS files, perhaps best kept as relational databases.

As indicated above, a hybrid approach may be the best way to develop the databases needed to support the models. Special care is necessary to minimize redundancy, using numerically based planning categories where possible, while ensuring that needed data are available to make the computations. Sizing the models to fit available computer technology is equally important and is discussed in the next section.

TECHNOLOGY TRENDS

The technology of the computers on which the models are run has a significant impact on implementation success, along with the model methodologies and databases. In the early days of human resource and many other models, the technical demands of the models far outstripped the capabilities of the computers available for running them. Considerable attention was focused on constructing efficient solution algorithms (Charnes, Cooper, Klingman, and Niehaus, 1973, 1975).

Management-oriented information support was a constant concern. From the start, efforts were made to embed the models in a user-oriented information system (Niehaus, 1972, 1979; Niehaus and Sholtz, 1976). Considerable research was done on interactive information systems well before they became today's standard user interface. (Niehaus, 1977, 1979; Niehaus, Sholtz, and Thompson, 1978).

The capabilities of large mainframe computers eventually caught up with the demands of the model structures and computer algorithms. The cycle was repeated with more complex models requiring even more extensive computer support. In recent years, for human resource models, mainframe computer capability reached the point that the existing solution algorithms were sufficient for a wide variety of problems. This is particularly true for corporate policy analysis models where study is concentrated on a relatively small number of alternative scenarios. Computer capacity remains an issue for large scale operational support models requiring the development of multiple reports for various communities of job categories or suborganizations. In this case, issues of data storage, interactive accessibility for end-users, and integration with complex reporting systems put more demand on computer environment requirements than did the actual computation of the model itself.

Using human resource models on microcomputers opened a new dimension and revived their use. In many cases, mainframe-based models became even more inaccessible to users who were unwilling to wait for the development and translation of results by modeling experts. The early microcomputers were too small for complex models, with most modeling limited to such applications as simple Markov models. This has all changed, and today many applications of complex microcomputer-based human resource models are being reported in the literature (e.g., see Niehaus, 1985, 1987, 1988; Niehaus and Price, 1988, 1990).

The Navy's shipyard studies have relied almost exclusively on microcomputers for their computation support. The concept of keeping the support simple and user-oriented was assumed from the start. The initial applications were spreadsheet models using simple Markov processes. As time progressed, a variety of goal programming models were used, tailored to run fully configured microcomputers. FORTRAN-based goal-arc modeling software, developed on a mainframe, was downloaded to a microcomputer and made operational with minimum effort. A shell was developed using LOTUS 1-2-3 spreadsheet software so that the inputs and outputs are expressed in terms familiar to users.

Figure 7.4 shows one of the current microcomputer-based software system designs used in the shipyard studies. The LINDO microcomputer linear programming package is used for solutions. Seventy-five job category, nine planning period models are routinely being used. While computation times run up to several hours, the results are immediately accessible to the analysts supporting the shipyard's top management. Many of the technical tricks developed in the early mainframe days are being used to get necessary computational results.

In the near future, many of the limitations of current microcomputer-based linear programming models will disappear. With the larger hard disks now available, the data currently developed on mainframe systems can be developed on the microcomputer. The extensive memory capabilities now available, coupled with the speed of the 80386 (or 80486) processor, should reduce the computation time by at least an order of magnitude. Follow-on generations of microcomputers and related software should permit the desktop solution of most of the human resource planning models now on larger computers.

Figure 7.4. Microcomputer Optimization Model Operation

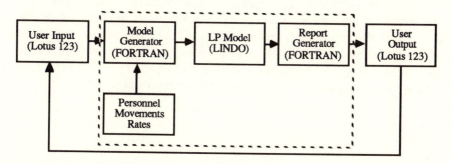

Source: Aguilar, Bres, Niehaus, and Sharkey, 1990.

SUMMARY

Human resource models have come a long way from the fundamental research days of the Navy's support of the Charnes, Cooper, and Niehaus collaborative effort, begun in the 1960s. The strategic thinker behind much of this program was Bill Cooper. He had the kind of vision to not only see the "big picture," but also relate this strategic thinking with the needed methodological and technological implementation concerns.

It is interesting that the more complex versions of these human resource models are reemerging with the increasing power of the microcomputer. Many of the specialized solution methods developed in the early days of more limited computational support are particularly useful in this desktop computer environment. Except for models requiring considerable interaction with very large databases, one can expect that most models will be based at desktop workstation.

As the model designs and solution methods reemerge in a "back-to-the-future" fashion, integrated approaches to human resource planning are also reemerging. In the Mare Island Naval Shipyard case, all elements of an integrated corporate decision-making system will soon be in place. Similarly, military manpower, personnel, and training decision and information support systems are entering the early prototype stages with all the concerns about database integration. The goal programming modeling methodologies from the initial fundamental research into integrated human resource planning will probably provide a contribution. As with the original research in this area, this renewed emphasis will probably take an integrated view with all the power of computer environments available in the 1990s.

It is not difficult to trace the original human resource modeling research to its diffusion to this class of problems in many applications in scores of organizations worldwide. The models have provided for better management and technical efficiencies. Perhaps more importantly, the better decisions have led to the improvement of individuals through more conscious career planning and the promotion of equal opportunities. Such contributions are directly traceable to the mind and heart of Bill Cooper—a pathfinder in this as well as many other areas of management and management science.

REFERENCES

Aguilar, M., E.S. Bres III, R.J. Niehaus, and F. S. Sharkey, "A Best Fit Planning Model for Managing Personnel Turbulence", in R.J. Niehaus and K.F. Price, eds., *Human Resource Strategies for Organizations in Transition*. New York: Plenum Press, 1990.

Atwater, D.M., E.S. Bres III, R.J. Niehaus, and J.A. Sheridan, "Integration of Technological Change into Human Resources Supply-Demand Models," in G. Mensch and R.J. Niehaus, eds., *Work, Organizations and Technological Change*. New York: Plenum Press, 1982.

Atwater, D. M., R. J. Niehaus, and J. A. Sheridan, "EEO Goals Development in the Naval Sea Systems Command." OASN (M, RA&L) Research Report No. 35. Washington, D.C.: Office of the Assistant Secretary of the Navy (Manpower, Reserve Affairs and Logistics), 1980.

Bres, E. S., III, D. Burns, A. Charnes, and W. W. Cooper, "A Goal Programming Model for Planning Officer Accessions," *Management Science* 26, no. 8 (August 1980): 773-783.

Bres, E. S. III, R. J. Niehaus, F. J. Sharkey, and C. L. Weber, "Use of Personnel Flow Models for Analysis of Large Scale Work Force Changes," in R.J. Niehaus, ed., *Strategic Human Resource Planning Applications*. New York: Plenum Press, 1987.

Bres, E. S. III, R. J. Niehaus, F. J. Sharkey, and C. L Weber, "Coping with Occupational Structure Issues at Large Public Industrial Organizations," in R. J. Niehaus, and K. F Price, eds., *Creating the Competitive Edge Through Human Resource Applications*. New York: Plenum Press, 1988.

Cass, D., A. Charnes, W. W. Cooper, and R. J. Niehaus, A Program for Navy Officer Distribution Models," Research Report No. CCS145. Austin: Center for Cybernetic Studies, University of Texas, August 1973.

Cass, D., A. Charnes, W.W. Cooper, and R.J. Niehaus, "A Multi-Page Goal Programming Model and Algorithm for Navy Officer Rotations," Management Sciences Research Report No. 350. Pittsburgh: Management Sciences Research Group, Graduate School of Industrial Administration, Carnegie-Mellon University, September 1974.

Charnes, A., and W. W. Cooper, *Management Models and Applications of Linear Programming*. New York: John Wiley & Sons, Inc., 1961.

Charnes, A., and W. W. Cooper, "Goal Programming and Multiple Objective Optimizations," *European Journal of Operational Research* 1 (January 1977): 37–54.

Charnes, A., W. W. Cooper, and R. Ferguson, "Optimal Estimation of Executive Compensation by Linear Programming," *Management Science* 1, no. 2 (January, 1955): 423–430.

Charnes, A., W. W. Cooper, B. Golany, V. Lovegren, W. T. Mayfield, and M. Wolfe, "A Goal Programming System for the Management of the U.S. Navy's Sea-Shore Rotation Program," in *Human Resource Policy Analysis: Organizational Applications*. New York: Praeger, 1985.

Charnes, A., W. W. Cooper, D. Klingman and R. J. Niehaus, "Static and Dynamic Biased Quadratic Multi-Attribute Assignment Models: Solutions and Equivalents," Research Report No. CCS115. Austin: Center for Cybernetic Studies, University of Texas, March 1973.

Charnes, A., W. W. Cooper, D. Klingman, and R. J. Niehaus, "Explicit Solutions in Convex Goal Programming," *Management Science* 22, no. 4 (December 1975): 438-448.

Charnes, A., W. W. Cooper, K. A. Lewis and R. J. Niehaus, "A Multi-Objective Model for Planning Equal Employment Opportunities," in M. Zeleny, ed., *Multiple Criteria Decision Making: Kyoto 1975*. New York: Springer Verlag, 1976.

Charnes, A., W. W. Cooper, K. A. Lewis, and R. J. Niehaus, "A Multi-Level Coherence Model for EEO Planning", in A. Charnes, W. W. Cooper, and R.J. Niehaus, eds., *Management Science Approaches to Manpower Planning and Organization Design*. New York: Elsevier North-Holland, 1978, pp. 13-29.

Charnes, A., W. W. Cooper, A. Nelson, and R. J. Niehaus. "Model Extension and Computation in Goal-Arc Network Approaches for EEO Planning," *INFOR* 20, no. 4 (November 1982): 315-335.

Charnes, A., W. W. Cooper, and R. J. Niehaus, "Mathematical Models for Manpower and Personnel Planning," in A. I. Siegel, ed., *Proceedings of U.S. Naval Personnel Research and Development Laboratory Symposium of Computer Simulation as Related to Manpower and Personnel Planning,*

Washington, D.C.: Naval Personnel Research and Development Laboratory, 1971.

Charnes, A., W. W. Cooper, and R. J. Niehaus, *Studies in Manpower Planning*, NTIS No. AD 055952. Washington, D. C.: U.S. Navy Office of Civilian Manpower Management, 1972a.

Charnes, A., W. W. Cooper, and R. J. Niehaus, "A Generalized Network Model for Training and Recruiting in Manpower Planning" in D. J. Bartholomew and A. R. Smith, eds., *Manpower and Management Science*, London: English Universities Press, 1972b.

Charnes, A., W. W. Cooper, and R. J. Niehaus, "A Prototype Test of a Multi-Level Model for Military-Civilian Manpower Planning," OCMM Research Report No. 19. Washington, D.C.: U.S. Navy Office of Civilian Manpower Management, May 1974.

Charnes, A., W. W. Cooper, and R. J. Niehaus, "Dynamic Multi-Attribute Models for Mixed Manpower Systems," *Naval Research Logistics Quarterly* 22, no. 2 (June 1975): 205-220.

Charnes, A., W. W. Cooper, and R. J. Niehaus, "A Goal Programming Model for Manpower Planning," in J. Blood, ed., *Management Science in Planning and Control.* New York: Technical Association of the Pulp and Paper Industry, 1968. (Also reprinted in D.J. Bartholomew, ed., *Manpower Planning*, Middlesex, England: Penguin Books, 1976.)

Charnes, A., W. W. Cooper, and R. J. Niehaus, eds. *Management Sciences Approaches to Manpower Planning and Organization Design.* New York: Elsevier North Holland, 1978.

Charnes, A., W. W. Cooper, R. J. Niehaus, and D. Padalino, "Integrated Manpower and Program Planning Models for Laboratory Management," *Journal of Navy Civilian Manpower Management* (September 1974): 17-23.

Charnes, A., W. W. Cooper, R. J. Niehaus, and A. P. Schinnar. "Measuring Efficiency and Tradeoffs in Attainment of EEO Goals," in G. Mensch and R.J. Niehaus, eds., *Work, Organizations, and Technological Change.* New York: Plenum Press, 1982.

Charnes, A., W. W. Cooper, R. J. Niehaus, and D. Sholtz, "A Model and a Program for Manpower Management and Planning," in N. Lieblich, ed., *Computer Impact on Engineering Management.* Pittsburgh: Instrument Society of America, 1968.

Charnes, A., W. W. Cooper, R. J. Niehaus, and D. Sholtz, "A Model for Civilian Manpower Management in the U.S. Navy," in A. R. Smith, ed., *Models of Manpower Systems.* London: English Universities Press, 1970.

Charnes, A., W. W. Cooper, R. J. Niehaus, and D. Sholtz, "An Algorithm for Multi-Attribute Assignment Models and Spectral Analyses for Dynamic Organization Design," paper presented at the Forty-first Operations Research Society of America Meeting, New Orleans, April 27, 1972.

Charnes, A., W. W. Cooper, R. J. Niehaus, and D. Sholtz,"Multi-Level Models for Career Management and Resource Planning," in D. J. Clough, C. C. Lewis, and A. L. Oliver, eds., *Manpower Planning Models*, London: English Universities Press, 1974.

Charnes, A., W. W. Cooper, R. J. Niehaus, and A. Stedry, "Static and Dynamic Assignment Models with Multiple Objectives with Some Remarks on Organization Design," *Management Science* 15, no. 8, Series B (April 1969): 365-375.

Cooper, W. W., R. J. Niehaus, and D. Nitterhouse, "Workforce Goals Planning for the Naval Laboratory System," OCP Research Report No. 31, Washington, D.C.: U.S. Navy Office of Civilian Personnel, 1977.

Eubanks, T., and G. L. Thompson, "Bargaining Assignment and Officer Rotation Models in the U.S. Navy," in D. Bryant and R.J. Niehaus, eds., *Manpower Planning and Organization Design*. New York: Plenum, 1977.

Lewis, K. A., "Manpower Planning for Equal Employment Opportunities— As Applied to the U.S. Navy Civilian Workforce," Ph.D. Dissertation, School of Urban and Public Affairs, Carnegie-Mellon University, May 1977.

Niehaus, R. J., "The Application of Computer-Assisted Multi-Level Manpower Planning Models in the Federal Government," D.B.A. Dissertation, School of Government and Business, George Washington University, 1972.

Niehaus, R. J., "Conversational Manpower Planning Models in a Telecommunications Environment," in D. Bryant and R. J. Niehaus, eds., *Manpower Planning and Organizational Design*. New York: Plenum, 1977.

Niehaus, R. J., *Computer-Assisted Human Resources Planning*, New York: Wiley Interscience, 1979.

Niehaus, R. J., ed., *Human Resource Policy Analysis*. New York: Praeger, 1985.

Niehaus, R. J., ed. *Strategic Human Resource Planning Applications*. New York: Plenum, 1987.

Niehaus, R. J., ed. "Models for Human Resource Decisions," *Human Resource Planning* 11, no. 2 (1988): 95-107.

Niehaus, R. J. and E. S. Bres, "Contributions of A. Charnes to Human Resource Planning," paper presented at the University of Texas Conference in Honor of Abraham Charnes on the Occasion of His 70th Birthday, Austin, Texas, October 14-15, 1987.

Niehaus, R. J., and D. Nitterhouse, "Planning and Accountability Systems for EEO and Affirmative Action Policy," OASN (M, RA&L) Research Report No. 38. Washington, D.C.: Office of the Assistant Secretary of the Navy (Manpower, Reserve Affairs and Logistics), 1980.

Niehaus, R. J., and K. F. Price, eds., *Creating the Competitive Edge Through Human Resource Applications*. New York: Plenum, 1988.

Niehaus, R. J. and K. F. Price, eds., *Human Resource Strategies for Organizations in Transition*. New York: Plenum, 1990.

Niehaus, R. J. and D. Sholtz, "A Navy Shore Activity Manpower Planning System for Civilians," OCMM Research Report No. 24. Washington D.C.: U.S. Navy Office of Civilian Manpower Management, 1976.

Niehaus, R. J., D. Sholtz, and G. L. Thompson, "Managerial Tests of Conversational Manpower Planning Models," in A. Charnes, W. W. Cooper, and R. J. Niehaus, *Management Science Approaches to Manpower Planning and Organization Design*, New York: Elsevier, 1978.

8

Tradeoffs between Efficiency and Effectiveness in Management of Public Services

Arie P. Schinnar

Following the publication of "Measuring the Efficiency of Decision-Making Units" by Charnes, Cooper, and Rhodes in 1978, we have applied at the University of Pennsylvania the data envelopment analyses (DEA) procedure in numerous studies of productivity in public health and human services delivery systems. Often these studies involved an inquiry into the determinants of efficiency to ascertain which factors are discretionary and under management control and which are not. Those factors that were statistically significant we selected to guide the development of policy instruments that would bring about improvements in service operations. Few of the results of our studies were ever implemented, however.

Although cost containment is a major concern of public administrators nowadays, the agency's direct service staff whereas in daily contact with the recipients of services, is primarily concerned with the effectiveness and quality of care delivered. Measures that are designed to streamline operations and achieve greater efficiency are frequently sidestepped by the direct service staff, who regard them as attempts to curtail services and compromise quality of care.

In three recent studies (Schinnar, Desai, and Ringle, 1983; Schinnar, Walters, Kusbiantoro, and Wood, 1984; Schinnar, Kamis-Gould, Delucia, and Rothbard, 1990) we have found corroboration for the concerns of public agencies' direct service staff. In two of these studies, efficiency and effectiveness were noted to be negatively correlated. In this chapter, I sketch a simple model of efficiency and effectiveness to explain the observed negative association between the two. I shall also demonstrate that the converse may be true: efficiency and effectiveness can complement each other as well.

A simple model is formulated to show that under quite reasonable conditions the highest level of service effectiveness is attained at moderate levels of efficiency. Thus, when service agencies operate at high levels of efficiency, further gains in efficiency will entail a loss of effectiveness. But when agencies operate at low efficiency levels, gains in efficiency will be complemented by improved effectiveness. I postulate therefore that managers of public health and human services organizations will steer their agencies' operations toward moderate levels of efficiency, where effectiveness is maximized. Hence, the concept of "best practice" in public management need not coincide with the most efficient operation.

OBSERVATIONS FROM THREE PRIOR STUDIES

Three recent studies correlated measures of efficiency and effectiveness, of which two revealed a negative association between the two. The first study entailed an analysis of the performance of the federal Work Incentive (WIN) program between 1976 and 1980. The program was designed to provide persons eligible for AFCE welfare benefits with job-skill training and job placement in the local labor market. The measure of efficiency used in the study reflects the conversion of staff time to service activities, such as training and job placement. The effectiveness measure reflects the rate at which service activities are transformed into program outcomes: job entries, welfare saving, and entry wages (Schinnar, Desai, and Ringle, 1983).

The second study compares efficiency and effectiveness of 145 public bus companies in the United States (Schinnar, Walters, Kusbiantoro, and Wood, 1984). Efficiency of bus operations is measured by the rate at which public transit resources (capital, employees, fuel) are converted into bus services (vehicle revenue miles and hours). Effectiveness is reflected in the rate at which bus services were consumed by the public (passenger trips and miles). The negative association between efficiency and effectiveness found in the two studies is shown in Figures 8.1 and 8.2. It leaves policy makers with a difficult decision: is productivity management worth the trouble? It requires that values be put on efficiency and effectiveness and that the two be considered together when the opportunity cost of any gains in service efficiency is realized as a loss in program effectiveness.

Initially, I dismissed the results by arguing that they are, by and large, an artifact of measurement. In the public sector, resources are often allocated by formula on a per capita basis through a variety of block and categorical grant mechanisms. As a result, the variance in resource utilization across observations may be quite small. In addition, outcomes attributed to public services may be as much a result of a variety of exogenous factors as they are a result of the direct services provided. For example, unemployment in the local labor market may affect the outcome of the WIN program more than does the training or the job placement service; congestion and population density may have more of an influence on transit effectiveness than does the availability of bus services to the public. Hence, the influence of large differences in direct service activities may not be reflected in the relatively inelastic outcomes. It is thus not surprising that we find that

$$\text{Efficiency} = \frac{\text{Service Activities}}{\text{Resources}}$$

and

$$\text{Effectiveness} = \frac{\text{Outcomes}}{\text{Service Activities}}$$

correlates negatively.

Figure 8.1
Outcome Effectiveness versus Resource Effectiveness

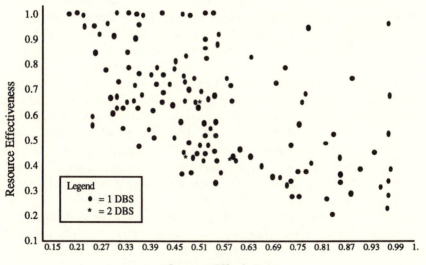

Figure 8.2. Cost Efficiency versus Effectiveness

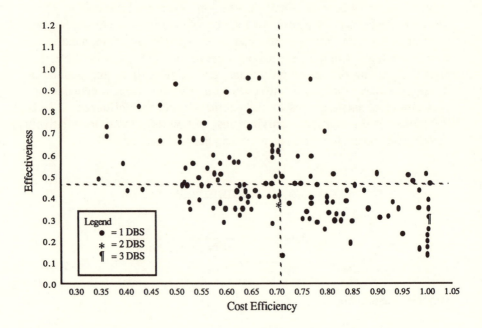

A third study (Schinnar, Kamis-Gould, Delucia, and Rothbard, 1990) provides an evaluation of staff productivity and service effectiveness of adult mental health partial care programs in New Jersey for 1984-85. In this study, staff productivity measures the conversion of direct staff hours (treatment, job-skill training, supervision of client activities) into client contact hours. Effectiveness is formulated to reflect the rate at which client contacts resulted in improvement in the clients' psychiatric and social conditions and in "successful" discharges. The study findings appeared to negate the results of the WIN and bus transit studies. Partial care progrms whose performance (efficiency level) was moderate showed significantly higher levels of effectiveness when compared with centers with low performance scores (see Figure 8.3). This was indicative of a positive association between efficiency and effectiveness. Furthermore, the statistical analysis had insufficient power to reject the null hypothesis that partial care centers with either moderate or superior performance on efficiency were equally effective. The previous conjecture that led me to dismiss the results of the WIN and bus transit studies failed to explain the positive relationship between efficiency and effectiveness in the public mental health sector. It was time for a new theory.

Figure 8.3. Average Program Effectiveness by Level of Productivity and Efficiency

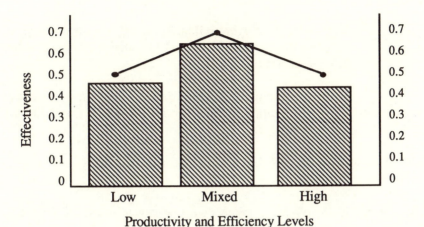

DEFINITIONS AND ASSUMPTIONS

The model I consider portrays an agency operating with a single input resource (R) and providing a single service activity (V) that is directed to achieve one output (P). Let

R = Amount of resources available, such as full-time-equivalent staff time per client per service episode

V = Amount of services delivered, such as the number of contacts or sessions per client during a service episode

P = The probability that the client's service goals have been attained within a service episode entailing the delivery of V units of service

A specific example will help clarify the definitions. Consider a psychiatric crisis episode requiring a person visit to a community mental health center (CMHC). Assume that gains in mental health status are related to that person's visits to a clinician. Successful treatment entails alleviating the symptoms of psychiatric distress. There are two random events in this example:

X = A random event reflecting an improvement in mental health status; when $X = 1$ the client's service goal has been attained

Y = A random event comprising the cumulative number of visits during a service (treatment) episode (at termination of service)

$p(X = 1, Y = y)$ = the probability of goal attainment of visit y

Thus, the probability of goal attainment within a service episode of V visits is

$$P(X = 1, Y \leq V) = \int_0^V p(X = 1, Y = y)dy$$

$$= \int_0^{v<1} p(X = 1, Y = y)dy + \int_0^v p(X = 1, Y = y)dy \quad (1)$$

To simplify notation, let $p(y) = p(X = 1, Y = y)$ and

$$P(V) = \int_0^v p(y)dy \qquad \text{prob. of goal attainment during the service episode}$$

$$P(0) = \int_0^{v<1} p(y)dy \qquad \text{prob. of goal attainment without service}$$

Hence, the residual gain in likelihood of goal attainment due to services is

$$P(V) - P(0) = \int_0^v p(y)dy \quad (2)$$

We later use the following properties and assumptions. Assume that P(V) is smooth and twice differentiable.

$$\frac{\partial}{\partial v} [P(V) - P(0)] = \frac{\partial P(V)}{\partial V} = p(V) \tag{3}$$

but

$$p(V) + p(X = 1 \mid V)p(V) = \text{we write } p(X \mid V)p(V) \tag{4}$$

Hence,

$$\frac{\partial^2 P}{\partial V^2} = \frac{\partial p(X \mid V)}{\partial V} p(V) + p(X \mid V) \frac{\partial p(V)}{\partial V} \tag{5}$$

We shall also assume

$$\frac{\partial p(X \mid V)}{\partial V} > 0 \tag{5A}$$

implying that additional services marginally increase the likelihood of goal attainment, but at a diminishing rate

$$\frac{\partial^2 p(X \mid V)}{\partial V^2} < 0$$

and assume   (5B)

$$\frac{\partial p(V)}{\partial V} < 0$$

implying that there are fewer people utilizing services as time goes on. The *negative exponential* has been observed in numerous studies of service utilization.

We can express the average effectiveness of the service (psychiatric treatment) during the service episode by the average gain in the likelihood of goal attainment per unit of service consumed (visits):

$$F = \frac{P(V) - P(0)}{V} \tag{6}$$

where $P(0) \geq 0$ is the probability that the client will achieve his goals (improvement in mental health) without consumping services (treatment), $V = 0$. In a recent paper, Frank (1988) reports that 75 percent of persons experiencing signs and sypmtoms of emotional distress exhibit a substantial reduction in the number of symptoms within a year, whether in treatment or not. Among those seeking treatment, visits to the clinicians contributed significantly to a reduction in the persistence of emotional distress.

Assuming F is smooth and twice differentiable, the marginal effectiveness of each unit of service is

$$\frac{\partial F}{\partial V} = \left(\frac{\partial P}{\partial V} - \frac{P(V) - P(0)}{V} \right) \frac{1}{V} \tag{7}$$

with a second order derivative

$$\frac{\partial^2 F}{\partial V^2} = \left[\frac{\partial^2 P}{\partial V^2} - \frac{2}{V} \left(\frac{\partial P}{\partial V} - \frac{P(V) - P(0)}{V} \right) \right] \frac{1}{V} \tag{8}$$

We similarly express the average efficiency by the ratio of service units consumed per client (average visits per client):

$$E = \frac{V(R)}{R(E)} \qquad (9)$$

or $V(R) = ER(E)$. By expressing services as a function of resources, $V(R)$, we reference the underlying production function. By making resource allocation dependent on efficiency, we acknowledge the fact that in the public sector, resource allocation usually follows historical patterns of resource utilization, thereby assuming a certain level of efficiency; there is rarely a competitor. We further assume that V is twice differentiable with respect to E and that

$$\frac{\partial V}{\partial E} > 0 \qquad (9A)$$

That is, we expect that gains in efficiency will result in an overall increase in the supply of services (V), although some resources may be reallocated to other purposes as the efficiency of service delivery improves. In the public or not-for-profit psychiatric sector this may allow more visits per client; in the private sector this increase in supply may reduce the price of each visit and spur further demand. However, we further assume that the marginal gains in service activities diminish as efficiency increases:

$$\frac{\partial^2 V}{\partial E^2} < 0 \qquad (9B)$$

A SIMPLE MODEL

It is apparent from equations (6) and (7) that effectiveness can be expressed as a function of efficiency. Now we differentiate F with respect to E.

$$\frac{\partial F}{\partial E} = \frac{\partial F}{\partial V} \frac{\partial V}{\partial E} \qquad (10)$$

and

$$\frac{\partial^2 F}{\partial E^2} = \frac{\partial^2 F}{\partial V^2}\left(\frac{\partial V}{\partial E}\right)^2 + \left(\frac{\partial F}{\partial V}\right)\frac{\partial^2 V}{\partial E^2} \tag{11}$$

By inserting equations (2) and (3) into equation (8) and collecting terms, we obtain

$$\frac{\partial^2 F}{\partial E^2} = \left[\frac{\partial^2 P}{\partial V^2} - \frac{2}{V}\left(\frac{\partial P}{\partial V} - \frac{P(V)-P(0)}{V}\right)\right]\frac{1}{V}\left(\frac{\partial V}{\partial E}\right)^2$$

$$+\left(\frac{\partial P}{\partial V} - \frac{P(V)-P(0)}{V}\right)\frac{1}{V}\frac{\partial^2 V}{\partial E^2} \tag{12}$$

The signs of equations (10) and (11) thus govern how a change in efficiency (E) affects effectiveness (F). When equation (10) is zero, we obtain from equation (7) the first-order optimality condition

$$\frac{\partial P}{\partial V} = \frac{P(V)-P(0)}{V} \tag{13}$$

If V* exists such that equation (10) holds then at that point equation (12) reduces to the second-order derivative of P(V). A negative value for equation (9B) thus suggests a local maximum in the neighborhood V*.

A brief digression to examine Figures 8.4 and 8.5 will help clarify equation (12). Consider an example in which the effect of services on the client is cumulative (e.g., education, mental health treatment) and the largest benefit of the service is realized at some critical level of service delivery. We associate this with a bell-shaped pattern to the derivative of P(V) shown in Figure 8.4 and a corresponding logistical curve for P(V) in Figure 8.5. The tangent to the curve in Figure 8.5 is the line P(V) = FV + P(0) whose slope provides the effectiveness (F) and the intercept P(0). The slopes of all lines originating at P(0) that intersect P(V) will provide the full range of effectiveness scores. It is apparent that all effectiveness scores associated with V = V* are lower than F(V*), the maximum effectiveness.

Figure 8.4. Relationship between Service Amount V and ∂P/∂V,
P Being Probability of Attaining Service Goals

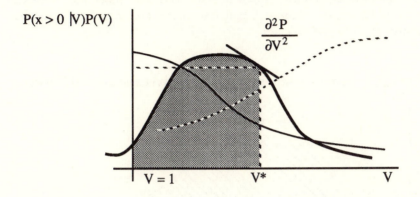

Figure 8.5. Relationship between Service Amount V and
Probability P of Attaining Service Goals

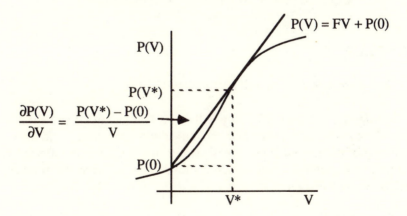

Figure 8.5 shows the components of the second-order derivative [equation (9B)]. The shaded area is P(V*) − P(0), which, when divided by

V*, equals $\partial P/\partial V$ evaluated at V*. At that point the second derivative of P(V) is negative, as required by equation (9B) to meet the condition for a maximum point.

The curve relating effectiveness and efficiency, (E) and (F), is drawn in Figure 8.6. The exact shape of the curve will depend on the functional forms that comprise the efficiency and effectiveness scales. Probability functions that resemble the shape of the curve in Figure 8.5 will result in a single peak of maximum effectiveness, which is associated with moderate levels of efficiency. Hence, our conjecture is that moderate efficiency levels may be indicative of higher effectiveness.

Figure 8.6. Relationship between Effectiveness and Efficiency

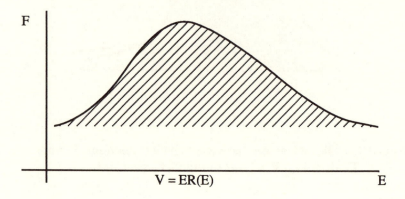

CONCLUSION

We summarize our conclusions as follows:

Tradeoffs. Gains in efficiency will result in a loss in effectiveness if a large number of clients attain their goal either with no services or at the very beginning of service utilization (one or two visits). This will be reflected in a function in Figure 8.5 whose mode is close to V = 0, or if it resembles a negative exponential function.

Complementarity. Gains in efficiency will yield improved effectiveness of service delivery if most clients attain their service goal (improved mental health) after a long or intensive service period. This will be associated with a functional form in Figure 8.5 that is skewed to the left.

Elasticity and Variance. The above conjectures are governed by the skewness of the function and the location of the mode in the feasible range of V. The degree of skewness and the "variance" jointly determine the rates of tradeoff or complementarity. The larger the "variance," the lower the tradeoff rate. A larger "variance" will be associated with large variations in the efficacy of the service intervention, which may be due to skill differences among providers of the service or variance in the responses of clients to the intervention. Generally this will be associated with low overall effectiveness levels and a low elasticity of effectiveness with respect to changes in efficiency.

Productivity Management. In health and human service systems, if gains in efficiency are perceived to compromise effectiveness, attempts to improve efficiency will meat considerable resistance. In fact, it is commonly assumed that the cost of measures taken to improve efficiency will be borne by the client whose benefits will be curtailed. It is therefore important to ascertain a priori whether efficiency and effectivenss are substitutes or complements. If they are complements, management of productivity is a "piece of cake"; if they are substitutes, productivity management entails finding a compromise solution; regrettably you cannot "have your cake and eat it, too."

NOTE

This research was supported by grants from the National Institute of Mental Health and The Pew Charitable Trusts.

REFERENCES

Charnes, A., W. W. Cooper, and E. Rhodes. "Measuring the efficiency of decision-making units." *European Journal of Operation and Research* 2 (1978): 429–444.

Frank, R. G. "Use of mental healt services and persistence of emotional distress." *Medical Care* 26, no. 2 (1988): 1203–1214.

Schinnar, A.P., A. Desai and M. Ringle. "Measuring the performance of work incentive programs." Paper presented at the ORSA/TIMS Joint National Meeting, Orlando, November 1983.

Schinnar, A. P., E. Kamis-Gould, N. Delucia, and A. B. Rothbard. "Organizational determinants of efficiency and effectiveness in mental health partial care programs." *Health Services Research* (in press).

Schinnar, A. P., L. C. Walters, B. Kusbiantoro and L. Wood. "Comparative Productivity Analysis of Public Transit Companies." Paper presented at the ORSA/TIMS Joint National Meeting, Dallas, November 1984.

9

Sensitivity of DEA to Models and Variable Sets in a Hypothesis Test Setting: The Efficiency of University Operations

Taesik Ahn
Lawrence M. Seiford

The primary purpose of this study is to empirically examine the sensitivity of data envelopment analysis (DEA) while analyzing the relative efficiencies of public and private doctoral-granting institutions of higher learning (IHLs) in the United States for the academic year 1985-86.

Conventional econometric approaches to estimating educational production functions can be found in the literature of educational economics. These approaches generally involve a priori specification of a hypothesized parametric form, after which a set of parameter values is estimated by minimizing some measures of distance from the thus selected function. As can be seen from survey papers of educational production behavior (e.g., Brinkman, 1986; Hanushek, 1987), differences in the choice of functional forms have produced considerable variation in the study results. Different investigators have reached different conclusions, and no consensus appears to be in sight.

Here we seek to follow a different direction by using DEA as an alternative to these parametric approaches in studying IHLs. While DEA does not require explicit specification of particular forms of functional relationships for the input and output relations, there are several different ways in which underlying DEA concepts can be modeled—via the ratio, additive, and multiplicative models. (See the following section for further details.) Given these multiple choices of DEA models for use in studying IHL production behavior, it is natural to ask whether DEA results are likely to be as sensitive to different DEA models as regression results are to different specifications of functional forms. The sensitivity of these results to DEA model selection is one issue examined in this study.

Different specifications of particular functional forms could have caused the inconsistent, sometimes contradictory results in previous educational economics literature (Brinkman, 1986; Hanushek, 1987). Another explanation for these anomalies could be the different variables used by different studies and/or the different measurements of these selected variables. Since there is no generally agreed upon variable set for use in studying IHL behavior, multiple sets of variables are available for analyses. In this case, the natural question is whether and how relative efficiency results (for public vs. private IHLs) change when selected variable sets for analyses are altered. Our study examines the effect of variable replacement as well as aggregation/disaggregation of variables.

Most regression methodologies used in the area of educational economics are geared toward describing "typical and average" production behavior without specific reference to individual units used in the sample. DEA, however, is targeted toward "individual and specific" efficiencies of the units included in the analyses. Because of inherent differences in efficiency characterizations across DEA models (Ahn, Charnes, and Cooper, 1988), it is inevitable that the efficiency of a particular unit may be rated differently across different models, while efficiencies of other units may remain constant across models. Our focus, however, is on stability of results. Thus, we do not wish to examine the efficiency rating changes on a unit-by-unit basis. We test DEA model sensitivity on an aggregate basis. Specifically, we test if, in a statistical test of the hypothesis, the conclusions remain constant.

The chapter proceeds as follows. The different DEA model formulations to be used for sensitivity testing are presented in the first section. The enxt section provides a background on relative efficiency of public versus private IHLs. The different sets of input and output variables used for DEA models and the research design are described in the third section section, followed by the results of the sensitivity testing. A discussion of results and implications for future research concludes the chapter.

ALTERNATIVE DEA MODELS

DEA actually encompasses a variety of alternative (but related) approaches to evaluating performance. Each of the models considered in this study (CCR ratio, BCC ratio, multiplicative, and additive) addresses managerial issues and provides useful results. However, the orientations are different.

DEA was first formulated as a nonlinear ratio programming problem (CCR ratio form) as reported in Charnes, Cooper, and Rhodes (1978). It was also shown that the linear fractional programming transformation of Charnes and Cooper (1962) could be used to obtain a corresponding pair of dual linear programming problems for use in evaluating the efficiency of not-for-profit organizations. This CCR ratio form, as given below, is a generalization of the usual single-output-single-input ratio definition of efficiency in science and engineering.

$$\text{Minimize} \quad \theta - \varepsilon \cdot e^T s^+ - \varepsilon \cdot e^T s^-$$
$$\theta, \lambda, s^+, s^-$$

subject to
$$Y \lambda - s^+ = Y_0$$
$$\theta X_0 - X\lambda - s^- = 0$$
$$\lambda, s^+, s^- \geq 0$$

$$(1)$$

This CCR ratio form was subsequently extended from equation (1) to equation (2), the BCC form, as given in Banker, Charnes, and Cooper (1984). The BCC form appends an additional convexity constraint ($\Sigma \lambda_i = 1$), which introduces a corresponding dual variable associated with the possible presence of increasing, decreasing, and constant returns to scale. Thus, one can distinguish between technical and scale inefficiences by estimating pure technical efficiency at the given scale of operation.

$$\text{Minimize} \quad \theta - \varepsilon \cdot e^T s^+ - \varepsilon \cdot e^T s^-$$
$$\theta, \lambda, s^+, s^-$$

subject to
$$Y \lambda - s^+ = Y_0$$
$$\theta X_0 - X\lambda - s^- = 0$$
$$e^T\lambda = 1$$
$$\lambda, s^+, s^- \geq 0$$

$$(2)$$

In addition to the CCR and BCC ratio forms other models have been developed utilizing underlying DEA concepts and principles. Charnes, Cooper, Seiford, and Stutz introduced a multiplicative ratio form (1982) which was subsequently extended to the units invariant version (1983) given below. These multiplicative models provide a log-linear envelopment or a Cobb-Douglas interpretation of the production process.

$$\text{Minimize} \quad -e^T s^+ - e^T s^-$$
$$\lambda, s^+, s^-$$

subject to
$$LOG(Y)\lambda - s^+ = LOG(Y_0) \tag{3}$$
$$LOG(X)\lambda + s^- = LOG(x_0)$$
$$e^T\lambda = 1$$
$$\lambda, s^+, s^- \geq 0$$

The additive model developed in Charnes, Cooper, Golany, Seiford and Stutz (1985) is based on the Charnes and Cooper (1961) test for Pareto efficiency. It allows connections with multiple criteria optimization and relates efficiency results to the economic concept of Pareto optimality.

$$\text{Minimize} \quad -e^T s^+ - e^T s^-$$
$$\lambda, s^+, s^-$$

subject to
$$Y\lambda - s^+ = Y_0 \tag{4}$$
$$X\lambda + s^- = X_0$$
$$e^T\lambda = 1$$
$$\lambda, s^+, s^- \geq 0$$

For all of these different DEA forms, multiple optimizations are performed to estimate the efficiency frontiers as opposed to once-only optimizations that are common in statistical approaches such as those used in least square regression estimation. Therefore, DEA efficiency frontiers are constructed in a piece-wise fashion—that is, piece-wise linear for the CCR ratio, BCC ratio, and additive forms and piece-wise loglinear for the multiplicative form.

BACKGROUND ON RELATIVE EFFICIENCIES

Our study focuses on the sensitivity of DEA across models, not on an individual basis, but on some aggregate level. This requires that we categorize IHLs in a meaningful fashion. In this chapter we categorize each IHL according to its institutional control, whether private or public. Since sensitivity, not relative efficiency per se, is our primary concern in this study, this grouping method will allow us to examine the consistency of hypothesis test results of relative efficiency.

The sample of IHLs examined in this study consists of 153 doctoral-degree-granting IHLs, defined by the National Center for Education Statistics as "an institution which places a significant emphasis on doctoral-level education as determined by (a) the number of doctoral degree recipients and (b) the diversity in doctoral program offerings." Among these universities 104 are public and 49 are private.

One of the notions used in studies of efficiency differentials of public and private sectors (Alchian, 1965; Caves and Christensen, 1980) is the economics of property rights. The claim is that, in contrast to private ownership, public ownership is diffused among all members of society, and no owner has a right to sell his ownership share. Hence, there is little economic incentive for any owner to monitor the behavior of management. This argument leads to a hypothesis that public ownership is inherently less efficient than private ownership. Following this notion, Davies (1977) compared two Australian air lines, Clarkson (1972) compared both types of ownership in a hospital management setting, and Pashigian (1976) examined the effects of public ownership on urban transit systems.

From a related, but more refined perspective, Lindsay (1976) proposed a theory of government enterprises in which the public sector directs more resources to visible output measures than to invisible output measures because funding resources are based on these more visible and hence more likely to be-monitored variables. In contrast to the notion of the economics of property rights, which argues that public institutions are less efficient than their private counterparts are, Lindsay claims that relative efficiency results depend on the characteristics of the output measures adopted for evaluation. Specifically, he hypothesizes that public institutions are more efficient when visible and closely monitored variables are used for output measures and evaluations and that the reverse is true when less visible and weakly monitored variables are used. This hypothesis has been tested in a hospital setting by comparing the patient days per cure of VA hospitals against those of proprietary hospitals. The prediction was that VA hospitals would focus more on generating patient days than on maintaining patient care quality because VA hospital funding is based more on patient days than on quality of patient care. Indeed, more patient days per cure were found for VA hospitals, supporting Lindsay's theory.

Sisk (1981) applied this theory to a higher education setting, comparing the number of enrollment years for a degree at public schools and at private schools. Sisk argued that public schools focus more on the enrollment headcounts or number of full-time-equivalent (FTE) students since their funding formulas are directly related to number of students enrolled rather than number of degrees awarded. Compared to private schools, Sisk found longer enrollment years per degree for public schools, supporting his hypothesis.

Some of the earlier studies on relative efficiency, such as the report by the Carnegie Commission on Higher Education (1972), used a simple ratio analysis to compare costs per student between public and private IHLs. The commission found that costs per student were higher for private schools than public counterparts. Most of these studies, including Lindsay's and Sisk's, were based on a single output measure (number of students) and a single input measure (a cost item).

In reality, IHLs utilize multiple inputs to produce multiple outputs. Thus, a more interesting question is whether this argument continues to hold in a realistic higher education setting of multiple outputs and multiple inputs. Utilizing DEA to handle the multiple outputs and multiple inputs, Rhodes and Southwick (1978) compared relative efficiency between public and private IHLs and found that private schools are more efficient then their public counterparts. This study was a significant improvement over earlier studies based on a single output and a single input.

For our purposes of comparing the relative efficiency of public and private IHLs, we may adopt either the argument of economics of property rights or Lindsay's argument. The first argument would lead us to predict that private IHLs are more efficient than public IHLs. This argument, however, may not be appropriate, considering the fact that the profit motive does not necessarily govern owners' incentives to monitor the management efficiency of IHLs, especially public IHLs.

Moreover, Lindsay's argument provides some flexibility in predicting the relative efficiency of IHLs, especially when there are no generally agreed upon variable sets to be used for IHL production behavior analysis. He predicts that public IHLs will be more efficient when visible and closely monitored output measures are used for efficiency evaluation and that the reverse will occur when more qualitative and less monitored output measures are used. What we want to study in this chapter in addition to DEA's model sensitivity is whether the relative efficiencies of public versus private IHLs change depending on the characteristics of the output variables chosen in this study. Hence, Lindsay's hypothesis will be adopted for our study. The prediction will then be that public IHLs will be more efficient than private IHLs when visible and directly monitored variables are selected as output variables. In contrast, when less closely monitored variables are used as output variables, we predict that public IHLs are less efficient than private universities.

VARIABLE SELECTION AND MEASUREMENTS

Even though outputs in higher education may be ill-specified, poorly measured, and only loosely connected to inputs (Bowen, 1980), the outputs of IHLs are broadly grouped into teaching, research, and service. It is extremely difficult, if not impossible, to find a "true" output measure for each of these dimensions. Considering the purpose of our chapter, little space will be devoted to discussing ideal measures for these outputs. Instead, alternative output measures will be identified and categorized according to their degree of visibility and monitoring by public funding institutions so that relative efficiency can be predicted based on different output characteristics.

Many researchers have used student years by itself as a main IHL output or as a teaching output along with other outputs. This output is measured in the form of total unadjusted enrollments as reported by IHLs, total full-time equivalent (FTE) enrollments, or FTE enrollments broken down into different levels of output (i.e., graduate and undergraduate enrollments). Headcount or FTE enrollment has been popularly used as a major output of IHLs not only because of data availability, but also because of its direct relation to state funding formulas.

Most of the state IHLs are funded on the basis of some form of enrollment-related output measure that is closely monitored by funding institutions. Lindsay's theory of government enterprise would then suggest that public IHLs focus more on these visible and closely monitored variables, and, hence, public IHLs will be rated as more efficient than their private counterparts when these measures are used as output variables.

Instead of enrollment headcounts, sometimes the number of degrees awarded is considered as a IHL output. Considering the fact that the number of degrees awarded is the result of the number of student years, it would appear to capture effectiveness of education better than enrollment measures do. Because of this, the degrees-awarded output measure is preferred to an enrollment output measure as a basis for funding (California Department of

Finance). Unlike enrollment numbers, however, the number of degrees granted has not been a popular output measure for IHL and has not been included in most public institutions' funding decisions. Measurement, and even identification, of research-related output is more problematic. In principle, research output should consist of the creation of "new" knowledge or the validation and correction of existing knowledge. A direct and completely satisfactory measure of increments to the stock of knowledge is almost impossible to obtain. Surrogates might consist of measures of various components of research output that can be quantified, such as publications, research reports, patents, and other such results of research efforts. These measures would involve difficulties even if the data were available in any reasonably complete and satisfactory form—which is not the case.

Brinkman (1981) employed the total amount spent on sponsored research by an IHL. This measure, however, is more of an input than an output. Other researchers, including Southwick (1969), Rhodes and Southwick (1989), and Cohn and Santos (1986) have used the amount of grants for research received by an IHL in an attempt to accord recognition to research output embodied in the evaluations of the granting bodies. These research output variables, however measured, are weakly monitored by state funding institutions. Our study uses federal grants and contracts received by IHLs as the research-related output variable.

Unlike enrollment-related output measures, degrees awarded and research related output measures seem to lack a direct linkage with funding decisions. Given these different characteristics of output variables, we may predict that public IHLs are less efficient when degrees earned and/or research grants are used as output variables.

The output variables discussed previously can be identified separately such as undergraduate and graduate enrollments versus total enrollments, or undergraduate and graduate degrees, or as an aggregate, such as total enrollments or total number of degrees awarded. Aggregation or separation of multiple variables may change the efficiency ratings of the units studies. DEA sensitivity to these variables' (dis)aggregation will also be analyzed in this study.

Inputs identified in this study will include faculty salaries as a direct labor input, total physical investment as a capital input, and overhead expenditures, including library, computing, administrative, and student support expenditures. [See Ahn (1987) for further discussion of these input measures.]

To be noted is that when the number of degrees awarded is used as an output variable, it is reasonable to include enrollment headcounts or FTE equivalents as input variables. Thus, we consider enrollment numbers as raw material in producing degrees, the final product. This approach is consistent with the two-stage DEA analysis where outputs of one stage (termed intermediate outputs) are used as inputs to the next stage (Charnes, Cooper et al., 1986).

Tables 9.1 through 9.5 summarize the design of this study. The tables cover four four different DEA models—CCR ratio, BCC ratio, additive, and multiplicative models. The row headings list four different variable combinations. The input variables—faculty salaries, total physical investment values, and overhead expenditures—are the same for the first two sets of variables in Tables 9.2 and 9.3. The input variables for the third and fourth sets include additional enrollment variables (undergraduate enrollment and graduate enrollment separately for Table 9.4 and total enrollments for Table 9.5).

Table 9.1. Experimental Design

| Table | Variable Sets | | DEA Models | | | |
	Inputs	Outputs Outputs	CCR Ratio	BCC Ratio	Additive	Multi-plicative
9.2	Faculty Salaries Physical Investment Overhead Expenses	Undergrad FTEs Graduate FTEs				
9.3	Faculty Salaries Physical Investment Overhead Expenses	Total FTEs				
9.4	Faculty Salaries Physical Investment Overhead Expenses Undergrad FTEs Graduate FTEs	Undergrad Degrees Graduate Degrees Grants				
9.5	Faculty Salaries Physical Investment Overhead Expenses Total Enrollment	Total Degrees Grants				

Output variables in the first two rows include heavily monitored enrollment variables—undergraduate and graduate enrollments for Table 9.2 and total enrollments for Table 9.3, respectively.

In contrast, output variables for the Table 9.4 include the less closely monitored variables: undergraduate degrees granted, graduate degrees granted, and federal research grants and contracts. Output variables for Table

9.5 include total degrees granted and total federal research grants and contracts awarded. As discussed earlier, the set of input variables used for Tables 9.3 and 9.5 includes those identified in the Tables 9.2 and 9.4. For Table 9.4, where undergraduate and graduate degrees awarded are used separately for output variables, undergraduate and graduate enrollments are also used separately for input variables in addition to the other three input variables. Similarly, for Table 9.5 where total degrees awarded is identified as one of the output variables, total enrollments will also be used as one of the input variables.

Table 9.2. Inputs: FacSal, PhyInv, OvhdExp; Outputs: UG-FTE, Grad-FTE

Ctrl	Model	N	X-bar	Var	Skew	#-eff
PR	CCR	49	.653	.042	.217	6
PU	CCR	104	.749	.147	.009	9
All	CCR	153	.719	.03	-.143	15
PR	BCC	49	.72464	.04516	-.06913	12
PU	BCC	104	.82892	.0206	-.46437	24
All	BCC	153	.79552	.0306	-.53539	36
PR	ADD	49	17326	2.4E8	.683	12
PU	ADD	104	14493	1.64E8	.793	24
All	ADD	153	15400	1.89E8	.795	36
PR	MULT	49	1.734	1.764	.099	21
PU	MULT	104	1.258	.831	.251	20
All	MULT	153	1.411	1.17	.39	41

Given this matrix of DEA models and variable sets, the sensitivity of DEA results to model selection will be analyzed by comparing the results of a selected row across columns. These across-column comparisons can be done for each row (Tables 9.2 through 9.5). If we compare the results down the rows for a selected column, then the sensitivity of efficiency results to the different variable sets can be analyzed. In addition, different sets of selected variables include variables in disaggregated forms (Tables 9.2 and 9.4) or in aggregated forms (Tables 9.3 and 9.5). Comparisons of efficiency results between Tables 9.2 and 9.3 (and between Tables 9.4 and 9.5) will also allow us to examine the effects of variable (dis)aggregation on efficiency analyses.

Table 9.3. Inputs: FacSal, PhyInv, OvhdExp;
Output: Total-FTE

Ctrl	Model	N	X-bar	Var	Skew	#-eff
PR	CCR	49	.521	.029	.758	2
PU	CCR	104	.723	.02	.065	5
All	CCR	153	.659	.032	-.081	7
PR	BCC	49	.587	.041	.504	2
PU	BCC	104	.795	.022	-.263	14
All	BCC	153	.728	.037	-.357	16
PR	ADD	49	25443	3.87E8	.607	4
PU	ADD	104	18095	2.322E8	1.355	14
All	ADD	153	20448	2.918E8	1.095	18
PR	MULT	49	2.659	1.809	-.316	4
PU	MULT	104	1.409	.744	.176	11
All	MULT	153	1.809	1.418	.499	15

RESULTS OF DEA

Tables 9.2 through 9.5 are the summary tables for the DEA analysis of IHLs. Each corresponds to a particular variable set. The variable sets employed in the analysis were

9.2:   Inputs—FacSal, PhyInv, OvhdExp
           Outputs—UG-FTE, Grad-FTE

9.3:   Inputs—FacSal, PhyInv, OvhdExp
           Outputs—Total-FTE

9.4:   Inputs—FacSal, PhyInv, OvhdExp, UG-FTE, Grad-FTE
           Outputs—UG-Deg, Grad-Deg, Grants

9.5:   Inputs—FacSal, PhyInv, OvhdExp, UG-FTE, Grad-FTE
           Outputs—Total-Deg, Grants

For the variable set selected in each table, four different DEA models are applied to the same data set, and the results in each table are grouped by model. For each model there are three lines. The first line is for the subset of 104 public universities. The second line is for the subset of 49 public universities. The third line is for the entire group of 153 universities. The column headings are N = the number in the set, X-bar = the mean efficiency score (for the CCR and BCC ratio models) or the mean of the objective function value, the sum of the slacks (for the additive and multiplicative models), var = variance, skew = measure of skewedness, # eff = the number of efficient decision making units (DMUs).

Table 9.4. Inputs: FacSal, PhyInv, OvhdExp, UG-FTE, Grad-FTE; Outputs: UG-Deg, Grad-Deg, Grants

Ctrl	Model	N	X-bar	Var	Skew	#-eff
PR	CCR	49	.879	.011	-.536	16
PU	CCR	104	.813	.013	.034	12
All	CCR	153	.834	.014	-.149	28
PR	BCC	49	.915	.009	-1.260	27
PU	BCC	104	.865	.013	-.372	35
All	BCC	153	.881	.012	-.618	62
PR	ADD	49	9984	1.33E8	.927	20
PU	ADD	104	16480	1.84E8	.568	24
All	ADD	153	14399	1.767E8	.688	44
PR	MULT	49	.607	.729	1.888	24
PU	MULT	104	1.135	.092	.092	32
All	MULT	153	.966	.556	.556	56

As seen in Table 9.2, the data set consisting of the entire group of universities (public and private) is used for the DEA efficiency evaluation. After the efficiency results are obtained for the entire group, the 153 universities are grouped with respect to their control, public or private. The mean efficiency ratings for the 49 private universities and for the 104 public universities are then compared to test the relative efficiency of public versus private IHLs. Under the variable set in Table 9.2, where enrollment-related variables UG-FTE and Grad-FTE, are used as output variables, public universities were found to be significantly more efficient (.749 > .653). Similar results are found with the BCC model (.725 for private and .829 for public at a significance level of .009).

Table 9.5. Inputs: FacSal, PhyInv, OvhdExp, UG-FTE, Grad-FTE; Outputs: Total-Deg, Grants

Ctrl	Model	N	X-bar	Var	Skew	#-eff
PR	CCR	49	.781	.014	.143	6
PU	CCR	104	.678	.01	.704	1
All	CCR	153	.711	.014	.562	7
PR	BCC	49	.845	.015	-.328	6
PU	BCC	104	.782	.018	.038	11
All	BCC	153	.802	.018	-.102	17
PR	ADD	49	12834	1.311E8	.585	12
PU	ADD	104	20893	1.618E8	.392	11
All	ADD	153	18312	1.653E8	.446	23
PR	MULT	49	.892	.705	1.199	15
PU	MULT	104	1.464	.612	-.453	14
All	MULT	153	1.281	.709	.049	29

In contrast to the CCR and BCC efficiency ratings ($0 \leq h \leq 1$), the objective function value for the additive and multiplicative models is the sum of the slacks (i.e., the distance from the efficient frontier). Hence, the larger the slacks, the lower the efficiency. Under the additive model, the mean of the sum of the slacks for the private universities is larger than that for the public universities at a significance level of .13. This indicates that, given the variable set in Table 9.2, public universities are found to be more efficient under the additive model. We reach an identical conclusion about the relative efficiency at a significance level of .01 with the multiplicative model. Based upon these consistent findings, we infer that public universities appear to direct more resources to those visible and closely monitored variables than do private universities. This may be because funding formulas of public universities directly incorporate those enrollment-related variables.

One result that should be noted is that the relative efficiency results are consistent across models; that is, the results of our hypothesis test are not sensitive to the particular DEA model selected.

Table 9.3 shows the results where the outputs of Table 9.2, UG-FTE and Grad-FTE, are combined into one output variable, Total-FTE. It is selected because of its popularity as an output variable in previous educational economics studies.

By comparing the overall efficiency levels under the variable sets of Tables 9.2 and 9.3, we can observe the decrease in overall efficiency ratings. As the output variables are aggregated, overall average efficiency for 153 universities decreased from .719 to .659 for the CCR model, from .796 to .728 for the BCC model, from 15400 to 20449 for the additive model[1] and from 1.411 to 1.809 for the multiplicative model. Aggregation of the variables reduces the number of dimensions used for relative comparison, which reduces the chance of IHLs being selected as efficient units *ceteris paribus*.

Relative comparisons of public versus private universities show that public universities are still more efficient than private universities. These results are consistent with the results shown in Table 9.2, where the total FTE output variable was separated into undergraduate FTEs and graduate FTEs. Additionally, four different models support the same conclusion, with statistical significance in all cases. Based on the results of Tables 9.2 and 9.3, we infer that public universities are more efficient than private universities when rather visible and closely monitored (by funding institutions) output variables are used for efficiency evaluation. Our hypothesis is consistently supported by these results.

Early studies showed that cost per FTE is smaller for public schools than for their private counterparts. Those early findings are analogous to the results obtained in Table 9.3 in the sense that total FTE is used as an output variable and cost items are used as input variables. The only difference is that a single input (cost) was used in early studies instead of multiple inputs, as is the case in Table 9.3.

Table 9.4 shows DEA results when important, but rather invisible and loosely monitored variables,[2] such as undergraduate degrees awarded, graduate degrees awarded, and external research grants, are used as output variables. As seen in this table, relative efficiency comparison results are the opposite of those obtained in Tables 9.2 and 9.3, that is private universities are here found to be more efficient than public universities. This leads us to conclude that public schools appear to direct fewer resources to these invisible and loosely monitored variables and more resources to visible and closely monitored variables.

As with the earlier cases, relative efficiency comparison results are consistent across all four models, again with no exceptions. In other words, the results were not sensitive to DEA model selection.

Table 9.5 uses two output variables: total degrees awarded, which is the aggregation of undergraduate degrees awarded and graduate degrees awarded, and external grants. As in the case of Table 9.3, aggregating two variables into one reduces the overall efficiency levels. For example, if we compare the efficient IHLs of Tables 9.4 and 9.5, we see that the number of efficient IHLs is reduced when the variables are aggregated (e.g., 28 IHLs to 7 IHLs under the CCR model). Other than this overall decrease in efficiency scores caused by aggregation, the results remain the same: private universities are again found to be more efficient than public universities are (as was true for Table 9.4). As before, this result is consistent across all four models (that is, our hypothesis testing results are not sensitive to DEA model selection.

CONCLUSION AND DIRECTIONS FOR FUTURE RESEARCH

Our DEA results strongly support the hypothesis that public schools are more efficient than private schools when visible and closely monitored output variables are used for evaluation. The reverse is true, however, when quality-related, but loosely monitored, output variables, such as degrees awarded or external grants, are used as output variables. Most state funding formulas for public schools directly incorporate enrollment-related variables, rather than degree-related or research-related variables. Hence, public schools have incentives to direct more resources to those variables. In contrast to their efficiency in generating enrollment years, public schools were found to be less efficient in converting enrollment years into degrees. Note that the two-phase analysis (Charnes, Cooper, et al., 1986) was used to incorporate the fact that the number of enrollment years is used as a teaching output, which in turn could be used as an input in generating degrees.

These findings should be useful for setting IHL policy and for determining public school funding formulas, in particular. Exclusive use of enrollment-related variables in a state funding formula may have negative impacts on the education quality of IHLs.

Given the alternative models available for DEA implementation, the choice of a specific DEA model for evaluation is an important issue. If DEA results are proved to be sensitive to the model selected for an analysis, the credibility of the results obtained would be seriously weakened. To our satisfaction, however, the CCR, BCC, additive, and multiplicative models generated the same hypothesis test results in each and every case for four different variable sets (Tables 9.2 through 9.5). Note that there are systematic differences between these different DEA models because of the differences in efficiency characterizations (Ahn, Charnes, and Cooper, 1988). Thus, different DEA models may generate different efficiency ratings for a *particular* IHL. In this chapter, however, our investigation focused on whether different models would result in different conclusions in a hypothesis test setting. With no exceptions, the hypothesis test results were consistent across both DEA models and variable aggregation, thus establishing the robustness of DEA.

NOTES

The authors wish to thank Professor Agha Iqbal Ali for making his DEA computer code available for use in this study and Mary Hawkins for her technical assistance. This research was partly supported by the Smith College Dual Degree Programs in Liberal Arts and Engineering and a University of Massachusetts faculty research grant.

1. Note that for the additive and multiplictive models, as the efficiency becomes lower, the sum of the slacks becomes larger.

2. In the sense that those variables are not explicitly monitored by state funding institutions.

REFERENCES

Ahn, T. "Efficiency and related issues in higher education: A data envelopment analysis approach," unpublished dissertation, University of Texas at Austin, 1987.

Ahn, T., A. Charnes, and W.W. Cooper, "Efficiency characterizations in different DEA models," *Socio-Economic Planning Sciences* 22 (1988): 253-257.

Alchian, A. A., "Some economies of property rights," *Politico* 30 (December 1965): 816-29.

Banker, R. D., A. Charnes, and W. W. Cooper, "Models for estimating technical and scale efficiencies," *Management Science* 30 (1984): 1078-1092.

Bowen, H. R., *The cost of higher education: How much do colleges and universities spend per student and how much should they spend?* San Fransisco: Jossey-Bass, 1980.

Brinkman, P. T., "Factors affecting instructional costs at major research universities," *Journal of Higher Education* 52 (1981): 265-279.

Brinkman, P.T., "The higher-education cost runctions," paper presented at the NSF Seminar on University Operations and Finance, Washington, D.C., June 9, 1986.

California, Department of Finance, *Quality and productivity in graduate education at the University of California: Department of Finance white paper.* Sacramento: California State Department of Finance, n.d.

Carnegie Commission on Higher Education, *The more effective use of resources.* New York: McGraw-Hill, 1972.

Caves, D. W., and L. R. Christensen, "The relative efficiency of public and private firms in a competitive environment: the case of Canadian Railroads," *Journal of Political Economy* 88 (1980): 958-976.

Charnes, A. and W. W. Cooper, *Management models and industrial applications of linear programming.* New York: Wiley, 1961.

Charnes, A. and W. W. Cooper, "Programming with Linear Fractional Applications of Linear Programming," *Naval Logistics Quarterly* 9 (3-4) (September-December 1962): 181-186.

Charnes, A. and W. W. Cooper, B. Golany, B. Halek, B. Klopp, E. Schmitz, and D. Thomas, "A two-phase Data Envelopment Analysis approaches to policy evaluation and management of army recruiting activities: tradeoffs between joint services and army advertising," Research Report CCS # 532. Austin: University of Texas, Center for Cybernetic Studies, March 1986.

Charnes, A. and W. W. Cooper, B. Golany, L. Seiford, and J. Stutz, "Foundations of Data Envelopment Analysis for Pareto-Koopmans Efficient Empirical Production Functions," *Journal of Econometrics* 30 (1985): 91-107.

Charnes, A. and W. W. Cooper, and E. Rhodes, "Measuring efficiency of decision making units," *European Journal of Operations Research* 3, no. 4 (July 1978: 429-444.

Charnes, A. and W. W. Cooper, L. Seiford, and J. Stutz, "A multiplicative model for efficiency analysis," *Socio-Economic Planning Sciences* 16, no. 15 (1982): 223-224.

Charnes, A. and W. W. Cooper, L. Seiford, and J. Stutz, "Invariant multiplicative efficiency and piecewise Cobb-Douglas Envelopments," *Operations Research Letters* 2, no. 3 (1983): 101-103.

Clarkson, K. W., "Some implications of property rights in hospital management," *Journal of Law and Economics* 15 (October 1972): 363-384.

Cohn, E. and M. C. Santos, "University as multi-product firms: Economies of scale and scope," mimeo, Department of Economics, University of South Carolina, 1986.

Davies, D. G., "The efficiency of public vs. private firms: the case of Australia's two airlines," *Journal of Law and Economics* 14 (April 1971): 149-165.

Hanushek, A. A., "The economics of schooling: production and efficiency in public schools," *Journal of Economic Literature* 24, no. 3 (September 1986): 1141–1177.

Lindsay, C. M., "A theory of government enterprise," *Journal of Political Economy* 84 (1976): 1061-1077.

Rhodes, E. L., and L. Southwick, "Determinants of efficiency in public and private universities," mimeo, School of Environmental and Public Affairs, Bloomington: Indiana University, 1986.

Sisk, D., "A theory of Government Enterprise: University Ph.D. production," *Public Choice* 37 (1981): 357-363.

Southwick, L., "Cost trends in Land Grant colleges and universities," *Applied Economics* 1 (1969): 167-182.

U.S. Department of Education, *Higher Education General Information Survey (HEGIS)*, No. 20.

Part IV

Organization Design

The Optimal Size of
a Law Firm and the
Contingency Fee Decision

Ferdinand K. Levy
Gerald L. Thompson

This chapter focuses on those law firms in the United States whose main objective is profit maximization. Particularly we are interested in firms that want to service all the legal needs of their present clients, to acquire new clients on a fixed fee basis, and to take clients on a contingency fee basis in order to expand their revenues and profits. The questions investigated are how many professional employees (lawyers) such firms should have, and, given their risk perferences, what the important conditions are for the firms to take cases on a contingency fee basis.

Even though the anlaysis is confined to law firms, parts of it are equally applicable to other professional groups, such as public accounting firms, medical clinics, and management consulting firms. Such entities need to know how large their professional staffs should be to service the present and near future needs of their present clients and to acquire and service new clients. Moreover, the contingency fee analysis presented here might be employed by a management consulting group willing to take as its fee some of a client company's stock whose future value in part depends upon the outcome of the advice rendered by the group.

Throughout the analysis, we consider an ongoing firm faced with the once-a-year task of deciding how many lawyers it should hire (or perhaps discharge) for the coming year. The analysis focuses on that part of this decision that is problematical. That is, we assume that the firm has a collection of clients on retainer fees whose total billings for standard services are accurately predictable. What we are interested in is the added new demands that might be placed on the firm's professional staff by both present and potential clients. We are thus concerned with incremental returns and costs. Further, the analysis, even though performed here for the firm as a whole, could be used by large firms on a departmental basis (e.g., litigation staff, corporate staff, labor staff, real estate staff, etc.). In looking at the contingency fee decision, we also posit an ongoing firm that as it makes the decision whether to accept such a case, already has a portfolio of cases including fixed hourly billing rates as well as other contingency fee cases. Thus, the analysis and hence the acceptance decision of a contingency fee case will depend upon how the case affects the portfolio and hence the risk preferences of the firm.

THE SIZE OF LAW FIRMS

We begin with some institutional data obtained confidentally from some large law firms in the eastern United States. Generally, the hiring of young lawyers or associates by these firms occurs only once during the year, although some firms maintain that they can expand their staffs continuously throughout the year. These associates or nonpartners are usually budgeted at 1900 hours per year.[1] That is, their yearly salaries (and, for that matter, those of the partners in the firm) are divided by 1900 to obtain an hourly cost rate. The hourly billing rate to a client is this hourly rate multiplied by a factor that from interiews was determined to be anywhere from 2.0 to 4.0.

As pointed out, large law firms handle

1.   Routine work for regular clients on a retainer basis.

2.   Extraordinary duties—such as litigation, new stock issues, and EEOC claims—for regular clients on a demand basis.

3.   New clients who wish to retain the firm on a regular basis for a specific matter.

4.   New clients who wish to use the firm for specific litigation on a contingency fee arrangement.

The workload demands of clients in the first two classes can be forecasted from past experience. Even if the regular clients have unusually large demands for legal services during a year, these demands can usually be met by the attorneys on hand by expanding the number of hours they bill upward to a maximum of 2300. Of course, as the workload from a particular client grows, the demands placed on the firm are predictably increased.

The last two types of clients are of particular interest because they represent incremental growth and sources of revenue. The firm must balance the forgone income from not having enough resources to service these clients with the cost of having excess resources (i.e., of hiring too many lawyers whom it is unable to keep busy). To solve this problem, let

C_0 be the hourly cost of hiring an additional attorney, including all setup costs (e.g., secretary, incremental office space, etc.),

$C_0^* = 1900\ C_0$ be the yearly cost,

C_1 be the hourly revenue billed when the above attorney is working for a client,

$C_1^* = 1900\ C_1$ be the average yearly revenue,

L be the number of potential lawyers to be hired, and

f(N) be the probability density function that N incremental hours will be required

Then the firm's expected profit, $E(\Pi)$, if it hires L additional lawyers, is given by

$$E(\Pi) = C_1^* \int_{-\infty}^{L} Nf(N)dN + C_1^* L \int_{L}^{\infty} f(N)dN - C_0^* L \quad (1)$$

where the first term on the right refers to revenue when the new lawyer demand N is less than the number of hires, the second term refers to the revenue when the demand is too great to be completely serviced by the newly hired attorneys, and the last term represents the additional cost of the new staff.

The expected profit $E(\Pi)$ is maximized when

$$\frac{d\ E(\Pi)}{d\ L} = 0 \quad (2)$$

where

$$\frac{d\ E(\Pi)}{d\ L} = C_1^* \left[Lf(L) + \int_{L}^{\infty} f(N)dN - Lf(L) \right] - C_0^* \quad (3)$$

Solving yields

$$C_1^* [1 - F(L)] - C_0^* = 0 \tag{4}$$

and, thus,

$$F(L) = \frac{C_1^* - C_0^*}{C_1^*} \tag{5}$$

where $F(L)$ is the distribution of the random variable N.
   Note that equation (4) states

$$C_1^* \int_L^\infty f(N)dN = C_0^*$$

which is the usual condition derived from economics, that at the margin, the expected return from hiring an additional hour of attorney time should equal its cost.

   Since the arrivals of new clients or cases can be considered to be independent, we assume that they are Poisson distributed with mean λ and variance λ, measured in lawyer workload per year. Now, if we assume that the distribution can be approximated by a normal one, then the expected profit from hiring the number of lawyers given in equation (5) can be derived by substituting equation (4) into equation (1) to yield

$$E(\Pi) = C_1^* \int_{-\infty}^L N f(N)dN \tag{7}$$

Using the normal approximation suggested above,

$$E(\Pi) = C_1^* \left[\lambda \left(\frac{C_1^* - C_0^*}{C_1^*} \right) \right.$$

$$-\sqrt{\lambda}\left(\frac{1}{2\pi}\left(\exp-\frac{1}{2}\left(\frac{L-\lambda}{\sqrt{\lambda}}\right)^2\right)\right)] \tag{8}$$

where the second set of parentheses refers to the standard normal deviate for the number of lawyers hired.

Data from the law firms surveyed indicate that the range of the ratio C_1/C_0 (i.e., the ratio of the hourly billing rate to the hourly cost of an additional hire) varies from 2.0 to 4.0. Table 10.1 shows the expected net revenues and the costs of uncertainty from hiring additional attorneys with different billing ratios.

Note that Table 10.1 is expressed in terms of number of attorneys; i.e., column 2 is the expected demand for incremental attorneys to service new cases and clients. Thus, if $\lambda = 2$, this implies that 2 x 1900 hours or 3800 hours of new work is expected.[2] The table is derived from equation (8), and its use is quite simple. If $(C_1^*/C_0^*) = 2$, it is easy to see that the number of new hires is exactly equal to the encremental demand. Suppose that a firm whose ratio of billing to costs (C_1^*/C_0^*) is 3.0 expects an incremental demand of 9500 hours next year. Assuming this represents five lawyers, look under column (1) for 3.0 and column (2) for $\lambda = 5$. Reading across the table shows that 5.96 lawyers should be hired, which yields an expected profit of 7.57 x yearly cost of a new lawyer. Obviously, 5.96 lawyers cannot be hired, but this problem can be solved by either hiring five and assuming they will each work (1 + .96/5) (1900) or 2265 hours or hiring six and calculating the expected profit from equation (1).[3] Column (8) of Table 1 shows the average yearly expected profit for various values of (C_1^*/C_0^*), assuming that those values do not change from year to year and that the actual demand can be forecasted perfectly each year. Column (9) represents the average cost of uncertainty to the firm.

It might be argued that there is a major difference in services declined by a law firm due to lack of personnel between those clients who present only one case on a contingency fee basis and those who wish to retain the firm as regular counsel indefinitely into the future. Obviously, these can be divided into two maximization equations with different means. Yet, it is not necessary because the present value of the future billings per hour is c_1/r, and the net present value of the hourly cost into the future is c_0/r, where r is the firm's discount rate. Hence, equation (5) holds as stated for the number of new hires. However, equation (7), showing the profit from the newly acquired perpetual clients, should be increased by the factor $1/r$. Thus, they are more valuable than one-time clients.

Table 10.1. Expected Profits, Optimal Hires, and Cost of Uncertainty Using a Normal Approximation to the Poisson Distribution for Different Billing Ratios and Various Means

(1) c_1^*/c_0^*	(2) Expected Demand λ	(3) Std. Dev. of Demand $\sqrt{\lambda}$	(4) $f(N)$	(5) $\dfrac{N-\lambda}{\sqrt{\lambda}}$ Std. Normal Dev.	(6) Optimal Hires	(7) $E(T)$	(8) Max. $E(T)$ under Certainty	(9) Cost of Uncertainty Col. (8)–Col. (7)
2.0	1	1	1/2	0	1	$.20\,C_0^*$	C_0^*	$.80\,C_0^*$
	2	1.414			2	$.87\,C_0^*$	$2\,C_0^*$	$1.13\,C_0^*$
	5	2.236			5	$3.22\,C_0^*$	$5\,C_0^*$	$1.78\,C_0^*$
	10	3.162			10	$7.48\,C_0^*$	$10\,C_0^*$	$2.52\,C_0^*$
	20	4.472			20	$16.43\,C_0^*$	$20\,C_0^*$	$3.57\,C_0^*$
2.5	1	1	3/5	.25	1.25	$.53\,C_0^*$	$1.5\,C_0^*$	$.97\,C_0^*$
	2	1.414			2.35	$1.63\,C_0^*$	$3.0\,C_0^*$	$1.37\,C_0^*$
	5	2.236			5.56	$5.33\,C_0^*$	$7.5\,C_0^*$	$2.17\,C_0^*$
	10	3.162			10.72	$11.94\,C_0^*$	$15.0\,C_0^*$	$3.06\,C_0^*$
	20	4.472			21.12	$25.67\,C_0^*$	$30.0\,C_0^*$	$4.33\,C_0^*$
3.0	1	1	2/3	.44	1.43	$.91\,C_0^*$	$2\,C_0^*$	$1.09\,C_0^*$
	2	1.414			2.61	$2.46\,C_0^*$	$4\,C_0^*$	$1.54\,C_0^*$
	5	2.236			5.96	$7.57\,C_0^*$	$10\,C_0^*$	$2.43\,C_0^*$
	10	3.162			11.36	$16.56\,C_0^*$	$20\,C_0^*$	$3.44\,C_0^*$
	20	4.472			21.92	$35.14\,C_0^*$	$40\,C_0^*$	$4.86\,C_0^*$
3.5	1	1	5/7	.565	1.57	$1.31\,C_0^*$	$2.5\,C_0^*$	$1,19\,C_0^*$
	2	1.414			2.80	$3.32\,C_0^*$	$5.0\,C_0^*$	$1.68\,C_0^*$
	5	2.236			6.26	$9.84\,C_0^*$	$12.5\,C_0^*$	$3.16\,C_0^*$
	10	3.162			11.79	$21.24\,C_0^*$	$25.0\,C_0^*$	$3.76\,C_0^*$
	20	4.472			22.52	$44.68\,C_0^*$	$50.0\,C_0^*$	$5.32\,C_0^*$
4.0	1	1	3/4	.675	1.68	$1.73\,C_0^*$	$3.0\,C_0^*$	$1.27\,C_0^*$
	2	1.414			2.95	$4.20\,C_0^*$	$6.0\,C_0^*$	$1.80\,C_0^*$
	5	2.236			6.51	$12.16\,C_0^*$	$15.0\,C_0^*$	$2.84\,C_0^*$
	10	3.162			12.13	$25.98\,C_0^*$	$30.0\,C_0^*$	$4.02\,C_0^*$
	20	4.472			23.02	$54.32\,C_0^*$	$60.0\,C_0^*$	$5.68\,C_0^*$

Further, some firms may obtain referral fees by sending clients whom they do not have the resources to handle to other firms. The question here is how this affects the optimal number of lawyers to be hired. If the expected referral fees for a firm on an average basis are higher than the expected profit from accepting the client, then answering that question is easy. Obviously, the firm will maximize its profits by sending all new clients to other firms and collecting the referral fees.

Suppose the referral fee, C_2^*, measured on a yearly basis, is less than the billing fee; then the firm maximizes its expected profits, $E(\Pi)$, where

$$E(\Pi) = C_1^* \int_0^L Nf(N)dN + C_1^* \int_L^\infty f(N)dN$$

(9)

$$+ C_2^* \int_L^\infty (N - L)f(N)dN - C_0^* L$$

In equation (9), the first term on the right refers to the expected revenues when demand is less than the number of lawyers hired, the second is the expected gain in billing fees from lawyers hired when the demand is greater than the number of hires, the third is the expected income from referral fees in this latter case, and $C_0^* L$ represents the cost of hiring L lawyers. Equation (9) is maximized when

$$F(L) = \frac{\left(C_1^* - (C_2^* + C_0^*) \right)}{C_1^* - C_2^*}$$

(10)

Obviously, the right-hand side of equation (10) is equivalent to equation (5) when $C_2^* = 0$. For $0 < C_2^* < C_1^*$, this right-hand side will be smaller, and fewer lawyers will be hired. This conclusion also follows logically from economic theory because the opportunity cost of not having sufficient attorneys on hand is reduced.

THE CONTINGENCY FEE DECISION

Consider an ongoing firm that has at the current time a portfolio of unassigned lawyer hours available for future clients. Some of these clients may be taken on a contingency basis; that is, instead of receiving a fixed fee, the law firm pays all the expenses in return for a payment of αy where y is the client's maximum award and is a fraction satisfying $0 < \alpha < 1$. Under what conditions should the firm accept a new client on a contingency fee basis?

To help answer this question, we use the model developed in Levy (1985). The problem treated there was that of a plaintiff embarking on a lawsuit having maximum payoff of y and a probability of winning p. He wishes to maximize the expected return of

$$E(\pi) = E(py - C) \tag{11}$$

where π is the net value of the suit and C is the total out-of-pocket expenditures that will be incurred if the suit is accepted. It was assumed that there was a (fixed) maximum probability $\bar{p}$ of winning the suit, and a (variable) miminum probability p* of winning. The probability p* starts at a low a priori value and moves toward $\bar{p}$ as expenditures are made and the case progresses. Levy showed that, under these assumptions, the maximum amount that should be spent on the suit was

$$C = (\bar{p} - p^*)y/e \tag{12}$$

where $e = 2.71828$ and is the base of natural logarithms. The learning function of the model then gives the probability of winning as

$$p = \bar{p} - (\bar{p} - p^*)/e \tag{13}$$

and the expected payoff to the plaintiff

$$E(\pi) = \bar{p}y - 2(\bar{p} - p^*)y/e$$

$$= y[(e-2)\,\bar{p} + 2p^*]/e \tag{14}$$

Table 10.2 shows the expected returns from litigation, assuming $y = 100$, that is, the table is expressed in percentages of the maximum return.

The actual decision whether to accept a specific contingency case depends upon

1   the contingency fee parameter α

2   the maximum and minimum probabilities $\bar{p}$ and p^*

3   the willingness of the firm to take risks

4   the out-of-pocket and opportunity costs of taking the case.

The first three factors will be discussed in this section; the fourth factor will be discussed in the next section.

Since the law firm's gain is directly related to the client's it is reasonable to assume that the firm will also be willing to make the maximum expenditure C. However, the firm will make a positive gain only if it can cover expected costs, giving the condition

$$\alpha py > C \tag{15}$$

Substituting from equations (12) and (13) gives a necessary condition for the firm to be willing to accept the suit as

$$(\bar{p} - p^*) < \frac{\alpha\,\bar{p}\,e}{\alpha + 1} \tag{16}$$

which can be rewritten as

$$p^* \geq \bar{p}\ \frac{1 - (e-1)\,\alpha}{1 + \alpha} \tag{17}$$

Since the numerator of equation (17) cannot be negative, it follows that if

Table 10.2. Plaintiff's Expected Gains and Maximum Costs from Litigation Expressed as a Percentage of the Most Likely Outcome[4]

(1) Maximum Probability of Success	(2) Minimum Probability of Success	(3) Expected Gross Return	(4) Maximum Expenditures	(5) Expected Net Return	(1) Maximum Probability of Success	(2) Minimum Probability of Success	(3) Expected Gross Return	(4) Maximum Expenditures	(5) Expected Net Return
1	.9	96.32	3.68	92.64	.7	.4	58.96	11.04	47.92
	.8	92.64	7.36	85.28		.3	55.29	14.72	40.57
	.7	88.96	11.04	77.92		.2	51.60	18.39	33.21
	.6	85.29	14.72	70.57		.1	47.92	22.07	25.85
	.5	81.60	18.39	63.21		.0	44.25	25.75	18.50
	.4	77.93	22.07	55.85					
	.3	74.25	25.75	48.50	.6	.5	56.32	3.68	52.64
	.2	71.57	29.43	41.14		.4	52.64	7.36	45.28
	.1	66.89	33.11	33.78		.3	48.96	11.04	37.92
	.0	63.21	36.79	26.42		.2	45.29	14.72	30.57
						.1	41.60	18.39	23.21
						.0	37.92	22.07	15.85
.9	.8	86.32	3.60	82.64					
	.7	82.64	7.36	75.28	.5	.4	46.32	3.68	42.64
	.6	78.96	11.04	67.92		.3	42.64	7.36	35.28
	.5	75.29	14.72	605.7		.2	38.96	11.04	27.92
	.4	71.60	18.39	53.21		.1	35.29	14.72	20.57
	.3	67.92	22.07	45.85		.0	31.60	18.39	13.21
	.2	64.25	25.75	38.50					
	.1	60.57	29.43	31.14	.4	.3	36.32	3.68	32.64
	.0	56.87	33.11	23.78		.2	32.64	7.36	25.28
						.1	28.96	11.04	17.92
.8	.7	76.32	3.68	72.64		.0	25.29	14.72	10.57
	.6	72.64	7.36	65.28					
	.5	68.96	11.04	57.98	.3	.2	26.32	3.68	22.64
	.4	65.29	14.72	50.57		.1	22.64	7.36	15.28
	.3	61.60	18.39	43.21		.0	18.96	11.04	
	.2	57.92	22.07	35.85					
	.1	54.25	25.75	28.50	.2	.1	16.32	3.68	12.64
	.0	50.27	29.43	21.14		.0	12.64	7.36	5.28
.7	.6	66.32	3.78	62.64	.1	.0	6.32	3.68	-2.64
	.5	62.64	7.36	55.28					

$$\alpha \geq \frac{1}{e-1} = \frac{1}{1.718} = .582 \tag{18}$$

then the firm can always expect to recover its costs, regardless of the value of p^*. However, the most common value is $\alpha = .4$, for which the inequality in equation (17) becomes $p^* \geq .548 \, \bar{p}$. Thus, if $\bar{p} = .8$, then the requirement from equation (17) is $p^* \geq .438$. Other critical values of p^* occur in column 10 of Table 10.3 for $\alpha = 1/3$ and in column 10 of Table 10.4 for $= 2/5$.

We now discuss the connection between the maximum probability $\bar{p}$ and the firm's willingness to take a risk. The expected value of the return from litigation is αpy, which has variance

$$\sigma^2(\pi) = \alpha^2 y^2 p(1 - p) \tag{19}$$

and standard deviation

$$\sigma(\pi) = \alpha y \sqrt{p(1 - p)} \tag{20}$$

One common measure of the risk of an uncertain return is the coefficient of variation, V, defined as the standard deviation divided by the expected value of the return, or

$$V = \frac{\alpha y \sqrt{p(1 - p)}}{\alpha yp} = \sqrt{\frac{1 - p}{p}} \tag{21}$$

A low value of V indicates the return has low risk, while a high value of V indicates it has high risk.

Suppose R is a number indicating the maximum risk the firm is willing to take. Then we must impose the constraint

$$V = \sqrt{\frac{1 - p}{p}} \leq R \tag{22}$$

which yields

$$p \geq \frac{1}{1 + R^2} \tag{23}$$

Substituting the value of p from equation (13) gives

Table 10.3. Expected Returns from Taking Cases on Contingency Fee Basis: Y = 100, α = 1/3

(1) p̄	(2) p̄ − p*	(3) αpy	(4) C₀	(5) Expected Net Cash Flow Col.(3)−Col.(4)	(6) Std. Dev. of Col.(3) σ	(7) Coefficient of Variation [Col.(6) ÷ Col.(3)]x100%	(8) Ratio of Billing to Cost Col.(3) ÷ Col.(4)	(9) Avg. Probability Cost Will Be Recovered	(10) Critical Values p*
1	.1	32.11	3.68	28.43	6.28	19.55	8.70	1.0000	
	.2	30.88	7.36	22.52	8.70	28.19	4.20	.9965	
	.3	29.65	11.04	18.61	10.45	35.23	2.69	.9625	.3204
	.4	28.43	14.72	13.71	11.81	41.53	1.93	.8770	
	.5	27.20	18.39	8.81	12.92	47.49	1.48	.7517	
	.6	25.98	22.07	3.91	13.82	53.22	1.18	.5714	
.9	.1	28.77	3.68	25.09	11.45	39.81	7.82	.9857	
	.2	27.55	7.36	20.19	12.63	45.83	3.74	.9452	
	.3	26.32	11.04	15.28	13.59	51.62	2.38	.8686	.2884
	.4	25.10	14.72	10.38	14.38	57.29	1.71	.7642	
	.5	23.87	18.39	5.48	15.03	62.98	1.66	.6406	
	.6	22.64	22.07	0.57	15.56	68.73	1.03	.5160	

.8	.1	25.44	3.68	21.76	14.17	55.70	6.91	.9382	
	.2	24.21	7.36	16.85	14.86	61.37	3.29	.8708	
	.3	22.99	11.04	11.95	15.42	67.09	2.08	.7794	.2563
	.4	21.76	14.72	7.04	15.86	72.91	1.48	.6700	
	.5	20.53	18.39	2.14	16.21	78.95	1.12	.5517	
.7	.1	22.11	3.68	18.43	15.75	71.26	6.01	.8790	
	.2	20.88	7.36	13.62	16.13	77.23	2.84	.7995	
	.3	19.65	11.04	8.61	16.40	83.43	1.78	.7019	.2203
	.4	18.43	14.72	3.71	16.57	89.92	1.25	.5871	
.6	.1	18.77	3.68	15.09	16.53	88.07	5.10	.8186	
	.2	17.55	7.36	10.19	16.64	94.85	2.38	.7291	
	.3	16.32	11.04	5.28	16.66	102.10	1.48	.6255	.1923
	.4	15.10	14.72	0.38	16.59	109.91	1.03	.5080	
.5	.1	15.44	3.68	11.76	16.62	107.65	4.20	.7611	
	.2	14.21	7.36	6.85	16.48	115.98	1.93	.6628	.1604
	.3	12.99	11.04	1.95	16.26	125.17	1.18	.5478	
.4	.1	12.11	3.68	8.43	16.03	132.41	3.29	.7019	
	.2	10.88	7.36	3.52	15.63	143.66	1.48	.5910	.1282
.3	.1	8.77	3.68	5.09	14.67	167.31	2.38	.6386	.0961
	.2	7.55	7.36	0.19	13.95	184.85	1.03	5040	
.2	.1	5.44	3.68	1.76	12.32	226.44	1.48	.5557	.0641

223

Table 10.4. Expected Returns from Taking Cases on Contingency Fee Basis: Y = 100, α = 2/5

(1) p̄	(2) p̄ − p*	(3) αpy	(4) C_0	(5) Expected Net Cash Flow Col.(3)−Col.(4)	(6) Std. Dev. of Col. (3) σ	(7) Coefficient of Variation [Col.(6)÷Col.(3)]×100%	(8) Ratio of Billing to Cost Col.(3)÷Col.(4)	(9) Avg. Probability Cost Will Be Recovered	(10) Critical Values p*
1	.1	38.53	3.68	34.85	7.53	19.55	10.47	1.0000	
	.2	37.06	7.36	29.70	10.44	28.19	5.04	.9977	
	.3	35.58	11.04	24.54	12.54	35.23	3.22	.9750	
	.4	34.12	14.72	19.40	14.16	41.53	2.32	.9147	.2233
	.5	32.64	18.39	14.25	15.50	47.49	1.77	.8212	
	.6	31.17	22.07	9.10	16.59	53.22	1.41	.7088	
	.7	29.70	25.75	3.95	17.49	58.89	1.15	.5910	
.9	.1	34.53	3.68	30.85	13.75	39.81	9.38	.9875	
	.2	33.06	7.36	25.70	15.15	45.83	4.49	.9554	
	.3	31.58	11.04	20.54	16.30	51.62	2.86	.8962	.2010
	.4	30.12	14.72	15.40	17.25	57.29	2.05	.8133	
	.5	28.64	18.39	10.25	18.03	62.98	1.56	.7157	
	.6	27.17	22.07	5.10	18.67	68.73	1.23	.6064	
.8	.1	30.52	3.68	26.84	17.00	55.70	8.29	.9429	
	.2	29.06	7.36	21.70	17.83	61.37	3.95	.8888	
	.3	27.58	11.04	16.54	18.51	67.09	2.50	.8133	

	.4	26.12	14.72	11.40	19.04	72.91	1.77	.7257	
	.5	24.64	18.39	6.25	19.45	78.95	1.34	.6255	.1788
	.6	23.16	22.07	1.09	19.75	85.23	1.05	.5239	
.7	.1	26.52	3.68	22.84	18.90	71.26	7.21	.8869	
	.2	25.06	7.36	17.70	19.35	77.23	3.40	.8186	
	.3	23.58	11.04	12.54	19.68	83.43	2.14	.7389	
	.4	22.12	14.72	7.40	19.89	89.92	1.50	.6443	
	.5	20.64	18.39	2.25	19.99	96.85	1.12	.5438	.1563
.6	.1	22.52	3.68	18.84	19.83	88.07	6.12	.8289	
	.2	21.06	7.36	13.70	19.97	94.85	2.86	.7549	
	.3	19.58	11.04	8.54	20.00	102.10	1.77	.6664	
	.4	18.12	14.72	3.40	19.91	109.91	1.23	.5675	.1340
.5	.1	18.52	3.68	14.84	19.95	107.65	5.03	.7704	
	.2	17.06	7.36	9.70	19.78	115.98	2.32	.6879	
	.3	15.58	11.04	4.54	19.51	125.17	1.41	.5910	.1117
.4	.1	14.52	3.68	10.84	19.24	132.41	3.95	.7123	
	.2	13.06	7.36	5.70	18.76	143.66	1.77	.6217	
	.3	11.58	11.04	0.54	18.14	156.62	1.05	.5120	.0993

$$p = \bar{p} - (\bar{p} - p^*)/e \geq \frac{1}{1+R^2} \tag{24}$$

This can be rewritten as

$$\frac{\bar{p} - p^*}{e} \leq \bar{p} - \frac{1}{1+R^2} \tag{25}$$

from which as the right hand side must be positive, it is evident that

$$\bar{p} \geq \frac{1}{1+R^2} \tag{26}$$

is a necessary condition of $\bar{p}$ in order for a firm whose risk level is R to accept a contingency fee case. Equation (24) can also be rewritten as

$$p^* \geq \frac{e}{1+R^2} - (e-1)\bar{p} \tag{27}$$

which gives a necessary condition of p^*, for given values of R and $\bar{p}$, for acceptance of the case. Note from equation (27) that if $\bar{p} = 1/(1 + R^2)$, then $p^* = \bar{p}$, which is unlikely to hold. Hence equation (26) usually holds as a strict inequality.

Table 10.5 shows some typical values for R and the corresponding lower bounds from equations (26) and (27) on $\bar{p}$ and p^*. The last column gives the minimum value of p^* when $\bar{p} = 1$, which is therefore the smallest acceptance value of p^*.

In order to decide whether to accept a contingency case the information in Table 10.3 for $\alpha = 1/3$ and Table 10.4 for $\alpha = 2/5$ can be used. Similar tables for other values of α could easily be generated. In these tables column (1) is the maximum probability $\bar{p}$ of winning the verdict y (assumed to be 100%); column (2) is the minimum (a priori) probability p^* of winning y; column (3) gives the firm's expected payoff αpy; column (4) gives the maximum amount that should be spent from equation (2); column (5) is the difference between columns (3), and (4) and represents the expected net return to the firm; column (6) is the standard deviation of column (3) calculated from equation (20); column (7) is the coefficient of variation from equation (21) times 100; column (8) is the ratio of expected return [column (3)] to expected cost [column (4)]; column (9) gives the probability that the out-of-pocket costs will be recovered; and column (10) gives the critical values of p* for the given $\bar{p}$, calculated from equation (17).

Table 10.5. Minimum Values of p and p* for Contingency Fee Cases to Be Acceptable at Various Risk Levels

R	Minimum $\bar{p}$ from (26)	Minimum p* from (27) when $\bar{p} = 1$
.25	.94	.84
.50	.80	.46
.75	.64	.02
1.00	.50	0.00
1.50	.30	0.00

Tables 10.3 and 10.4 contain the key variables that the firm may wish to use in deciding whether to take the case. If it is a profit maximizer regardless of risk, it should take all cases whose values of p* are greater than those in column (10) for the $\bar{p}$ given in column (1). This will guarantee recovery of costs in half of the cases. On the other hand, if the firm wishes to recover at its usual ratio of billing rate to cost (or even more, due to uncertainty), it can make use of the ratios given in column (8). The firm can also use the coefficients of variation listed in column (7) to choose its proper level of risk.

Risk can be taken into account on a global level by considering the amount of risk in the current portfolio of cases before and after the new case would be added. If its current portfolio contains only low-risk cases, then it may well want to accept a risky new contingency case. But if it has a high-risk portfolio, then it may reject the new case. A similar analysis for the acceptance of new department store charge customers appears in Cyert and Thompson (1968).

OPPORTUNITY AND OUT OF POCKET COSTS

In the early part of this chapter it was shown that when the billing ratio was greater than 2, the optimal number of lawyers to be hired was greater than the expected need for lawyers. This, in turn, means that the lawyers will be underemployed and will not on the average be able to bill all of their hours; that is, there will be excess capacity in the firm. In such a case the opportunity costs of assigning them to a new contingency fee case is small. We give a macro and then a micro analysis of this phenomenon.

The macro analysis uses the notation of the second section. Assume that N is the number of lawyer hours currently available, that n* hours will be required for a new contingency fee case, and that f(n) is the density function of hours demanded for the regular cases. Then

$$C_1 \int_{N-n*}^{N} nf(n)dn \tag{28}$$

is the maximum opportunity cost of accepting the case. Thus equation (28) gives the mimimum expected revenue that the contingency fee case should yield if it is accepted. Note that the density function, f(n), changes as the end of the current period approaches, which tends to make the decision to accept the case depend more on future out-of-pocket costs and also on the firm's risk preferences.

The micro analysis of opportunity costs to be discussed next requires more data and computation, but could easily be handled by a personal computer.

A legal case usually goes through several stages of activity over a number of months or years with each stage having a fairly predictable demand for lawyer hours. However, in between active stages there is only nominal or zero demand for professional time. An example of the lawyer-hour demand profile is shown in Figure 10.1. In that figure, T is the planning horizon—hat is, the length of time over which future planning is to be made.

Suppose the firm assumes a reasonable load profile for each of its current cases and then cumulates the total load profile. A typical total load profile is shown in Figure 10.2. The dotted line in that figure represents the total number of lawyer-hours available each day during the planning period, which depends on the current size of the firm. Note that the total load profile sometimes is greater than and sometimes is less than the available number of hours. Excess demand can be handled by overtime if it is not too great. Some of the unbilled hours can be used by doing anticipatory work on cases that are near to an active stage. However the rest of the unbilled hours wil disappear if some use cannot be found for them.

Figure 10.1. Expected Lawyer-Hour Demand Profile for a Case during the Planning Horizon

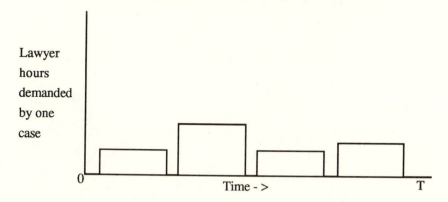

Suppose a contingency fee case with a load profile such as the one in Figure 10.1 is being considered for acceptance. If we add its demands to the current total load profile shown in Figure 10.2, we can find out how much of its demand can be covered by unbilled hours and how much will have to be covered by overtime hours. In this way a much more accurate picture of both the true opportunity costs and the true out-of-pocket costs can be found.

SUMMARY

The chapter employs elementary management science techniques to assist law firms in deciding how fast to expand their professional staffs and when to take cases on a contingency fee basis. Planning for new hires is based on a simple inventory model that assumes a Poisson arrival rate for new demands, which should be easily estimated from past data with the inclusion of a trend as necessary. Shortage costs or the inability to satisfy new clients can be estimated with some degree of accuracy in this model.

The contingency fee model is based on Levy (1985), which gives a learning model illustrating when an issue can be litigated and the maximum amount that should be spent. To this is added the coefficient of variation as a measure of risk, so that firms can use the model based on their own risk preferences to decide when to accept cases on a contingency fee basis. Both models are intended to stimulate further research in management science techniques for professional firms and to be of practical use to actual firms.

Figure 10.2. Total Cumulative Lawyer-Hour Demand Profile during the Planning Horizon

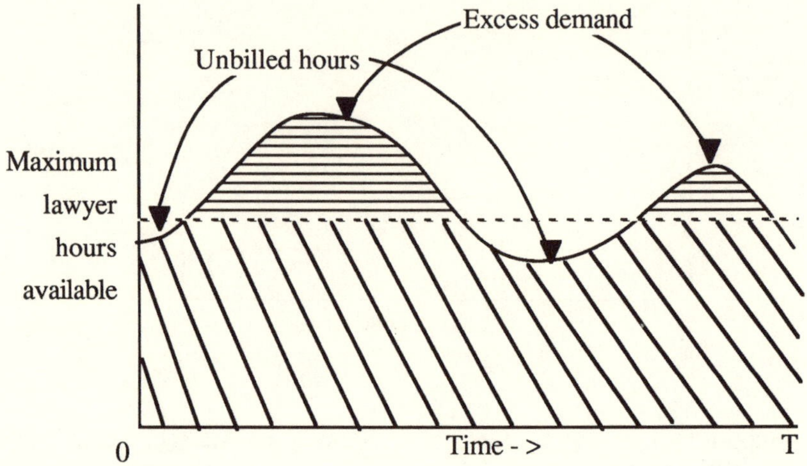

NOTES

The chapter is dedicated to our teacher, friend, and colleague William W. Cooper. An earlier version was sent to him and used as one basis for the dissertation of his doctoral student, Hong Chul Shin, at the University of Texas.

1. In a survey of fourteen firms with a miminum size of twenty-two professionals, the range of yearly hours budgeted ran from 1700 to 2200. Nine reported 1900 hours.

2. Obviously, the mean arrival λ_1 of contingency fee cases differs from that of new "regular clients," λ_2. Thus, $\lambda = \lambda_1 + \lambda_2$. If a firm budgets y hours per lawyer, the expected average demand for new hires will then be λ = (number of hours)/y.

3. Note that equation (8) will not give the correct profit because it is derived from equation (1) with the substitution $F(N) = (C_1^* - C_2^*)/C_1^*$. For the example in the text, the expected profit from hiring seven lawyers term by term in equation (1) is

$$E(\Pi) = (3C_0^*)(2.53) + (3C_0^*)(6)(.3264) - 6C_0^* = 7.46C_0^*$$

Similarly, if only five were hired, and we assume that each worked a maximum of 1900 hours,

$$E(\Pi) = (3C_0^*)(2.44) + (3C_0^*)(5)(.5) - 5C_0^* = 7.38C_0^*$$

Thus, six is obviously better if 1900 hours is the maximum.
4. Table 10.2 was a reproduced from Levy (1985).

REFERENCES

Cyert, Richard M., and Gerald L. Thompson, "Selecting a Portfolio of Credit Risks by Markov-Chains," *Journal of Business* 41, no. 1 (1968): 39-46.

Levy, F.K., "The Managerial Economics of Civil Litigation," *Management Science* 31, no. 3 (1985) 323-342.

11

A Fractal Analysis
of Capital Structure
Bertil Näslund

During a liquidity crisis, the cash flows from projects are assumed to be affected by the debt burden of the firm. The firm is assumed to have a hierarchical structure, and some ideas from fractal geometry are used to derive the probability of bankruptcy for the firm as a whole. This procedure gives a precise value for the optimal debt ratio, which depends upon the risk and return of the individual projects of the firm and the form of the hierarchical structure of the enterprise.

Studies of financial structure usually make the analysis at the firm level, rather than at the project level. The better known "theories" are

1. Modigliani-Miller (M.M) theory combined with taxes and bankruptcy. Capital structure in determined by equalizing tax savings on debt and bankruptcy cost (Modigliani and Miller,1958).

2. Miller's theory in which aggregate capital structure is determined by personal income taxes and corporate taxes. The point at which the marginal taxes paid by the marginal investor (in corporate debt) offset the corporate tax saving determines the debt ratio (Miller, 1977).

3. Managerial theories (agency theory and signaling) that consider various costs associated with equity (e.g., perquisites associated with equity and loan covenants associated with debt) or the value of correct signals and the costs of wrong ones, which give

       plausible arguments for the existence of some optimal capital structure (Jensen and Meckling, 1976; Ross, 1977).

4.   Various behavioral theories such as Miller's idea of "neutral mutation." (Firms fall into financial habits that managers like, but that have very little effect on the value of the firm. related to that is the "pecking order theory," which is more precise about the nature of these preferences.) (See Miller, 1977; Donaldson, 1961.)

For reviews of these and other theories, see Myers, 1984 and Weston, 1989.

Capital structure plays an important role in the capital budgeting decision since it affects the cost of capital. Even if the relationship between financing and investing is complex, it is often suggested that the capital structure is determined in some way (e.g.,by using one of the theories above), which determines the cost of capital for capital projects and thus influences their acceptance.

We shall use the opposite sequence in the analysis here and begin with the typical investment of the firm and treat it as a minifirm that is responsible for its share of the total debt burden of the firm. Using this as our starting point and assuming that investments, departments, divisions, and subsidiaries are organized in a hierarchical fashion we shall determine the optimal capital structure for the firm as a whole.

FRACTAL GEOMETRY

Fractal geometry has currently been applied in many fields of science. The basic work is focused in Mandelbrot (1982) and many texts have been written recently (e.g., Feder, 1988; Barnsley, 1988). An intuitive definition of a fractal is given in Feder (1988): "A fractal is a shape made of parts similar to the whole in some way" (p. 11).[1]

The Cantor sets give a simple illustration of fractal sets which also give a very direct image of a business organization (see Figure 11.1 for an example). The initial distance is divided into three equal parts deleting the middle one. The same principle is applied to the remaining levels.

The important aspect that we shall be using here is self-similarity. At each level the levels below look the same. Self similarity in organizations has to do with human behavior and organization structure in ways that will be specified below.

No prior knowledge of fractals is necessary to continue reading, but fractal trees (see, e.g., Solla, 1986) have been an inspiration for this chapter.

Figure 11.1. Construction of the Triadic Cantor Set

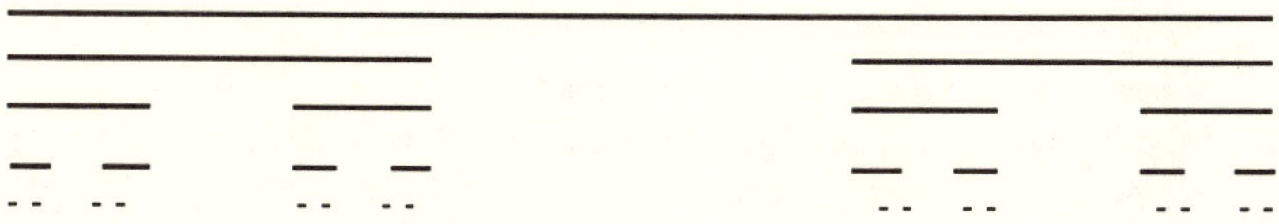

THE MODEL

The decision making in the firm is assumed to be hierarchical. At the bottom of the hierarchy are projects of a "typical size," which might vary between firms. The firm makes capital budgeting decisions for these typical projects and normally makes rather detailed cash-flow analyses.

We assume that the projects are organized such that those that are most similar form groups, as shown in Figure 11.2. Other forms of organization are discussed in the next section.

Figure 11.2. Grouping of Projects

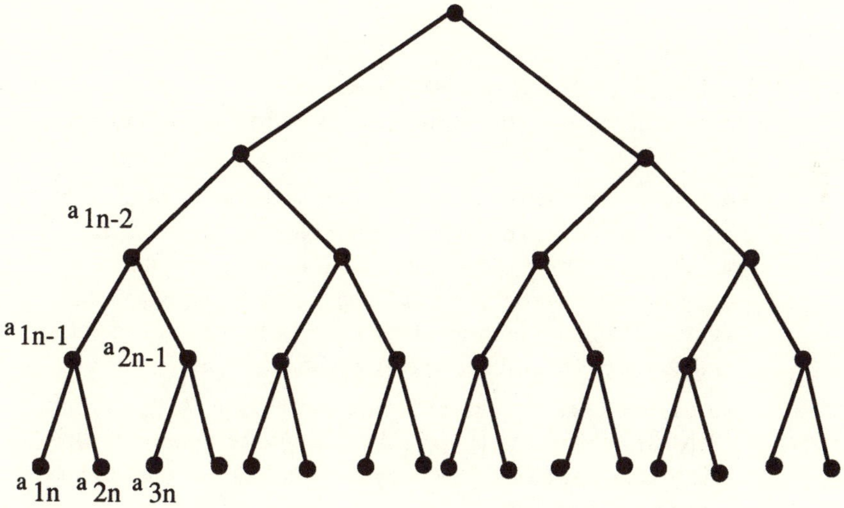

As an illustration we can think of a chain of restaurants, which, for administrative reasons, combine the two closest relationships into one profit center. At one level higher, the two closest profit centers form one larger profit center, and so on. The "typical" investment is the investment in one restaurant.

The basic assumption in the following analysis is self-similarity. At each level of the hierarchy, an assessment is made as to how well the two projects[2] are going to perform, and at each level the probability distribution has the same analytic form.

We assume that the "typical" project has an investment a_n that must be financed and that the amount of debt allocated to the project is D_n. The total debt of the firm is allocated to the projects in such a way that each project has the same debt ratio. The cash flow from the project during a liquidity crisis is αa_n which is stochastic, where a_n is the investment in the project. The average cash flow is αa_n. The annual financial charges due to the borrowing is a certain fraction d of the borrowing D_n. We assume that the probability that the cash flow generated by the project is insufficient can be written using the Weibul distribution[3]

$$\Pr(\alpha a_n \le dD_n) = 1 - e^{-\left(\frac{dD_n}{v_n}\right)^m} \tag{1}$$

where m and V_n are parameters of the distribution.

The level of debt will influence the cash flow from a project in different ways.

1. A firm under distress will put departments under pressure to deliver cash flow to meet debt service charges. This will lead to activities of various sorts (e.g., reduced repair, less R&D, less advertising) as discussed by Donaldson (1961) and Shapiro and Titman (1986). These activities may reduce the net present value of the project, but will improve short-term cash flow.

2. As has been emphasized by Mason and Merton (1985), a firm often has an option to temporarily close projects during periods of low cash flow. This is more likely to happen when a firm has to service a large debt.

3. A serious problem for a firm that has liquidity problems is that it cannot take new opportunities, may be attacked by competitors, may lose customers who are worried about the survival of the

firm etc. These aspects are further discussed in Modigliani and Miller (1958) and Piper and Weinhold (1982).

We represent the effects of debt on the cash flow by setting $\alpha a_n = f(dD_n)$ when $\alpha a_n < dD_n$. Projects are interdependent in many ways. The strongest interdependence is assumed to be associated with project failure.

If a project a_{in} fails to pay the financing it goes "bankrupt." However, other projects might earn cash flows above dD_n, and therefore, their cash flow can be used to pay part of the remaining payment for project a_{in}.[4]

Due to the organization of the firm, typical investments are organized in groups, departments, divisions, etc., in a hierarchical fashion, as shown in Figure 11.2 and it is the investment in the same group that is used first to cover the inability of project a_{in} to cover its financial costs. Call this other project a_{jn}. Thus at the very bottom of Figure 11.2, we have two investments, a_{in} and a_{jn}, which together form a group, as in Figure 11.3. In the following section, we discuss other organizational forms.

Figure 11.3. Two Investments Forming a Group

a_{1n-1}

a_{1n} a_{jn}

The probability that the group consisting of a_{in} and a_{jn} will go "bankrupt" is determined by the probability (1) that a_{jn} will go "bankrupt" and no be able to get support from a_{jn}, (2) that a_{jn} will go "bankrupt" and not be able to get support from a_{in}, and (3) that both of them will go "bankrupt" simultaneously. We begin by assuming that the projects are similar and that they are independent, except for the administrative relationship described above. These assumptions will be relaxed in the next section. When project a_{in} does not cover its financial charges, we will assume that it covers a fraction μ of $d \cdot D$, where $0 \le \mu \le 1$. The remaining part $(1 - \mu) = \gamma$, must come from a_{jn}.

The probability that project a_{jn} cannot support a_{in} and provide the necessary extra financing such that the node $n - 1$ does not go bankrupt is

$P_n^{1,2}$ (that $\alpha a_{jn} \leq (1 + \gamma)dD_n$, given that $\alpha a_{jn} > dD_n$). Setting $1 + \gamma = \beta$, we can write[5]

$$P_n^{1,2} = 1 - (1 - P_n)^{\beta^m - 1} \qquad (2)$$

If the "department" originating from a_{n-1} goes "bankrupt" the "bankruptcy" is transmitted to level $n - 1$. The probability that this will happen is determined by

$$P_{n-1} = P_n^2 + 2P_n(1 - P_n) P_n^{1,2} \qquad (3)$$

which means the probability that both will go "bankrupt" plus the probability that either one will go "bankrupt" and not be able to get support of the other. Inserting equation (2) in equation (3) gives

$$P_{n-1} = 2P_n (1 - (1 - P_n)^{\beta^m}) - P_n^2 \qquad (4)$$

Equation (4) shows how the "bankruptcy" at the project level is transmitted, which might result in the bankruptcy of the total firm.

The assumption therefore is that due to overhead at every department and due to human behavior (bounded rationality, organization slack, etc.), the form of the probability distribution of cash flows is the same at each level in the organization.

Thus, when funds are generated at level $n - 1$, the probability of "bankruptcy" of department n is determined by equation (3). The form of the probability distribution of cash flows at level n is still a Weibul distribution.

The fixed point equation $P_{n-1} = P_n$ gives the values $P = 0$, $P = 1$ and the "critical value" P_c determined by

$$P_c = 1 - \left(\frac{1}{2}\right)^{\frac{1}{\beta^m - 1}} \qquad (5)$$

Figure 11.4 shows the relationship between P_n and P_{n-1}

Figure 11.4. The Relationship between p_n and p_{n-1}

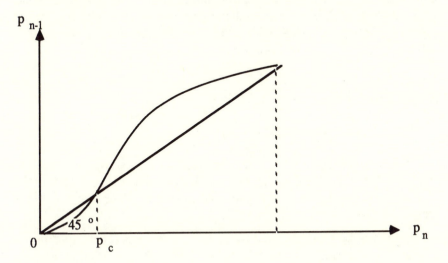

The probability P_c is the critical probability of bankruptcy of the typical investment. If the debt is such that $P_n < P_c$, the debt service of the failed projects can be taken over by the successful ones. If, however, $P_n > P_c$, the failing departments continue to grow as we move up in the hierarchy and if the levels in the hierarchy are many, bankruptcy becomes certain.

Due to the tax advantage of debt, the firm tries to make debt as large as possible provided that bankruptcy can be avoided. It therefore remains to determine the critical debt D_c at the project level that corresponds to P_c.

Using equations (1) and (5) we find that D_c is determined by

$$D_c = \left[\frac{\ln 2}{\beta^m - 1} \right]^{\frac{1}{m}} \cdot \frac{v_n}{d} \tag{6}$$

Some further aspects of equation (6) are discussed in the final section.

The advantage of the analysis illustrated here is that it uses relatively simple and often readily available data on cash flows at the project level to estimate the parameters of the probability distribution.

The analysis then follows technical, administrative, and behavioral constraints on the firm to analyze how the failures at the project level can bankrupt the firm. It is, after all, at the project level where problems—loss of customer support, new competing products, new technologies—most often start.

ANALYSIS

The Critical Probability

The critical probability is not exactly reached in most situations due to a limited number of projects, and thus levels as shown in Figure 11.2. If the size of a typical project is $100,000 and the value of the firm's assets is $1,000,000,000 then $n \approx 13$.

As a specific example, we take $m = 2$ and $\beta = 1.5$. Then equation (3) moves $P_n = 0.1$ to $P_{n-1} = 0.0322$, $P_{n-2} = 0.0035$, $P_{n-3} = 0.00004$, etc. and we see that the probability of bankruptcy goes rapidly to zero. From this, we would predict that small firms (firms with few hierarchical levels) have less debt since the probability of "bankruptcy" does not go to zero. This has some empirical support (see Titman and Wessels, 1985).

If, on the other hand, $P_n = 0.6$, the sequence becomes $P_n = 0.6$, $P_{n-1} = 0.687$, $P_{n-2} = 0.802$, $P_{n-3} = 0.919$, $P_{n-4} = 0.987$, and the probability of bankruptcy approaches 1 as we move up the hierarchy in Figure 11.2.

The parameter V_n is used together with m to fit the Weibul distribution to the cash-flow probabilities associated with the project. For the actual determination of the debt ratio of the firm, we can instead use the average cash flow from the project during a liquidity crisis, αa_n, which is estimated during normal capital budgeting procedures.

The Debt Ratio

The average cash flow from the project during a liquidity crisis can be approximated using equation (1). The average value of the cash flow is

$$\bar{\alpha} a_n = \int_0^\infty m \frac{x^m}{V_n^m} e^{-\left(\frac{x}{V_n^m}\right)^m} dx$$

(7)

Set

$$\left(\frac{x}{V_n}\right)^m = t$$

Differentiating both sides, we obtain

$$m \frac{x^{m-1}}{V_n^m} dx = dt$$

and we can write

$$\bar{\alpha} a_n = \int_0^\infty x e^{-t} dt$$

From equation (7) we have

$$x = t^{\frac{1}{m}} \cdot V_n$$

and we can write

$$\bar{\alpha} a_n = \int_0^\infty V_n \cdot t^{\frac{1}{m}} \cdot e^{-t} dt$$

This is the gamma distribution

$$\Gamma(z) = \int_0^\infty t^{z-1} \cdot e^{-t} dt$$

using

$$z = \frac{1}{m} + 1$$

and therefore

$$\bar{\alpha} a_n = \Gamma(\frac{1}{m} + 1) V_n \tag{8}$$

Using equations (6) and (8), we can relate Table 11.1 for the $\beta = 1.5$.

Table 11.1. The Optimal Debt Ratio

	I	II	III
m	dD_c/V_n	$\bar{\alpha} a_n/V_n$	$D_c/a_n \cdot d/\bar{\alpha}$
2	0.744	0.8862	0.839
3	0.663	0.8930	0.742
5	0.637	0.9182	0.694
10	0.644	0.9513	0.677
20	0.655	0.9735	0.673

Since d is the known service charges on debt and is the average "return" from the typical investment during a liquidity crisis, the optimal debt ratio D_c/a_n follows from the third column. Firms that earn a large average return during a crisis can have more debt, with the constraint that $D_c/a_n < 1$. Empirical tests have focused on project or firm profitability and have found no support for the hypothesis that a profitable firm can use more leverage. It might be more appropriate to test the effects of firm performance during a liquidity crisis.

We can see from Table 11.1 that the optimal debt ratio declines with m. The standard deviation of the Weibul distribution increases with larger m for a given V_n.[6] Therefore, Table 11.1 illustrates how increased risk affects the debt ratio. For m larger than 3, the effect of risk on the optimal debt ratio is small. Empirical studies of the effect of risk on leverage are ambiguous, (see e.g. Kester, 1986).

The sensitivity of the debt capacity with respect to β can be determined by differentiating equation (7) with respect to β

$$\frac{dD_c}{D_c} \Big/ \frac{d\beta}{\beta} = - \frac{\beta^m}{\beta^m - 1}$$

Since $\beta > 1$, an increase in β will cause a decline in D_c.

SOME EXTENSIONS

We have assumed that all projects of the firm are identical. This is similar to the assumption that is used when the weighted average cost of capital is used and projects are assumed to be a "blueprint of the firm." This is obviously a very strong assumption. We will discuss this and other assumptions.

The Firm Consists of Different Divisions with Different Types of Projects

When the divisions of the firm are different and each consists of its own typical projects, the optimal debt ratio can be determined for each division as described above. The debt ratio for the firm is then the weighted average of the optimal debt ratios for the divisions. This assumes that the divisions consist of many layers such that a debt ratio above the critical one leads almost certainly to "bankruptcy."

The Firm Consists of Different
Kinds of "Typical" Projects

A firm might have two kinds of projects with different distributions for the return characterized, that is by different values for the parameter V_{n0}. Let us assume that we have two types of projects, one with the value V_{n0} and the other with the value V_{n1}.

The failure probability at the nth level is then

$$P_r(\alpha a_n \leq dD) = \eta \left(1 - e^{-\left(\frac{dD}{V_{n0}}\right)^m} \right)$$

$$+ (1 - \eta) \left(1 - e^{-\left(\frac{dD}{V_{n1}}\right)^m} \right)$$

(9)

where η and $(1 - \eta)$ denotes the fractions of the two types of projects.

The conditional probabilities shown in equation (2) cannot be expressed in a simple analytic form in this case. The analysis can, however, be made using numerical methods and opens the possibility for using this method in other, perhaps more realistic situations.

Organizational Form

In Figure 11.2 we describe an organization in which every department manages two departments below it. What happens if the number of departments is more than two? In Figure 11.5 we describe the situation where each department branches into three lower ones. The analysis above for two projects can now be repeated with three projects. A department "goes bankrupt"

1. when all three projects go bankrupt or
2. when two go bankrupt and the remaining one cannot provide sufficient cash flow to save all three from going bankrupt or
3. when one project fails and the other two cannot make up the difference.

The analysis of this case is straightforward, but it cannot be solved in analytic form, and numerical methods are necessary.

Figure 11.5. An Organization with Three Lower Departments

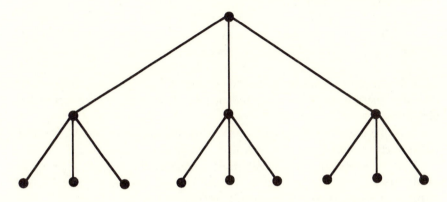

One interesting aspect of this is that the method described here makes it possible to analyze the effects of the organizational form on optimal capital structure.

Long-Term Effects of Cash-Flow Adjustments

As mentioned above, firms facing a liquidity crisis may generate cash by reducing R&D, maintenance, etc., which will have long-term costs. These costs can then be compared with the benefits of using debt rather than equity and determine β and D_c in equation (6) such that the cost advantage of debt equals—at the margin—the cost of the above-mentioned short-term adjustments to R&D, etc.

CONCLUSIONS

The capital structure decision has previously been approached from various points of view at the level of the total firm. This gives a cost of capital, which used to be used to assess the value of individual projects. These projects, however, are themselves the foundation of the firm and its riskiness and thus the determinants of capital structure. This is the position taken here and the starting point for the analysis.

The method used is characterized by an emphasis on the similarity of processes and behavior across various levels in an organization. This is an idealization with certain deficiencies but it might be appropriate for analysis of certain problems in organizations. The method can be used to study divisionalized firms, and it can be extended to allow projects within divisions to have different characteristics.

NOTES

1. Mandelbrot (1982) gives this definition: "A fractal is by definition a set for which the Hausdorff-Besicovitch dimension strictly exceeds the topological dimension," (p. 15).

2. At the lowest level, two projects are a_{1n} and a_{2n}, and at the level above, two projects are, that is a_{1n-1} and a_{2n-1}.

3. This distribution is frequently used in engineering to study the stability of different types of structures. For further discussion of the Weibul distribution, see Råde and Westergren (1988).

4. The fact that a project must pay its financial charges is in practice reflected in required return and target cash flows from a project and department.

5. We assume that β is independent of the parameters of the Weikal distribution.

6. $\sigma^2 = V^2_n (\Gamma(1+2/m) - \Gamma^2(1+1/m))$ (see Råde and Westergren, 1988).

REFERENCES

Barnsley, M., *Fractals Everywhere*, New York: Academic Press, 1988.

Donaldson, G., *Corporate Debt Capacity: A Study of Corporate Debt Policy and the Determination of Corporate Debt Capacity*, Harvard Graduate School of Business, 1961.

Feder, J., *Fractal*, New York: Plenum Press, 1988.

Jensen, M. C., and W. Meckling, "Theory of the Firm: Managerial Behavior, Agency Costs and Capital Structure," *Journal of Financial Economics* 3 (October 1976): 11-25.

Mandelbrot, B., *The Fractal Geometry of Nature*, San Francisco: Freeman, 1982.

Mason, S.P., and R. C. Merton, "The Role of Contingent Claims Analysis in Corporate Finance" in E.I. Altman and M.G. Subrahmanyam (eds.), *Recent Advances in Corporate Finance*, Irwin, 1985.

Miller, M., "Debt and Taxes," *Journal of Finance* 32, no. 2 (May 1977): 261-275.

Modigliani, F., and M. Miller, "The Cost of Capital, Corporate Finance and the Theory of Investment," *American Economic Review* 53 (June 1958): 261-297.

Myers, S. C., "The Capital Structure Puzzle," *The Journal of Finance* (July 1984): 575-592.

Piper, T. R., and Weinhold, W. A., "How Much Debt Is Right for Your Company?" *Harvard Business Review* 60, no. 4 (July-August 1982): 106-114.

Råde, L., and B. Westergren, *Beta: Mathematics Handbook*, Lund, Sweden: Chartwell-Bratt 1988.

Ross, S. A., "The Determination of Financial Structure; The Incentive-Signalling Approach," *Bell Journal of Economics* 8 (Spring 1977): 23-40.

Shapiro, A. C., and Titman, S. "An Integrated Approach to Corporate Risk Management" in J.M. Stern and D.H. Chew (eds.), *The Revolution in Corporate Finance*, Oxford, United Kingdom: Blackwell, 1986.

Solla, S. A., "Collapse of Loaded Fractal Trees," in L. Pietronero and E. Tossatti (eds.), *Fractals in Physics*, New York: Elsevier North Holland 1986, pp. 185-188.

Titman, S., and R. Wessels, "The Determinants of Capital Structure Choice," Working Paper, UCLA, 1985.

Weston, J.F., "What MM Have Wrought," *Financial Management* (Summer 1989): 29-38.

12

Applying the Audit Risk Model to the Organization Design of the Firm

Arie Y. Lewin

In April 1979, the H.J. Heinz Company revealed that some of its divisions had engaged in widespread improper billing, recognition of sales, recognition of expenses, and other practices. Major divisions involved included Heinz USA, Ore-Ida, Star-kist, and a number of foreign operations. Many of the improper practices mirror the game of budget control—understatement of revenues and overstatement of expenses (Hofstede, 1967; Schiff and Lewin, 1970). Vendors, particularly advertising firms, were enlisted to cooperate in improper invoicing. At Heinz USA alone, improper invoicing involved ten vendors at the division level and eight vendors at the department level, presumably with the tacit approval of division management.

There was also some indication that Heinz world headquarters management was aware of these practices. For example, in FY 1974, when world headquarters realized that Heinz USA might report profits in excess of those allowed by wage and price controls, they sought to have Heinz USA report lower profits. Heinz USA management is reported to have been reluctant to reduce its profits; nevertheless, it obtained a $2 million invoice from an advertising agency for services that were not performed, but were recorded as an expense for 1974. In calculating Heinz USA net profit after taxes (NPAT) for the purpose of awarding bonuses under the management incentive plan (MIP), world headquarters allowed an adjustment of $1 million (after taxes) for advertising. As a result the adjustment, Heinz USA management achieved its outstanding goal (40% bonus) for FY 1974.

From the perspective of auditing, the accumulated effect on shareholders' equity and working capital was not material (less than 2%). However, in several fiscal years the effect on the company's reported total revenues and income could be considered material: annual net income after taxes ranged from an understatement of 10.3 percent in 1973 to an overstatement of 3.27 percent in 1975. Nevertheless, it could be concluded that Peat Marwick, Mitchell and Co. (PM), Heinz auditors for all these years, managed the audit within the acceptable bounds of audit risk. It is a matter of speculation whether PM would have expanded the scope of the audit had it anticipated the business risk of losing the account. At its meeting on May 7, 1980, the Heinz board of directors accepted the recommendations of the audit committee that terminated the engagement of PM as the company's auditors.

Using the Heinz case as an illustration, this chapter considers audit effectiveness in terms of research in organization design and the components of the audit risk model. It is motivated by the belief that organization design research can inform the practice and effectiveness of auditing. The chapter also identifies fruitful areas of research collaborations between auditing and organization design scholars.

RESEARCH ON THE BEHAVIORAL
ASPECTS OF ACCOUNTING

Linking organization design and auditing is a logical extension of behavioral accounting, a research stream that was spawned by early nonaccountants in organization theory and psychology (Argyris, 1952, 1953; Simon, 1957a, 1957b; Hammond, 1955; Edwards, 1962). One topic of behavioral accounting has been the impact of budgets, planning, and control on individuals and subunits. A second line of research focuses on the use of accounting information in decision making (for recent reviews, see Ashton, 1982; Libby, 1981). The first line of research is grounded in managerial theories of the firm, and the second in human information processing theories.

Although behavioral and organization research in accounting has become a highly respected element of accounting research, with major implications for the practice of accounting, such research has been criticized on many grounds (e.g., Green, 1973; Hofstedt, 1975; American Accounting Association, 1974). The criticisms have some validity, but they do not address the predominance of research on one variable at a time, the need to employ methodologies that permit hypothesis testing and validation of theory using small samples, the importance of learning from outliers, inductive theorizing on the basis of processual ethnographic research, or the need to make the organization, rather than the individual, the unit of analysis. All of these are of great concern in organization theory and thus pertain to any bridge between organization design and auditing. In the context of auditing, too, there is a need to create a more encompassing framework that integrates research on and constructs of organization design with research on individual decision making. The context of the audit risk model is an example of where such a framework can be applied.

ORGANIZATION DESIGN AND AUDITING

The H.J. Heinz case illustrates the need for a more encompassing framework. The recommendations for changes made by the audit committee affected every element of the Internal Environment shown in Figure 12.1.

Figure 12.1. Modeling the Design of Organizations

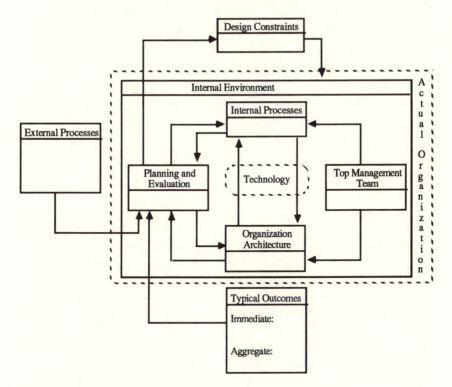

The recommendations related to the organization culture of H.J. Heinz in terms of control consciousness and ethical climate. They resulted in changes to the formal organization (architecture) in terms of a realignment of the reporting structure for corporate control and internal audit. The report recommended changes in internal processes, such as standardizing accounting policies and procedures (e.g., using a chart of accounts, authorizations, and procedures) and strengthening internal audit functions and procedures. The audit committee also recommended that top management reevaluate the mechanisms for planning and goal setting of the divisional MIP, as well as establishing at world headquarters a greater capacity for monitoring and evaluating division financial performance. Table 12.1 presents a retrospective summary assessment of control risk and inherent risk for the H.J. Heinz Company prior to 1979 and after 1980. These are ex-post assessments, based on analysis and interpretation of the audit committee recommendations.

Table 12.1. Retrospective Summary of Inherent and Control Risk of the H.J. Heinz Company

	Prior to 1979	After 1980
Control Risk	High	Minimal
Inherent Risk	High	Minimal

In hindsight, it seems that control risk should have been considered to be relatively high. Management at world headquarters enacted its belief in fostering autonomy and entrepreneurship at the division level through a decentralized organization design. The organization design lacked a corporate control structure; the division controller was an integral part of division management and did not have a formal reporting relationship to the corporate controller. Similarly, the director of corporate audit was not directly responsible for the internal audit function at the divisions. In addition, the corporate culture did not stress either control consciousness or ethics.

Inherent risk should also have been considered to be relatively high. Consistent with an entrepreneurial management philosophy and a decentralized organization design, H.J. Heinz operated with decentralized accounting procedures. There was no attempt to establish a uniform chart of accounts. The timing and format of quarterly financial reports varied by division. Accounting policies for timing, valuation, and recording of transactions were not uniform across divisions and foreign affiliates. In addition, marketing accountants (who were responsible for approving marketing expenditures) reported to marketing executives at the division level, and standards for authorization procedures were often not formalized and also varied across divisions and foreign affiliates.

Other variables contributing to an ex-post assessment of a relatively high combined risk (IR x CR) relate to the MIP, which required division management to resolve a clear conflict of interest involving their personal ethics, and goals for advancement and income (bonuses), with company goals for financial performance. In addition, the company did not have programs ensuring compliance with the Foreign Corrupt Practices Act (FCPA) or with its own Corporate Ethical Policy, which was first adopted in 1976.

In hindsight, it seems that PM assessed the combined risk as minimal and therefore, consistent with the audit risk (AR) model, its auditing procedures did not place heavy reliance on compliance and substantive testing activities. These contradictory assessments of the combined risk may result from several interacting factors: (1) the science of assessing the underlying audit risk of a client's organization design in terms of inherent and control risk is not well developed, so auditors tend to rely on intuitive judgments; (2) the internal organization design of PM, its management of audit assignment, and the skills of its specialists may be incompatible with a periodic independent reassessment of client organization and business; and (3) the lengthy relationship (Cook, 1977; Cook and Emerson, 1978; Macaulay, 1963) between PM and Heinz may have reinforced perceptions of minimal combined risk, which could lead to audit practices that further increase the likelihood of undetected errors (audit risk) by the auditor.

ORGANIZATION DESIGN AND THE AUDIT RISK MODEL

Application of the audit risk model in directing, planning and implementing an audit requires that the auditor develop an understanding and assessment of the client organization's business, organization structure, internal operating environment, legal structure, industry and economic conditions, and attitudes and credibility of management, as well as the potential for management fraud, existence of related party transactions, possibility of illegal acts, and likelihood of business failure. Public accounting firms have developed structures or heuristics for guiding the design of their audit approach plans. However, there is relatively little published empirical work relating elements of the AR model and auditing to the analysis and assessment of specific organization designs.

Figure 12.1 describes the major building blocks for modeling the design of organizations. Lewin and Minton (1986) noted that organization design reflects tradeoffs in achieving certain attributes of performance or other organization characteristics (e.g., ethical climate) as a function of external environmental constraints and other limiting factors. Organization design is the means by which management implements its strategic perspective and plans, consistent with its management philosophy, style, and values. In other words, the direction and allocation of resources are achieved through choices about the architecture of the organization (structure), internal processes (coordination, control, compensation policies, information processing, socialization, etc.); technology; organization culture, and form and function of the planning and evaluation system.

Environmental Uncertainty

Organization theorists have suggested that the external environment of the organization should be analyzed as a function of two major variables— environmental rate of change and environmental complexity. The greater the environmental rate of change and the greater the environmental complexity, the higher the environmental uncertainty. The greater the environmental uncertainty is, the more informal and decentralized the organization structure should be, and the greater the organization differentiation, number of departments, and boundary roles should be. Internal processes will thus be characterized by low formalization and standardization of procedures and by informal control and many integrating roles for internal coordination. Thus, all else being equal, the greater the environmental uncertainty, the higher the combined risk (IR x CR).[1]

A further environmental factor relates to the scarcity of resources and therefore to the extent that the organization is dependent on external resources. The greater the firm's external resource dependency is, the greater will be the desire of the firm to negotiate its environment (Cyert and March, 1963; Pfeffer and Salancik, 1978) and/or to increase its control over the external environment will be. Negotiating the environment may involve vertical and horizontal integration, contractual hedges and joint ventures, establishment of accepted industry practices, co-optation and interlocking directorates (Pennings, 1980), capturing and defending market shares, etc. Controlling the environment may involve entering new markets (or changing domain) where the firm can be dominant, political activities, and illegal activities, such as price fixing, stock manipulation, restraint of trade, or payoffs to foreign governments. Thus, all else being equal, the greater the external resource dependency of the firm, the greater the combined risk. Table 12.2 summarizes the relationships among environmental uncertainty, resource dependency, and the assessment of combined risk.

Table 12.2. Relationships among Environmental Uncertainty, Resource Dependency, and the Assessment of Combined Risk

		Low	High
Environmental Uncertainty	Low	Combined Risk IR Lower CR Lower	Combined Risk IR Lower* CR Higher*
	High	Combined Risk IR Higher CR Lower	Combined Risk IR Higher CR Higher*
		Low	High

Resource Dependency

*In particular if emphasis is on controlling the environment in contrast to negotiating the environment.

Organization Architecture and Internal Processes

Choices about organization structure require simultaneous consideration of technology, size, product lines and markets, and the environment. Departmental technology can be considered along the dimensions of variety (the frequency of unexpected and novel situations that occur in the production process) and analyzability (the extent to which the production process can be broken down into identifiable, replicable, and standardized tasks and sequences) (Duncan, 1979). Departmental technology can therefore be characterized along a routine/nonroutine dimension. The more routine the technology the higher its analyzability, and the lower its variety. Routine departmental technologies are best matched with functional organization structures characterized by high formulation of standard operating procedures, centralized decision making, hierarchical referral and control systems, and, all else being equal, low combined risk (IR x CR). Nonroutine departmental technologies are best matched with decentralized organic structures (such as matrix organizations) characterized by little formalization of standard operating procedures, decentralized decision making, informal coordination and control, and, all else being equal, high combined risk (IR x CR).

Departments may be dependent on each other to accomplish tasks. These interdependencies can be reciprocal (several departments have to provide coordinated services), sequential (one department uses as its inputs the outputs of the preceding department), or pooled (no interdependence exists between departments and very little day-to-day coordination between departments is required). Reciprocal technologies require a high level of lateral interdepartmental coordination and communication involving unplanned face-to-face meetings and mutual adaptation. Coordination of sequential technologies is best accomplished through plans and schedules, whereas coordination of pooled technologies can be accomplished by the use of standard operating procedures. Thus, all else being equal, the combined risk inceases as an organization depends more on increasing technological interdependence among departments.

The design of organizations also involves choices about the best way to group individuals into departments, about the design of vertical and horizontal linkages, and about internal processes and procedures. In general, choices about structures reflect tradeoffs in creating the organization's capacity for information processing. This capacity is a funcion of the degree to which the organization design incorporates vertical and horizontal linkages (Galbraith, 1974). Vertical linkages include structural devices, such as formal control structures and management information systems, strategic planning departments, and levels and positions in the hierarchy, as well as internal processes and procedures, such as budgets, plans, standard operating procedures, and decision referral rules. Horizontal linkages involve lateral relations, such as liaison functions, task forces, frequent unplanned meetings, and the use ot formalized integrator roles.

From the perspective of the AR model, all else being equal, the greater the organization's requirements for intormation processing capacity, the greater the requirements for vertical and/or horizontal coordination and control linkages, and the higher the combined risk (IR x CR). Furthermore, the greater the dependency on horizontal (over vertical) linkages for creating organization capacity for information processing, the higher the combined risk.

These organization designs are based on theories of high congruence (best fit) among structure, internal processes, environment, size, and technology. To the extent that the organization design congruence departs from optimality (Mackenzie, 1986), organization efficiency and effectiveness will decrease, and the combined audit risk should increase.

Top Management

Maximizing the fit between the strategic perspective of top management and the organization design as the means of implementing this perspective is another important condition. The greater the fit, the more effective the organization. Audit risk will vary as a function of the strength of management values and core beliefs that affect inherent and control risk.

The effective enactment of any organization design depends on the mystical social glue (informal processes, organization culture) that creates and reinforces a sense of shared purpose, beliefs, and commitment and that guides individual behavior and decision making. A strong, focused organization culture seems to be directly related to organization effectiveness (Kilman and Saxton, 1983; Nadler and Tushman, 1988). But strong, focused maladaptive cultures can be dysfunctional to effectiveness.

Organization culture can be analyzed along several dimensions (Nadler and Tushman, 1988). In particular, it is important to diagnose (1) core values and beliefs, (2) expected behaviors that guide and direct conduct, and (3) organization climate norms that embody how things are done, such as commitment, teamwork, and ethical conduct.

Top mangement has a major role in shaping organization culture, which to a large extent reflects its philosophy and values. One mechanism, amongst many, that it has for doing so is establishing accounting policies and procedures consistent with strategy and core values. From the perspective of the AR model, the analysis of organization culture also needs to assess the extent to which the core values and beliefs are articulated and embodied in norms of expected behavior that affect inherent or control risk. For example, to what extent are values of honesty, integrity, and fairness embedded in practices involving work and external relationships?

Empirical research on specific dimensions and characteristics of organization culture (e.g., ethical climate) and its relationship to organization effectiveness is rare (see Lewin and Minton, 1986). From the perspective of the AR model, however, it is clear that organization culture should be directly related to inherent and control risk. For example, companies with deeply articulated and carefully internalized ethical climates should, all else being equal, have lower combined risk. At Heinz, explicit top management concern with ethical behavior is absent. The management incentive plan placed the burden of resolving conflict of interest dilemmas on individual managers, without direction or guidance from an articulated policy on ethical conduct.

EFFECTIVENESS AND EFFICIENCY
OF AUDIT STRUCTURES

Research on the effectiveness and efficiency of the audit and how to best design audit approaches has begun to explore tradeoffs between organic and mechanistic approaches (Dirsmith and McAllister, 1982a, 1982b). When Cushing and Loebbecke (1986) analyzed the audit process of twelve major public accounting firms in terms of the levels of formalization and standardization of the firms' audit approach, they found that the major differences among firms lay in the structure and procedures used to implement widely shared phases of an audit approach: of the twelve firms, the audit approaches of two were classified as unstructured, two as highly structured, four as semi-structured, and four as partially structured. They also suggested that increased efficiency is directly related to higher formalization and standardization, a finding supported by Elliot (1981), Holstrum (1981), Kinney (1986), and Stringer (1981). However, Cushing and Loebbecke (1986) also noted that efficiency could be a function of fit between the design of a structured audit approach and the audit environment. A poor fit could result in inefficiencies.

Lewin and Minton (1986) noted that different organization designs are associated with different features of organization effectiveness and that performance measures associated with efficiency (e.g., resource productivity measures) are present in every model of organization effectiveness. The implication for the debate on the efficiency of audit structures is that, empirically, efficiency could be associated with all modes of structure. However, the effectiveness (as reflected in loss of client, regulatory sanctions, reputation, discovery of material errors, litigation) of audit firms might be distinguished in their approach to understanding the client organization and how that analysis is used to modify and adapt the firm's audit approach. Cushing and Loebbecke (1986) noted that although all audit firms acquire knowledge of the business as part of their planning phase, it is not at all clear what heuristics these firms use to do so and how the information is used in planning the audit. Regardless of audit structure, the greater the capacity of a firm to understand the client organization and adapt audit methodologies is the greater the efficiency and effectiveness of the audit should be. All else being equal, this capacity should increase with industry specialization. However, the greater the firm's industry specialization, the higher the degree of structure, and the lower the felt need to invest in a capacity to understand the client.

The institutional structure of the audit-client relationship should also affect efficiency and effectiveness. Levinthal and Fichman (1988) report that the hazard rate of a dissolution of the auditor-client relationship is very low in the first two years of the relationship, is greatest (.035) in the third and fourth years, and declines sharply thereafter. The overall hazard rate was also affected by the likelihood the auditor would issue a qualified opinion, which also declines as the duration of the relationship increases and is highest (.030) in the third and fourth years.

Various factors may explain the longevity of the auditor-client relationship, including the transaction cost of replacing the auditor (Williamson, 1981; Monteverde and Teece, 1982). As the duration of the auditor-client relationship increases, perceived commitment to the relationship also increases because of the development of assets specific to the relationship (Cook, 1977; Cook and Emerson, 1978; Nelson and Winter, 1982).

The audit-client relationship involves a repeated exchange process. Thus, as the duration of the relationship increases, the auditor's felt need to continuously develop and update his understanding of the client organization diminishes, and the probability of undetected error rises because the auditor's subjective assessment of inherent and control risk decreases.

Thus, we have come full circle. The efficiency and effectiveness of the audit are directly related to the capacity of the firm to understand the client organization. The willingness to invest in and maintain this capacity diminishes with the duration of the relationship (once it survives the early years), which leads to an increase in the hazard rate of eventual dissolution of the relationship because of unacceptable performance. These concepts are exemplified in the Heinz case, as is an understanding of the relationship between organization design and audit risk.

RESEARCH STRATEGIES AND METHODS

Incorporating organization-level variables in research on the assessment of inherent and control risk could proceed along several paths. Although this list is by no means exhaustive, several possibilities come to mind: (1) descriptive studies of procedures and heuristics utilized by public accounting firms for conducting and integrating an analysis of the client organization into the planning of the audit; (2) empirical investigations of the relationship between organization design variables (as discussed in this chapter) and components of the AR model; (3) human information processing research involving organization design variables, institutional structure of the audit relationship, and assessment of AR; (4) diagnoses of organization culture for AR-related dimensions, such as control consciousness and ethical climate; and (5) the organization design of the audit process.

Devising approaches for studying variable-rich phenomena such as those present in auditing and organization design, represents a major challenge and will require new approaches. Campbell (1977) suggested that "very intensive and very thorough case studies" (p. 54) might provide the basis for advancing theory and practice. Case research implies a researcher/practitioner partnership. However, as Beyer and Trice (1982) suggested, it has been difficult to engineer such relationships and lack of utilization of research findings may be due to the lack of attention by researchers to the needs of practitioners and to the political realtities of the organization being studied.

Case studies, however intense and thorough, have provided rich insights. It has proven difficult, nevertheless, to aggregate and generalize findings from a collection of single cases which are not comparable on many dimensions, such as organization context, variables studied, and data collected.

Recently, however, new approaches to case research have been appearing in the literature. Such research involves multiple longitudinal enthnographic precessual research (Van De Ven, Angle, and Poole, 1989). Like single case research, it requires access and cooperation from real-world organizations (i.e., public accounting firms and/or their clients). The research involves a collaborative effort of a multidisciplinary team (e.g., with a background in auditing, organization theory, ethnographic methods, and qualitative data analysis).

This approach to case study research "investigates a contemporary phenomenon within its real life context; when the boundaries between phenomenon and context are not clearly defined; and in which multiple sources of evidence are used" (Yin, 1984, p. 23). As Yin (1984) points out, the multiple sequential case approach has many of the characteristics of a field experiment, without the artificialty of the laboratory or the limitation of single case studies. The replicated case method allows the researcher to validate and generalize "theoretical propositions" (Yin, 1984, p. 21) on the assumption that each replication represents a separate, independent experiment. As Leonard-Barton (1988) noted that because the context of each case will vary, the grounded theory derived from a series of cases should generalize across a range of situations. Such an approach reduces the need for large samples, but it also does not purport to generalize to a given population. It does, however, provide the means for deriving processual theories, which can be further tested on large samples using traditional survey instruments.

A further variation to the replicated case research approach involves what Lewin and Minton (1986) described as the engineering of organization effectiveness or administrative experimentation (Berlin, 1978). The basic idea is to transform an organization intervention into a carefully planned research episode with the objective of testing causal relationships. The replicated case approach involves observations, interviews, and archival data analysis, and, unlike the engineering approach, it involves no intervention in the process. Thus, the replicated case approach is appropiate when the objective is to compare the planning process of an audit for a totally new client, during the early years of the auditor-client relationship, for various longer durations, and at the time an auditor-client relationship is terminated. The intervention approach is appropriate if the objective is to study the effect of a change in procedures (e.g. the introduction of new heuristics for analyzing client organization design) and comparr the resulting audit planning process with prior practice.

The major obstacle to undertaking replicated case or intervention research is a lack of researchers experienced in the design implementation of such research as well as in the analysis of multiple data sources (see, for example, Leonard-Barton and DeLacy, 1987; Bourgeois and Eisenhardt, 1988). Many of these issues were discussed at the National Science Foundation Conference on Longitudinal Processual Research Methods in Organizations (Austin, Texas September 14-16, 1988). The collection of papers from this conference published in *Organizational Science* (Volume 1, No. 3, 1990) provide a solid basis for researchers interested in such approaches. In addition to the problem of access to field sites and measurement and data analysis issues, there are the limitations that arise from the bounded rationality of principal investigators. These are reflected in the type and scope of research being undertaken (e.g., single retrospective case studies, exploratory or pilot studies, laboratory experiments, and questionnaire surveys) and in the advocacy for simplified theories or for a few qualitative organizing concepts. Much of the information processing research on judgment and auditing reflects these limitations.

The human information processing paradigm, however, can provide opportunities for new directions. Following Libby, Artman, and Willingham (1985), it should be feasible to explore the assessment of inherent and control risk by designing experimental situations that incorporate information on a combination of organization-level variables and that attempt to directly test some of the propositions developed in this chapter.

A more difficult challenge involves research on organization culture, using dimensions that can be hypothsized to be related to components of the AR model. The diagnosing of organization culture is not well developed. Kilman and Saxton (1983) have developed the Culture Gap[sm] Survey, which assesses work-group norms. However, it remains to relate such norms to observed behaviors in organizations or to specific outcomes. In the context of auditing, it would be useful to measure control consciousness or ethical climate and to relate these measures in causal or correlational terms to audit risk.

The complexity of organizations as a function of the large number of variables, as well as the complexity of the audit process and the audit judgments auditors are called upon to make, is not in dispute. However, auditing and organization scholars must accept the challenge of complexity and the imperative of devising appropriate research strategies. This challenge is taking on a new urgency as societal expectations about the role of the auditing profession are being debated and redefined and as practitioners increasingly turn to academic research for answers.

NOTE

1. For large divisionalized, multi-market multi-product firms, the environmental analysis must be undertaken for each business.

REFERENCES

American Accounting Association, Report of the Committee on the Relationship of Behavioral Science to Accounting, Sarasota, FL: American Accounting Association, 1974.

Argyris, C., *The Impact of Budgets on People,* Controllership Foundation, 1952.

Argyris, C., "Human Problems with Budgets," *Harvard Business Review* 31, no. 1 (1953): 97-110.

Ashton, R. H., "Human Information Processing in Accounting," *Studies in Accounting Research,* no. 17, Sarasota, FL: American Accounting Association, (1982).

Berlin, V. N., "Administrative Experimentation: A Methodology for More Rigorous Muddling Through," *Management Science* 24 (1978): 789-799.

Beyer, J. M., and H. M. Trice, "The Utilization Process: A Conceptual Framework and Synthesis of Empirical Findings," *Administration Science Quarterly* 27 (1982): 591-622.

Bourgeois, L .J., III, and K. M. Eisenhardt, "Strategic Decision Processes in High Velocity Environments: Four Cases in the Microcomputer Industry," *Management Science* 34, no. 7 (1988): 616-835.

Campbell, J. P., "On the Nature of Organizational Effectiveness," in P. S. Goodman and J.M. Pennings, eds., *New Perspectives on Organizational Effectiveness*, San Francisco: Jossey-Bass, 1977, pp. 13-55.

Clinard, M. B., *Corporate Ethics and Crime*, Beverly Hills, CA: Sage, 1983.

Cook, K., "Exchange and Power in Networks of Interorganizational Relations," *Sociological Quarterly* 18 (1977): 62-82.

Cook, K. S., and R. M. Emerson, "Power, Equity and Commitment in the Exchange Networks," *American Sociological Review* 43 (1978): 721-739.

Cushing, B. E., and J. K. Loebbecke, "Comparison of Audit Methodologies of Large Accounting Firms," Accounting Research Study No. 26, American Accounting Association, 1986.

Cyert, R. M. and J. G. March, *A Behavioral Theory of the Firm*, Englewood Cliffs, NJ: Prentice-Hall, 1963.

Derry, R., "Moral Reasoning in Work Related Conflicts," in W. Frederick, ed., *Research in Corporate Social Performance and Policy*, vol. 9, Greenwich, Conn.: JAI Press, 1987.

Dirsmith, M. W., and J. P. McAllister, "The Organic vs. the Mechanistic Audit," *Journal of Accounting, Auditing and Finance* (1982a): 214-228.

Dirsmith, M. W., and J. P. McAllister, "The Organic vs. the Mechanistic Audit: Problems and Pitfalls (Part II)," *Journal of Accounting, Auditing and Finance* 6, no. 1 (Fall 1982b): 60-74.

Duncan, R., "What Is the Right Organization Structure? A Decision Tree Analysis Provides The Answer," *Organizational Dynamics* (Winter 1979): 59-80.

Edwards, W., "Utility Subjective Probability, Their Interaction, and Variance Preferences," *Journal of Conflict Resolution* 6, no. 1 (March 1962): 42-51.

Elliot, R. K., "The Future of Audit Research," *The Auditor's Report* (1981): 1-12.

Galbraith, J. R., "Organization Design: An Information Processing View," *Interfaces* 4, no. 3 (May 1974): 28-36.

Green, D. O., "Behavioral Science and Accounting Research," in N. Dopuch and L. Revsine (eds), *Accounting Research 1960-1970: A Critical Evaluation*, Urbana: University of Illinois, 1973, pp. 93-104.

Hammond, K. R., "Probabilistic Functioning and the Clinical Method," *Psychological Review* 62, no. 4 (July 1955): 255-262.

Hofstede, G. H., *The Game of Budget Control*, New York: Van Nostrand, 1967.

Hofstedt, T. R., "A State-of-the-Art Analysis of Behavioral Accounting Research," *Journal of Contemporary Business* 4, no. 4 (Autumn 1975): 27-49.

Holstrum, G. L., "Audit Judgment Research," *The Auditor's Report* (1981): 4-5.

Kilman, R. H., and M .J. Saxton, *Culture Gap^sm Survey*, Organization Design Consultants Inc., 1983.

Kinney, W. R., "Audit Technology and Preferences for Auditing Standards," *Journal of Accounting and Economics* 8 (1986): 73-89.

Leonard-Barton, D., "Implementation as Mutual Adaptation of Technology and Organization," *Research Policy* 17, no. 5 (October 1988): 251-267.

Leonard-Barton, D., and B. DeLacy, *Skunkworks at Digital Equipment Corporation: The Tale of ECON*, Harvard Business School Case Services, 1987.

Levinthal, D. A., and M. Fichman, "Dynamics of Interorganizational Attachments: Auditor-Client Relationships," *Administrative Science Quarterly* 33 (1988): 345-369.

Lewin, A. Y., and J. W. Minton, "Determining Organizational Effectiveness: Another Look, and An Agenda for Research," *Management Science* 32, no. 5 (May 1986): 514-538.

Libby, R., *Accounting and Human Information Processing: Theory and Applications*, Englewood Cliffs, NJ: Prentice-Hall, 1981.

Libby, R., J. T. Artman, and J. J. Willingham, "Process Susceptibility, Control Risk, and Audit Planning," *Accounting Review* 60, no. 2 (1985): 212-225.

Macaulay, S., "Non-Contractual Relations in Business," *American Sociological Review* 28 (1963): 55-70.

Mackenzie, K. D., "Virtual Positions and Power," *Management Science* 32, no. 5 (May 1986): 622-642.

March, J. G., and Z. Shapira, "Behavioral Decision Theory and Organizational Decision Theory," in G. R. Ungson and D. N. Braunstein (eds.), *Decision Making: An Interdisciplinary Inquiry*, Boston, Mass.: Kent Publishing, 1982, pp. 92-115.

Monteverde, K., and D. Teece, "Supplier Switching Costs and Vertical Integration in the Automobile Industry," *Administrative Science Quarterly* 23 (1982): 434-453.

Nadler, D., and M. Tushman, "Concepts, Tools, and Processes," *Strategic Organization Design*, Greenwood, Ill.: Scott, Foresman, 1988.

Nelson, R., and S. Winter, *An Evolutionary Theory of Economic Change*, Cambridge, Mass.: Harvard University Press, 1982.

Pennings, J. M., *Origins and Consequences of Connections Among Directorates*, San Francisco: Jossey-Bass, 1980.

Pfeffer, J., and G. R. Salancik, *The External Control of Organizations: A Resource Dependent Perspective*, New York: Harper and Row, 1978.

Schiff, M., and A. Y. Lewin, "The Impact of People on Budgets," *Accounting Review* 45, no. 2 (1970): 259-268.

Simon, H. A., *Administratiive Behavior*, 2nd ed. New York: Macmillan, 1957a.

Simon, H. A., *Models of Man,* New York: John Wiley & Sons, 1957b.

Stringer, K. W., "Future Directions for Auditing Research," *Auditor's Report* (1981): 3-4.

Van De Ven, A. H., H. L. Angle, and M. S. Poole, *Research on the Management of Innovation: The Minnesota Studies,* New York: Harper and Row/Ballinger, 1989.

Victor, B., and J. B. Cullen, "The Organizational Bases of Ethical Work Climates," *Administrative Science Quarterly* 33 (1988): 101-125.

Weiss, W. L., "Minerva's Owl: Building a Corporate Value System," *Journal of Business Ethics* 5 (1986): 243-247.

Williamson, O. E., "The Economics of Organization: The Transaction Cost Approach," *American Journal of Sociology* 87 (1981): 548-577.

Yin, R. K., *Case Study Research: Design and Methods,* Beverly Hills, Calif.: Sage Publications, 1984.

Part V

Industry and Economy

13

Longitudinal Analysis of Industries: An Ordinal Time Series Approach

Timothy W. Ruefli
Ana R. Adaniya
J. Armando Gallegos
Seong-Joon Limb

While studies emphasizing industry as the unit of analysis may be the rule in industrial organization economics (for a survey, see, e.g., Shepard, 1979), the firm is clearly the unit of analysis of choice in strategic management studies. In the strategic management literature, the industry *per se* has been the primary unit of analysis in studies by Reilly and Drzycimski (1974), Dess and Beard (1984), Conrad and Plotkin (1968), Bowman (1980), Figenbaum and Thomas (1985, 1986, 1988), Wernerfelt and Montgomery (1986), and a few others. Aside from these few instances, industry-level concerns appear in strategic management research primarily as the context for interfirm rivalry. The emphasis on the industry context varies from very important in population-ecology studies [Aldrich (1979); Aldrich and Pfeffer (1976); McKelvey and Aldrich (1983)] and resource dependence theories [Pfeffer (1972); Jacobs (1974); Midlin and Aldrich (1975), Pfeffer and Salancik (1978)], to moderately important, in the works of Ansoff (1965), Hambrick (1982), Hofer (1975), Hitt and Ireland (1985), Huff (1982), and Porter (1980, 1985), among others, to an effect to be controlled or tested [e.g., Christensen and Montgomery (1981), Bettis and Hall (1981), Gupta (1969), Rumelt (1982)]. Techniques to aid practitioners in determining or evaluating corporate strategy often include consideration of industry attributes, whether in the relatively precise form of industry growth in the BCG matrix (Gale, 1972) or in the vague industry attractiveness of General Electric's Business Screen (Hofer and Schendel, 1978; Hax and Majluf, 1983).

A series of studies (Ruefli, 1990; Ruefli and Wilson, 1987; Ruefli, 1988) has shown the applicability of ordinal time series analysis to firms in the context of an industry or to firms in the context of an economy. This chapter will present an exploratory study to ascertain the suitability of ordinal analysis when the industry is the focus of analysis. The investigation will start with a brief overview of the ordinal methodology and of the information statistics employed in ordinal analysis. This will be followed by an empirical analysis of 101 industries and an examination of the rank behavior over time of selected industries. Information statistics will be used to examine interindustry behavior on nine dimensions. To complement this analysis and address in a preliminary way some of the questions raised by the interindustry analysis, information statistics for internal analysis of two selected industries will be presented. The chapter will conclude with implications of the findings to date and directions for further study.

APPROACH

Ordinal Time Series Analysis

The approaches to interindustry analysis found in the literature have been based on cardinal (absolute) data in cardinal space (see, e.g., Reilly and Drzycimski, 1974; Dess and Beard, 1984; Conrad and Plotkin, 1968; Bowman, 1980; Figenbaum and Thomas, 1985, 1986, 1988; Wernerfelt and Montgomery, 1986). In so doing, the emphasis inherent in the data is on the relation of an industry to its own historical performance. Relative effects are introduced only in terms of aggregate interactions in the selected methodology or in comparisons of results after the analysis has been run. In this study we will employ ordinal time series analysis (Ruefli and Wilson, 1987; Ruefli, 1990) in which cardinal data are transformed into ordinal data through a simple ranking procedure. Analysis will thus be accomplished in ordinal space. Such a transformation has a number of salutary effects on the analysis. First, the relative effects among and within industries, since they are represented in the ordinal data, are incorporated in a study prior to the analysis, in contrast to the case of cardinal analysis, wherein relative effects are not developed until the analysis phase or later. The relative nature of the ordinal data and methodology has the effect of placing a strategic emphasis on the analysis. Second, only relative effects (i.e., differential impacts across industries) are shown by the ordinal data; the common effects of business cycles or other macroeconomic impulses are removed by the ordinal transformation. Third, in a like manner, temporal effects in the data are removed, so the need for indexing for inflation, etc., is not present in ordinal analysis. Fourth, ordinal analysis is not sensitive to errors in the data (Brockett and Kemperman, 1980) unless they are large enough to induce rank shifts; thus, the technique works with "dirty" data that might render cardinal analysis unusable. Fifth, ordinal analysis improves the comparability among results on different dimensions. Because the ordinal transformation also introduces a common scaling factor, there is no need for further interdimensional scaling. As a byproduct of the common scaling, graphical display of interindustry results is enhanced.

Ordinal Production Functions

One of the problems in a strategic analysis is to establish a reference point from which evaluations can be made i.e., a bench mark against which to measure behavior; a similar situation obtains in interindustry analysis. To compare industry behaviors, it would be desirable to have a starting point. Analysis in ordinal space is able to establish such a reference point via the concept of an ordinal production function. Cardinal production functions relate inputs to outputs in cardinal space (Henderson and Quandt, 1980, p. 65). By analogy, ordinal production functions relate input ranks to output ranks in ordinal space. That is, for the $\mathcal{L}^{th}$ output, the ordinal production function for the ith industry is

$$qr_{i,\mathcal{L}} = f_i (xr_{i,1}, xr_{i,2}, \dots xr_{i,n1}; yr_{i,1}, yr_{i,2}, \dots yr_{i,n2}) \qquad (1)$$

where $qr_{i,\mathcal{L}}$ is the rank of the $\mathcal{L}^{th}$ output, $xr_{i,j}$ is the rank of the jth input, and $yr_{i,k}$ is the rank of the kth process or intermediate product. Relation (1) holds for all industries and outputs.

Given this function and the fact that each industry, for a given dimension, has a unique rank, assigned from a finite set of ranks, we can establish a reference point for each industry by assuming that scale effects predominate. In this case, for a given industry the rank across all dimensions would be the same; that is, $qr_{i,\mathcal{L}} = xr_{i,j} = yr_{i,k}$ for all i, j, k, $\mathcal{L}$. This is the ordinal equivalent of a cardinal production function that is homogeneous of degree one (Henderson and Quandt, 1980, pp. 111-114).

The equi-rank production function provides a basis for evaluating the behavior of industries, albeit a relative basis. This is possible because a finite number of ranks are employed, and if one industry has a better rank on dimension A than it does on dimension B, there is at least one other industry for which the opposite is true. This characteristic will serve as a basis for the first part of the interindustry analysis.

Ordinal Statistics

Ordinal time series analysis employs a set of rank statistics (Ruefli and Wilson, 1987, pp. 648-654) and a set of information statistics (Ruefli and Wilson, 1987, pp. 654-658) to describe the relative behavior of the entities being analyzed. Only the information statistics will be used here, and these will be outlined below.

Given a set of industries, ranked along a given dimension in each year, it is possible to generate an incidence matrix, T, whose elements, $(t_{i,j})$, are the number of times an industry made a transition from rank i to rank j. This incidence matrix can be converted to a transition matrix by dividing each element by the total number of transitions to yield a transition matrix, P, whose elements, $[p_{i,j}] = [t_{i,j}/(\Sigma_i \Sigma_j t_{i,j})]$, are the probabilities (in frequency terms) of transitions from rank to another (see Figure 13.1).

Figure 13.1. Transition Matrix
(p_{ij} = the frequency of observed transitions from rank i to rank j)

		1	2	3	. .	n
			RANK T + 1			
R		1	2	3	. .	n
A						
N	1	$p_{1,1}$	$p_{1,2}$	$p_{1,3}$	. .	$p_{1,n}$
K	2	$p_{2,1}$	$p_{2,2}$	$p_{2,3}$	. .	$p_{2,n}$
	3	$p_{3,1}$	$p_{3,2}$	$p_{3,3}$	. .	$p_{3,n}$
T	.	.	.	.	. .	.
	.	.	.	.	. .	.
	n	$p_{n,1}$	$p_{n,2}$	$p_{n,3}$	. .	$p_{n,n}$

Having developed a transition matrix for the sample of industries, the next step is to compute information statistics that give the amount of uncertainty associated with the rank transition process. This is accomplished by employing a variation of the entropy function (Ruefli and Wilson 1987). For the cell representing the transition from rank i to rank j, the total uncertainty associated with the transformation is

$$H_{i,j} = -p_{i,j} \ln (p_{i,j}); \quad 0 \le p_{i,j} \le 1 \tag{2}$$

The total uncertainty for the whole process is simply the sum of entropies over all cells:

$$H_{i,j} = -\Sigma_i \Sigma_j \, p_{i,j} \ln (p_{i,j}); \Sigma_i \Sigma_j \, p_{i,j} = 1 \tag{3}$$

To allow for comparisons between processes with differing numbers of industries, equation (3) must be normalized. This is accomplished by dividing the expression in equation (3) by the maximum possible uncertainty that can be generated in a process represented by an n-by-n matrix. Such a matrix would have $1/n^2$ in each cell and a total uncertainty of $2\ln(n)$. Dividing equation (3) by this value gives an expression for the total relative uncertainty:

$$H_{rel} = -\Sigma_i \Sigma_j \, p_{i,j} \frac{\ln (p_{i,j})}{2\ln(n)}; \; \Sigma_i \Sigma_j \, p_{i,j} = 1 \tag{4}$$

Total relative uncertainty has a component that is of interest in assessing inter-industry and intraindustry behavior, and that is the uncertainty associated with industries losing position in the rank transition process. The total uncertainty associated with loss of position is called total risk and can be computed by noting that in a transition matrix, those entries that lie above the main diagonal are associated with loss of rank position (see Figure 13.2). To find total relative risk for a process, all that is necessary is to sum the relative entropies of those cells above the diagonal:

Figure 13.2. Partitioning of Total Uncertainty

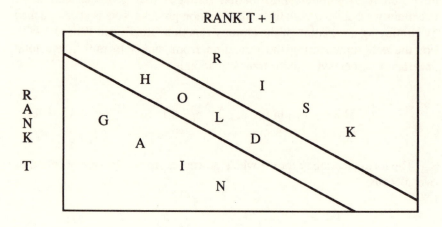

$$\text{Risk}_{rel} = -\Sigma_i\ \Sigma_{i<j}\ p_{i,j}\ \frac{\ln\ (p_{i,j})}{2\ln(n)};\ \Sigma_i\ \Sigma_j\ p_{i,j} = 1 \qquad (5)$$

The measures of total relative uncertainty and total relative risk developed above will be computed for the rank transition process on each of nine dimensions of the sample set of industries and for the rank transition process of the firms in two selected industries. The results will allow the comparison across dimensions and across levels of the industrial economy of the uncertainties associated with both levels of the hierarchy.

DATA

The data for this study were drawn from the COMPUSTAT aggregate file of 282 industries (*Standard and Poor's,* 1989), which is organized at the four-digit SIC code level (U.S. Office of Management and Budget, 1972). Industries with the most complete data for the period 1969 to 1988 were selected, yielding 101 industries for analysis. (The Appendix lists the industries in the sample.) While these industries were not selected on a randomized basis, the only known bias introduced by the selection procedure was toward good reporters, and, thus, the sample is felt to be fairly representative of all industries.

For each industry, data on eight dimensions of size and performance (assets, revenues, employees, common equity, net income, ROA, ROE,

ROS) over the period 1969 to 1988 were assembled, while R&D expenditures for the period 1975 to 1988 were compiled, yielding nine dimensions for analysis. To provide a perspective on intraindustry behavior, data on the same nine dimensions were collected for all of the COMPUSTAT firms in two of the industries in the sample, petroleum refining and pharmaceuticals. These latter two industries were selected for reasons that will become clear shortly.

Data for R&D expenditures at the industry level were available only for the fourteen-year period 1975 to 1988; thus, for this dimension, statistics were computed only for this period. To provide comparability, statistics for the other dimensions were computed on a longitudinal basis with a fourteen-year rolling window. Not only did this permit comparison across all dimensions in the last fourteen-year period calculated, but also it allowed comparisons over time on the other eight dimensions.

RESULTS

Interindustry

Rank Positions. To illustrate the ability of ordinal statistics to characterize the relative performance of industries over time, the position statistics on all nine dimensions were grouped by industry. Figures 13.4 through 13.8 depict examples of the types of ordinal profiles represented in the sample. Figure 13.3 shows the ordinal behavior of the aluminum industry on nine dimensions for the period 1969 to 1988. Most noticeable here is the cyclic pattern of relative returns for this industry. Note that these cycles are not due to economywide fluctuations that affect all industries. The ordinal transformation eliminates the common effects of such global swings. What remain are the differential effects, from industry to industry, of global and local economic activities. In the case of aluminum, the most recent upswing was completed in 1988, and if past cyclic experience holds, it can be predicted that the industry is in for a period of relative declines in returns. Note that revenue position, which is equivalent to industry share of the total economy, has declined at a slow, but steady pace until the last two years, when a slight recovery began. Note also that in terms of an ordinal production function for this industry, the departure from the equi-rank case is such that the ranks of assets, employees, equity, revenue, and net income are all generally better than return ranks.

Figure 13.3. Aluminum Industry Ordinal Behavior

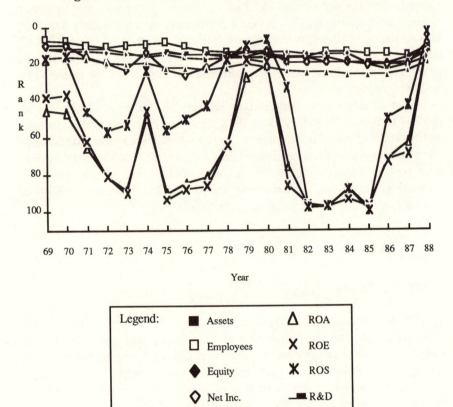

Figure 13.4 depicts the relative performance of the computer and office equipment industry. It indicates that this industry has a high and stable position relative to other industries in the sample on revenues, employees, assets, net income, equity, and R&D expenditures. Returns for this industry are less cohesive than they were for the aluminum industry, and they have a less clear cyclic pattern. In terms of an ordinal production function, the pattern for computers and office equipment is similar to that for aluminum.

General industrial machinery and equipment is an industry that is clearly in relative decline, as Figure 13.5 indicates. The decline on almost all dimensions was clear from the outset, and only in the last year studied does there appear to be a general increase. Note that, in terms of an ordinal production function, return ranks were better than other ranks in the period 1969 to 1975, but since then they have been at best equivalent in rank.

Figure 13.4.   Computer and Office Equipment Industry Ordinal Behavior

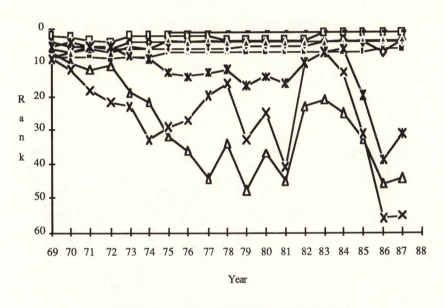

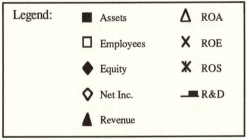

Petroleum refining in Figure 13.6 displays a cyclic pattern in returns that is characterized by sharp relative improvements, coupled with gradual worsenings in positions. All other dimensions are relatively stable and follow an exaggerated pattern similar to that shown by the aluminum industry with respect to return and other ranks.

Pharmaceutical industry data were available for the period 1973 to 1988 and display the pattern in Figure 13.7. While there is some cyclicality in returns, with the exception of ROE, it takes place in a very narrow band of rank positions. In terms of an ordinal production function, the graph does reveal that the industry was relatively more labor-intensive than asset-intensive (since rank by employees was better than rank by assets in all years) and that the industry gained position over time on almost all dimensions.

Figure 13.5. General Industrial Products Industry Ordinal Behavior

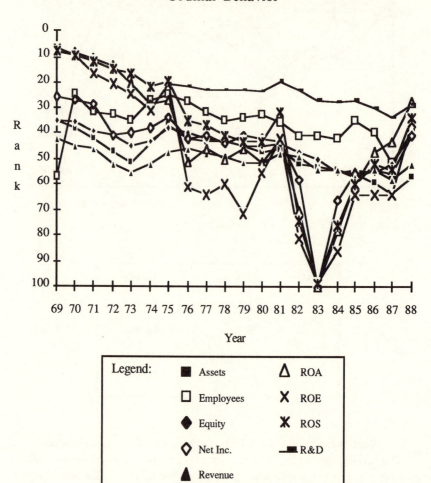

One conclusion that can be drawn from the foregoing is that, as maintained by industrial organization theory and in the strategic management literature by Dess and Beard (1984), industries do have different longitudinal patterns and levels of performance. Further, from the graphs it is clear that industry-level studies that examine periods of half a decade or even a decade are likely to be biased (especially in terms of returns) by their selection of time period and are therefore limited in their generalizability. Clearly, such studies should be characterized by longer time periods.

Figure 13.6. Petroleum Industry Ordinal Behavior

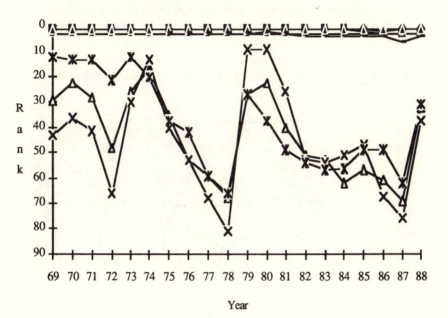

Information Statistics. Total uncertainty statistics for the sample of
101 industries were computed on all dimensions except R&D for the period
1969 to 1988. Data for aggregate R&D expenditures were available only for
the period 1975 to 1988. Total uncertainty was calculated on a fourteen-year
rolling-window basis for all dimensions. The results are shown in Figure
13.8. Interestingly, the pattern of information statistics over time was quite
stable. The uncertainty associated with return positions was the highest and
clustered at about one-third of the maximum possible uncertainty. Levels of
uncertainty associated with rank shifts in terms of numbers of employees and
levels of net income were roughly comparable, as were the levels of
uncertainty for the other four dimensions. While the small number of
dimensions prohibited meaningful computation of levels of significance for
the differences in the three groups, their differences are obvious in the graph.

Figure 13.7. Pharmaceutical Industry Ordinal Behavior

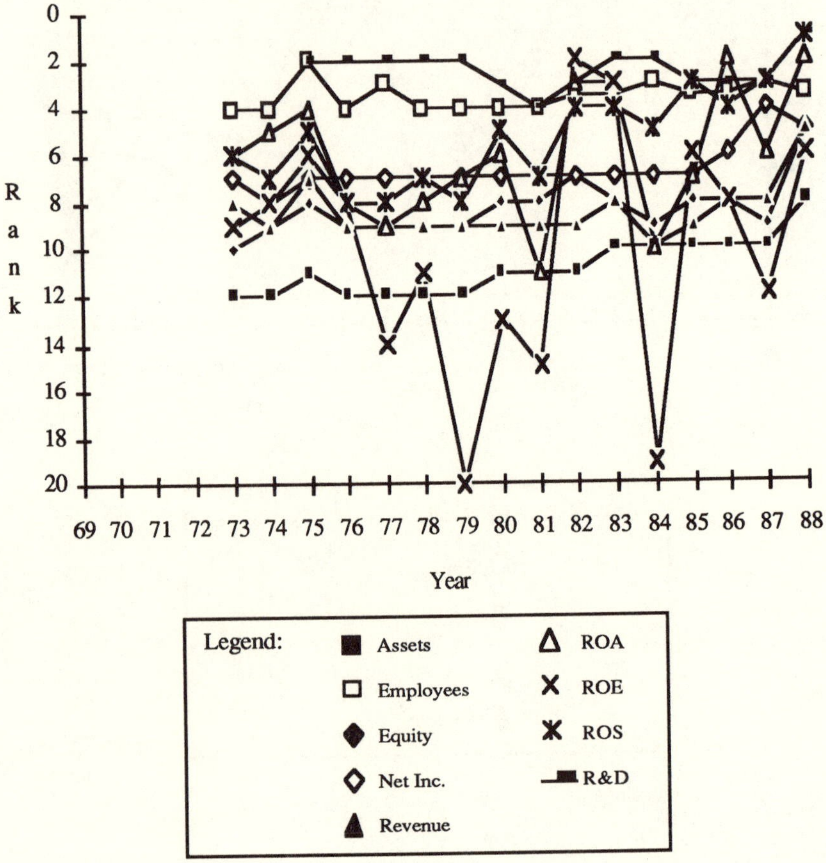

Figure 13.8. Total Uncertainty for Entire Sample of Industries

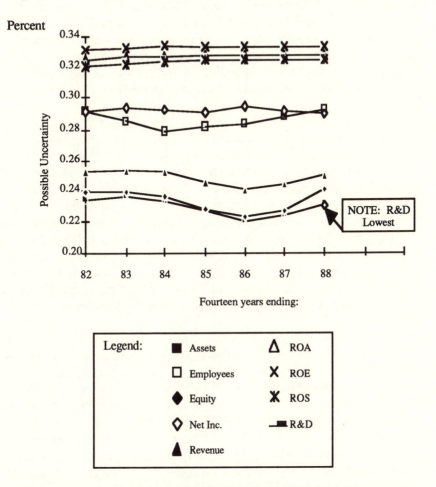

The levels of uncertainty reported above indicate that while there was a moderate amount of uncertainty associated with rank shifts, the level was far from that which would characterize a random walk. There was a slight upward trend in these statistics over time, reflecting some change in the rank shift process among industries in the later years of the study. Levels of uncertainty for revenues, equity, and assets moved together and showed a decrease through the period ending in 1986, with a slight increase in the next two periods.

The most surprising finding of this research was that the most stable dimension in terms of position shifts in the period 1975 to 1988 was dollar expenditures on R&D. Uncertainty associated with this dimension was about

23 percent of the total possible and indicated that each industry's share of expenditures on R&D remained relatively stable over time across the 101 industries in the sample. As Figure 13.8 indicates, rank transitions for R&D expenditures were slightly more certain than were transitions for assets. This implies that industries are stratified by R&D expenditures, and this result holds over time. Closer reexamination of Figures 13.3 through 13.7 will reveal considerable stability in the R&D expenditure rank of the industries graphed.

While this research found no definitive explanation for this surprising result, it is possible to speculate on the reasons for its existence. For one thing, industries in the COMPUSTAT database are defined by SIC codes, which, in turn, are based on product line commonalties, which, in turn, are related to a specific technology. The result may be therefore due, in part, to the effectiveness of the SIC code definitions. The stratification by R&D expenditures implies that each technology carries with it a set of opportunities that are subscribed to by the firms in the associated industry. These opportunities are such that the expected marginal return from a dollar investment in one technology is equal to a dollar cost at a cumulative level of investment (across firms in an industry) that is roughly in the same proportion to the similar cumulative levels of investment in other technologies over time.

While the total uncertainty associated with a system is of broad interest, of more specific interest is information associated with the chance of loss of position. This information is available by simply adding the entropy levels of those cells that are above the diagonal in the transition matrix. When this is done for each dimension on a fourteen-year rolling-window basis, the results are as graphed in Figure 13.9. The relative positions of the dimensions are as they were for total uncertainty. The risk associated with industry rank shifts has, over the seven periods examined, declined for all dimensions for which data were available. R&D rank shifts had the lowest risk level in the only period for which there were R&D expenditure data.

Conclusions. The results of the interindustry ordinal analysis indicate that while there is a considerable degree of stability among industries, there are enough differences in levels and patterns to support the contention that the interindustry level is significant as a strategic context. The results at this level clearly suggest that a analysis similar to that applied above should be applied with industries to determine if the degree of stability exhibited between industries is replicated by firms within industries.

Figure 13.9. Interindustry Risk for Sample of 101 Industries

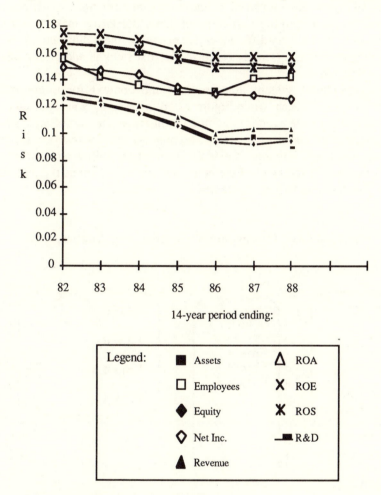

Intraindustry

The findings above raise the question of whether the uncertainty and risk levels and patterns observed at the interindustry level, especially those regarding R&D expenditure positions, are duplicated at the intraindustry level. This question is at the heart of the historical differences between industrial organization economics and strategic management research. The former has traditionally maintained the primacy of interindustry effects, while the latter has emphasized the importance of management and intra-industry effects. In the last decade or so, a number of articles (Caves and Pugel, 1980;

Cubbins and Geroski, 1987; Martin, 1983; Ravenscraft, 1983; Gale, 1972; Shepard, 1972) in the industrial economics literature have questioned traditional beliefs by noting that intraindustry differences may be more important than interindustry differences. By extending the ordinal analysis to the intraindustry level, this study can take the first steps in addressing this issue in ordinal terms.

The hierarchical system that provides the context for inter- and intraindustry analysis is shown in Figure 13.10. Interindustry analysis takes place at the level of the economy, with an industry as the unit of analysis. Intraindustry analysis takes place at the level of an industry, with a firm as the unit of analysis. Implicit in this framework is a third possibility, and that is to carry out analysis at the level of the economy, with the firm as the unit of analysis. This last case will not be treated in this research.

Figure 13.10. Hierarchical Context for Analysis

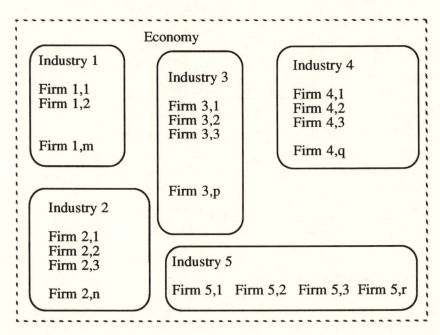

The traditional input/output (I/O) paradigm maintains that interindustry behaviors predominate over intraindustry effects. To examine this proposition in a preliminary fashion, intraindustry (firm-level) data were gathered for two industries of the 101 included in the industry sample. These two industries, petroleum refining and pharmaceuticals, were selected because they were mature and presumably stable industries. Such stability should bias the results of the intraindustry analyses against uncertainty in rank shifts, so that any findings of uncertainty here should be more meaningful.

Data on the same dimensions and time periods employed in the inter-industry analysis were collected from the COMPUSTAT database for twenty-eight petroleum refining firms and for forty-seven pharmaceutical firms. Data equivalent to those used in the industry analysis were not available for lines of business, so consolidated corporate data were used. However, since most of the firms in each of these industries obtain the bulk of their revenues and earnings from one line of business, any discrepancy was felt to be mitigated and, in any case, was biased in the direction of stability.

Petroleum Refining Industry. Uncertainty and risk statistics were computed for both industries in a fashion analogous to that used at the industry level. Figure 13.11 graphs the fourteen-year window results for total uncertainty for petroleum refiners. Several interesting points can be made from this graph. First, the levels of total uncertainty concerning rank shifts within the petroleum refining industry are about half those found in the interindustry study. This is as would be expected for a stable industry. Second, R&D expenditure rank shifts are the most uncertain of all the dimensions for all periods. Third, the uncertainties associated with return positions are at the middle levels of uncertainties on all dimensions. Risk levels for the petroleum refining industry are relatively stable (Figure 13.12). R&D expenditures are the most unstable in the first two periods, they are replaced by number of employees for four periods, and ROA rank shifts are the most uncertain in the last period. The patterns of intraindustry rank behavior thus differ significantly from those found at the interindustry level.

Pharmaceutical Industry. Information statics for the pharmaceutical industry are graphed in Figures 13.13 and 13.14. Total uncertainty in Figure 13.13 shows an increasing trend on all dimensions except R&D expenditures, which stayed steady at about 22 percent of total possible uncertainty. In the period ending in 1982 uncertainty levels were below those of the interindustry analysis, but above those found for petroleum refining. Return uncertainty levels were the highest and were clustered in the same fashion as in the interindustry findings. Shifts in position by number of employees emerged as the most stable. Risk measures for the pharmaceutical firms showed the same upward trend and patterns as did the total uncertainty statistics, with R&D expenditures maintaining the same level over all seven periods (see Figure 13.14)

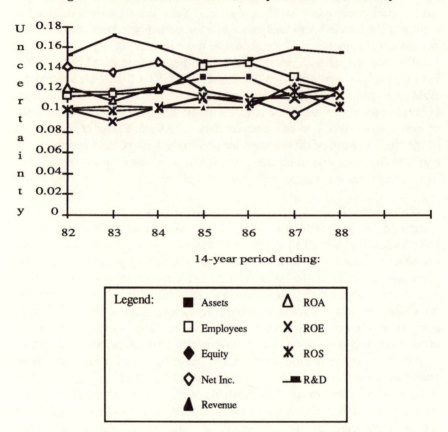

Figure 13.11. Petroleum Industry Total Uncertainty

14-year period ending:

Legend:
- ■ Assets
- □ Employees
- ◆ Equity
- ◇ Net Inc.
- ▲ Revenue
- △ ROA
- X ROE
- ✖ ROS
- ■— R&D

Conclusions. The intraindustry analysis of two industries indicated that the patterns of rank shift behavior found at this level differ from those found at the interindustry level. While results from a sample of two do not provide conclusive evidence, the findings are strongly suggestive that different processes are at work at different levels of the economy. For example, the relative stability found in R&D expenditure rank shifts at the interindustry level was not replicated at the intraindustry level for either industry examined. This implies that while there may be rank stability across industries, within an industry the firms invest different amounts in R&D from year to year. Jockeying for position within the industry, firms have invested in R&D and then have been surpassed in expenditures along this dimension in subsequent periods. Clustering of rank statistics and patterns over time differed considerably from level to level, thus arguing for treating each level as a distinct area of research.

Figure 13.12. Petroleum Industry Strategic Risk

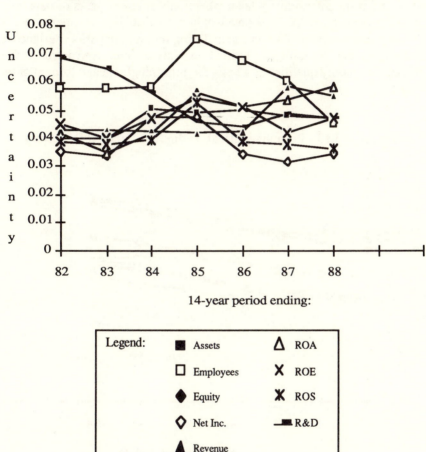

IMPLICATIONS

The findings of this research should be placed in the context of the limitations under which the study operated. First, only twenty years worth of industry data for 101 industries were used. While this far exceeds the data usually employed by studies reported in the strategic management literature (notable exceptions do exist at the firm level—e.g., Cool and Schendel,

1987; Miller and Friesen, 1982—in particular, and among population-ecology studies in general), the results show that these data were barely enough to identify relevant patterns in some cases and, by implication, were inadequate to reveal other long-term patterns. This data constraint is especially relevant to the findings regarding the stability of R&D expenditure positions at the interindustry level where only fourteen years of data were available. Finally, as has been noted, only two substudies were performed at the intraindustry level. This was quite fitting for an initial effort designed to investigate the suitability of ordinal analysis to inter- and intraindustry studies, but hardly qualifies as a basis for a meaningful generalization of the results.

Figure 13.13. Pharmaceutical Industry Total Uncertainty

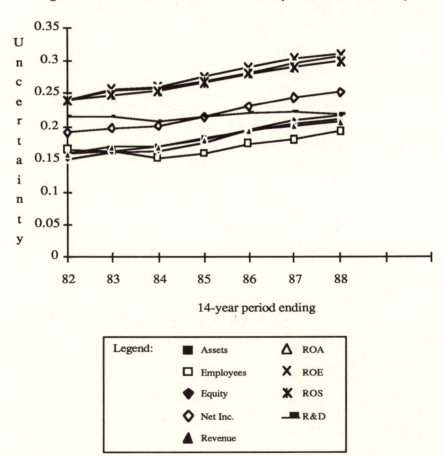

Figure 13.14. Pharmaceutical Industry Strategic Risk

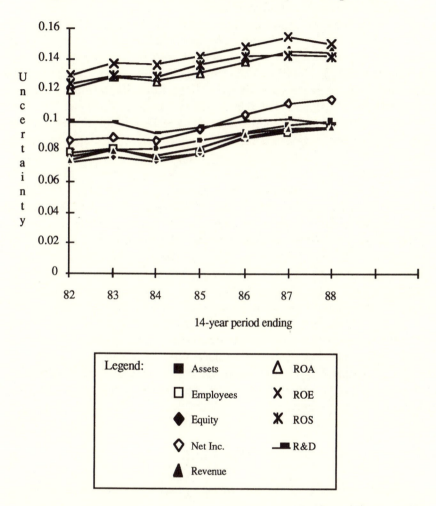

Given the limitations cited above, several conclusions can be drawn from the analysis. First, in regard to the counterintuitive findings on the relative stability of R&D expenditure positions, it appears that technologies offer a set of investment opportunities that differ in relative magnitude across technologies, that these differences remain over time, and that firms within an industry will subscribe to these opportunities, but at levels that differ in a relative fashion over time. These results can be partially motivated by noting that SIC definitions are based on groups of similar product lines, which, in turn, are related to technologies. The findings of stability in terms of R&D

expenditures may be due, in part, to the efficacy of the SIC code definitions in relation to the underlying technologies.

A second important result is that for the types of studies implied by inter- versus intraindustry issues, multidecade periods are required. As the findings here indicate, half-decade or even decade results may not be sufficient because they may suffer from bias introduced by industry cycles or random impulses. Further, the results strongly suggest that some form of relative analysis is beneficial in reducing the effects of business cycles, etc.

The empirical results reported here support the findings of stratification in relative industry performance found in other studies. This lends support to the industrial organization model regarding the importance of choice of industry, but modifies it to make it contingent on the cyclical nature of industry performance. The results also lend support to diversification strategy models. Qualifying these implications, which are drawn at the interindustry level, are the findings at the intraindustry level. Shifts in rank position on all dimensions support the relative emphasis placed on management by the strategic management approaches. Even in mature, stable industries, such as petroleum refining and pharmaceuticals, there is substantial uncertainty regarding rank transitions and, by implication, room for management expertise in guiding individual firms to higher relative levels of performance.

Finally, even the preliminary findings reported here demonstrate that ordinal analysis provides a new perspective that has not been provided by cardinal analysis. Because of the relative nature of the ordinal data and results, an ordinal analysis yields a perspective that is particularly appropriate for strategic management studies, be they at the level of the firm, the industry, or the economy.

DIRECTIONS FOR FURTHER RESEARCH

One measure of the success of an exploratory study is its ability to identify research projects with potential. The set of projects outlined below demonstrates the exploratory power of ordinal analysis.

First, with respect to the theoretical issue of the relative importance of inter- versus. intraindustry effects, the results reported here are not conclusive; rather, they are suggestive. Additional evidence must be sought by developing intraindustry statistics for a random sample of the other 99 industries in the industry sample. In this fashion arguments can be developed that shed light on the relative importance of inter- versus intraindustry effects.

An intriguing, but less straightforward project suggested by the results reported here would be the investigation of the reasons underlying the relative stability of R&D expenditure rankings across industries. Such research would go well beyond the ordinal methodology presented here.

A third project arising out of the research reported here would be the categorization of the contribution of individual industries to interindustry risk and total uncertainty. Collins and Ruefli (1989) have developed a measure of strategic risk that partitions system uncertainties over the entities comprising the system. Applied to the industry data developed for this study, this technique would generate longitudinal measures of the relative uncertainties associated with each industry in the sample. Such information would complement that available in the literature (e.g., Dess and Beard, 1984) and would aid researchers who wish to select industries of various levels of stability (e.g., Fredrickson, 1984; Fredrickson and Mitchell, 1984).

A fourth project would be analogous to the third and would generate uncertainty levels for the firms investigated in the first project mentioned above. Using the same data employed in the first project, Collins and Ruefli's measure of strategic risk could be developed for each firm in each industry sample. The resulting information would be of potential interest to practitioners and academics alike.

Still another research effort would be to attempt to empirically fit an ordinal production function to one or more industries. A preliminary attempt at this has been made in the case of the microelectronics industry (Ruefli, Kozmetsky, and Yue, 1990), with interesting results.

Finally, an interesting empirical study would be to investigate the cyclical nature of relative returns uncovered for some industries in this study. Reasons for the relative cyclical nature of some industries and not others should be sought, and for those industries with cyclic behavior, the types of cyclical behavior should be investigated.

REFERENCES

Aldrich, Howard E., *Organization and Environments*, Prentice-Hall, Englewood Cliffs, NJ (1979).

Aldrich, Howard E., and Jeffrey Pfeffer, "Environments of Organizations," in A. Inkeles (ed.), *Annual Review of Sociology*, Vol. 2, Annual Reviews, Palo Alto, CA (1976): 79-105.

Andrews, K., *The Concept of Corporate Strategy*, 2nd ed., Dow Jones-Irwin, Homewood, IL (1987).

Ansoff, H.I., *Corporate Strategy: An Analytic Approach to Business Policy for Growth and Expansion*, New York: McGraw-Hill (1965).

Bain, J.S., "Relation of Profit Rate to Industry Concentration: American Manufacturing, 1936-40," *Quarterly Journal of Economics* 65 (1951): 293-324.

Baker, S.H., "Risk, Leverage and Profitability: An Industry Analysis," *Review of Economics and Statistics* 55, no. 4 (November 1973): 503-507.

Bass, F. M., P. Cattin, and D. R. Wittink, "Firm Effects and Industry Effects in the Analysis of Market Structure and Profitability," *Journal of Marketing Research* 15, no. 1 (1988): 3-10.

Beard, D., and G. Dess, "Industry Profitability and Firm Performance: A Preliminary Analysis of the Business Portfolio Question," *Academy of Management Proceedings* (February 1979): 123-127.

Bettis, R. A., and W. K. Hall, "Risks and Industry Effects in Large Diversified Firms," *Academy of Management Proceedings* (1981): 17-20.

Biduault, F., "Strategic Management and Resources of Industrial Organization," in J. McGee and H. Thomas (eds), *Strategic Management Research: A European Perspective*, John Wiley & Sons (1986), pp. 109-121.

Bowman, E. H., "A Risk/Return Paradox for Strategic Management," *Sloan Management Review* 2, no. 3 (Spring 1980): 17-31.

Brockett, P. L., and J. H. B. Kemperman, "Statistical Recognition of Trends in Health Monitoring Systems," *Methods of Information in Medicine* 19, no. 2 (April 1980): 106-112.

Caves, R., *American Industry: Structure, Conduct, Performance*, Prentice-Hall, Inc., Englewood Cliffs, NJ (1972).

Caves, Richard E., "Industrial Organization, Corporate Strategy, and Structure," in Robert B. Lamb (ed.), *Competitive Strategic Management*, Prentice-Hall, Englewood Cliffs, NJ (1984), ch. 5.

Caves, R., and Pugel, T., *Intraindustry Differences in Conduct and Performance, Viable Strategies in U.S. Manufacturing Industries*, New York University Press (1980).

Chakravathy, Balaji, S., "Measuring Strategic Performance," *Strategic Management Journal* 7 (1986): 737-758.

Chandler, A. D., Jr., "The Structure of American Industry in the Twentieth Century: A Historical Overview," *Business History Review* 43 (1969): 255-298.

Christensen, H. Kurt, and C. A. Montgomery, "Corporate Economic Performance: Diversification Strategy versus Market Structure," *Strategic Management Journal* 2 (1981): 327-343.

Collins, James M., and Timothy W. Ruefli, "An Ordinal Approach to Strategic Risk," IC^2 Institute, The University of Texas, Austin, TX, 1989.

Comanor, W., "The Political Economy of the Pharmaceutical Industry" *Journal of Economic Literature* 24, no. 3 (September 1986): 1178-1217.

Conrad, G.R., and I.H. Plotkin, "Risk-Return: U.S. Industry Pattern" *Harvard Business Review* 46, no. 2 (March-April 1968): 90-99.

Cool, K.O., and D. Schendel, "Strategic Group Formation and Performance: The Case of the US Pharmaceutical Industry, 1963-1982," *Management Science* 33 (1987):1102-1124.

Cubbin, J., and P. Geroski, "The Convergence of Profits in the Long Run: Inter-Firm and Intra-Industry Comparisons," *The Journal of Industrial Economics* 35, no. 4 (June 1987): 427-442.

Dess, G. G., and D. W. Beard, "Dimensions of Organizational Task Environments," *Administrative Science Quarterly* 29 (1984): 52-73.

Figenbaum, A., and H. Thomas, "An Examination of Bowman's Risk-Return Paradox," *Academy of Management Proceedings* (1985): 7-11.

Figenbaum, A., and H. Thomas, "Dynamic and Risk Measurement Perspectives on Bowman's Risk-Return Paradox for Strategic Management: An Empirical Study," *Strategic Management Journal* 7 (1986): 395-407.

Figenbaum, A., and H. Thomas, "Attitudes Toward Risk and the Risk-Return Paradox: Prospect Theory Explanations," *Academy of Management Journal* 31, no. 1 (1988): 85-106.

Fredrickson, J. W., "The Comprehensiveness of Strategic Decision Processes: Extension, Observations, Future Directions," *Academy of Management Journal* 27, no. 3 (1984): 445-466.

Fredrickson, J. W., and T. R. Mitchell. "Strategic Decision Processes: Comprehensiveness and Performance in an Industry with an Unstable Environment," *Academy of Management Journal* 27 (1984): 399-423.

Gale, Bradley, "Market Share and Rate of Return," *Review of Economics and Statistics* 54 (November 1972): 412-423.

Gupta, M. C., "The Effect of Size, Growth, and Industry on the Financial Structure of Manufacturing Companies," *Journal of Finance* 2 (1969):517-529.

Hambrick, D. C., "Environmental Scanning and Organizational Strategy," *Strategic Management Journal* 3, no. 2 (1982): 159-174.

Hannan, Michael T., and John Freeman, "The Population Ecology of Organizations," *American Journal of Sociology* 82 (1977): 929-964.

Harrigan, K. R., *Strategies for Declining Businesses*, Lexington, Mass.: D. C. Heath, 1980.

Hax, A.C., and N. S. Majluf, "The Use of the Industry Attractiveness-Business Strength Matrix in Strategic Planning," *Interfaces* 13, no. 2 (April 1983): 54-71.

Henderson, J. M., and R. E. Quandt, *Microeconomic Theory: A Mathematical Approach*, 3rd edition, McGraw-Hill, New York, 1980.

Hitt, M. A., and R. D. Ireland, "Corporate Distinctive Competence, Strategy, Industry and Performance," *Strategic Management Journal* 6 (1985): 273-293.

Hofer, C. W., "Toward a Contingency Theory of Business Strategy," *Academy of Management Journal* 18 (1975): 784-810.

Hofer, C. W., and D. Schendel, *Strategy Formulation: Analytical Concepts*, West Publishing, St. Paul, Minn. (1978).

Huff, A.S., Industry Influences on Strategy Formulation, *Strategic Management Journal* 3 (1982): 119-131.

Jacobs, D., "Dependency and Vulnerability: An Exchange Approach to the Control of Organizations," *Administrative Science Quarterly* 19 (1974): 45-59.

McKelvey, B., and H. Aldrich, "Populations, Natural Selection, and Applied Organizational Science," *Administrative Science Quarterly* 28 (1983): 101-128.

Midlin, S., and H. E. Aldrich, "Interorganizational Dependence: A Review of the Concept and a Reexamination of the Findings of the Aston Group," *Administrative Science Quarterly* 20 (1975): 382-392.

Miller, D., and P. Friesen, "The Longitudinal Analysis of Organizations," *Management Science* 28, no. 9 (September 1982): 1013-1034.

Nightengale, J., "On the Definition of 'Industry' and 'Market,'" *The Journal of Industrial Economics* 27 (1978): 31-40.

Pfeffer, J., "Mergers as a Response to Organizational Interdependence," *Administrative Science Quarterly* 17 (1972): 382-394.

Pfeffer, J., and G. Salancik, *The External Control of Organizations: A Resource Dependence Perspective*, New York: Harper & Row, 1978.

Porter, M., "Structure within Industries and Companies' Performance," *Review of Economics and Statistics* 61 (February 1979): 214-228.

Porter, M., *Competitive Strategy*, New York: The Free Press, 1980.

Porter, M., *Competitive Advantage*, New York: The Free Press, 1985.

Ravenscraft, D., "Structure-Profit Relationships at the Line of Business and Industry Level," *Review of Economics and Statistics* 61 (February 1983): 22-31.

Reilly, F. K., and E. F. Drzycimski, "Alternative Industry Performance and Risk," *Journal of Financial and Quantitative Analysis* 9, no. 3, (June 1974): 423-446.

Ruefli, T. W., "Impacts of Deregulation on Performance and Management of the Largest American Transportation Companies," *Technovation* 5 (1986): 35-60.

Ruefli, T. W., "Ordinal Measures for Strategy and Management Control: Application to the U.S. Airline Industry," *Technovation* 8, nos. 1-3 (1988): 43-70.

Ruefli, Timothy W., ed., *Ordinal Time Series Analysis: Methodology and Applications in Management Strategy and Policy*, Quorum Books, Westport, CT, 1990.

Ruefli, T. W., G. Kozmetsky, and P. Yue, "International Competition in the Microelectronics Industry: The Balance Between Returns and Share," in Timothy W. Ruefli (ed), *Ordinal Time Series Analysis: Methodology and*

Applications in Management Strategy and Policy, Quorum Books, Westport, CT, 1990, ch. 9.

Ruefli, T. W., and Wilson, C. L., "Ordinal Time Series Methodology for Industry and Competitive Analysis," *Management Science* 33, no. 5 (May 1987): 640-661.

Rumelt, R. P., "Diversification Strategy and Profitability," *Strategic Management Journal* 3 (1982): 359-369.

Schmalensee, R., "Do Markets Differ Much?," *American Economic Review* 75 (June 1985): 341-351.

Shepard, W. G., "The Elements of Market Structure," *Review of Economics and Statistics* 54 (February 1972): 25-37.

Shepard, W. G., *The Economics of Industrial Organization*, Prentice-Hall, Englewood Cliffs, NJ, 1979.

Standard and Poor's COMPUSTAT PC-Plus, New York, 1989.

Standard and Poor's Industry Surveys, New York, 1987.

Teece, D., *Vertical Integration and Vertical Divestiture in the U.S. Oil Industry*, Institute for Energy Studies, Stanford, CA, 1976.

U.S. Office of Management and the Budget, *Standard Industrial Classification Manual*, U.S. Government Printing Office, Washington, DC, 1972.

Wernerfelt, B., and Montgomery, C., "What Is an Attractive Industry?" *Management Science* 32, no. 10 (1986): 1223-1230.

APPENDIX A

COMPUSTAT Industrial Aggregates Sample Analyzed

Industry Name	SIC
ABRASIVE,ASBESTOS,MISC MINRL	3290
ADHESIVES AND SEALANTS	2891
ADVERTISING AGENCIES	7311
AIRCRAFT	3721
AIRCRAFT ENGINE,ENGINE PARTS	3724
AIRCRAFT PARTS, AUX EQ, NEC	3728
APPAREL & OTHER FINISHED PDS	2300
BAKERY PRODUCTS	2050
BEVERAGES	2080
BLDG MATL,HARDWR,GARDEN-RETL	5200
BOLT,NUT,SCREW,RIVETS,WASHRS	3452
BOOKS:PUBG, PUBG & PRINTING	2731
BRDWOVEN FABRIC MILL, COTTON	2211
BRDWOVN FABRIC MAN MADE,SILK	2221
CAN FRUIT,VEG,PRESRV,JAM,JEL	2033
CAN,FROZNPRESRV FRUIT & VEG	2030
CEMENT,HYDRAULIC	3241
CHEMICALS & ALLIED PRODS	2800
COMMERCIAL PRINTING	2750
COMMUNICATIONS EQUIP, NEC	3669
COMPUTER & OFFICE EQUIPMENT	3570
CONCRETE,GYPSUM,PLASTER PDS	3270
CUTLERY,HAND TOOLS,GEN HRDWR	3420
DETECT,GUARD,ARMOR CAR SVCS	7381
DRILLING OIL AND GAS WELLS	1381
ELEC APPARATUS & EQUIP-WHSL	5063
ELECTR, OTH ELEC EQ, EX CMP	3600
ELECTRIC & OTHER SERV COMB	4931
ELECTRIC LIGHTING,WIRING EQ	3640
ELECTRIC SERVICES	4911
ELECTRONIC COMP, ACCESSORIES	3670
ELECTRONIC COMPONENTS, NEC	3679
ELECTRONIC CONNECTORS	3678
ENGINES AND TURBINES	3510
FABRICATED PLATE WORK	3443

FABRICATED RUBBER PDS, NEC	3060
FACILITIES SUPPORT MGMT SVCS	8744
FARM MACHINERY AND EQUIPMENT	3523
FINANCE-SERVICES	6199
FINANCIAL-COMPOSITE	0004
FOOD AND KINDRED PRODUCTS	2000
FOOTWEAR,EXCEPT RUBBER	3140
GEN BLDG CONTRACTORS-NONRES	1540
GENERAL INDL MACH & EQ, NEC	3569
GENERAL INDUSTRIAL MACH & EQ	3560
GRAIN MILL PRODUCTS	2040
GUIDED MISSILES & SPACE VEHC	3760
HOSPITALS	8060
HOUSEHOLD AUDIO & VIDEO EQ	3651
HOUSEHOLD FURNITURE	2510
NDL COML FANS,BLOWRS,OTH EQ	3564
NDL TRUCKS,TRACTORS,TRAILRS	3537
NDUSTRIAL MEASUREMENT INSTR	3823
NS AGENTS,BROKERS & SERVICE	6411
RON AND STEEL FOUNDRIES	3320
KNITTING MILLS	2250
LAB ANALYTICAL INSTRUMENTS	3826
LIFE INSURANCE	6311
LUMBER & OTH BLDG MATL-RETL	5211
MACHINE TOOLS, METAL CUTTING	3541
MACHINERY AND EQUIPMENT-WHSL	5080
MANIFOLD BUSINESS FORMS	2761
MEAT PACKING PLANTS	2011
MEN,YTH,BOYS FRNSH,WRK CLTHG	2320
METAL FORGINGS AND STAMPINGS	3460
METALS SERVICE CENTERS-WHSL	5051
MILLWORK,VENEER,PLYWOOD	2430
MISC CHEMICAL PRODUCTS	2890
MISC FOOD PREPS, KINDRED PDS	2090
MISC INDL, COML, MACHY & EQ	3590
MISC PLASTICS PRODUCTS	3080
MOTOR VEH SUPLY,NEW PTS-WHSL	5013
MOTOR VEHICLE PART,ACCESSORY	3714
MOTORS AND GENERATORS	3621
NATIONAL COMMERCIAL BANKS	6021
NATURAL GAS DISTRIBUTION	4924
NATURAL GAS TRANSMIS & DIST	4923

OFFICE FURNITURE	2520
OFFICE FURNITURE, EX WOOD	2522
OPERATORS-NONRES BLDGS	6512
PAINTS,VARNISHES, LACQUERS	2851
PAPER MILLS	2621
PERFUME,COSMETIC,TOILET PREP	2844
PERIODICAL:PUBG,PUBG & PRINT	2721
PETROLEUM REFINING	2911
PHARMACEUTICALS	2834
PHOTOGRAPHIC EQUIP & SUPPL	3861
PREFAB METAL BLDGS & COMP	3448
PRIM PRODUCTION OF ALUMINUM	3334
PROF & COML EQ & SUPPLY-WHSL	5040
PUMPS AND PUMPING EQUIPMENT	3561
RAILROADS,LINE-HAUL OPERATNG	4011
REFRIG & SERVICE IND MACHINE	3580
SAWMILLS, PLANING MILLS, GEN	2421
SHOE STORES	5661
SOAP,DETERGENT,TOILET PREPS	2840
SPECIAL CLEAN,POLISH PREPS	2842
SPECIAL INDUSTRY MACHY, NEC	3559
STEEL PIPE AND TUBES	3317
SVCS TO DWELLINGS, OTH BLDGS	7340
TIRES & RUBBER GOODS	3011

14

An Analysis of the Financial Competitiveness of Defense Industry Firms
William F. Bowlin

Since 1982, over twenty laws have been enacted that have impacted on the acquisition policies and procedures of the Department of Defense (DoD). Some of these laws have placed an additional burden on the government. However, most of these changes have affected defense industry firms (Math, 1989). In addition to legislative actions, changes to internal management procedures and policies have caused changes to the DoD's acquisition policy. These changes include reducing progress payments, requiring more competition for defense contracts, requiring warranties, requiring capitalization of special tools and equipment instead of immediate reimbursement by the government, increasing the use of the percentage of completion approach for revenue recognition an approach to the completed contract approach, and reducing recovery of independent research and development (IR&D) and bid and proposal (B&P) costs, among other policy changes. Figure 14.1 is a time line presentation of the policy changes. Also, see Appendix A for additional details on some of these changes.[1]

These changes have the potential to adversely impact the financial competitiveness (e.g., profitability, cash flow, market value) of defense industry firms. The purpose of this study is to empirically assess the impact of these acquisition policy changes on the financial competitiveness of the aerospace defense industry. Using data envelopment analysis (DEA), this research assesses and compares the financial performance of aerospace-defense firms and nonaerospace defense firms.

Figure 14.1. Procurement Policy Revisions

Warranties required for aircraft engines	1983	Grace Commission urged competition in contracting
Warranties required for all new weapon systems	1984	Competition in Contracting Act passed
Reduced progress payment rate from 85% to 80%	1985	
Stronger preference for dual/multiple sourcing indicated by Congress	1986	Packard Commission urged greater competition in contracting
Reduced value of completed contract method		Reduced progress payment rate to 75%
	1987	
DoD to reduce pre-negotiation profit objective by 1%		Require contractor to capitalize and amortize 50% of special tooling costs

This chapter is organized in the following manner. The first section reviews prior industry and government reports on this subject. This is followed by a description of the methodology used in this research. Finally, the third section reports the results of the analyses.

PRIOR STUDIES

A number of industry and government reports on the impact of DoD acquisition policy changes on the financial health of the defense industry have been completed over the past few years. Industry reports have been completed by the Financial Executives Institute (FEI), the Defense Industry Advisory Group, the MAC Group, and others. Government studies have been done by the Department of Defense (DoD) and the General Accounting Office (GAO).

The Financial Executives Institute (July 1987) issued a report that shows that the cash flows and profit for a representative (but unidentified) weapon system acquisition contract would be negatively affected. PaineWebber Incorporated (1988) concluded, from a professional investment advisor's point of view, that the performance of the aerospace defense industry has been disappointing. The firms lost 50 percent of their market value relative to S&P 500 stocks, and their price-earnings ratio is about 60 percent of the market average. The Defense Industry Advisory Group (1988) reported to Congress that legislative and regulatory changes reduced contractor profit, discouraged capital investment by the defense industry, and reduced the rewards of doing business with DoD below those necessary to be commensurate with the risk.

The most extensive industry report, and the one receiving the most publicity, was the MAC Group (1988) report. The MAC Group was awarded a contract by the Aerospace Industries Association, the Electronic Industries Association, and the National Security Industrial Association to analyze the impact of statutory, regulatory, and managerial practice changes affecting defense procurement risks and returns. They projected the impact of the acquisition policy changes on defense program and companywide financial data provided by nine companies for one year, 1985.[2] This is one year before any of the changes could have had a material impact on any actual reported data. The MAC Group concluded that, under the revised procedures and policies, the return on investment for the defense programs analyzed would have been less than the return necessary to preserve stockholder value. In addition, profits on the companies' defense business segment would have been reduced an average of 23 percent.

The government has also analyzed the profitability of defense firms. DoD (1985) studied seventy-six corporations from 1975 to 1983, comparing the financial results of contractors' defense segments with those of the companies' commercial segments and with those of durable goods manufacturers. DoD concluded that procurement policies were enabling the defense industry to achieve an equitable return for its involvement in the defense business.

Recently, the General Accounting Office (1989) reviewed the MAC Group study and concluded that based on the limited data used by the MAC Group, the MAC Group's conclusions could not be validated for the defense industry as a whole. The cumulative effect of the procurement policy changes may negatively impact contractor profitability and cash flow, but the data are not available to determine their significance. The MAC study did not ascertain the industrywide level of profitability of contractors either before or after these policy changes.

The industry studies provide anecdotal evidence that the financial health of the defense industry is deteriorating. In addition, some market evidence supports the same conclusion. However, none of the studies has compared the financial conditions of defense companies with those of nondefense companies before and after the acquisition policy changes were made in order to determine whether the defense firms were placed at a financial disadvantage (i.e., became financially noncompetitive). Primarily, the industry studies have assessed the financial impact (profitability, cash flows, etc.) of the revised policies on defense contracts that have already been completed. That is, they have assessed what the financial performance of completed defense contracts would have been under the new policies and compared these financial results to the actual financial results. They did not compare the financial performance of defense firms with that of nondefense firms before and after the policy changes. Hence, these studies did not consider the possibility that the firms were making excess profits prior to the policy changes. It is possible that even though the financial condition of defense firms is deteriorating, they are not worse off than other firms. It is also possible, as the General Accounting Office (1989) points out, for the firms to make behavioral changes that would allow them to remain financially competitive.

The purpose of this study is to address these two limitations. It compares the financial competitiveness of defense firms with that of nondefense firms before and after implementation of the policy changes.

METHODOLOGY

Data Envelopment Analysis

The methodology used in this research is a nonparametric frontier estimation technique called data envelopment analysis (DEA). DEA, developed by Charnes, Cooper, and Rhodes (CCR) (1978), can be accorded the form of a fractional-programming model which can be related to the work of Farrell (1957). It can also be accorded other forms, as described in Banker et al. (1989), and related to work in Pareto-Koopman efficiency evaluation, as in Charnes and Cooper (1957). Originally intended as a technique for measuring the performance (i.e., efficiency) of nonprofit organizations, DEA has since been used in other applications, including applications involving the activities of private, for-profit entities.[3]

In this research, we use DEA to create a "frontier" consisting of the "best" organizations operating in a multiple output and multiple input environment in order to measure whether aerospace defense industry firms are financially competitive with other firms. However, instead of viewing the model results as a measure of efficiency, we call the results a measure of financial competitiveness. This approach involves a cross-sectional comparison of financial competitiveness measures from a sample of aerospace defense firms and a sample of firms not part of the aerospace defense industry (a comparison group). This is done for the ten-year period, 1979-1988. Then the financial competitiveness measures are reviewed for changes over the ten-year period. Using Banker's (1989) statistical test of significance, we test whether there is a statistically significant difference between the financial competitiveness measures of the two samples before and after the policy changes. We then have a crosssectional comparison analyzed over time from which to see whether the policy can be associated with any changes in financial performance.

Hypotheses

Two hypotheses have been put forth concerning the affect of the procurement policy changes. The first one is that these changes have had a negative impact on the firms' earnings and cash flows, making the aerospace defense industry firms financially noncompetitive since 1985. Prior to these changes, the industry was financially competitive, so the argument runs, and it was the changes that caused the industry to become financially noncompetitive.

If the aerospace defense industry's contention is true, we would expect the defense industry's financial competitiveness measures to deteriorate in relation to the measures for the comparison group. Prior to 1985, we would expect no difference in the financial competitiveness measures between the two groups, but after 1985, we would expect to see a widening difference between the two groups, with the defense industry's rating deteriorating progressively in relation to that of the comparison group as the cumulative effects of the policy changes become apparent.

The second hypothesis is one that is sometimes thought of as the "government's" position. In this case, it is argued that prior to 1985 the defense industry earned excess profits and that acquisition policy changes would have the desirable effect of bringing the firms in other industries. If this contention is true, we would expect to find that the financial competitiveness measures for defense industry firms prior to 1985 were significantly higher than those for firms in other industries—indicating excess returns for those years. After 1985, the measures for defense industry and the comparison group should become progressively closer—indicating that the excess profits are being eliminated where, as is customary, "excess profit" is to be viewed as a relative term.

Variables

Two factors are considered in selecting the variables used in the DEA model. One consideration is the production function nature of the DEA (CCR version) model we are using, and the second consideration is the financial analysis nature of the research. We develop these in turn.

From a production function standpoint, one might ask what a firm is attempting to produce in financial terms. Market share, profitability, liquidity, and market value can be considered important financial outputs of a firm, and these can be regarded as outputs produced through consuming capital (e.g., plant and equipment, and personnel). In addition, analysis of the financial performance of firms oftentimes involves using financial ratios. Following a financial ratio analysis approach, we would use ratios such as return on assets, sales per employee, and return on stockholders' equity to compare the financial performance of firms.

Combining these two concepts, we select net income, cash flow from operations, net sales, and end-of-year market value as output measures to use to determine our financial competitiveness measure. The input variables are total assets, stockholders' equity, plant and equipment, and number of employees. Each of these output and input variables is described in the following paragraphs. For ease of reference, the measures are summarized in Table 14.1.

Net Income (NI). Net income after taxes is selected as the profitability measure over other possibilities, such as income from operations. The primary reason is that net income reflects changes in tax laws, interest expense, and extraordinary items that would not be evident in other profitability measures such as income from operations. The defense industry contends that the new acquisition legislation and policies significantly increase their borrowing requirements and consequently their interest expense. Furthermore, some companies (e.g., Northrop Corp.) have taken charges to their income for inventory adjustments and written off receivables that are related to their defense-business segment. Hence, we believe that net income is the appropriate measure of return or profitability since it captures these items.

Table 14.1. Output and Input Variables

Variable	Description
Outputs	
Net Income (NI)	Net income after taxes
Cash Flow from Operations (CFO)	Net income adjusted for noncash expenses and revenues and changes in current assets (excluding cash and cash equivalents) and current liabilities
Net Sales (S)	Net sales as reported on end-of-year income statement
End-of-Year Market Value (MV)	Stock market close price for the fiscal year multiplied by the company's common shares outstanding
Inputs	
Total Assets (TA)	Net book value of assets as reported on end-of-year balance sheets
Stockholders' Equity (SE)	Dollar value of the common stockholders' equity reported on end-of-year balance sheets
Plant and Equipment (P&E)	Net book value of plant and equipment as reported on end-of-year balance sheets
Employees (EMP)	Number of employees as reported in Securities and Exchange Commission Form 10K

Cash Flow From Operations (CFO). There are several definitions of cash flow that could be used as the liquidity measure. One such measure is cash flow from operations as presented on cash-flow statements in accordance with Statement of Financial Accounting Standard #95. However, this measure is available only for 1988 and thus is not usable for this study. We therefore use a modified measure of cash flow from operations. This measure is computed by adjusting net income for noncash expenses and revenues and for changes in current assets (not including cash and cash equivalents) and current liabilities. This measure is a close approximation to the cash flow from operations presented in cash-flow statements and includes increases in receivables and inventories that can cause problems that will require attention in our analyses.

Net Sales (S). Net sales is selected as the variable to represent market share. Also, sales is normally considered an output of the firm.

End-of-Year Market Value (MV). An objective of the firm that has considerable appeal to economists is to maximize the market value of the firm for its shareholders (Van Horne, 1986, p. 5). Market value can also serve a purpose similar to that of an error term in regression analysis in that it captures unknown factors (e.g., factors considered important by the market that are not explicitly treated in this study). Finally, this is a relevant measure because both the PaineWebber and the MAC Group studies indicate that the policy changes should have a negative impact on market value. Hence, market value has the potential for identifying the financial deterioration of defense firms. This output measure is defined as the market close price for the fiscal year multiplied by the company's common shares outstanding.

Total Assets (TA). This variable, treated as an input, represents the net book value of assets from all sources devoted to the business as reported on end-of-year balance sheets. It can be regarded as an input used to produce income, sales, and cash flow and thereby provides return-on-assets measures common in financial ratio analyses. Also, the value of assets is a factor in the market value of a firm.

Stockholders' Equity (SE). This variable is the dollar value of the common stockholders' equity as reported on the end-of-year balance sheets. It provides a return on owners-investment measure.

Plant and Equipment (P&E). This input variable is the net book value of plant and equipment as reported on end-of-year balance sheets. It provides an indication of the return on and productivity of capital investment (capital turnover).

Employees (EMP). Employees are an important nonbalance sheet assets of a firm and thus are included as an input in the DEA model. In this study, the measure used for this input is the number of employees as reported on Securities and Exchange Commission Form 10K. Including number of employees as an input variable is justified by analogy with its common use in productivity measures such as sales per employee and earnings per employee.

Using the ratio form of DEA, we may symbolize our financial competitiveness measure as

$$\frac{NI + CFO + S + MV}{TA + SE + P\&E + EMP} \qquad (1)$$

where the symbols are as defined previously. As can be seen, it includes several financial ratios of the type commonly used for evaluating the financial performance and health of an organization, but generalizes them to a composite measure which we will examine in more detail below.

One limitation of using dollar values as surrogate measures for inputs and outputs, as we do in this study, is that DEA requires all inputs and outputs to be positive values. There is the possibility that net income, cash flow, and stockholders' equity are negative values. In these cases, a small positive value is substituted for the negative values.[4]

Databases

Input and output data for this study come from COMPUSTAT, which contains financial data for firms that are publicly traded. The sample of defense firms are those that are categorized as aerospace defense firms by Value Line. There are thirty-two such firms, and they are listed in Appendix B. Data for all input and output measures are not available in COMPUSTAT for all years. Thus, the number of defense firms used in the DEA model varied from year to year and ranged from a low of 27 for 1988 to a high of 32 for 1987 and 1986.

Two different comparison groups are used in this study. One group consists of a random sample of forty-six S&P 500 firms listed in Appendix C. As with the defense industry sample, data are not available for all the firms in all years. The number of companies ranged from forty-one in 1979 to forty-five in 1987. Dow Jones industrials, excluding those firms identified in the defense industry sample, are the second comparison group. They are shown in Appendix D. The number of Dow Jones firms for which data are available ranged from twenty-five in 1988 to twenty-eight in 1979 and 1982.

RESULT

Appendix E contains the year-by-year, individual company financial competitiveness measures computed with the data envelopment analysis model to obtain a comparison between the aerospace defense firms and the S&P 500 firms, and Appendix F contains the same measures for comparing the defense firms with the Dow Jones industrials. To determine whether there is a statistically significant difference between the two samples for each year, we use an approach suggested by Banker (1989).

Using Banker's test, the null hypothesis is H_0: $\sigma_1 = \sigma_2$, indicating that the two samples come from the same distribution. The alternate hypothesis is

H_a: $\sigma_1 > \sigma_2$, which is interpreted to mean that the aerospace-defense firms (Group 1) are financially less competitive, on average, than the comparison group, Group 2 (e.g., S&P 500 firms).

We assume that the financial competitiveness measures follow an exponential distribution since this probability distribution has the appropriate skewness as well as non-negativity characteristic associated with the DEA scalar measure. The test statistic for this distribution is

$$[\sum_{n_1 \varepsilon G_1} (1/T_j - 1)/n_1]/[\sum_{n_2 \varepsilon G_2} (1/T_j - 1)/n_2] \quad (2)$$

where

T_j = The financial competitiveness measure computed with the DEA model

n_1 = The number of firms included in Group 1

n_2 = The number of firms included in Group 2

This test statistic follows an F-distribution with $(2n_1, 2n_2)$ degrees of freedom.

S&P 500 Comparison

In this analysis, we test whether, on average, the aerospace defense firms are financially competitive with the S&P 500 firms. Table 14.2 shows the test-statistic values computed via equation (2) for this comparison and their statistical significance. A test-statistic value less than one indicates that the aerospace defense industry sample is, on the average, financially healthier than the firms in the S&P 500 sample. on the other hand, a test-statistic value greater than one indicates that the firms in the aerospace defense industry sample are not as financially competitive as the firms in the S&P 500 sample. The significance level associated with these values determines whether the difference between the two samples is significant enough to conclude that the two samples come from different populations.

Table 14.2. Financial Competitiveness Statistical Analysis—Aerospace Defense versus S&P 500

Year	Test-Statistic Value	Level of Significance
1979	.8639	.28
1980	1.1378	.29
1981	1.5881	.03
1982	1.4464	.06
1983	1.0376	.43
1984	1.5380	.04
1985	1.2735	.15
1986	1.0891	.35
1987	1.4513	.05
1988	1.2743	.16

To illustrate the table's information, we use the 1979 results. Note that in 1979 the test-statistic value is .8639—an indication that the aerospace defense firms are financially competitive with (possibly even healthier than) their S&P 500 counterparts. However, the level of significance is only .28. Thus, from the standpoint of statistical significance, we conclude that there is no difference in the financial health of the aerospace defense firms and the S&P 500 companies in 1979.

Reviewing the results in Table 14.2, we conclude that the evidence fails to support either the "industry" or the "government" position. Following the "industry" position, we would expect a test-statistic value of about one, with no statistical significance for 1984 and prior years—indicating that the aerospace defense firms were on a financial par with the S&P 500 firms. After 1984, we would expect a test-statistic value trend moving from around one to significantly greater than one. This would indicate that the DoD acquisition policies and procedures implemented after 1984 had an adverse impact on the financial health of the aerospace-defense firms.

For ease of review, we present in Figure 14.2 the test-statistic values from Table 14.2. As can be seen, the trend in the financial competitiveness measure test statistic after 1984 is the same as before 1984. Except for 1979, the test-statistic value is consistently greater than one—indicating that the S&P 500 sample of firms were financially healthier than the aerospace defense sample companies both before and after 1984. Furthermore, a three-year cycle is apparent in the test-statistic value, peaking in 1981, 1984, and 1987, and each of these peak values is statistically significant at the .05 level. Thus, although our results show that the financial health of the aerospace defense industry was significantly worse than that of S&P 500 firms in 1987, this same situation existed in 1981 and 1984, which was prior to the changes in acquisition policy. In addition, in 1988 the difference between the two samples is not statistically significant.

Figure 14.2. S&P 500 versus Aerospace Defense Financial Competitiveness Test Statistics

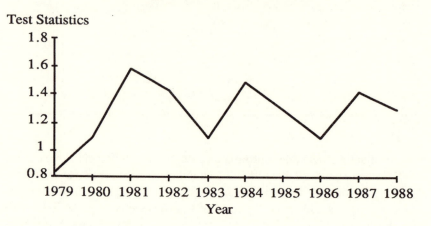

Hence, the evidence does not support the "industry" scenario. Statistical support for the aerospace defense firms' contention that their financial position has been deteriorating (i.e., they are becoming financially noncompetitive) since 1984 because of the cumulative effects of DoD acquisition policy changes is not evident. There is no apparent deterioration trend, and the cycle of results is basically the same after 1984 as it was prior to 1984.

Nor does the evidence support the hypothesis that (1) the defense industry was earning excess returns prior to implementation of the revised acquisition policies and (2) the revised policies brought the defense industry returns in line with the returns earned by nondefense firms. However, the results do indicate that the defense firms are just as financially competitive with nondefense companies before and after adoption of the revised policies.

It appears the defense firms are able to modify their behavior to meet the demands imposed on them by the new policies.

Dow Jones Comparison

Table 14.3 shows the statistics for comparing the financial competitiveness measures of the aerospace defense companies and the Dow Jones companies. Prior to 1984, there is no significant difference between the financial competitiveness measures of the two groups. Even at its lowest level of .07 in 1988, the test-statistic value of 1.5244 fails to achieve any of the customary significance levels, and in most other years the risk of a Type I error is far higher than can be regarded acceptable. However, the 1988 test-statistic value of 1.5244 does indicate that for 1988 the aerospace defense firms were financially worse off than the Dow Jones companies.

Table 14.3. Financial Competitiveness Statistical Analysis—Aerospace Defense versus Dow Jones

Year	Test-Statistic Value	Level of Significance
1979	.6956	.09
1980	.8001	.20
1981	.8730	.31
1982	.7996	.20
1983	.8599	.29
1984	.9548	.43
1985	1.1978	.25
1986	.9710	.45
1987	1.1447	.31
1988	1.5244	.07

However, there are some indications that the "industry" position (i.e., that the financial competitiveness of the aerospace defense industry has deteriorated since the change in DoD acquisition policies and procedures were implemented) is valid. Figure 14.3 illustrates these findings. Prior to 1985, the test-statistic value was less than one—suggesting that aerospace defense firms were financially healthier than the Dow Jones companies. In three of the four years after 1984, the test statistic is greater than one—indicating that the aerospace defense firms were financially noncompetitive with the Dow Jones firms. Hence, the situation warrants watching as to the possibility that a trend may be setting in, and there is a transition in the financial position of aerospace defense firms from being better off financially to being worse off financially in comparison with the Dow Jones companies. Although these results provide some preliminary indications that the aerospace defense firms are adversely impacted by the DoD acquisition changes, they are statistically inconclusive.

Figure 14.3. Dow Jones versus Aerospace Defense Financial Competitiveness Test Statistics

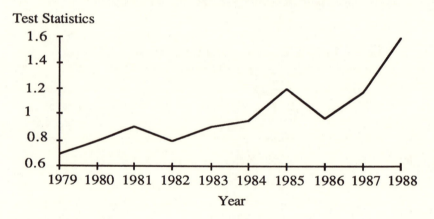

Sensitivity Analysis

The study's results are tested as to their sensitivity to a change in probability distribution assumption and definition of cash flow. These analyses are discussed in turn.

Half-Normal Distribution. An analysis of the financial competitiveness measures is accomplished using a half-normal probability distribution assumption instead of an exponential distribution.[5] The results parallel those for the exponential distribution for both the S&P 500 and the Dow Jones comparisons. They are inconclusive as to whether the aerospace defense firms are financially worse off than nondefense firms as a result of changes in DoD acquisition policy. The cyclical trends apparent in the exponential distribution for both the test-statistic values and their statistical significance are also evident with the half-normal distribution assumption.

Adjusted Cash Flow. The sensitivity of the above results to the cash flow measure is also tested. The cash -flow output variable is changed to measure net income adjusted for noncash expenses and revenues. This mitigates the impact of changes in receivables and inventories captured by the first cash-flow output variable. The conclusions reached previously are not sensitive to the change in the cash flow measure. In comparison to the S&P 500 and Dow Jones firms, it is not apparent that the aerospace defense companies' financial position is deteriorating as a result of changes in DoD acquisition policies and procedures.

SUMMARY AND CONCLUSIONS

In recent years several legislative, management practice, and policy changes have affected DoD's procurement process. Some prior studies have indicated that these changes have adversely impacted the financial health of the defense industry. The defense industry claims that neither Congress nor the DoD has properly assessed the cumulative effect of all of the procurement process changes.

Public policy decisions require that problems be studied in a variety of ways so that limitations inherent in any study or methodology do not bias the decisions to be made.[6] For example, see the different conclusions reached by Evans and Heckman (1983) and Charnes, Cooper, and Sueyoshi (1988) concerning the breakup of American Telephone & Telegraph Co. If different methodologies or research approaches produce the same conclusion, then public policy makers can feel more certain that their decisions are correct. Hence, in order to determine if the defense industry's concerns over DoD acquisition policy changes could be validated, we undertook an approach different from tha of the defense industry.

The results of this study do not corroborate the defense industry's findings. Our results indicate that the revisions to DoD acquisition policies and procedures implemented since 1983 have yet to adversely impact the financial position of aerospace defense firms in comparison to the S&P 500 firms and Dow Jones industrials. It is not evident that the financial health of defense firms has deteriorated and that these firms have consequently become financially noncompetitive. The financial competitiveness measures for the aerospace defense firms generally are not significantly different (statistically) from those for the S&P 500 and Dow Jones firms and indicate that the financial health of the defense firms is no different from that of the S&P 500 and Dow Jones companies—both before and after implementation of the acquisition policy changes. Furthermore, the cyclical trend evident in the data over the ten-year period covered by this study indicates that the financial health of the defense firms has not changed in relation to that of the comparison groups.

There are limitations associated with this research do need to be noted. First is the choice of data, which were limited here to data publicly reported by the firms covered in this study. A more desirable database would involve access to company records and reports which are not readily available. Second, differences in accounting practices and reporting procedures of the firms may influence the conclusions reached in this study, and this can (and should) be treated in various ways.[7] Third, the DEA methodology that we have used requires that all output and input variables be represented in positive amounts. This forced us to use an artificial process in which very small positive values were used in place of the negative values for net losses and negative cash flows.

This study does not purport to show whether defense-business *segments* and defense *contracts* are providing sufficient return, but it does provide evidence that defense firms, taken as a whole, remain as financially healthy and competitive as nondefense companies before and after adoption of the revised procurement policies. Either the changes did not have the adverse impact predicted by the defense industry or the defense industry firms were able to modify their behavior (e.g., by cost reduction, asset diversification, or asset divestiture strategies), in order to mitigate the adverse impact of the policy changes.

Further research on the financial health of the defense-industrial base should be pursued. Econometric or experimental design methodologies could be used to corroborate or refute the findings of this study. Likewise, the financial health of other defense industries, such as the defense electronics industry, should be reviewed for the same reason. Also, the profitability of defense-business segments and defense contracts should be analyzed in order to further assess the impact on the aerospace defense industry of public policy decisions. Finally, company-specific research could identify characteristics of successful and healthy defense firms. DEA's ability to focus on individual organizations would be particularly advantageous in this process.

NOTES

I gratefully acknowledge the assistance provided by Ms. Virginia Goetzinger. The views expressed herein are those of the author and do not necessarily reflect the views of the United States Air Force nor the Department of Defense.

1. Also see the MAC Group (1988), General Accounting Office (1989), and Waelchi (1988) for additional discussion of DoD acquisition policy and procedure revisions.

2. The MAC Group will not release the data used in its study due to confidentiality promised to participating companies.

3. See Charnes and Cooper (1985) and Banker et al. (1989) for a detailed description of the data envelopment analysis methodology and a discussion of the CCR and other DEA models.

4. See Charnes et al. (1989) for alternative procedures for handling this limitation, such as subtracting the absolute value of the negative amount from a large positive constant.

5. The test statistic for the half-normal distribution assumption provided by Banker (1989) is

$$[\sum_{n_1 \varepsilon G_1} (1/T_j - 1)^2/n_1]/[\sum_{n_2 \varepsilon G_2} (1/T_j - 1)^2/n_2]$$

In this case, the test statistic follows an F-distribution with (n_1, n_2) degrees of freedom.

6. Additional discussion of the importance of using different methodologies (e.g., econometric, management science, and experimental design approaches) in public policy research can be found in Allison et al. (1989).

7. Bowlin (1984) provides some possible ways to treat problem data in the DEA model.

REFERENCES

Allison, J., A. Charnes, W. W. Cooper, and T. Sueyoshi, "Uses of Modelling in Science and Society," *Research Report*, Center for Legal and Regulatory Studies, Graduate School of Business, The University of Texas at Austin, September 1989.

Banker, R.D., "Econometric Estimation and Data Envelopment Analysis," *Research in Governmental and Nonprofit Accounting* 5 (1989).

Banker, R.D., A. Charnes, W.W. Cooper, J. Swarts, and D. Thomas, "An Introduction to Data Envelopment Analysis with Some of Its Models and Their Uses," *Research in Governmental and Nonprofit Accounting* 5 (1989).

Bowlin, W. F., "A Data Envelopment Analysis Approach to Performance Evaluation in Not-for-Profit Entities with an Illustrative Application to the U.S. Air Force," doctoral dissertation, Graduate School of Business, The University of Texas at Austin, 1984.

Charnes, A., and W. W. Cooper, "Management Models and Industrial Applications of Linear Programming," *Management Science* 4 (October 1957): 38-91.

Charnes, A., and W. W. Cooper, "Preface to Topics in Data Envelopment Analysis," *Annals of Operations Research* 2 (1985): 59-94.

Charnes, A., W. W. Cooper, Z.M. Huang, and D.B. Sun, "DEA Cone-Ratio Approaches for Use in Developing Decision Support Systems to Monitory Performance in a Collection of Banks," *CCS Report*, Center for Cybernetic Studies, College of Business Administration, The University of Texas at Austin, September 1989.

Charnes, A., W.W. Cooper, and E. Rhodes, "Measuring the Efficiency of Decision Making Units," *European Journal of Operational Research* 2, no. 6 (November 1978): 429-444.

Charnes, A., W.W. Cooper, and T. Sueyoshi, "A Goal Programming/Constrained Regression Review of the Bell System Breakup," *Management Science* 34, no. 1 (January 1988): 1-25.

Defense Industry Advisory Group, *Report to the Subcommittee on Defense Industry and Technology, Senate Armed Services Committee*, February 5, 1988.

Department of Defense, *Defense Financial and Investment Review*, June 1985.

Evans, D. D., and J. J. Heckman, "Multiproduct Cost Function Estimates and Natural Monopoly Tests for the Bell System," in D.S. Evans (ed.), *Breaking Up Bell*, Elsevier Science Publishers, Amsterdam, 1983, ch. 10.

Farrell, M. J., "The Measurement of Productive Efficiency," *Journal of the Royal Statistical Society* 120, no. 3 (1957): 253-281.

Financial Executives Institute, *Recent Developments in Government Profit Policy*, Washington Office: 1100 Seventeenth Street, N.W., Washington, D.C. 20036, April 1987.

Financial Executives Institute, *The Impact of Government Policies on Defense Contractors*, Washington Office: 1100 Seventeenth Street, N.W., Washington, D.C. 20036, July 1987.

General Accounting Office, *Government Contracting, Effect of Changes in Procurement and Tax Policy on the Defense Industry*, May 1989 (GAO/NSIAD-89-121).

MAC Group, *The Impact on Defense Industrial Capabilities of Changes in Procurement and Tax Policy*, February 1988.

Math, P.F., "DOD Acquisition Reform Efforts," Statement before the Subcommittee on Defense Industry and Technology, Senate Armed Services Committee, May 11, 1989 (GAO/T-NSIAD-89-23).

Paine Webber, Inc., "Professional Investment Adviser's View of the Defense Industry," Briefing presented to the Directorate of Program Planning and Integration, Office of the Assistant Secretary of the Air Force (Acquisition), August 3, 1988.

Van Horne, J.C., *Financial Management and Policy*, 7th ed., Prentice-Hall, Englewood Cliffs, N.J., 1986.

Waelchi, F., "A Capital Crisis in the Defense Industry?" *Program Manager* (July-August 1988): 31-36.

APPENDIX A

Summary of Procurement Policy Changes

Following is a summary of the more significant procurement policy changes that have occurred recently. Additional discussion of these changes can be found in the MAC Group (1988), Waelchi (1988), and General Accounting Office (1989). The potential effect of these policy changes is to reduce income and cash flow through either forgone interest income from investments or increased interest expense from borrowing.

Tax Law Changes. Many companies within the defense industry have deferred tax payments by using the completed contract method to account for their revenues and expenses. Because this method defers profit recognition to the end of the contract, it consequently defers tax payments. In 1982, 1986, and 1987, legislation restricted the use of the completed contract method and increased the use of the percentage of completion method for profit recognition. The potential effect of these legislative changes is to reduce income and cash flow through either forgone interest income from investments or increased interest expense from borrowing.

Progress Payments. Progress payments are made to contracts with fixed-price contracts to assist them in financing their work-in-process. This, in effect, is interest-free government financing. The progress payment rate has been progressively reduced from 85 percent to 80pecent in 1985 and then to 75 percent in 1986. Consequently, defense contractors are required to finance more of their work-in-process.

Special Tooling Investment. Historically, the cost of special tooling and test equipment required for a defense contract was considered a direct contract expense, and contractors were reimbursed as these costs were incurred. Legislative changes in 1986 and 1987 required contractors to capitalize and amortize 50 percent of this investment. This delays the government's reimbursement to the contractor for these costs.

Fixed-Price Contracts. There is a percentage point within the defense industry that the government is increasingly requiring fixed-price contracts for research and development efforts instead of the cost-reimbursement contracts used previously. The potential impact of this change is to have contractors absorb a greater portion of the research and development cost.

Profit Policy. In response to the Department of Defense (1985), DoD revised its profit policy that applied to negotiated (noncompetitive) contracts. Their objective was to reduce prenegotiation profit objectives by 1 percent.

Competition in Contracting. The Competition in Contracting Act passed in 1984, emphasized competition in all government contracts. It also indicated congressional preference for dual or multiple sourcing. Congress's preference for dual or multiple sourcing was reiterated in the FY 86 defense authorization law.

APPENDIX B

Aerospace Defense Industry Sample

AAR Corporation	Adams Russell Incorporated
ARX Incorporated	Boeing Company
E-Systems Incorporated	EDO Corporation
Fairchild Industries Incorporated	Gencorp Incorporated
General Dynamics Corporation	General Motors—Class H
Grumman Corporation	Hexcel Corporation
Hi-Shear Industries	Lockheed Corporation
Logicon Incorporated	Loral Corporation
M/A-Com Incorporated	Martin Marietta Corporation
McDonnell Douglas Corporation	Moog Incorporated—Class A
Northrop Corporation	Raytheon Company
Rockwell International Corporation	Rohr Industries
Sparton Corporation	Sundstrand Corporation
Transtechnology Corporation	TRW Incorporated
UNC Incorporated	United Industrial Corporation
Watkins-Johnson Company	Wyman-Gordan Company

APPENDIX C

S&P 500 Sample

Advanced Micro Devices
Andrew Corporation
Ball Corporation
CBS Incorporated
Consolidated Rail Corporation
Deere & Company
Gannett Company
GTE Corporation
Intergraph Corporation
International Paper Company
K Mart Corporation
Masco Corporation
Monsanto Company
NL Industries
Pitney-Bowes Incorporated
Public Service Enterprise
Santa Fe Southern Pacific Corp.
Southwestern Bell Corporation
Sysco Corporation
Tandy Corporation
Trinova Corporation
USX Corporation
Xerox Corporation

American Home Products Corporation
Avery International
Brunswick Corporation
Consolidated Freightways Incorporated
CSX Corporation
Donnelley (RR) & Sons Company
Giant Food Incorporated—Class A
Hasbro Incorporated
International Business Machines Corp.
Johnson & Johnson
Marion Laboratories
Mead Corporation
Moore Corporation Ltd.
Pacific Telesis Group
Prime Computer
Quantum Chemical Corporation
Sonat Incorporated
Stanley Works
Tandem Computers Incorporated
Texaco Incorporated
Unocal Corporation
Worthington Industries
Zayre Corporation

APPENDIX D

Dow Jones Industrials Sample

Allied Signal Incorporated
American Express
Bethlehem Steel Corporation
Coca-Cola Company
Eastman Kodak Company
General Electric Corporation
Goodyear Tire & Rubber Company
International Paper Company
Merck & Company
Navistar International
Procter & Gamble Company
Texaco Incorporated
United Technologies Corporation
Westinghouse Electric Corporation

Aluminum Company of America
American Telephone & Telegraph
Chevron Corporation
Du Pont (E.I.) De Nemours
Exxon Corporation
General Motors Corporation
International Business Machines Corp.
McDonald's Corporation
Minnesota Mining & Manufacturing Co.
Philip Morris Companies Incorporated
Sears Roebuck & Company
Union Carbide Corporation
USC Corporation
F.W. Woolworth Company

APPENDIX E

Defense Industries—S&P 500 Sample Financial Competitiveness Measures

Defense Industries

Company	1988	1987	1986	1985	1984	1983	1982	1981	1980	1979
AAR Corp	0.2585	0.6508	0.6509	0.6203	0.6460	0.5394	0.6033	0.4991	0.7240	0.9042
Adams Russell		0.2756								
ARX Inc	0.2853	0.3502	0.4817	0.5734	0.5441	0.8306	0.7107	0.7370	0.7532	0.8023
Boeing	0.6976	0.5368	0.8347	1.0000	0.9354	0.8947	0.4862	0.7085	0.8765	1.0000
E-Systems	0.6206	0.5704	0.7223	0.7241	0.9502	1.0000	0.9553	0.6857	0.6049	0.6830
EDO Corp	0.3700	0.3538	0.4376	0.5234	0.6373	1.0000	1.0000	0.7573	0.5464	0.6016
Fairchild	0.5703	0.6222	0.9397	0.7264	0.3878	0.5795	0.7021	0.6809	0.5500	1.0000
Gencorp	1.0000	1.0000	0.7226	0.4600	0.3754	0.4781	0.3817	0.4629	0.5166	0.4841
Gen Dynamics	0.6216	0.6292	0.8780	1.0000	1.0000	0.9364	0.8111	0.6382	0.6763	0.7844
GM-Class H	0.4463	0.6013	0.5027							
Grumman	0.5328	0.4980	0.5871	0.6657	0.8836	0.9870	1.0000	0.7662	0.7375	0.6964
Hexcel	0.8083	0.3819	0.4733	0.4808	0.4923	0.4857	0.4892	0.4096	0.5700	0.6016
Hi-Shear		0.3988	0.6406	1.0000	1.0000	1.0000	0.5524	1.0000	0.7617	1.0000
Lockheed	0.7700	0.7381	0.8873	1.0000	1.0000	1.0000	1.0000	1.0000	1.0000	1.0000
Logicon		1.0000	1.0000	1.0000	1.0000	1.0000	1.0000	1.0000	1.0000	1.0000
Loral		0.4084	0.4655	0.6460	0.6600	0.5760	0.6716	0.6023	0.6625	0.7355
M/A-Com	0.6461	0.2427	1.0000	0.3782	0.4318	0.4849	0.4858	0.6987	0.7337	0.7820
Martin Marietta	0.6983	0.5831	1.0000	1.0000	1.0000	0.8652	0.7739	0.6279	0.6233	0.8403
McDonnell Doug	0.5237	0.5642	0.6155	0.6485	0.7531	0.8537	0.6619	0.8805	0.5817	0.6227
Moog	0.3675	0.3289	0.4310	0.4874	0.4416	0.4501	0.3625	0.5045	0.5390	0.8528
Northrop	0.5783	0.6339	1.0000	0.9251	0.8137	0.8686	0.6792	0.4988	0.8290	0.6823
Raytheon	0.7515	0.7706	0.8454	0.7670	0.5939	0.7145	0.7415	0.7769	0.7364	0.7712

Company	1988	1987	1986	1985	1984	1983	1982	1981	1980	1979
Rockwell	0.5600	0.8190	0.8825	0.7535	0.7599	0.7147	0.5936	0.6944	0.6300	0.7054
Rohr	0.4787	1.0000	0.6277	0.6842	1.0000	0.8616	0.7497	0.7342	0.7413	0.9893
Sparton	0.6714	0.6792	0.7720	0.7272	0.6659	0.8716	0.6439	0.8211	0.4918	0.6358
Sundstrand	1.0000	0.6754	0.3588	0.5144	0.5718	0.5181	0.6572	0.7801	0.6506	0.6697
Transtechnology		0.6852	0.4942	0.4173	0.6096	0.6480	0.5745	0.8914	0.8586	0.9183
TRW	0.5185	0.6946	0.7757	0.8541	0.5785	0.7784	0.5826	0.6827	0.5939	0.6656
UNC	0.4728	0.5020	0.9345	0.4392	0.5762	0.3717	0.3138	0.2866	0.3757	1.0000
United Ind	0.5284	0.7606	0.4030	0.8387	0.8634	0.8680	0.7658	0.7539	0.6660	0.6464
Watkins-Johnson	0.6315	0.6575	0.6744	0.6519	0.6135	0.6760	0.5376	0.5513	0.5146	0.7062
Wyman-Gordan	0.3065	0.3968	0.4110	0.4238	0.6733	0.9659	1.0000	1.0000	0.6640	0.6396

S&P 500 Firms

Company	1988	1987	1986	1985	1984	1983	1982	1981	1980	1979
Advanced Micro	0.5872	0.5781	0.2618	0.5253	1.0000	1.0000	0.8560	0.9452	0.7064	0.8425
Am Home Prod	0.7916	0.9157	1.0000	1.0000	1.0000	1.0000	1.0000	1.0000	1.0000	1.0000
Andrew	0.5241	0.5812	0.4814	0.5220	0.6674	0.7666	0.9555	0.6459	0.5364	
Avery	0.4912	0.4623	0.5494	0.6264	0.6847	0.6823	1.0000	0.6872	0.6285	0.5998
Ball	0.4462	0.8326	0.6214	0.7485	0.6725	0.7327	0.6531	0.6650	0.5169	0.6418
Brunswick	0.6448	0.7344	0.5533	0.6933	0.6818	0.9335	1.0000	0.6034	0.4075	0.4244
CBS	1.0000	1.0000	1.0000	1.0000	0.7817	0.7989	0.7061	0.7653	0.7773	0.9778
Con Freightways	0.6071	0.6179	0.7610	0.5990	0.5891	0.6230	0.6246	1.0000	0.6616	0.7618
Con Rail	0.3194	0.4319								
CSX	0.3767	0.5634				0.3565	0.7323	0.4965	0.4282	0.4502

Company	1988	1987	1986	1985	1984	1983	1982	1981	1980	1979
Deere	0.4673	0.4410	0.3424	0.3848	0.4756	0.3558	0.4234	0.5144	0.5814	0.7244
Donnelley		0.5935	0.6318	0.6380	0.6791	0.7992	0.7144	0.7136	0.6931	0.8171
Gannett	0.4829	0.5017	0.6980	0.6959	0.7266	0.7095	0.7251	0.8751	0.7875	0.8734
Giant Food		0.9172	1.0000	1.0000	1.0000	1.0000	1.0000	1.0000	1.0000	1.0000
GTE	0.3494	0.5091	0.6182	0.4754	0.8468	0.7217	0.5545	0.7122	0.5274	0.6517
Hasbro	0.7879	0.6984	0.8658	1.0000	0.7369	1.0000	1.0000	0.8197	1.0000	0.7889
Intergraph	0.5243	0.6091	0.6999	1.0000	1.0000	1.0000	1.0000	1.0000		
IBM	0.4934	0.5721	0.7530	0.9450	0.9779	1.0000	1.0000		1.0000	1.0000
Intl Paper	0.5120	0.5452	0.5815	0.5488	0.5678	0.5140	0.5538	0.7592	0.4878	0.9617
John & John	0.6641	0.5090	1.0000	0.7894	0.7248	0.6884	0.7833	0.7912	0.7789	0.8201
K Mart		0.6561	0.8021	0.8560	0.7600	0.7593	0.6458	0.6118	0.5992	0.7385
Marion	1.0000	1.0000	1.0000	1.0000	1.0000	1.0000	0.6798	1.0000	0.7620	0.7330
Masco	0.4795	0.5156	0.5405	0.7586	1.0000	0.7145	0.8497	0.7181	0.7853	0.8797
Mead	0.6535	0.7121	0.5010	0.5856	0.8875	0.5937	0.5401	0.5720	0.6763	0.7902
Monsanto	0.5642	0.6190	0.6351	1.0000	0.6885	0.7503	0.5871	0.6259	0.4890	0.6203
Moore	0.5309	0.6609	0.6163	0.6812	0.7095	0.6040	0.7910	0.7090	0.6784	0.6809
NL Industries	1.0000	0.5141	0.2871	0.4861	0.5588	0.6614	0.8035	1.0000	0.7749	0.5927
Pacific Telesis	0.4387	0.6122	0.9353	1.0000						
Pitney-Bowes	0.7502	0.4586	0.7104	0.6806	0.6268	0.7123	0.5330	0.5541	0.5614	0.5687
Prime	0.4485	0.5897	0.6402	0.7350	0.6650	0.6177	0.8882	1.0000	1.0000	1.0000
Quantum Chem	1.0000	0.7711	0.7594	0.6856	0.8507	0.5667	0.7443	0.9127	0.6732	0.7905
Santa Fe	0.4779	0.4579	0.3593	0.5070	0.5525	0.5992	0.3219	0.3772	0.3406	0.3954
Sonat		1.0000	0.7110	0.7787	1.0000	1.0000	1.0000	0.8751	0.8753	1.0000
SW Bell	0.8913	0.5484	0.9343	0.7520						
Stanley	0.4793	0.4439	0.5199	0.6472	0.6259	0.5718	0.5686	0.6538	0.5463	0.6633
Sysco	1.0000	1.0000	1.0000	1.0000	1.0000	1.0000	1.0000	1.0000	1.0000	1.0000

Company	1988	1987	1986	1985	1984	1983	1982	1981	1980	1979
Tandem	0.5390	0.7063	0.8778	0.5934	0.6707	0.9108	0.8180	1.0000	1.0000	1.0000
Tandy	1.0000	0.7838	1.0000	0.7608	0.9840	1.0000	1.0000	1.0000	1.0000	1.0000
Texaco	1.0000	1.0000	1.0000	1.0000	1.0000	1.0000	1.0000	1.0000	1.0000	1.0000
Trinova	0.4203	0.4383	0.8483	0.4689	0.5392	0.5393	0.3869	0.6432	1.0000	0.5651
Unocal	0.8378	1.0000	1.0000	1.0000	1.0000	1.0000	1.0000	1.0000	1.0000	1.0000
USX	0.6325	0.5672	1.0000	0.6009	0.8486	0.5532	0.5227	0.7244	0.4692	0.3851
Worthington		0.6021	0.7098	0.7954	0.7451	0.6736	0.8112	0.6966	0.8057	0.6845
Xerox		0.6003	0.6305	0.4747	0.6037	0.6098	0.5957	0.7921	0.6791	0.8050
Zayre	1.0000		1.0000	0.9063	0.8699	0.8145	0.7731	0.7571	0.7779	0.8891

APPENDIX F

Defense Industries—Dow Jones Sample Financial Competitiveness Measures

Defense Industries

Company	1988	1987	1986	1985	1984	1983	1982	1981	1980	1979
AAR Corp	0.5643	0.9970	1.0000	0.9938	1.0000	0.9705	0.8823	0.8386	1.0000	1.0000
Adams Russell	0.4673	0.4949								
ARX Inc	0.8093	0.4721	0.7186	0.7542	0.7007	1.0000	1.0000	1.0000	1.0000	0.8494
Boeing	1.0000	0.6338	1.0000	1.0000	0.9942	1.0000	0.7787	0.8651	1.0000	1.0000
E-Systems	1.0000	0.8408	0.9265	1.0000	1.0000	1.0000	1.0000	1.0000	0.9320	0.9300
EDO Corp	0.5396	0.5541	0.6926	0.6609	0.8395	0.7288	0.8738	0.8125	0.8299	0.7925
Fairchild	0.7579	0.6352	0.9071	0.6109	0.6111	0.6106	0.5703	0.9049	0.7549	1.0000
Gencorp	1.0000	1.0000	0.8718	0.8181	0.7298			0.5891	0.6997	0.6689
Gen Dynamics	0.9251	0.9524	0.9643	1.0000	1.0000	1.0000	1.0000	0.9403	1.0000	0.9990
GM-Class H	0.6006	0.5698	0.7067							

Company	1988	1987	1986	1985	1984	1983	1982	1981	1980	1979
Grumman	0.8541	0.7618	0.8660	0.8771	0.8883	0.9912	1.0000	0.9439	0.8952	0.8995
Hexcel	0.7660	0.6931	0.7139	0.6998	0.6902	0.6725	0.6781	0.7232	0.8296	0.8299
Hi-Shear		0.5953	1.0000	1.0000	1.0000	1.0000	0.7479	1.0000	1.0000	1.0000
Lockheed	0.9635	0.9300	0.9863	1.0000	1.0000	1.0000	1.0000	1.0000	1.0000	1.0000
Logicon		1.0000	1.0000	1.0000	1.0000	1.0000	1.0000	1.0000	1.0000	1.0000
Loral		0.5990	0.5448	0.9382	0.8422	0.7345	1.0000	0.9120	1.0000	1.0000
M/A-Com	1.0000	0.4441	1.0000	0.5873	0.6439	0.7936	0.7290	1.0000	1.0000	1.0000
Martin Marietta	1.0000	0.9436	1.0000	1.0000	1.0000	0.8724	0.9793	0.7356	0.7773	0.8381
McDonnell Doug	0.7800	0.8052	0.8559	0.8728	0.8939	0.9890	1.0000	1.0000	1.0000	0.8128
Moog	0.5709	0.5230	0.5611	0.5677	0.5448	0.5964	0.5327	0.6400	0.7584	0.8875
Northrop	1.0000	1.0000	1.0000	0.9879	0.8535	0.9374	0.9034	0.7671	1.0000	0.8219
Raytheon	1.0000	0.9816	1.0000	0.9461	0.7828	0.8421	0.9526	1.0000	1.0000	0.9533
Rockwell	0.8006	0.8798	0.9721	0.7978	0.7806	0.7920	0.7824	0.7880	0.8965	0.8025
Rohr	0.7419	1.0000	0.9198	0.8334	1.0000	0.9012	0.8825	0.8779	0.7839	1.0000
Sparton	0.9688	0.9564	1.0000	0.8525	0.7253	0.9285	0.7897	1.0000	0.8848	0.7952
Sundstrand	0.5917	0.6282	0.6110	0.6140	0.5909	0.6204	0.7595	0.9740	0.8505	0.7648
Transtechnology		0.6922	0.6882	0.4678	0.8210	0.8887	0.7917	1.0000	1.0000	0.9846
TRW	0.9029	0.8426	0.8230	1.0000	0.6783	0.8065	0.7647	0.8133	0.8751	0.8257
UNC	0.6039	0.6412	0.8042	0.4811	0.7404	0.4130	0.4398	0.3239	0.4287	1.0000
United Ind	0.7320	0.8217	0.6344	1.0000	1.0000	0.8787	0.9097	0.9642	0.9650	0.7601
Watkins-Johnson	0.8633	0.7927	0.8815	0.8656	0.7992	0.8667	0.6770	0.6599	0.7564	0.7481
Wyman-Gordan	0.5197	0.5512	0.6349	0.6576	0.7453	0.9449	1.0000	1.0000	0.8279	0.7893

Company	1988	1987	1986	1985	1984	1983	1982	1981	1980	1979
Allied Signal	0.7085	0.6110	0.6775	0.4638	0.6664	0.6893	0.6233	0.6648	0.7062	0.6855
ALCOA	0.7869	0.5118	0.6196	1.0000	0.5999	0.6245	0.4862	0.4776	0.8678	0.9694
AT&T	0.9493	0.7919	0.9689	0.8943	0.8010		0.6061	0.7394	0.7325	0.6936
Bethlehem	1.0000	0.6222	0.6361	0.6800	0.7045	0.6942	0.8236	0.6252	0.6923	0.7209
Chevron	0.6727	0.7593	0.7346	0.9844	1.0000	1.0000	1.0000	1.0000	1.0000	1.0000
Coca-Cola	1.0000	1.0000	1.0000	1.0000	1.0000	1.0000	1.0000	1.0000	1.0000	1.0000
Du Pont	0.8093	0.7879	0.9219	0.8305	0.9169	0.9507	0.8053	0.6271	0.8653	0.8952
Eastman Kodak	0.5579	0.6228	0.6877	0.6669	0.7245	0.6898	0.7986	0.9392	0.9926	0.9274
Exxon	1.0000	1.0000	1.0000	1.0000	1.0000	1.0000	1.0000	1.0000	1.0000	1.0000
Gen Electric	0.7395	0.6993	0.7508	0.8009	0.7433	0.7732	0.8172	0.9344	0.8577	0.7568
Gen Motors	0.7460	0.7396	0.7944	0.8575	0.9437	0.9235	0.7627	0.7202	1.0000	1.0000
Goodyear	0.7920	0.6672	0.5597	0.6561	0.6954	0.7796	0.7613	0.7584	0.8124	0.7686
IBM	0.6038	0.6540	0.8646	1.0000	1.0000	1.0000	1.0000	1.0000	1.0000	0.9133
Intl Paper	0.7719	0.6279	0.5551	0.5573	0.5518	0.5354	0.5571	0.7370	0.5317	1.0000
McDonald's	0.6912	0.5032	0.7464	0.9185	0.7782	0.7586	0.8055	0.8832	0.9063	0.7400
Merck	1.0000	1.0000	1.0000	1.0000	1.0000	1.0000	1.0000	1.0000	1.0000	1.0000
MMM	0.9320	0.8170	0.9955	0.9974	0.9459	0.8512	0.8913	0.9840	1.0000	0.8813
Navistar	1.0000	1.0000	1.0000	1.0000	1.0000	1.0000	1.0000	0.8022	0.6878	0.8808
Philip Morris	1.0000	0.8522	0.9781	1.0000	0.9301	1.0000	1.0000	0.9194	0.9089	0.8696
Proctor&Gamble	0.8856	0.8932	0.8735	1.0000	0.9795	1.0000	1.0000	0.9575	0.9013	1.0000
Texaco	1.0000	1.0000	0.9945	1.0000	1.0000	1.0000	1.0000	1.0000	1.0000	1.0000
Union Carbide	0.9876	0.7955	1.0000	0.5767	0.5097	0.5247	0.4891	0.6027	0.8023	0.6139
United Tech	0.8253	0.7288	06822	0.6949	0.7392	0.7797	0.8005	0.8282	0.9003	0.8547
USX	0.8855	0.6370	1.0000	0.7233	0.7785	0.7265	0.6141	0.8550	0.5882	0.6334
Westinghouse	0.7167	0.6917	0.9452	0.9400	0.6211	0.6327	0.6604	0.8455	0.8001	0.5788
Woolworth		0.9786	0.9922	1.0000	0.9503	0.9210	0.9165			1.0000

15

A Multiregional Model
for India, 2000 A.D.

Ranajit Dhar
Sanjay Goel
M. R. Rao

Construction of models with a regional breakup of the national economy dates back to as early as 1951 when Walter Isard (1951) presented his model of "Inter-Regional and Regional Input Output Analysis." Not only do such interregional input output models (IRIO) require data on intersector transactions as in a national model, but also each transaction has to be further broken down into its region of origin. Japan is one of the few countries where such IRIO models are constructed regularly under the Ministry of International Trade and Industry (MITI) (1970) for every five years since 1960. Oosterhaven (1981) has developed a five-region IRIO model of the Dutch economy.

The difficulty of getting detailed data for IRIO models has led to research on inter-regional commodity flows and has given birth to the development of multiregional input output (MRIO) models. Pioneering work on the development of MRIO models has been done by Chenery et al. (1953) for the Italian economy and by Moses (1955) and Polenske (1980) for the U.S. economy.

Leontief (1953) developed a "balanced regional" model considering "local" and "national" groups of sectors. Later, Leontief and Hoffenberg (1961) used this model to study the effect of a compensated 20 percent cut in armament expenditures on the output and employment of the various regions of the U.S. economy. Leontief and Strout (1963) developed a "gravity" model for multiregional analysis. This model treats trade variables as a function of both demand and supply simultaneously and calculates a gravity coefficient instead of using trade coefficients as in the Chenery/Moses model.

All the models discussed above may be considered a multiregional consistency models where trading relations are assumed to be fixed.

Construction of multiregional programming models with a provision for varying trading relations started in late 1950s. Such programming models were developed either for a single sector in a multiregional framework, as Henderson (1958) did for the coal industry, or in a multiregional, multisectoral framework, as in Moses (1960).

A number of multiregional models—consistency as well as single- and multisectoral optimizing models—were constructed for the Indian economy. The construction of such models was taken up in the early 1960s. Ghosh and Dhar (1965) prepared a single-sector optimizing model for the cement industry of India to study the efficiency of that sector's interregional flows. The first multiregional input output model for the Indian economy was constructed by Dhar (1965) for the year 1953-54. This table was used by Dhar, Venning, and Berry (1966) and Ghosh (1967) to make certain interesting projections for various regions of the Indian economy. The same table was also used by Dhar to study the implications for income leakages (1972) and to study the nature of spatial clusters (1973) of the Indian economy.

Bhatia (1961) made a study to delineate an interindustry, interregional, and intertemporal linear programming model of technological transformation of the Indian economy from a traditional one to a modern one. Narain and Sardesai (1967) developed a four-regiol, five-sector model to test a methodology for determining the optimal location of industries in various regions of India by minimizing transport costs. Mathur and Hashim (1970) have experimented with a four-region, twenty-three-sector model to obtain optimal levels of production and trading by minimizing transport costs. Mathur (1972) has also developed a dynamic model with five regions and twenty-seven sectors for India, which he has used to offer various alternative solutions under different assumptions regarding trade balance and output growth rate constraints by minimizing the transport costs.

For two decades after that there was a lull in the area of construction of multiregional models for the Indian economy. This was partly due to the large magnitude of work involved in the construction of such an elaborate model and partly due to emphasis on a centralized planning framework.

Dhar and Rao (1983) have developed an EMPOV model to analyze the feasibility of a basic need strategy of growth for tackling the problems of poverty and unemployment. An empirical analysis of the model was conducted for the regional economy of the Bangalore district of Karnataka State in India. Subsequently, the above EMPOV model was extended in terms of the methodology used, by the same authors along with Goel (1988), and an empirical analysis was conducted for the Indian economy for the eighth and ninth plans simultaneously.

Of late there is a growing realization that important tasks such as the reduction of employment and poverty cannot be taken up at the aggregative national level alone and that there is a need for decentralized planning, which necessitates the construction of multiregional models. Recently Dhar (1989) has constructed a multiregional fixed trading model for five regions and thirteen sectors in order to obtain consistent projections for each of the sectors of each region for the eighth plan period (1989-90 to 1994-95) for India.

The objective of the proposed study is to construct a multiregional and multisectoral optimizing model for the Indian economy. This model, unlike multiregional models attempted in the past, specifically deals with the problems of availability of basic needs in all the regions simultaneously by reducing the existing inequality between regions in per capita aggregate household consumption levels. An appropriate consumption target is fixed, and GDP or value added is maximized to achieve a more equitable distribution of income across the regions. The model is designed in such a way that it will also help in studying the trading and thereby, the transport implications for each region.

This model takes into consideration various limitations on capacity expansion, household consumption levels, and trading activities of each sector of each region. Implications for net fixed investment requirements are obtained endogenously from this model for each region. Although a free flow of funds across regions is assumed, aggregate net fixed investment for the country as a whole will be constrained by the expected availability of savings from both within and outside the country.

The software for the model was developed on a PC/AT to obtain results for the target year (1999-2000) for five regional and thirteen sectoral groupings (including the transport sector) of the national economy.

The mathematical framework of the model is presented in the next section. The results relating to (1) reduction of regional disparity in income and consumption, (2) sectoral growth profiles of each region, (3) investment implications, and (4) implications for domestic and foreign trading are analyzed in the following section. A summary of conclusions and limitations concludes the chapter.

MATHEMATICAL FORMULATION

The multiregional optimizing model (MROM) is a target year, multiregional and multisectoral optimizing model.

The model deals with three sets of variables for each region: (1) sectoral output levels, (2) sectoral consumption levels, and (3) sectoral interregional trade levels. There are two sets of exogenous variables for each region: (1) sectoral foreign exports and (2) sectoral replacement investment. The model contains a number of equality and inequality constraints, including upper and lower bounds. These are discussed below.

Consider r regions and s sectors in the economy. The indices i and j correspond to the sectors, while the indices p and q correspond to the regions. All values and variables, unless otherwise specified, refer to the target year.

Demand = Supply

The demand D_i^p for each sector i of region p is given as follows:

$$D_i^p = \sum_j x_{ij}^p + C_i^p + NFI_i^p + RI_i^p + INV_i^p \qquad (1)$$

where

x_{ij}^p = Output of sector i (from any of the regions) used in sector j of region p

C_i^p = Consumption of output of sector i of region p

NFI_i^p = Net fixed investment demand in sector i of region p

RI_i^p = Replacement investment demand in sector i of region p

INV_i^p = Inventory demand in sector i of region p

Here, x_{ij}^p is the output of sector i used by sector j to produce an output of x_j^p. So, if we assume fixed technological coefficients over the plan horizon, then

$$x^p_{ij} = a^p_{ij} \cdot X^p_j \tag{1.1}$$

where, a^p_{ij} = current input coefficient indicating the value of input from sector i (from any source) required per unit of output of sector j in region p and x^p_j = output of sector j in region p.

The next fixed investment demand NFI^p_i can also be written in terms of capital input coefficients, which reflect the capital requirement for increasing the capacity of a sector. So we have

$$NFI^p_i = \sum_j b^p_{ij} \cdot \Delta X^p_j \tag{1.2}$$

where b^p_{ij} = capital input coefficient indicating the value of input from sector i required to increase the output of sector j in region p by one unit after the period of gestation lag for sector j, and ΔX^p_j = increment in the output of sector j in region p. If T is the target year, X^p_j refers to the output during the year T, and ΔX^p_j refers to the increment in output during the year $T + \phi_j$ from the previous year $T + \phi_j - 1$, where ϕ_j is the gestation lag for sector j.

Hence,

$$\Delta X^p_j = X^p_j (1 + \alpha^p_j)^{\phi j} - X^p_j (1 + \alpha^p_j)^{\phi j - 1}$$

$$= X^p_j \cdot r^p_j$$

where

$$r^p_j = \alpha^p_j \cdot (1 + \alpha^p_j)^{(\phi j - 1)}$$

and α_j^p = post-terminal growth rate of output of sector j in region p.

This growth rate is exogenously specified.

The inventory demand is also a derivative of increment in outputs and is given as follows:

$$INV_i^p = \mu_i^p [X_i^p (1 + \alpha_i^p) - x_i^p]$$ (1.3)

where μ_i^p = inventory requirement to increase the output of sector i by one unit. This is known as the inventory coefficient.

The replacement investment is defined as follows:

$$RI_i^p = RI_{io}^p \cdot (1 + RIGR_i)^T$$ (1.4)

where

RI_{io}^p = Base year replacement investment demand
for sector i in region p

$RIGR_i$ = Annual growth rate of replacement investment
in sector i

T = Plan period in years

So the demand equation (1) may now be written as

$$D_i^p = \sum_j a_{ij}^p \cdot X^p + \sum_j b_{ij}^p \cdot X_j^p \cdot r_j^p + C_i^p$$

$$+ RI_{io}^p \cdot (1 + RIGR_i)^T + \mu_i^p \cdot \alpha_i^p \cdot X_i^p$$ (2)

The supply side of the equation can be written as follows:

$$S_i^p = X_i^p + M_i^p - E_i^p + \sum_{\substack{q \\ q \neq p}} T_i^{qp} - \sum_{\substack{q \\ q \neq p}} T_i^{pq} \tag{3}$$

where

X_i^p = Output of sector i in region p

T_i^{pq} = Trade of sector i from region p to region q

M_i^p = Foreign import in sector i of region p.

This import is taken to be a function of the demand in sector i. In particular, the import in sector i of region p is assumed to be specified fraction of the demand in the same sector of the same region.

Hence

$$M_i^p = f(D_i) = m_i^p \cdot D_i^p$$

where m_i^p = ratio of base year import to base year total demand in sector i of region p.

We have

E_i^p = Foreign export of sector i from region p

$$= E_{io}^p (1 + EXGR_i)^T$$

where

E_{io}^p = Base year foreign export of sector i from region p

$EXGR_i$ = Annual growth rate of foreign export of sector i

The supply demand equation $S_i^p = D_i^p$ can now be written combining equations (1) and (3) and rearranging as follows:

$$\sum_j A_{ij}^p \cdot X_j^p + \sum_{\substack{q \\ q \neq p}} T_i^{qp} - \sum_{\substack{q \\ q \neq p}} T_i^{pq}$$

$$- (1 - m_i^p) \cdot C_i^p = R_i^p \tag{4}$$

where,

$$A_{ij}^p = - (1 - m_i^p) \cdot (a_{ij}^p + b_{ij}^p \cdot r_j^p) \quad \ldots \text{ for } i \neq j$$

$$= 1 - [(1 - m_i^p) \cdot (a_{ii}^p + b_{ii}^p \cdot r_i^p + \mu_i^p \cdot \alpha_i^p)] \text{ for } i = j$$

and

$$R_i^p = (1 - m_i^p) \cdot RI_{io}^p \cdot (1 + RIGR_i)^T + E_{io}^p (1 + EXGR_i)^T$$

Equation (4) can be written for all regions and for all the sectors except the transport sector, since the output of the transport sector depends upon the trade values. The transport sector equation consists of the following components: (1) direct use in the households, (2) self input requirement, and (3) requirement of transport for intraregional, interregional, and foreign trade flows.

Let k denote transport sector. Then we have

$$X_k^p = \sum_{\substack{i \\ i \neq k}} [(X_i^p - \sum_{\substack{q \\ q \neq p}} T_i^{pq} - E_i^p) \cdot CD_i \cdot d^{pp}$$

$$+ \sum_{\substack{q \\ q \neq p}} T_i^{qp} \cdot CR_i \cdot d^{qp} + M_i^p \cdot CF_i \cdot d^{fp}]$$

$$+ C_k^p + a_{kk} \cdot x_k^p \tag{5}$$

where

CD_i = Cost per km of transporting the output of sector i within the region

d^{pp} = Average distance for internal trade in region p

CR_i = Cost per km of transporting the output of sector i between regions p and q

d^{pq} = Average distance between regions p and q

CF_i = Cost per km of transporting foreign export/import of sector i

d^{fp} = Average distance for foreign trade of region p

a_{kk} = Self-input for transport sector k

Substituting for M_i^p and rearranging, equation 5 may be written as follows:

$$B_k^p \cdot X_k^p + \sum_{\substack{j \\ j \neq k}} B_j^p \cdot X_j^p + \sum_{\substack{j \\ i \neq k}} \sum_{\substack{j \\ q \neq p}} T^{pq} \cdot CD_i \cdot d^{pp}$$

$$\tag{6}$$

$$- \sum_{\substack{j \\ i \neq k}} \sum_{\substack{j \\ q \neq p}} T_i^{qp} \cdot CR_i \cdot d^{qp} - C_k^p - \sum_{\substack{j \\ i \neq k}} C_i^p CF_i d^{fp} m_i^p = RI^p$$

where

$$B_k^p = (1 - a_{kk}^p) - \sum_{\substack{j \\ i \neq k}} CF_i \, d^{fp} \cdot m_i^p \, (a_{ik}^p + r_k^p \cdot b_{ik}^p)$$

$$B_j^p = - CD_j \cdot d^{pp} - \sum_{\substack{j \\ i \neq k}} m_i^p \cdot CF_i \cdot d^{fp} \, (a_{ij}^p + r_j^p \cdot b_{ij}^p)$$

$$- \mu_j \cdot \alpha_j^p$$

$$\ldots \text{ for } j \neq k$$

$$RI^p = - \sum_{\substack{j \\ i \neq k}} [E_{io}^p \cdot (1 + EXGR_i^p)^T \cdot CD_i \cdot d^{pp}]$$

$$+ \sum_{\substack{j \\ i \neq k}} [RI_{io}^p \cdot (1 + RIGR_i^p)^T \cdot CF_i \cdot d^{fp} \cdot m_i^p]$$

So, equations (4) and (6) make up the set of demand-supply constraints for the model.

Surplus/Deficit of Aggregate Domestic Trade of Each Region

Two constraints are put on the net domestic trade of each of the regions to restrict its trade deficit and surplus. These constraints are

$$\sum_i \left(\sum_{\substack{q \\ q \neq p}} T_i^{pq} - \sum_{\substack{q \\ q \neq p}} T_i^{qp} \right) \leq SL^p \tag{7.1}$$

$$\sum_i (\sum_{\substack{q \\ q \neq p}} T_i^{qp} - \sum_{\substack{q \\ q \neq p}} T_i^{pq}) \leq DL^p \qquad (7.2)$$

where

$$SL^p = \text{Net domestic trade surplus limit for region } p$$

$$DL^p = \text{Net domestic trade deficit limit for region } p$$

Growth Rate of Domestic Trade of the Country

There is one constraint on the growth rate of total domestic trade in the country. This constraint states that the implied annual growth rate of total domestic trade is to be below a specified value.

$$\sum_i \sum_p \sum_{\substack{q \\ q \neq p}} T_i^{pq} \leq \sum_i \sum_p \sum_{\substack{q \\ q \neq p}} T_{io}^{pq} \cdot (1 + GRDT)^T \qquad (8)$$

where T_{io}^{pq} = base year trade of commodity i from region p to region q and GRDT = permissible annual growth rate of aggregate domestic trade over the base year.

Net Fixed Investment

There is one constraint on the total net fixed investment during the plan period. This is again related to the base year value and is written as follows:

$$\sum_p \sum_i \sum_j b_{ij}^p \cdot r_i^p \cdot x_j^p \leq I_{io} \cdot (1 + IGR)^T \qquad (9)$$

where I_{io} = total base year investment and IGR = permissible annual growth rate of net fixed investment.

Upper Limit on Aggregate Net Imports of the Country

One constraint is put on the net foreign imports in order to keep it below a certain specified level. This is given as

$$(\sum_i \sum_p M_i^p - \sum_i \sum_p E_i^p) \leq ML \tag{10}$$

where ML = net import limit.

Lower and Upper Bounds on Outputs

For each sectoral output, the lower and upper bounds are specified as

$$X_i^p \geq X_{io}^p \cdot (PROPOUT) \tag{11.1}$$

$$X_i^p \leq X_{io}^p \cdot (1 + \alpha_i^p)^T \tag{11.2}$$

where

$$X_{io}^p = \text{Base year output in sector i of region p}$$

PROPOUT = a percentage value.

Lower and Upper Bounds for Trade

Lower and upper bounds are also specified for individual trade levels. These are given by

$$T_i^{pq} \geq T_{io}^{pq} \cdot (DLO) \tag{12.1}$$

$$T_i^{pq} \leq T_{io}^{pq} \cdot (DUP) \tag{12.2}$$

where DLO and DUP are, respectively, the specified lower and upper percentage limits.

Lower and Upper Bounds on Per Capita Consumption

The bounds on consumption are specified using a basic needs approach model. The lower and upper bounds for consumption are given as follows.

$$C_i^p \geq PCL_i^p \cdot (POP^P) \tag{13.1}$$

$$C_i^p \leq PCU_i^p \cdot (POP^P) \tag{13.2}$$

where $\quad PCL_i^p = Max\ (RO_i^p\ ;\ Min\ [RO_i^p \cdot (1 + \beta_i^p)^T;\ PCT_i])$

$PCU_i^p = PCL_i^p \cdot (1 + CUP)$

PCT_i = Minimum specified per capita consumption for sector i

RO_i^p = Base year per capita consumption of sector i in region p

β_i^p = Desired growth rate of per capita consumption of sector i in region p.

CUP = A percentage value (expressed as a fraction) to determine the upper limit.

POP^P = Population in region p

Thus, the model contains r · s supply-demand constraints, one investment constraint, 2r net trade constraints, one total trade growth constraint, and one net import constraint. The number of variables are r · s for output; r · s for consumption and r · (r-1) · s for domestic trade.

The Objective Function. The objective function of the model is to maximize the weighted sum of value added in all the regions. This is expressed as follows:

$$\text{Max } Z = \sum_p \sum_j w^p \cdot (1 - \sum_i \alpha_{ij}^p) \cdot X_j^p$$

where w^p = weight given to the value added of region p.

ANALYSIS OF RESULTS

The multi-regional model discussed in the previous section is solved for the target year, 1999-2000, with 1989-90 as the base year. The model considers the following five regional groupings of the states:

1.	Eastern region:	Assam, West Bengal, Orissa, Arunachal Pradesh, Meghalaya, Nagaland, Manipur, Mizoram, Tripura, Andaman, Nicobar Islands
2.	Central region:	Bihar & Uttar Pradesh
3.	Northern region:	Rajasthan, Madhya Pradesh, Punjab, Haryana, Himachal Pradesh, Jammu, Kashmir, and Delhi
4.	Southern region:	Andhra Pradesh, Karnataka, Tamil Nadu, Kerala, and Pondicherry
5.	Western region:	Maharashtra, Gujarat, Goa, Daman, and Diu

The main reason for selecting this particular regional groupings is the availability of data. These regional groupings are the same as those used in the study by Dhar (1965, 1989). Thus, it was possible to obtain the necessary base year transactions using appropriate indicators.

The following thirteen sectoral groupings were considered in this model. These sectors have been classified as basic, nonbasic, or intermediate, as shown in the parentheses below:

1. Foodgrains (basic)
2. All other agriculture (basic)
3. Mining (intermediate)
4. Textiles (basic)
5. Chemicals (basic)
6. Petroleum (intermediate)
7. Cement (intermediate)
8. Metals & engineering (nonbasic)
9. All other industries (nonbasic)
10. Electricity (intermediate)
11. Construction (basic)
12. Transport (intermediate)
13. All other services (basic)

The sectoral groupings used here are again the same as those used in the study by Dhar and Rao (1983), Dhar, Rao, and Goel (1988), and Dhar (1989). As explained in the earlier studies by the same authors, the above sectoral groupings are too broad and cover certain elements of basic, nonbasic, and intermediate components in almost all of them. The above classification has been made based on their principal use either as basic, nonbasic, or intermediate. Thus, foodgrains which includes ordinary quality grains for general use as well as superior varieties of grains used mostly by the richer sections of the population, is considered as a basic need sector because the former constitutes a larger proportion. Similar explanations can easily be offered for the classification of other sectors also.

The base year transactions for each region, giving sectoral output, interindustry transactions, household consumption, net fixed investment, replacement investment, inventory, foreign exports and imports, and domestic trade of each sector for every pair of regions are provided in the study by Dhar (1989). The same data are used in the present study but only some of them, such as output, consumption, and interregional trade, are presented here in various tables.

In the model separate current and capital coefficient matrices are assumed for each region. However, due to lack of data the same matrices as given in Dhar (1989) are used for all regions. Tables 15.1 to 15.5 contain the values of the rest of the input data.

The model allows for differential weights in the objective function for different regions. However, preliminary test runs indicated that differential weights may not provide significantly different results, possibly due to the broad sectoral and regional groupings used in the present study. Hence, in solving this model, equal weights have been used for all the regions.

Table 15.1. Parameter Values

Item		Alternative 1	Alternative 2
1.	Time horizon in years (T)	10	10
2.	Number of regions (r)	5	5
3.	Number of sectors (s)	13	13
4.	Percentage annual growth rate of population (PGR); same for all regions	2	2
5.	Upper limit for sectoral consumption expressed as a percentage above the lower limit (CUP)	5	5
6.	Inventory coefficient (gamma); same for all sectors, all regions	0.25	0.25
7.	Sectoral percentage annual growth rate of replacement investment (RIGR); same for all sectors, all regions	6.5	6.5
8.	Maximum percentage annual growth rate of net fixed investment (IGR)	11	12
9.	Lower limit on the target year sectoral output expressed as a proportion of the corresponding base year value (PROPOUT)	1	1
10.	Lower and upper limits on the individual sectoral interregional trade expressed as a percentage of the corresponding base year value (DLO, DUP)	50 & 200	25 & 400
11.	Upper limit on net interregional trade surplus and deficit for each region (SL & DL) [in Rs. crores]*	16,000	20,000
12.	Upper limit on percentage annual growth rate of aggregate inter-regional trade for the country	7	7
13.	Net foreign import (ML) [in Rs. crores]*	6849	0
14.	Export growth rates in percentage, same for all sectors	5	5 (10 for sectors 3 & 4 and 15 for sector 9)

*1 crore = 10 million

Table 15.2. Transportation Costs
(in Rs. per Rs. 1000 of output transported) at 1984-85 Prices

Sector	Intraregional for 500 kms	Interregional per 1000 kms	Foreign for 10000 kms
Foodgrains	60	100	360
Other Agriculture	35	60	210
Mining	85	150	500
Textiles	6	10	36
Chemicals	40	65	240
Petroleum	60	100	360
Cement	120	200	720
Metals & Engineering	18	30	100
Other Industries	18	30	100
Electricity	-	-	-
Construction	-	-	-
Transport	-	-	-
Services	-	-	-

Table 15.1 contains parameter values, Table 15.2 contains various transportation costs, and Table 15.3 gives the average interregional distances. In the present study a liberal growth of the transport sector is allowed, again in line with the objective of this study. However, growth of the transport sector has been constrained by specified upper and lower limits on the interregional trade of each commodity, specified upper and lower limits on the aggregate net domestic imports of each region, and a specified upper limit on annual growth rate of aggregate interregional trade in the country. This is done to avoid a large increase in the interregional trading and transport costs of the economy. The upper limits on the output growth rates for individual sectors in each region are the same as the post-terminal growth rates, as presented in Table 15.4.

The sectoral growth rates of per capita household consumption are presented in Table 15.5. These rates are fixed at a relatively higher level for the basic need items, while for the nonbasic needs items, they have been fixed at a lower level in line with the objective of this study to make available all the basic needs in all the regions in a more equitable manner.

**Table 15.3. Average Interregional Distance
(in 000 kms)**

	E	C	N	S	W
E	-				
C	1.0	-			
N	2.0	1.0	-		
S	2.5	2.1	2.3	-	
W	2.3	1.5	1.3	1.5	-
From/To	E	C	N	S	W

The empirical analysis is done in order to test the model and offer some broad guidelines for the required sectoral growth rates of outputs together with investment allocation, consumption targets, and interregional trading pattern. In order to highlight the sensitivity of the model to changes in the various parameters, two significantly different alternatives have been presented here. Alternative 1 results assume limitations on the availability on aggregate saving resources as well as limitations on export demands. Alternative 2 results on the other hand, assume larger availability of saving resources and a higher market for export. The other differences between the two alternatives lie in the upper limit on net imports, the lower and upper limits on individual sectoral trade between pairs of regions, the maximum allowable net regional surplus or deficit, and the post-terminal growth rates of outputs. The values used are given in Tables 15.1 and 15.4

For both the alternatives, the model is first run with an assumed set of post-terminal output growth rates, which were decided on the basis of technological, managerial, and economic considerations. From the results obtained, the sectoral output growth rates achieved in each region are calculated. The post-terminal sectoral output growth rates are then interactively adjusted to be comparable as far as possible to the sectoral output growth rates achieved.

Table 15.6 presents the macroeconomic balances for 1999-2000, the final year of the ninth plan, under the two alternatives along with the corresponding base year values.

The data in Table 15.6 indicate that the per capita GDP for the country is Rs.3256 in the base year, 1989-90. Regarding the regional disparity of per capita GDP, the Western region has the highest per capita GDP, which is about 1.55 time the country average. On the other hand, the lowest per capita GDP is for the central region (which is Rs.2266) and is roughly 70 percent of the country average. The per capita GDP in the other three regions—namely, the Eastern, Northern and Southern regions are within ± 10 percent of the country average. The regional disparity of per capita GDP, as measured by the Lorenz ratio, is 0.137 during the base year.

Table 15.4
Sectoral Post-Terminal/Maximum Specified Growth Rates of Output for Each Region and Gestation Lag (in years)

Sector\Region	E	C	N	S	W	Lag
Foodgrains	[.030	.045	.035	.030	.030]*	1
	(.030	.045	.035	.030	.025)	
Other Agriculture	[.050	.070	.070	.050	.040]	1
	(.050	.070	.070	.050	.050)	
Mining	[.040	.070	.065	.040	.020]	5
	(.060	.080	.065	.065	.040)	
Textiles	[.050	.050	.060	.040	.030]	2
	(.050	.090	.060	.040	.045)	
Chemicals	[.040	.050	.075	.060	.040]	2
	(.080	.090	.030	.060	.045)	
Petroleum	[.070	.080	.000	.040	.050]	4
	(.075	.090	.000	.040	.050)	
Cement	[.055	.110	.090	.060	.020]	2
	(.055	.110	.100	.070	.050)	
Metals & Engineering	[.080	.150	.100	.110	.050]	3
	(.075	.150	.110	.110	.100)	
Other Industries	[.050	.080	.070	.050	.020]	2
	(.070	.120	.080	.065	.025)	
Electricity	[.060	.085	.060	.060	.030]	4
	(.070	.090	.060	.060	.045)	
Construction	[.070	.130	.090	.070	.020]	3
	(.070	.125	.095	.070	.040)	
Transport	[.040	.060	.050	.050	.040]	2
	(.065	.060	.050	.055	.040)	
Services	[.050	.070	.050	.050	.030]	1
	(.050	.070	.055	.050	.045)	

* [ ] For alternative 1
( ) For alternative 2

Table 15.5. Sectoral Specified Per Capita Consumption Growth Rate for Each Region

Sector\Region	E	C	N	S	W
Foodgrains	.020	.020	.015	.020	.020
Other Agriculture	.030	.035	.025	.035	.025
Mining	.010	.010	.010	.020	.010
Textiles	.020	.025	.020	.030	.020
Chemicals	.020	.015	.015	.015	.015
Petroleum	.040	.050	.045	.030	.010
Cement	-	-	-	-	-
Metals & Engineering	.010	.018	.010	.015	.010
Other Industries	.010	.019	.010	.013	.010
Electricity	.060	.080	.025	.020	.010
Construction	.050	.060	.050	.060	.060
Transport	.015	.025	.015	.025	.015
Services	.020	.040	.020	.020	.020

The results of alternative 1 pertaining to GDP show a 5.3 percent growth rate for the country, with growth rates varying from as low as 2.8 percent for the western region to as high as 7.6 percent for the central region. The growth rates for the eastern, northern, and southern regions are 4.9 percent, 5.7 percent, and 5.4 percent respectively. These growth rates imply a substantial reduction in the regional disparity of income, as measured by the Lorenz ratio—from 0.137 in the base year to 0.059 in the target year, indicating an annual reduction of about 10 percent. This is possible mainly because of the selection of appropriate upper limits on sectoral output growth rates in the various regions. Relatively higher upper limits are given for regions having lower per capita income, and correspondingly lower values are given for regions having higher per capita income in the base year. Simultaneously, the constraints on net domestic trade of each region are fixed in such a way that it also helps to achieve the same objective of reducing the regional disparity. Alternative 2 projections are worked out with higher growth rates of foreign exports. This gives a higher GDP growth rate of about 6 percent for the country and between 5.7 percent and 7.9 percent for the different regions. The regional disparity of per capita GDP under this alternative is less equitable, compared to alternative 1, because the growth rate differences are not significant. The Lorenz ratio for alternative 2 is 0.0857.

Table 15.6. Macro-Economic Balances
(in Rs. Crores [10 million] at 1984-85 Prices)

Indicators	Country	Regions				
		E	C	N	S	W
Gross Domestic Product	267323	44859	49053	49674	65253	58484*
	[448572	72296	102017	86403	110857	76999]
	(476683	73567	104632	90308	113292	94884)
Annual Growth Rate of GDP in Percentage	[5.3	4.9	7.6	5.7	5.4	2.8]
	(5.9	5.1	7.9	6.2	5.7	5.0)
Consumption	210745	33785	50111	45241	48773	32835
	[315056	49176	81364	63620	74139	46757]
	(313122	49594	80474	62726	74607	45721)
Savings	56577	11074	-1058	4433	16479	25649
	[133516	23120	20653	22783	36718	30242
	(163561	23973	24158	27582	38684	49164)
Gross Investment	63426	9035	9481	11268	17705	15937
	[139872	19162	37848	27764	35879	19319]
	(161350	20993	41235	30842	37541	30738)
Total Investment for 10 years	[994495	139826	219431	191300	266504	177434]
	(1091300	147899	232279	204347	273963	232812)
Domestic Net Exports	-	2563	-9527	-6348	734	12578
	-	[3930	-14830	-4751	3206	12445]
	-	(1379	-15706	-5245	830	18741)
Foreign Net Exports	-6849	-524	-1013	-487	-1959	-2866
	[-6356	28	-2365	-130	-2367	-1522]
	(2212	1601	-1370	1985	312	-316)
Population (in crores)	82.1	12.75	21.65	16.40	19.70	11.60
	[100.1	15.50	26.40	20.00	24.00	14.10]
	(100.1	15.50	26.40	20.00	24.00	14.10)
Per capita GDP (in Rs.)	3256	3518	2266	3029	3312	5042
	[4482	4652	3866	4322	4616	5445]
	(4763	4733	3965	4517	4718	6710)
Per Capita Consumption (in Rs.)	2567	2650	2315	2759	2476	2831
	[3148	3164	3083	3182	3087	3306]
	(3129	3191	3049	3138	3107	3233)
Per Capita Consumption Growth Rate	[2.0	1.8	2.9	1.4	2.2	1.6]
	(1.9	1.9	2.8	1.3	2.3	1.3)

*Values without any parentheses - Base Year
    Values with [ ] - Alternative 1
    Values with ( ) - Alternative 2

The total gross investment requirement for the country for the ten-year plan period works out to be Rs.994495 crores for alternative 1 and a higher value of Rs.1091300 crores under alternative 2. The distribution of total gross investment across the regions under alternative 1 is 14 percent, 22 percent, 19 percent, 27 percent, and 18 percent for the eastern, central, northern, southern, and western regions respectively, whereas the corresponding values for alternative 2 are 14 percent, 21 percent, 19 percent, 25 percent, and 21 percent, respectively. This means that the share of investment to the western region increases under alternative 2 with proportional reductions in the shares of the central and southern regions. As the savings figures indicate, investment ranges for different regions will have to be achieved through a substantial increase in the savings of each region from internal sources. Regarding the inflow of savings from the other regions, as seen from domestic trade, alternative 1 indicates that the inflow into the central region from the other regions would have to be substantially increased, while for the Northern region the inflow of savings from the other regions would have to be reduced. The outflow of savings from the western region to the rest of the regions is to remain almost at the same level as in the base year while the outflow from the eastern and southern regions will have to increase substantially. The savings flow in Alternative 2 is almost similar to Alternative 1 except that the outflow of the savings form the Eastern region will have to reduce from its base year level while the Western region will have to substantially increase its contribution of savings into other regions. The larger contribution of savings from the western region to other regions in alternative 2 is possible because of its higher GDP growth rate.

Table 15.6 gives the values of the net foreign exports for the country as well as for all the regions. Thee values indicate the role of foreign savings in the development of each of the regions. In the base year, the different regions experienced varying degrees of foreign savings contribution in their development. In alternative 1, although for the country, the net foreign import has remained almost the same as that in the base year; there is however, a substantial change in its distribution among the regions. The inflow of foreign savings has increased in the central and southern regions and decreased in the northern and western regions, while the eastern region has an outflow of its savings outside the country, although at a very low level.

Table 15.6 also gives data on per capita consumption for the country and the various regions for the base year as well as under alternatives 1 and 2. Base year per capita consumption for the country is Rs.2567, with the values for the western, northern, and eastern regions being higher than the country, average and for the central and southern regions, they are below the country average. In fact the western region has the highest per capita consumption at Rs.2831, and the central region has the lowest at Rs.2315. The western region value is 10 percent above the country average, and the Central region value is 9 percent below the country average. This indicates that the regional disparity in the levels of per capita consumption of the various regions is not significant. The Lorenz ratio for this regional disparity is 0.042.

The disparity in per capita consumption is sought to be reduced by appropriately selecting the minimum sectoral growth rates of per capita consumption. Thus, as can be observed from the data provided in Table 15.5, the upper limits on the growth rates of almost all the sectors for the central region are assumed to be at a higher level, compared to the other regions, while the corresponding upper limits are assumed to be at a lower level for the western region, except for the construction sector. The rankings of regions according to the per capita construction under alternative 1 are exactly the same as in the base year, but the disparity has been reduced substantially. The regional consumption disparity under alternative 1 is only 0.013 (i.e., a reduction of about 11% per annum). The results relating to the per capita consumption for the country and the various regions under alternative 2 are almost similar to those under alternative 1. This is to be expected because all the relevant constraints on consumption were kept the same under the two alternatives. Certain differences have occurred, mainly due to changes in the other constraints. The Lorenz ratio of regional consumption disparity under alternative 2 is 0.012.

Table 15.7 gives secotral gross output for each region and Table 15.8 gives the results regarding the per capita consumption achieved under the two alternatives. It may be noticed that in Table 15.8, of the six basic need sectors (foodgrains, other agriculture, textiles, chemicals, construction, and services), the targets are achieved in three of them (foodgrains, textiles, and services) under both alternatives. In the case of the other agriculture sector, the targets are achieved in all the regions except for the southern region under both the alternatives and except for the western region under alternative 2 only.

In the chemicals sector, the targets are reached in the eastern, southern, and western regions, while for the central and northern regions the two targets are narrowly missed. In the construction sector, the targets are reached for the eastern, northern, and western regions, while for the central region the shortage is about 10 percent and for the southern region the shortage is slightly higher than 13 percent. Hence, again, the marginal differences in per capita consumption as observed between the two alternatives are due to changes in the constraints other than those relating to consumption.

Aggregate domestic trade for the country has been projected to increase at a rate of 4.15 percent in alternative 1 and at a slightly higher rate of 4.29 percent in alternative 2. In both the alternatives, the growth rate of interregional trade is lower than the growth rate of GDP. This is due to the upper limits on the growth rate of transport sectors and the upper limits on the surplus/deficit of aggregate trading of each region.

Table 15.7. Sectoral Gross Output for Each Region (in Rs. Crores [10 million] at 1984-85 Prices)

Sector\Region	E	C	N	S	W
Foodgrains	5918	12340	14015	7464	4608*
	[7953	19163	19769	10032	6193]
	(7953	19163	19769	10032	5899)
Other	12860	12326	5746	19446	12036
Agriculture	[20949	24247	11304	31676	17535]
	(20949	24247	11304	31676	19605)
Mining	1268	1441	899	293	415
	[1878	2834	1689	434	506]
	(2272	3111	1610	550	615)
Textiles	4825	1588	4778	4423	9495
	[7860	2587	8557	6548	12760]
	(7860	3759	8557	6548	14745)
Chemicals	2628	1844	3420	6628	10994
	[3890	3005	6283	11870	16247]
	(5674	4367	4341	11870	17074)
Petroleum	1329	2003	-	1961	4391
	[2616	4324	-	2410	7152]
	(2740	4742	-	2903	7152)
Cement	233	351	226	433	532
	[366	997	536	776	532]
	(398	882	588	853	867)
Metals &	10718	7922	11964	13245	15319
Engineering	[21889	32050	29035	36148	18858]
	(17717	30031	33154	35223	39489)
Other Industries	9657	6583	11230	16389	14404
	[15731	14213	20447	26696	16927]
	(18997	18848	24246	30765	18438)
Electricity	1978	2136	2745	3317	3279
	[3401	4718	4524	5552	4322]
	(3543	4866	4672	5679	5012)
Construction	7230	6795	7097	10539	13144
	[12057	20689	15267	19630	13891]
	(12869	22067	16687	20368	18790)
Transport	3863	5016	4922	6384	5754
	[5718	8983	7707	10399	8343]
	(7251	8983	8018	10905	8517)
Services	21739	25718	25839	33124	27370
	[33531	50302	41625	52783	35947]
	(34264	50591	43411	53955	42039)

*Values without any parentheses - Base year
    Values with [ ] - Alternative 1
    Values with ( ) - Alternative 2

Table 15.8. Sectoral Per Capita Consumption (in Rs. at 1984-85 prices)

Sector\Region	E	C	N	S	W	Target
Foodgrains	478.1	457.6	511.2	444.8	427.1*	510.0
	[535.5	535.5	536.7	529.9	535.5]	
	(535.5	533.3	511.2	527.2	510.0)	
Other	409.0	391.3	437.2	347.4	421.2	550.0
Agriculture	[577.1	577.5	577.5	514.5	566.2]	
	(549.7	577.5	557.4	514.5	539.2)	
Mining	3.2	2.9	2.9	2.5	3.1	3.0
	[3.2	3.0	3.0	3.0	3.1]	
	(3.4	3.1	3.1	3.1	3.2)	
Textiles	177.1	156.4	189.3	150.4	207.0	200.0
	[200.0	204.9	200.0	200.0	217.3]	
	(207.6	210.0	200.0	210.0	207.0)	
Chemicals	42.9	43.8	44.6	44.7	46.6	55.0
	[55.0	53.3	54.3	54.5	56.8]	
	(55.0	53.3	54.3	54.5	56.8)	
Petroleum	24.1	12.4	14.1	29.2	67.1	40.0
	[35.7	20.2	21.9	39.2	67.1]	
	(35.7	20.2	21.9	39.2	67.1)	
Cement	-	-	-	-	-	-
	-	-	-	-	-	-
	-	-	-	-	-	-
Metals &	77.2	60.0	75.6	62.9	80.0	90.0
Engineering	[89.5	75.0	87.7	76.7	92.7]	
	(89.5	75.0	87.7	76.7	92.7)	
Other Industries	432.2	343.9	434.3	361.6	447.3	450.0
	[472.5	429.5	472.5	432.0	472.5]	
	(472.5	429.5	472.5	432.0	472.5)	
Electricity	21.6	14.9	40.2	36.6	60.3	45.0
	[40.7	33.5	47.3	46.9	63.4]	
	(40.7	33.5	47.3	46.9	63.4)	
Construction	29.0	24.0	29.0	23.1	29.9	50.0
	[49.6	45.2	49.6	43.4	52.5]	
	(49.6	45.2	49.6	43.4	52.5)	
Transport	80.0	77.3	86.2	82.7	131.7	140.0
	[95.7	103.9	105.0	105.8	147.0]	
	(97.5	101.7	100.0	110.4	141.7)	
Services	776.0	650.6	784.2	777.2	800.1	850.0
	[892.5	892.5	892.5	892.5	892.5]	
	(892.5	857.6	892.5	892.5	892.5)	

* Values without any parentheses - Base year
Values with [ ] - Alternative 1
Values with ( ) - Alternative 2

The trading of each commodity between every pair of regions has undergone substantial changes between the base and the target years, as can be seen from the Table 15.9. In both the alternatives, the domestic trading in individual commodities between pairs of regions is such that in most instances upper or lower limits are binding. The results of alternative 1, when compared to the results of alternative 2, show less drastic changes in the trading of several commodities between pairs of regions because under Alternative 1 relatively more stringent limits are fixed on individual sectoral trade between the pairs of regions. Furthermore, in certain cases a region that is a net domestic exporter (importer) of a particular commodity during the base year has become a net domestic importer (exporter) of the same commodity during the target year. Such changes comparing the base year and the results of alternative 1 and also comparing the results of the two alternatives are summarized in Table 15.10. For instance, the other industries sector in the eastern region, which is a net domestic importer in the base year, has become a net domestic exporter under alternative 1. This is because of changes in demand and supply conditions in the model. Thus, the consumption demand as a proportion of this sector's output is lower under alternative 1 than in the base year. The interindustry demand as a proportion of output is also marginally lower in the target year, compared to that in the base year. These shortages were compensated by proportionately higher domestic exports, compared to domestic imports. Similar explanations apply to other instances given in Table 15.10.

The above results indicate the sensitivity of sectoral production, consumption, and trading for each region as well as the sensitivity in the reduction of regional disparity in per capita income and consumption between alternatives 1 and 2.

CONCLUSIONS AND LIMITATIONS

In past attempts to construct multiregional models, researchers have essentially tried to minimize transport costs or production and transport costs taken together. In the present study, the emphasis is on the reduction of regional disparity in income and consumption, while ensuring the availability of basic need items in all the regions. Two implicit assumptions are made in the above model to achieve the above objectives. The first assumption is that, given the resource limitations, regional disparity in per capita income level can be reduced only by curtailing the output growth rates of the more developed regions and correspondingly assuming higher growth rates for the less developed regions. The second assumption is that to achieve the desired target of speedy availability of basic need items, the growth rates of nonbasic items will have to be curtailed. When resources limitations are not so acute and there are no market limitations, high growth rates can be achieved simultaneously in more developed regions as well as for the nonbasic need sectors.

Table 15.9. Domestic Trade between Regions (in Rs. Crores [10 million] at 1984-85 prices)

From\To	E	C	N	S	W	
For Sector "Foodgrains"						
E		104	88	337	181	by*
	-	52	176	168	362	Alt. 1
		416	352	1348	724	Alt. 2
C	510		272	1038	551	by
	1020	-	544	2076	1102	Alt. 1
	127		68	4152	137	Alt. 2
N	1106	695		2251	1194	by
	1171	1115	-	4299	2276	Alt. a
	4406	173		3093	2046	Alt. 2
S	66	300	573		110	by
	33	600	1146		221	Alt. 1
	265	1200	2076		27	Alt. 2
W	208	89	77	220		by
	416	178	154	441	-	Alt. 1
	52	22	19	55		Alt. 2
For Sector "Other Agriculture"						
E		658	2035	649	389	by
	-	1316	1359	894	779	Alt. 1
		1639	6981	162	97	Alt. 2
C	175		841	268	161	by
	87		716	536	322	Alt. 1
	539		210	67	40	Alt. 2
N	141	219		216	129	by
	282	109	-	432	165	Alt. 1
	564	54		864	32	Alt. 2
S	974	1318	4076		654	by
	487	735	7921		1308	Alt. 1
	3898	329	3403		163	Alt. 2

Table 15.9 (continued)

From\To	E	C	N	S	W	
W	169	69	48	1101		by
	339	139	96	2202	-	Alt. 1
	678	278	192	711		Alt. 2

For Sector "Mining"

From\To	E	C	N	S	W	
E		73	18	187	427	by
	-	36	9	93	705	Alt. 1
		19	4	748	339	Alt. 2
C	51		17	175	418	by
	102	-	8	267	718	Alt. 1
	12		4	43	936	Alt. 2
N	50	67		176	363	by
	100	134	-	352	683	Alt. 1
	200	16		225	662	Alt. 2
S	4	6	1		46	by
	9	12	neg	-	92	Alt. 1
	19	24	neg		185	Alt. 2
W	7	9	2	58		by
	14	18	5	117	-	Alt. 1
	28	36	10	14		Alt. 2

For Sector "Textiles"

From\To	E	C	N	S	W	
E		48	208	263	766	by
	-	24	104	265	1532	Alt. 1
		192	52	647	191	Alt. 2
C	38		58	73	74	by
	76	-	116	146	148	Alt. 1
	9		14	18	18	Alt. 2
N	81	60		157	424	by
	162	120	-	314	849	Alt. 1
	20	240		305	106	Alt. 2
S	77	311	118		150	by
	38	155	105	-	300	Alt. 1
	19	77	29		37	Alt. 2
W	524	2502	728	913		by
	262	4734	364	1726	-	Alt. 1
	131	3599	182	1650		Alt. 2

Table 15.9 (continued)

From\To	E	C	N	S	W	
For Sector "Chemicals"						
E		165	135	79	127	by
	-	267	67	158	254	Alt. 1
		660	540	316	508	Alt. 2
C	88		120	74	114	by
	176	-	240	142	228	Alt. 1
	22		30	17	28	Alt. 2
N	146	245		117	189	by
	73	490	-	234	378	Alt. 1
	36	61		468	47	Alt. 2
S	54	90	73		1740	by
	27	110	36	-	3480	Alt. 1
	13	22	294		2399	Alt. 2
W	1393	2315	1965	1071		by
	2544	4630	3043	1315	-	Alt. 1
	2878	3461	3632	267		Alt. 2
For Sector "Petroleum"						
E		39	145	69	82	by
	-	19	134	138	164	Alt. 1
		156	580	276	328	Alt. 2
C	159		67	267	820	by
	318	-	126	534	1640	Alt. 1
	39		268	1068	1146	Alt. 2
N						by
	-	-	-	-	-	Alt. 1
	-	-	-	-	-	Alt. 2
S	95	91	149		385	by
	47	45	74	-	409	Alt. 1
	380	364	37		96	Alt. 2
W	387	480	1913	728		by
	193	960	3755	1456	-	Alt. 1
	1220	120	3268	734		Alt. 2
For Sector "Cement"						
E		2	6	2	2	by
	-	1	3	1	4	Alt. 1
		8	24	8	7	Alt. 2

Table 15.9 (continued)

From\To	E	C	N	S	W	
C	36		46	13	12	by
	73	-	92	26	24	Alt. 1
	48		47	17	3	Alt. 2
N	11	4		4	4	by
	22	3	-	8	8	Alt. 1
	44	16		1	1	Alt. 2
S	11	5	15		4	by
	11	10	7	-	8	Alt. 1
	45	20	3		16	Alt. 2
W	5	14	16	5		by
	10	14	8	2	-	Alt. 1
	21	56	66	20		Alt. 2

For Sector "Metals & Engineering"

From\To	E	C	N	S	W	
E		679	364	1333	370	by
	-	1358	182	666	740	Alt. 1
		665	91	333	92	Alt. 2
C	74		104	379	105	by
	37	-	52	189	210	Alt. 1
	18		26	94	26	Alt. 2
N	98	251		494	137	by
	196	502	-	247	274	Alt. 1
	392	1004		1976	548	Alt. 2
S	167	235	99		573	by
	334	470	198	-	1146	Alt. 1
	668	940	24		143	Alt. 2
W	494	1004	591	2055		by
	247	1320	295	1027	-	Alt. 1
	1976	4018	2223	901		Alt. 2

For Sector "Other Industries"

From\To	E	C	N	S	W	
E		465	131	133	109	by
	-	871	65	266	218	Alt. 1
		1860	375	33	436	Alt. 2
C	112		183	184	156	by
	57	-	91	368	312	Alt. 1
	28		45	46	162	Alt. 2

Table 15.9 (continued)

From\To	E	C	N	S	W	
N	109	627		178	148	by
	218	1254	-	356	296	Alt. 1
	27	2508		44	37	Alt. 2
S	252	2608	736		815	by
	126	4936	368	-	1630	Alt. 1
	895	652	184		3260	Alt. 2
W	430	1510	420	985		by
	215	1005	210	1970	-	Alt. 1
	107	377	105	656		Alt. 2

* by = Base year
Alt. 1 = Alternative 1
Alt. 2 = Alternative 2

Table 15.10. Changes in the Direction of Net Domestic Trade (in Rs. Crores [10 million] at 1984-85 Prices)

Sector	Region	Base Year	Alternative 1	Alternative 2
Textiles				
	Northern	-389*	756	395
Cement				
	Southern	11	-1	39
	Western	18	-8	136
Metals & Engineering				
	Eastern	1913	2133	-1872
	Northern	-178	491	1555
	Southern	-3187	17	-1529
Other Industries				
	Eastern	-66	805	1646
	Northern	-376	1389	1907
	Western	2119	945	-2649

* (-) Indicates more imports than exports

Two sets of results, alternatives 1 and 2, have been obtained in this study. Essential differences between these two alternatives involve assumptions on savings and market potential. Alternative 1 assumes relatively lower savings and foreign exports, compared to alternative 2.

The empirical analysis done here has shown that it is possible to substantially reduce the regional disparity in income and consumption while at the same time sustaining a national GDP growth rate of 5.5 percent and 6 percent, respectively, for alternatives 1 and 2. The results of Alternative 1 pertaining to the GDP of individual regions show the lowest growth rate of 2.8 percent for the western region and the highest growth rate of 7.6 percent for the central region. The growth rates for the eastern, northern, and southern regions are 4.9 percent, 5.7 percent, and 5.4 percent, respectively. These regional growth rates imply a substantial reduction in the regional disparity of income as measured by the Lorenz ratio, from 0.137 in the base year to 0.059 in the target year. The regional growth rates for the regions under alternative 2 are 5 percent, 5.1 percent, 5.7 percent, 6.2 percent, and 7.9 percent for the western, eastern, southern, northern, and central regions, respectively. The corresponding Lorenz ratio for regional income disparity in alternative 2 is 0.0857.

The gross investment requirements for the country for the ten-year plan period are Rs.994495 crores and Rs.1091300 crores, respectively, for alternatives 1 and 2. The distribution of gross investment across the regions under alternative 1 is 14 percent, 22 percent, 19 percent, 27 percent, and 18 percent, respectively, for the eastern, central, northern, southern, and western regions, whereas the corresponding values under alternative 2 are 14 percent, 21 percent, 19 percent, 25 percent, and 21percent, respectively.

The disparity in per capita consumption is sought to be reduced by appropriately selecting the minimum sectoral growth rates of per capita consumption in each region. The regional consumption disparity under alternative 1 is 0.013 against the base year value of 0.042. The same figure under alternative 2 is 0.012, close to that of alternative 1. The target base need consumption for the foodgrains, textiles and services sectors has been fully met in all the regions under both alternatives. For the other agriculture sector, the target is met in all the regions except the southern region in both the alternatives, except the western region in alternative 2, where the results are short by a very small margin. In the chemical sector also, the target is narrowly missed in the central and northern regions, while in other regions it is met fully. In the construction sector, the target is reached in the eastern, northern, and western regions, while the results are short by 10 percent in the central region and by 13 percent in the southern region. As expected, there are only marginal differences in the per capita consumption achievements under alternatives 1 and 2.

The aggregate domestic trade in the country has been projected to increase at 4.15 percent and 4.29 percent under alternatives 1 and 2, respectively. The trading of each commodity between every pair of regions has undergone substantial changes between the base year and the target year. In most instances, upper or lower limits are observed to be binding, and, as a result, the trading pattern under alternative 1 showed less drastic changes, compared to that of alternative 2. Furthermore, in certain cases, a particular commodity that had a domestic import surplus (export surplus) during the base year turned into an export surplus (import surplus) during the target year. This indicates a very strong sensitivity of the trading relationship to changes in the various parameters in this model.

All the regions were net importers, although in varying degrees, during the base year so far as foreign trade is concerned. Under alternative 1, the aggregate net imports of the country remain the same as those of the base year, but the eastern region becomes a net exporter while all the other regions continue to be net importers. Under alternative 2, the country has an export surplus of Rs.2212 crores, with the eastern, northern, and southern regions becoming net exporters, while the central and western regions continue to be net importers. This shows striking regional differences in foreign trade when compared with the national aggregate.

The objective function used in the model is to maximize the GDP. Alternatively, it is possible to minimize the transport costs with appropriate constraints on the achievement of a target level of consumption of basic needs and income levels in the various regions. In this context, a goal programming approach may be more appropriate. It is also possible to consider multiple objectives, such as maximization of the GDP and minimization of transportation cost, together in a single objective function. However, such approaches are left for future work.

The software for the model, which was developed on the PC/AT, is portable and user-friendly. While only two alternatives have been studied in detail in the present study, it is possible to consider various other alternative scenarios and choose for implementation the most appropriate one from the point of view of the development goals of the country.

One of the limitations in the use of a multiregional model is the lack of regional data, especially with reference to current and capital coefficient matrices. Such data have to be explicitly developed to make a comprehensive multiregional study, and particularly to analyze the relevant comparative advantages of various sectors of various regions.

The multiregional model developed here is essentially a supply-side model. However, the availability of basic need items does not automatically ensure their demand. This will have to be done by adopting appropriate pricing and/or income policies. The pricing and income policies and the appropriate basic need supply policies are complementary. Development of such a demand-side model is left for the future work.

REFERENCES

Bhatia, V. G. (December 1961), "Interregional Allocation of Investment in Development Programming," unpublished thesis, Harvard University.

Chenery, H.B., Clark, P.G., and Cao-Pinna, Vera (1953), *The Structure and Growth of the Italian Economy*, Rome: U.S. Mutual Security Agency.

Dhar, R. (1965), "Inter-Regional Input Output Analysis: A Study of Inter-Regional Inter-Sectoral Relations of the Indian Economy, 1953-54," Ph.D. thesis, Jadaypur University, Calcutta, India. (Summary published in *Economic Analysis in Input Output Framework*, R. K. Bjaradwaj and P. N. Mathur (eds.), 1965.

Dhar, R. (1972), "Implications of Income Leakages in a Multi-Regional Framework," *Indian Journal of Regional Science* 4, no. 12.

Dhar, R. (June-December 1973), "The Nature of Spatial Clusters of the Indian Economy," *Anvesak.*

Dhar, R. (1989), "A Multi-Regional Model for India's Eighth Plan (1989-90 to 1994-95): With Analysis of Basic Needs," Indian Institute of Management at Bangalore (unpublished).

Dhar, R., and Rao, M.R. (April 1983), "The EMPOV Model," United National Centre for Regional Development (UNCRD) Working Paper No. 83-7, Nagoya.

Dhar, R., Rao, M.R., and Goel, S. (1988), "An Optimizing Model for India's Eighth and Ninth Plans: With Analysis of Basic Needs," presented at the seminar on Modeling and Analysis of Large Systems, IIM, Ahmedabad, India, August 19-21, 1988. (Proceedings are being published by Oxford and IBH Publishing Company.)

Dhar, R., Venning, R., and Berry, B.J.L. (1966), "Inter-Regional Inter-Sectoral Relations of the Indian Economy," in *Essays on Commodity Flows and the Spatial Structure of the Indian Economy*, B. J. L. Berry (ed.). Research Paper No. 111, Chicago: Department of Geography, University of Chicago.

Ghosh, A., with Chakravarty, A. (June 1967), "An Inter-Industrial Programming Model for Production and Transportation of Commodities for Different Regions of India," *Artha Vijnana* 9.

Ghosh, A., and Dhar, R. (1965), *Efficiency in Location and Inter-Regional Flows: The Study of Cement Industry in India under the Five Year Plans*, Amsterdam: North Holland.

Henderson, J.J. (1958), *The Efficiency of Coal Industry*, Cambridge, Mass.: Harvard University Press.

Isard, W. (November 1951), "Inter-Regional and Regional Input Output Analysis: A Model of a Space Economy," *Review of Economics and Statistics* 33, no. 4: 318-328.

Leontief, W. (1953), "Inter-Regional Theory," in *Studies in the Structure of American Economy*, W. Leontief (ed.), New York: Oxford University Press.

Leontief, W., and Hoffenberg, M. (April 1961), "The Economic Effect of Disarmament," *Scientific American* 204, no. 4: 47-55.

Leontief, W., and Strout, A.S. (1963), "Multi-Regional Input Output Analysis," in *Structural Interdependence and Economic Development*, T. Barna, ed. London: Macmillan; New York: St. Martin's Press.

Mathur, P.N. (1982), "An Inter-Industry and Inter-Regional Dynamic Model for Planning (a tentative outline)", in *Input Output Techniques*, A. Brody and A. P. Carter (eds.), Amsterdam: North Holland.

Mathur, P.N., and Hashim, S.R. (1970), "A Model for Optimum Location Flows," in *Economic Analysis in an Input Output Framework*, vol. 2, P. N. Mathur and P. Venkatramaiah (eds.). Poona, India: Input Output Research Association.

Ministry of International Trade and Industry (MITI), Japan (1970), "The Inter-Regional Input Output Table for Japan (1960 and 1965 Tables), Tokyo: Japanese Government.

Moses, L.N. (December 1955), "The Stability of Inter-Regional Trading Pattern and Input Output Analysis," *American Economic Review* 45, no. 1: 803-832.

Moses, L.N. (November 1960), "A General Equilibrium Model of Production, Inter-Regional Trade and Location of Industry," *Review of Economics and Statistics* 42, no. 4: 373-392.

Narain, D., and Sardesai, D.B. (1967), "Location of Industries in India—Transport Cost Minimization," *Artha Vijnana* 9 (special issue).

Oosterhaven, J. (1981), *Inter-Regional Input Output Analysis and Dutch Regional Policy Problems*, Aldershot, Hampshire (UK): Gower Publishing Co.

Polenske, K.R. (1980), *The U.S. Multi-Regional Input Output Accounts and Models*, Lexington, Mass.: Heath/Lexington Books.

Part VI

Programming Models

Improved Linear and Integer Programming Models for Discriminant Analysis

Fred Glover

There is a growing recognition that a variety of classical statistical problems can be approached advantageously using tools from the field of optimization. Reexamination of these problems and their underlying model assumptions can sometimes lead to refreshing new perspectives and alternative lines of attack. Discriminant analysis is high on the list of problems of this type and has been drawing increased attention recently because it straddles the areas of management science and artificial intelligence as well as statistics. Management science applications of discriminant analysis include decisions to make or buy, lend or invest, hire or reject (see Charnes, Cooper, and Rhodes, 1981; Kazmier, 1967; Spurr and Bonini 1976). Artificial intelligence applications involve the challenging realm of pattern recognition, including problems of signal differentiation, diagnostic classifications, code signatures, and data types (see Bobrowski, 1986; Kazmier, 1967; Tou and Gonzalez, 1974; and Watanabe, 1969).

An effort to wed statistical discrimination with optimization has come about through proposals to capture the goals of discriminant analysis in a collection of linear programming (LP) formulations (see Freed and Glover, 1981 and 1987; and Glover, Keene, and Duea, 1988). The objectives of initial forms of these models included minimizing the maximum deviation and the sum of deviations of misclassified points from a reference hyperplane, together with weighted variants of these objectives. Although the more advanced earlier variants and their recent derivatives have gone largely unexplored (a condition that deserves to be remedied), empirical testing of the simpler variants has disclosed the "minimum sum of deviations" model to be competitive in effectiveness with the classical approach of Fisher (see Kazmier, 1967 and Markowski and Markowski, 1985). This comparative testing was carried out in contexts determined by the limited goals and assumptions of classical discriminant analysis and did not examine settings that could be advantageously exploited by the more flexible objectives of the LP discriminant approaches. Moreover, no use was made of LP postoptimization to re-weight borderline misclassified points to obtain refined solutions, one of the strategic options of the LP approaches proposed with their earliest formulations. Consequently, the effective performance of the LP discriminant analysis models under these circumstances gave encouraging evidence of their potential value in wider applications.

At the same time, however, empirical tests also disclosed that the LP formulations gave counterintuitive and even anomalous results. Follow-up examination of specially anomalous results demonstrated that these formulations are attended by certain subtleties not found in other areas to which linear programming is commonly applied (see Bajgier and Hill, 1982; Freed and Glover, 1987; and Markowski and Markowski, 1985).

Analysis has indicated that the anomalous behavior of the LP formulations stems from the implicit use of normalizations in order to avoid "null solutions" that assigned zero weight to all data elements. Several normalizations have been identified (see Freed and Glover, 1987 and Glover, Keene, and Duea, 1988) in an attempt to overcome this difficulty. The most recent of these has been demonstrated to exhibit desirable invariance properties lacking in its predecessors and has produced encouraging experimental outcomes, yielding solutions generally better than those obtained by earlier studies (see Glover, Keene, and Duea, 1988).

In spite of these advances, however, the full power of the LP models for discriminant analysis has not been achieved because the best normalization proposed to date distorts the solutions in a manner not previously anticipated. The consequences of this distortion not only inhibit the quality of "first pass" solutions obtained by the LP formulations, but also can confound the logical basis of obtaining more refined solutions by differential weighting of deviations in the objective functions and LP postoptimization.

The purpose of this chapter is to remedy these defects and to demonstrate some of the consequences for improved modeling capabilities that result. We introduce a new normalization that eliminates the previous distortions in the LP models and that has attractive properties enabling it to obtain demonstrably superior solutions.

The new normalization further allows a generalization to integer conditions and causes the integer programming problem of minimizing the number of misclassified points to have as its continuous relaxation the LP problem of minimizing the cumulative deviations of misclassified points, permitting the latter to serve as an approximation to the former. The value of this approximation is reinforced by the demonstration that the new normalization also endows the LP formulation with an integer local optimality property, which yields a "balanced" number of misclassified points. These links between continuous and discrete solutions, and the lack of distortion that attended the most effective previous normalization, give new scope to the LP models. Finally, we show that the ability to place any desired relative emphasis on classifying particular points correctly leads to a conditionally staged application of the model, called the successive goal method, for achieving progressively more refined discrimination for both two-group and multigroup analysis.

A HYBRID LP DISCRIMINANT MODEL

We take as our starting point the hybrid LP model of Jurs (1986), which integrates features of the previous LP discriminant formulations (Freed and Glover, 1981 and 1987). Attention will initially be restricted to the two-group discriminant problem, which constitutes the main focus of our development.

We represent each data point by a row vector A_i, where membership in Group 1 or Group 2 is indicated by $i \in G_1$ or $i \in G_2$, respectively. (Different points can have the same coordinates, and efficient adaptations for this are indicated below in "Model Manipulation and Simplifications.")

To discriminate the points of the two groups, we seek a weighting vector x and a scalar b, which may be interpreted as providing a hyperplane of the form $Ax = b$, where A takes the role of representing A_i for each i. The goal is to assure as nearly as possible that the points of Group 1 lie on one side of the hyperplane and the points of Group 2 lie on the other, which translates into the conditions that $A_i x < b$ for $i \in G_1$ and $A_i x > b$ for $i \in G_2$.

Refining this goal as in Glover, Keene, and Duea (1988), we introduce external and internal deviation variables, represented by the symbols α_i and β_i, which refer to the magnitudes by which the points lie outside or inside (and hence "violate" or "satisfy") their targeted half spaces. Upon introducing objective function coefficients h_i to discourage external deviations and k_i to encourage internal deviations and defining $G = G_1 \cup G_2$, we may express the LP model as follows:

Minimize $h_0\alpha_0 + \sum_{i \in G} h_i\alpha_i - k_0\beta_0 - \sum_{i \in G} k_i\beta_i$ (1)

subject to

$$A_ix - \alpha_0 - \alpha_i + \beta_0 + \beta_i = b \qquad i \in G_1 \qquad (2)$$
$$A_ix + \alpha_0 + \alpha_i - \beta_0 - \beta_i = b \qquad i \in G_1 \qquad (3)$$

$$\alpha_0, \beta_0 \geq 0 \qquad (4)$$

$$\alpha_i, \beta_i \geq 0 \qquad i \in G \qquad (5)$$

x, b unrestricted in sign (6)

Many variations of this model framework are possible. For example, in the "$\in$ version" of the model, the variable b that constitutes the boundary term for the hyperplane can be replaced by b - $\in$ for Group 1 and by b + $\in$ for Group 2, where $\in$ is a selected positive constant, to pursue the goal of compelling elements of Group 1 and Group 2 to lie strictly inside the half space whose boundary is demarked by *b*. (Different values of $\in$ may be chosen for different points. However, under the choice of a uniform value, the $\in$ version is also equivalent to a "one-sided $\in$ model" that replaces *b* by b + $\in$ for Group 2 only, where the $\in$ value in this case is twice as large as in the "two-sided" case.)

The objective function coefficients will generally be assumed to be non-negative, although it is possible to allow the coefficients of the variables to be negative. In this latter variation the hybrid model represents a generalized form of a standard goal programming model. We also stipulate that the objective function coefficients should satisfy $h_i \geq k_i$ for i = 0 and i $\in$ G. Otherwise, it would be possible to take any feasible solution and increase the value of α_i and β_i (for $h_i < k_i$) an indefinite amount to obtain an unbounded optimum. More complete conditions for avoiding unbounded optimality, both necessary and sufficient, are identified subsequently.

From an interpretive standpoint, the α_0 variable provides a component to weight the "maximum external deviation," while the β_0 variable provides a component to weight the "minimal internal deviation." This interpretation is suggestive rather than exact, however, due to the incorporation of the individual point deviation variables, α_i and β_i, in the same equations as α_0

and β_0. The effects of these variables can be segregated more fully by introducing separate constraints of the form $A_i x - \alpha_0 + \beta_0 \leq b$ for $i \in G_1$, and $A_i x + \alpha_0 - \beta_0 \geq b$ for $i \in G_2$, at the expense of enlarging the model form. By deleting the α_0 and β_0 variables in equations (1) through (6) or, alternatively, by deleting the α_i variables and setting the k_i coefficients to zero, the foregoing model corresponds to one of the models first proposed in Freed and Glover (1981).

THE NORMALIZATION ISSUE

To understand the potential difficulties that underlie the preceding discriminant analysis formulation, it is useful to review in greater detail the history of its development and attempted application. In the form given, the model in fact is incomplete, for it must be amended in some fashion to avoid an optimal solution that yields the null weighting $x = 0$. If the two groups can be separated by a hyperplane (or "nearly" so) and if the k_i coefficients are positive, the null weighting will be automatically ruled out, but in this case the model must be amended to assure that it is bounded for optimality. Broadly speaking, the more challenging applications of discriminant analysis arise where the two groups significantly "overlap," and in these cases a solution yielding the null weighting $x = 0$ typically will be optimal if it is not somehow rendered infeasible.

The early implementations of LP formulations for discriminant analysis undertook to avoid the null weighting by the logical expedient of setting b to a nonzero constant. It was tacitly assumed that different choices of b would serve only to scale the solution (provided at least the proper sign was chosen), and the approximation to optimality in the special case where b ideally should be 0 still would be reasonably good.

However, experimental tests of different LP model variants soon disclosed that assigning b a constant value still permitted the null weighting to occur for certain data configurations. More generally the models responded with nonequivalent, and sometimes poor, solutions to different translations of the same underlying data, where each point A_i is replaced by the point $A_i + t$ for a common vector t (see Bajgier and Hill, 1982; and Markowski and Markowski, 1985).

These unexpected outcomes prompted the observation that setting b to a constant value could be viewed as a "model normalization," and it was soon discovered that other normalizations could be identified that affected the model behavior in different ways (see Freed and Glover, 1987). Let N denote the index set for components of the x vector. Then the first two proposals for alternative normalizations to remedy the problems of setting b to a constant can be written in the following form:

$$b + \sum_{j \in N} x_j \quad = \quad \text{a constant}$$

$$\sum_{j \in N} x_j \quad = \quad \text{a constant}$$

Of these alternatives, the latter proved in Freed and Glover (1987) to yield solutions that were equivalent for different translations of the data, a property not shared by the other normalizations. This advantage was not enough to rescue the latter normalization from defects, however. First, to use the normalization, the LP formulation had to be solved for both signs of the constant term to assure that the right sign was selected. Second, the variables had to be either directly or indirectly bounded (in a sense, yielding an auxiliary normalization) to assure bounded optimality. Third, the normalization continued to produce nonequivalent solutions for different rotations (in contrast to translations) of the problem data, where each point A_i is replaced by the point A_iR, and R is a rotation matrix.

The most recent attempt to settle the normalization issue occurred in Jurs (1986) with the "β normalization"

$$\beta_0 + \sum_{i \in G} \beta_i \quad = \quad 1$$

The need to allow for different signs of the constant term was eliminated with this normalization. More significantly, it was proved that the normalization succeeded in yielding equivalent solutions for both translations and rotations of the problem data. Experimentation further shows that the normalization provided solutions uniformly as good or better than solutions obtained with previous normalizations for the problems examined. In spite of these advances, however, this latest normalization likewise suffers undesirable limitations, which continue to distort the solutions obtained by the LP formulations.

In the following sections we illustrate the nature of the distortion inherent in the ß normalization and then show that it is compounded by a related defect that limits the generality and flexibility of the LP model when this normalization is used. We then provide a new normalization that is free of these limitations, while exhibiting the appropriate invariance properties for transformations of data. The attributes of this normalization are explored in results that establish additional features of the LP formulations not shared by alternative approaches. Finally, we amplify the implications of these results for obtaining discrimination approaches of increased power.

LIMITATIONS TO BE OVERCOME

The limitations of the β normalization will be illustrated in an example applicable to the standard discriminant analysis context as a means of clarifying the properties that need to be exhibited by an improved normalization. Consider the simple case where each point A_i has a single coordinate, and hence the weight vector x may be treated as a scalar variable. For illustrative purposes we will use the form of the hybrid model in which α_0 and β_0 are deleted. In addition, for further simplicity, we suppose all the k_i coefficients are 0.

The relevant data for the example are given in Table 16.1, indicating the coordinates and the penalties for being classified in the wrong group.

Table 16.1. The Coordinates and the Penalties for Being Classified in the Wrong Group

Group 1 Points		Group 2 Points	
Coordinates	Penalties	Coordinates	Penalties
$A_1 = 0$	$h_1 = 15$	$A_4 = -1$	$h_4 = 25$
$A_2 = 1$	$h_2 = 25$	$A_5 = 0$	$h_5 = 25$
$A_3 = -2$	$h_3 = 25$	$A_6 = 2$	$h_6 = 25$
	(all $k_i = 0$)		

A graph of the points is shown in Figure 16.1, where Group 1 points are indicated by circles and Group 2 points are indicated by squares. The misclassification penalties are shown above each point.

The values from -2 to +2 on the line segment correspond to the values of b. It is easy to show that the best way to separate the Group 1 and Group 2 points on the line segment is to choose the value b = 0, where Group 1 points are counted as misclassified if they fall to the right of the selected value and Group 2 points are counted as misclassified if they fall to the left. Then, only A_2 and A_4 are misclassified, each with a deviation of 1 unit from the value b = 0, hence giving a total penalty cost of (1 x 25) + (1 x 25) = 50.

Without a normalization constraint, the LP model falls into the trap of finding a meaningless "optimal" solution, x = 0 and b = 0, which makes all external deviations 0 and hence also makes the total penalty cost 0. Consider the result of using the β normalization to overcome this limitation. We can choose any positive constant term for the right-hand side of this normalization, and specify the normalization to be $\Sigma\beta_i = 4$, since 4 is the sum of the internal deviations, β_i, in the case identified as best by graphical analysis. Indeed, we then obtain x = 1, b = 0 (with $\alpha_4 = \alpha_2 = 1$, $\beta_3 = \beta_6 = 2$, all other α_i and $\beta_i = 0$) as a feasible solution for the LP model, yielding a total penalty cost of 50, as before.

Figure 16.1. Group 1 and Group 2 Points
with Misclassification Penalties

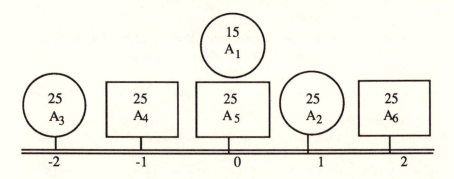

This solution turns out not to be optimal, however. Rather, the β normalization causes the inferior solution based on x = 1 and b = -1 to appear even better. From a graphical standpoint, the deviation variables with positive values for this solution are $\alpha_1 = 1$, $\alpha_2 = 2$, $\beta_3 = 1$, $\beta_5 = 1$, and $\beta_6 = 3$, which yield a total penalty cost of 65. However, the sum of the β_i variables equals 5, and to rescale the solution to satisfy the β normalization with a right-hand side of 4, the value of each variable must be multiplied by 4/5. The result is to multiply the total penalty cost of 65 likewise by 4/5, yielding a penalty cost for the LP model of 42. This is better than the "best case" penalty cost of 50, causing the model to favor a less desirable solution.

This outcome is made more remarkable by noting that an earlier normalization, Σx_j = a constant (in this case chose 1 as the constant), will correctly identify the "best solution" as optimal. Yet for multidimensional problems this earlier normalization suffers from distortions not encountered by the β normalization, and empirical testing has found it generally to provide solutions that are not as good as those produced by the β normalization. Consequently, we are motivated to seek a new type of normalization that is more broadly effective and reliable.

As a step toward identifying additional properties this new normalization ideally should have, and pitfalls it should avoid, we next examine the behavior of the normalization in the context of an integer programming formulation.

The Integer Programming Case

An integer programming (IP) discriminant model for minimizing the *number* of misclassified points can be formulated as a simple variant of the LP model. We write the IP model as follows.

Minimize $\quad \displaystyle\sum_{i \in G} z_i$ $\qquad\qquad\qquad\qquad\qquad\qquad\qquad$ (7)

subject to

$$A_i x - U z_i + \beta_i = b \qquad\qquad i \in G_1 \qquad\qquad (8)$$

$$A_i x + U z_i - \beta_i = b \qquad\qquad i \in G_2 \qquad\qquad (9)$$

$$\beta_i \geq 0 \qquad\qquad\qquad\qquad\quad i \in G \qquad\qquad\; (10)$$

$$z_i = 0 \text{ or } 1 \qquad\qquad\qquad i \in G \qquad\qquad\; (11)$$

$$x, b \text{ unrestricted in sign} \qquad\qquad\qquad\qquad (12)$$

The constant U is assumed to be chosen large enough that the inequality of $A_i x \leq b + U z_i$ will be redundant for $i \in G_1$ and the inequality of $A_i x \geq b -$

Uz_i will be redundant for $i \in G_2$, when z_i is set equal to 1. The β_i variables may be interpreted as slack and surplus variables for these inequalities. More generally, the constant U can be replaced by different constants U_i for each i in G. Likewise a constant can be added to the right-hand side of equation (8) and subtracted from the right-hand side of equation (9) to seek a minimizing solution for strict group separation.

To apply the β normalization to the IP formulation, we need to know how large the U should be. From equations (8) and (9), we note the normalization can be expressed as

$$\sum_{i \in G_1} (b - A_i x + U z_i) + \sum_{i \in G_2} (A_i x - b + U z_i) = 1$$

Hence, in particular this yields:

$$U = [1 - \sum_{i \in G_1} (b - A_i x) - \sum_{i \in G_2} (A_i x - b)] / \sum_{i \in G} z_i$$

Thus, we see that the value of U depends intimately on the optimal values of the problem variables, which cannot be known in advance. If the IP formulation is applied to points A_i of the numerical example of Table 16.1 and Figure 16.1, the value of U must uniquely be selected to be 1/4 to permit the optimal integer solution to be found. This serious deficiency of the β normalization from an integer programming model standpoint identifies a further type of limitation an improved normalization should seek to overcome.

THE NEW NORMALIZATION

The normalization we propose is

$$(- n_2 \sum_{i \in G_1} A_i + n_1 \sum_{i \in G_2} A_i)x = 1 \qquad (N)$$

where n_1 and n_2 are respectively, the number of elements in G_1 and G_2, and the right-hand side of 1 is an arbitrary scaling choice for a positive constant.

(An alternative scaling that tends to yield x_j values closer to an average absolute value of 1 is to choose this constant to be $2n_1n_2$.) An equivalent form of this normalization occurs by adding n_2 times each equation of (1) and subtracting n_1 times each equation of (3) to yield the constraint

$$2n_1n_2 \, (\beta_0\alpha_0) + n_2 \sum_{i \in G_1} (\beta_i - \alpha_i) + n_1 \sum_{i \in G_2} (\beta_i - \alpha_i) = 1 \qquad (N^*)$$

Expressing the normalization in the form (N) has certain advantages for analysis, while expressing it in the form (N*) is convenient for incorporation into the LP formulation [since the coefficients of the variables do not require calculation as in (N)]. It may be noted that the weights h_i and k_i in the objective function should not be chosen in proportion to the coefficients of corresponding variables in (N*), or else the normalization effectively constrains the objective function to equal a constant, and the minimization goal becomes superfluous. [If the k_i coefficients are proportional to corresponding coefficients of (N*), then a similar effect occurs in the case where it is possible to completely separate Group 1 and Group 2 points— where all α_i become 0.]

To understand the properties of the normalization given by (N) and (N*), let d_i denote the *net internal deviation* of the point A_i from the hyperplane generated by the discriminant model; that is

$$d_i = b - A_i x \qquad \text{for } i \in G_1$$

$$d_i = A_i x - b \qquad \text{for } i \in G_2.$$

Hence, d_i is positive (or zero) if A_i lies within its targeted half space and negative otherwise. [The "$\in$ version" of the model for seeking strict separation replaces the quantity b by $b - \in$, for a positive constant $\in$, in the definition of d_i. This results in increasing the constant term of the normalization (N) by the quantity $\in (n_1 + n_2)$, while leaving the constant term of the normalization (N*) unchanged.]

Note that if Group 1 and Group 2 have the same number of points and are "separable" to any meaningful extent by a hyperplane, then the internal deviations should sum to a larger value than the external deviations, and, hence, the sum of all the d_i values should be positive. More broadly, if

Group 1 and Group 2 have a different number of points, then upon weighting the d_i values to give equal representations to the groups relative to their sizes (i.e., multiplying each d_i in Group 1 by n_2 and each d_i in Group 2 by n_1), a meaningful separation should yield a positive value for this weighted sum. We embody this observation in the following definition.

A hyperplane creates a *meaningful separation* of Group 1 and Group 2 if

$$n_2 \sum_{i \in G_1} d_i + n_1 \sum_{i \in G_2} d_i > 0.$$

On the basis of this definition we may at once state the following result.

Theorem 1

The normalization (N) is equivalent (under scaling) to requiring a meaningful separation and eliminates the null weighting $x = 0$ as a feasible solution.

Proof. First, (N) reduces to an inconsistent equation when $x = 0$ and hence renders the null solution infeasible. To see that (N) is equivalent to requiring a meaningful separation, expand the inequality that defines a meaningful separation by substituting the appropriate values for d_i, according to membership of i in G_1 or G_2, thereby obtaining

$$n_2 \sum_{i \in G_1} (b - A_i x) + n_1 \sum_{i \in G_2} (A_i x - b) > 0$$

Algebraic manipulation and reduction permit this inequity to be reexpressed in the form

$$- n_2 \sum_{i \in G_1} A_i x + n_1 \sum_{i \in G_2} A_i x > 0$$

whose left-hand side corresponds to the left-hand side of (N). Given any feasible solution to the LP formulation that satisfies this inequality, upon dividing the values of all variables in the solution by the positive left-hand-side quantity, the result is again feasible for the LP problem and satisfies (N). Hence, allowing for scaling, the solutions are equivalent. Similarly, any feasible solution that satisfies (N) automatically satisfies the definition of a meaningful separation. This completes the proof.

Corollary

A meaningful separation exists if and only if there exists a hyperplane such that $n_2 \sum_{i \in G_1} d_i + n_1 \sum_{i \in G_2} d_i \neq 0$.

It also exists if and only if there exists some component A_{ij} of each point A_i, $i \in G$, such that $n_2 \sum_{i \in G_1} A_{ij} \neq n_1 \sum_{i \in G_2} A_{ij}$

Proof. The corollary is a direct consequence of Theorem 1 and the form of (N).

It may be noted by the proof of Theorem 1 that upon choosing non-negative scalars u_i such that $\sum_{i \in G_1} u_i = \sum_{i \in G_2} u_i > 0$, a normalization of the form

$$(- \sum_{i \in G_1} u_i A_i + \sum_{i \in G_2} u_i A_i)x = 1$$

will correspondingly eliminate the null solution and be consistent with a biased meaningful separation defined by the inequality

$$\sum_{i \in G_1} u_i d_i + \sum_{i \in G_2} u_i d_i > 0$$

Specifically, if there is reason to ensure that a weighted sum of internal deviations should exceed a correspondingly weighted sum of external deviations (as where particular points command more importance, and hence larger weights, than others), then such a biased normalization can be employed. We will not undertake to pursue the issue of these biased normalizations further, but simply note that our subsequent results can be readily adapted to treat them as well.

Useful additional insights into the nature of (N) and its consequences for the hybrid LP discriminant formulation are provided by examining the linear

programming dual of equations (1) through (6) with (N) attached. To create
this dual, it is convenient first to rewrite the constraint equation (2) by
multiplying it through by -1. Then, associating a variable v_i with the
equations (2) and (3) for each $i \in G$ and a variable v_0 with (N), we obtain the
following result.

Dual Model Formulation

Maximize v_0

subject to

$$A_0 v_0 - \sum_{i \in G_1} A_i v_i + \sum_{i \in G_2} A_i v_i = 0$$

$$h_0 \geq \sum_{i \in G} v_i \geq k_0$$

$$h_i \geq v_i \geq k_i \quad i \in G$$

$$\sum_{i \in G_1} v_i - \sum_{i \in G_2} v_i = 0$$

where

$$A_0 = - n_2 \sum_{i \in G_1} A_i + n_1 \sum_{i \in G_2} A_i$$

Our interest is analyzing this dual is to determine circumstances that
provide a feasible dual solution and hence that assure that the LP discriminant
formulation is bounded for optimality.

Necessary conditions for bounded optimality of the formulation (1)
through (6) are immediately evident from the dual formulation, as are
necessary conditions in order for certain variables of the LP discriminant

formulation to be nonzero at optimality. The following is established by reference to the quality theory of linear programming.

Necessary Conditions for Bounded Optimality

$$h_i \geq k_i \qquad i \in G \text{ and } i = 0,$$

$$\sum_{i \in G} k_i \leq h_0$$

Necessary conditions for Variables to be Nonzero

$$\text{For } \beta_0: \quad h_0 < \sum_{i \in G} h_i$$

$$\text{For } \beta_0: \quad k_0 > \sum_{i \in G} k_i$$

To avoid trivial solution values for dual variables, it is appropriate to stipulate $h_i > k_i$ for $i \in G$. In general, interpretation of the inequalities for bounded optimality in the context of the LP discriminant formulation suggests they reasonably may be required to be strict. It may be noted that $h_i > k_i$ implies that at most one of α_i and β_i will be positive, an outcome that also holds when $h_i = k_i$ in the case of extreme point solutions. (This is not true for the β normalization.)

We seek to go beyond the foregoing observations, however, by providing sufficient as well as necessary conditions for bounded optimality.

Theorem 2

The LP discriminant model in equations (1) - (6) with the normalization (N) is bounded for optimality whenever

$$\text{Min } (h_0/2, n_1 h_1 : i \in G_1, n_2 h_i : i \in G_2)$$

is at least as large as

$$\text{Max } (k_0/2,\ n_1 k_1 : i \in G_1,\ n_2 k_i : i \in G_2)$$

Proof. Replace (N) by (N*) in the primal formulation, whereon the dual problem becomes

Maximize v_0

subject to

$$-\sum_{i \in G_1} A_i v_i \ + \sum_{i \in G_2} A_i v_i = 0$$

$$h_0 \geq -2n_1 n_2 v_0 + \sum_{i \in G} v_i \geq k_0$$

$$h_i \geq -n_2 v_0 + v_i \geq k_i \qquad i \in G_1$$

$$h_i \geq -n_1 v_0 + v_i \geq k_i \qquad i \in G_2$$

Here v_0 is the same variable as in the preceding dual formulation, but the v_i variables, $i \in G$, are different. In this new dual formulation, we set $v_i = 0$ for all $i \in G$. The resulting partial solution satisfies the first problem constraint and leaves the remaining inequalities in the form of bounds on v_0. Expressing these as bounds on $-n_1 n_2 v_0$ in each case, and then comparing terms, yields the inequalities stated in the theorem. This completes the proof.

The sufficiency conditions of Theorem 2 are generally more restrictive than required to assure bounded optimality. When the theorem is applied to the model variant where α_0 and β_0 is deleted the corresponding term involving h_0 or k_0 is deleted from its statement. Where both α_0 or β_0 are deleted, and the two groups have the same number of elements, the conditions of the theorem simplify to $\text{Min}(h_i : i \in G) \geq \text{Max}(k_i : i \in G)$.

Theorem 2 has an additional attractive feature. Suppose that h_i and k_i values initially have been chosen subject only to the condition that all h_i (including h_0) are positive. If the inequality of Theorem 2 is not satisfied, let R be the ratio of the Max term to the Min term of the theorem. Then upon replacing each h_i by Rh_i in the objective (1), the condition of the theorem is satisfied. This modification of the coefficients of objective (1) leaves the relative magnitudes of the h_i coefficients, and also of the k_i coefficients, of objective (1) to reflect any desired *relative emphasis* on the correct classification of particular points, and bounded optimality can be assured by a simple adjustment of the objective function coefficient that preserves this relative emphasis.

Our next goal is to show that the normalization (N) is stable across rotations and translations of problem data. For this, we employ a useful result from Glover, Keene, and Duea (1988). Consider the following pair of related problems:

I.   Minimize $g(y)$

subject to
$$A_i x + \beta_i(y) = b \qquad i \in G \qquad\qquad (13)$$
$$y \in Y$$

II. Minimize $g(y)$

subject to
$$(A_i R + t)x + \beta_i(y) = b \quad i \in G \qquad (14)$$
$$y \in Y$$

The terms $g(y)$ and $\beta_i(y)$ for $i \in G$ in these problems represent arbitrary functions of y. To connect these problems to the LP and IP discriminant formulations, the vectors A_i and the variables x and b may be construed the same as indicated previously. The vector of variables y may accordingly include all remaining variables of the LP and IP formulations, while the condition $y \in Y$ may summarize non-negativity and integer requirements.

It is important to note that $y \in Y$ can also incorporate the normalization constraint (N), using the observation in the proof of Theorem 2 that reexpresses this constraint in terms of the α and β variables [which similarly leads to an expression for (N) in terms of the z and β variables for the IP problem]. The objective function $g(y)$ and the constraints function $\beta_i(y)$ of I and II may likewise encompass the associated linear functions of the LP and IP discriminant models as a special case.

The constraints that differentiate the two problems are constraints (13) and (14). The latter constraint set achieves the effect of transforming each point A_i by means of a rotation matrix R and translating the point by means of point A_i by means of a rotation matrix R and translating the point by means of a row vector t. More generally, we assume that R is nonsingular and disregard the stipulation that the transpose of a rotation matrix is also its inverse. Then we may state the following result (stability theorem—see Glover, Keene, and Duea, 1988).

Stability Theorem

The optimum objective function values for Problems I and II are the same. Moreover, if Y' and Y" represent the optimal solution sets Y for Problems I and II, respectively, then Y' = Y".

Proof. We show more particularly that if the solution (y', x', b') is optimal for I, then (y', $R^{-1}x'$, b' + $tR^{-1}x'$) is optimal for II, and if (y", x", b") is optimal for II, then (y", Rx", b" - tx") is optimal for I. By substituting and rearranging terms, it is clear that the solutions claimed to be optimal for problems I and II, given the assumed optimality of (y', x', b') and (y", x", b"), must respectively be feasible for these two problems. By feasibility for II we obtain g(y') ≥ g(y"), and by feasibility for I we obtain g(y") ≥ g(y'). Consequently g(y') = g(y") and the stated conclusions are established.

By our observations linking the LP and IP discriminant formulations to Problems I and II, the Stability Theorem gives the desired result.

Theorem 3

The optimum objective function values and optimal values for the α and β deviation variables in the LP discriminant formulation and for the z and β variables in the IP formulation, are unchanged for all rotations and translations of the problem data.

Proof. This theorem is a direct consequence of the preceding observations.

It may be noted that the general form of Problems I and II also makes the foregoing results applicable to the case where strict group separation is sought by replacing b with b - ϵ in the constraints applicable to Group 1 and with b + ϵ in the constraints applicable to Group 2.

We conclude this section by observing that the defect illustrated in Table 16.1 and Figure 16.1 for the β normalization is overcome by (N). In particular, the distortion of the solution caused by the β normalization in this example occurred because a shift of b (from its "best value" of 0) caused the to satisfy the β normalization. As a result, it was impossible to hold x constant to find the optimal b value, given x, since moving b forced x to change as well. The normalization (N) is free of this defect for the important reason that it is entirely possible to hold x constant and change b without any effect on the normalization constraint. Thus, the normalization (N) gives the same objective function values as the graphical analysis of the example of Table 16.1 and Figure 16.1, and identifies the same solution as optimal.

MODEL MANIPULATION AND SIMPLIFICATIONS

Our primary goal will be to identify how the model (1) - (6) can be manipulated to achieve an "equal representation" of the points in Group 1 and Group 2. This hinges on another more basic observation, which makes it possible to reduce the size of the model in the case where some points may have the same coordinates as others [to avoid including a separate constraint equation (and corresponding α_i and β_i variables) for each duplicate point].

Specifically, let S denote a collection of points all in G_1 or all in G_2, such that $A_p = A_q$ for each p, q in S. If S is a subset of G_1, then the equations of (2) corresponding to $i \in S$ can be replaced by a single representative equation $A_r x - \alpha_0 - \alpha_r + \beta_0 + \beta_r = b$, where A_r is the common vector A_i for all $i \in S$. If S is a subset of G_2, the equations of (3) corresponding to $i \in S$ can similarly be replaced by the representative equation $A_r x + \alpha_0 + \alpha_r - \beta_0 - \beta_r = b$. In each case, assuming that the h_i and k_i values are chosen in accordance with the stipulations of the preceding section and that the normalization (N) is employed, it follows that an optimal solution before the replacement occurs must yield the same values of α_i and β_i for each $i \in S$, and, hence, we are at liberty to interpret the values received by α_r and β_r as representing the common values.

To assure that the optimal solutions before and after replacement are the same under this interpretation, it suffices to let h_r and k_r, respectively, equal the sums of the h_i and k_i coefficients for $i \in S$. (It is reasonable in the original model to give these coefficients the same two values—say, h* and k*, for all $i \in S$, in which case $h_r = h*|S|$ and $k_r = k*|S|$.) The necessary and sufficient conditions for bounded optimality identified in the previous section will hold after the replacement if they held before the replacement.

The manner in which this model simplification can be used to achieve an "equal representation" of Group 1 and Group 2 is as follows. If the two groups are of different sizes, we make n_2 copies of each point in G_1 and n_1 copies of each point in G_2, so that the two groups effectively are given the same number of elements. The resulting representation does not enlarge the model formulation, since by the foregoing observation we may replace each h_i and k_i by $n_2 h_i$ and $n_2 k_i$ for $i \in G_1$, and by $n_1 h_i$ and $n_1 k_i$ for $i \in G_2$, without requiring the creation of additional variables or constraints in order to handle the implicitly generated copies of the original points.

By analogy with the case where all h_i (and all k_i) begin with the same value for the two groups, we may generally regard the objective function coefficients to be unbiased with respect to the sizes of the sample groups G_1 and G_2, if after the indicated adjustment, $\sum_{i \in G_1} h_i = \sum_{i \in G_2} h_i$ and $\sum_{i \in G_1} k_i = \sum_{i \in G_2} k_i$.

In the integer programming case, if the numbers of points in the two groups are not the same, then instead of minimizing the number of misclassified points, it may be more reasonable to minimize a weighted sum that gives Group 1 and Group 2 equal representation in the foregoing sense. Using the approach indicated for the LP case, we may minimize the number of misclassifications for this adjusted problem by replacing the IP objective (7) with

$$\text{Minimize} \quad n_2 \sum_{i \in G_1} z_i + n_1 \sum_{i \in G_2} z_i$$

On the basis of the preceding observations, we now examine connections between the LP and IP formulations.

LINKS BETWEEN THE LP AND IP DISCRIMINATION MODELS

Our first result link in the IP and LP formulations is to show that the LP formulations using (N) enjoy a special property that causes an optimal solution to "balance" the number of misclassified points across the two groups, whenever the objective weights each point equally.

We focus attention on the *Min Sum LP Model*, where α_0 and β_0 are deleted and the objective function takes the following simple form:

$$\text{Minimize:} \quad \sum_{i \in G} \alpha_i$$

It is to be emphasized that our results also apply to problems more general than the Min Sum model by making use of the constructions of the previous section.

We define the number of misclassified points to be balanced between Group 1 and Group 2 if the number of points with $\alpha_i > 0$ in each group does not exceed the number of points with $\alpha_i \geq 0$ in the other group. In the absence of points with $\alpha_i = 0$, this condition implies the number of misclassified points in each group will be the same.

Theorem 4

An optimal solution to the Min Sum LP model using normalization (N) yields a balanced number of misclassified points.

Proof. Since at most one of α_i and β_i will be positive for each i, it follows that $\alpha_i > 0$ for $i \in G_1$ only if $A_i x > b$, and that $\alpha_i > 0$ for $i \in G_2$ only if $A_i x < b$. Let n_k^+ and n_k^0, respectively denote the number of positive and zero α_i for $i \in G_k$ and k=1, 2. If b is increased by a small positive value ϵ, then all $\alpha_i > 0$ for $i \in G_1$ are decreased by ϵ, and all $\alpha_i \geq 0$ for $i \in G_2$ are increased by ϵ, yielding a net increase in $\Sigma \alpha_i$ of $(n_2^+ + n_2^0)\epsilon - n_1^+ \epsilon$. Since this value must be non-negative, we conclude that $n_2^+ + n_2^0 \geq n_1^+$. Consideration of decreasing b by ϵ similarly yields $n_1^+ + n_1^0 \geq n_2^+$. This completes the proof.

One consequence of Theorem 4 for linking the LP and IP formulations is that a balanced number of misclassified points must be "close" to a minimum number of misclassified points, when x is held constant and b is allowed to vary. This is expressed more precisely in the following result.

Corollary

Starting from an optimal LP solution, the greatest reduction in the number of misclassified points that can be obtained by holding x constant and varying b cannot exceed Min (n_1^+, n_2^+).

Proof. By the reasoning of the proof of Theorem 4, if b is increased, the largest possible reduction in the number of misclassified points is n_1^+ —

n_2^0, which is at most n_2^+ (as well as at most as n_1^+). The corresponding conclusion for decreasing b yields the result of the corollary.

The foregoing observations also make it possible to identify a value b that minimizes the number of misclassified points subject to holding x at its optimal LP value. That is, instead of relying on the worst case bound of the corollary, we may apply a method that identifies precisely the amount of reduction in misclassified points that is possible by shifting *b* and that further identifies the value of b that achieves this reduction. The method is as follows.

Method to Optimize b, Given x

0. Begin with $\theta^* = n_1^+ + n_2^+$, and perform the following steps for each Group k, k = 1, 2, such that $n_k^+ > 0$. Upon termination, θ^* will be the minimum number of misclassified points.

1. Restrict attention to those $i \in G_k$ such that $\alpha_i > 0$, and arrange these α_i in ascending order, reindexing for simplicity so that $\alpha_1 \le \alpha_2 \le ... \le \alpha_r$, where $r = n_k^+$.

2. Examine the α_i, i = 1, 2, ..., r in sequence, considering in turn that $\alpha_h < \alpha_{h+1}$ (or such that h = r).

    a. Define $b_h = b = \alpha_h$ for k = 1 and $b_h = b - \alpha_h$ for k = 2. If b is given the value b_h, the number of misclassified points is $\theta_h = n_1 + n_2 - n_k^0 + \Delta_h - h$, where Δ_h is the number of points A_i, for $i \in G_k$, such that $0 < \beta_i < \alpha_h$.

    b. If $\theta_h < \theta^*$, let $\theta^* = \theta_h$. Stop for the current value of k if $\theta_h - n_k^+ + h > \theta^*$; otherwise, return to Step 2a for the next value of h $\le$ r.

The stopping criterion of step 2b is based on the observation that the number of positive α_i not yet examined is $n_k^+ - h$, and hence this number represents an upper limit on the possible decrease in θ_h. The justification of the method derives from the logic underlying the proof of Theorem 4, from which it follows that an optimal b value is identified as the one that yields θ^*.

It is natural to ask whether a connection between the LP and IP formulations can be established that gives an indication of the quality of the LP solution for the IP problem in a more global sense, in contrast to the local sense of holding x constant, while b varies. The following answers this affirmatively.

Theorem 5

Assume that Group 1 and Group 2 have a meaningful separation and that the normalization (N) is employed. Then there exists a finite positive U^* such that for all $U \geq U^*$, the Min Sum LP formulation is a valid continuous relaxation of the IP formulation (7) - (12) under the scaling $\alpha_i = Uz_i$, $i \in G$.

Proof. Starting with the IP formulation and substituting a_i/U for z_i causes equations (8) and (9) to become the same as equations (2) and (3), while equation (10) becomes $\alpha_i = 0$ or U, which relaxes to $0 \leq \alpha_i \leq U$, for i $\in$ G. The objective (7) then becomes Minimize $(1/U) \sum_{i \in G} \alpha_i$, and, hence, the Min Sum LP formulation with $\alpha_i \leq U$, $i \in G$, has the same set of optimal solutions as the IP formulation upon relaxing $z_i = 0$ or 1 to $0 \leq z_i \leq 1$, $i \in G$. The key is therefore to demonstrate the existence of U^* such that the IP formulation achieves its intended purpose of minimizing the number of positive α_i, while simultaneously assuring the relaxation is valid for all $U \geq U^*$.

Replace the objective of the Min Sum formulation by Minimize $\sum_{i \in G} f(\alpha_i)$, where $f(\alpha_i) = 1$ if $\alpha_i > 0$ and $f(\alpha_i) = 0$ otherwise. This problem has an optimal solution x^*, b^*, α_i^*, and β_i^*, $i \in G$, under normalization (N) with all α_i^* finite, and we can require that at least one of α_i^* and β_i^* is 0 for all i. (To see this, minimize $\sum_{i \in S} \alpha_i$ for every subset S of G, holding $\alpha_i = 0$ for i $\in$ S. A smallest cardinality subset that has a feasible solution yields the indicated finite solution.) Then for $U^* = Max(\alpha_i^* : i \in G)$ and any $U \geq U^*$, the solution determined by setting $x = x^*$, $b = b^*$, and $\alpha_i = U$ if and only if $\alpha_i^* > 0$, is optimal for the Min Sum problem subject to the added condition $\alpha_i = 0$ or U. This follows from the fact that increasing α_i^* and β_i^* by the same amount, $U - \alpha_i^*$, for all i such that $\alpha_i^* > 0$, yields a solution that continues to satisfy all problem constraints and the normalization (N) without changing x* and b*, giving an objective function value of U $\sum\limits_{i \in G} f(\alpha_i^*)$. There cannot be a better solution to the Min Sum problem subject to $\alpha_i = 0$ or U, using (N), since by reversing the preceding derivation we would thereby obtain a solution better than the one assumed optimal for the problem of minimizing $\sum\limits_{i \in G} f(\alpha_i)$. The proof is completed by allowing U* to increase, if necessary, so that the constraint $\alpha_i \leq U^*$, $i \in G$, is redundant for the Min Sum LP formulation.

   We note that the crucial aspect of the preceding theorem was to establish the ability to choose any $U \geq U^*$, something not possible with the β normalization. In the case of the (N) normalization, we can additionally replace U by positive values $U_i \geq \alpha_i^*$ for each $i \in G$, provided the objective for the LP problem is correspondingly replaced by Minimize $\sum\limits_{i \in G} \alpha_i/U_i$. (If this is done, the relaxation theoretically may be tightened by adding the constraints $\alpha_i \leq U_i$ for $i \in G$, yielding progressively better relaxations as U_i is chosen closer to α_i^*. However, approximate knowledge of α_i^* values, and of relative differences between them, is not typically possible.)

   The proof of Theorem 5 in fact shows that the Min Sum solution, where the bound $U \geq \alpha_i$ is disregarded, yields a relaxation that cannot be improved for all U that are at least as large as the maximum α_i value in the LP solution. If this value is no larger than U*, the Min Sum relaxation is as good as choosing $U = U^*$.

   We now show that the IP problem can be solved without knowing (or provisionally selecting) a value for U. Consider the process of solving the IP problem by branch and bound, where an appropriate value of U is known. A branch that sets $z_i = 1$, or equivalently $\alpha_i = U$, replaces the associated constraint by

$$A_i x + \beta_i = b + U \qquad \text{if } i \in G_1$$

$$A_i x - \beta_i = b - U \qquad \text{if } i \in G_2$$

   For U large, the effect of this replacement is simply to make the associated constraint redundant since α_i is not a given weight in the objective function and takes any value necessary to product equality. Thus, in particular, the branch of setting $\alpha_i = U$ can be handled by removing the associated constraint or simply by changing the objective function coefficient of α_i to 0, which also effectively makes the constraint redundant. (The latter has the further advantage of allowing the branch and bound process to continue by primary feasible postoptimization.) Accompanying this change, the variable α_i is replaced by the objective function by the constant term U. Recording this modified form of the objective can be simply a bookkeeping formality, with no need to give a value to U.

It may also be noted that the proof of Theorem 5 implies that the Min Sum objective in fact can be replaced by any other that weights all α_i positively, still yielding a valid relaxation of the IP problem for some set of U_i values. This observation leads to the possibility of a postoptimizing strategy for modifying the LP objective function coefficients to come closer to minimizing the number of positive α_i. One approach for doing this is as follows.

Postoptimizing Heuristic to Minimize the Number of Misclassifications

1. Replace the objective for the Min Sum LP problem by
    Minimizing $\sum_{i \in G} h_i \alpha_i$, where all h_i are chosen to be positive
    (e.g., initially let all $h_i = 1$), and solve the resulting LP problem.
2. If the current LP solution yields a smaller number of positive α_i values than any solution so far, record this as the best candidate solution. (The first solution is automatically recorded as such a candidate.)
3. If $h_i \alpha_i = 0$ for all $i \in G$, the method terminates. Otherwise, select $h_p \alpha_p = Max(h_i \alpha_i : i \in G)$, and set $h_p = 0$.
4. Postoptimize to solve the resulting LP problem, and return to step 2.

The motivation for this procedure is that $x_i = 0$ must result for all i such that $h_i > 0$ if such a solution is feasible. The variable α_p may be viewed as one that most strongly resists being driven to 0. Hence, h_p is set to 0, forcing remaining variables α_i to 0. After the procedure terminates the strategy can be reversed by choosing α_p to be the smallest positive α_i such that $h_i = 0$, if any exist, and by making h_p positive. (If the process is repeated a few steps beyond where improvement results, then the original strategy can be activated once again.) The method can be coupled with the earlier method for optimizing b, given x.

In applying the procedures of this section, it should be remembered that the Min Sum formulation may give a weight of n_2 to points of G_1 and a weight of n_1 to points of G_2 to create an equal representation relative to size, and the case of duplicate points can cause the h_i values to vary in additional ways. The foregoing discussion of the Min Sum model applies to all of these cases under the interpretation that h_i = the number of times (possibly fractional) that point i occurs. Then, in the heuristic for minimizing the number of misclassifications, candidate solutions are evaluated by reference to the sum of these original h_i values over those i such that $\alpha_i > 0$. A corresponding observation applies to the solution of IP problems where the h_i values represent costs of misclassification.

A SUCCESSIVE GOAL APPROACH

A particularly significant use of the model results by a successive application employing hierarchically weighted deviation terms, which were proposed for its early special cases consisting of the MMD and MSD forms in Freed and Glover (1981 and 1987) and which can now be implemented without distortion by reliance on (N). The relevance of the IP results to this process derives from the fact that each stage involves a valid relaxation of a corresponding IP formulation. Such an approach is applicable to settings where multiple groups are to be differentiated or where two groups are treated as multiple groups by redefining subsets of points improperly classified at one stage of the application as new groups to be differentiated at the next. For the multiple group case, any subset of groups can be defined to be Group 1 and the remaining subset defined to be Group 2, thus encompassing alternatives ranging from a binary tree form of separation to a "one-at-a-time" form of separation.

By this approach, when the two currently defined groups are incompletely separated at a given stage, the hyperplane dividing them may be shifted alternately in each direction (increasing and decreasing b) by an amount sufficient to include all points of each respective group. (The magnitude of the two shifts will be the same for the MMD model, which minimizes both the maximum value and the sum of these shifts.) Upon identifying the shift for a given group, all points of the alternate group that lie strictly beyond the shifted hyperplane boundary become perfectly differentiated by this means, and such perfectly differentiated points can be segregated from the remaining points before applying the next stage. The number of stages devoted to creating perfect separation (before accepting the current hyperplane, without shifting) is a decision parameter of the process.

It is important in such a process, if a superior set of differentiating hyperplanes is sought, to retain points in the model that have been segregated as perfectly differentiated, rather than dropping them from consideration during subsequent stages. To reflect the fact that these segregated points should not inhibit the goal of differentiating among remaining points, their deviation terms are assigned objective function weights that are hierarchically of a lower order than are those assigned to points not yet segregated. The relative magnitudes of these lower order weights may reasonably be scaled to become progressively smaller for points segregated earlier in time. (In addition, to reduce problem size, a subset of the points most recently segregated may be discarded at each stage, where this subset is identified to consist of points lying beyond a chosen *magnified shift* of b. It is easy to shift b, for example, to a depth that excludes any selected percentage of most recently segregated points belonging to a specified group.)

We call this approach the *successive goal method* because the introduction of hierarchical differences in deviation weights, with diminishing weights for points segregated earlier, constitutes a natural partitioning of problem points into subset by reference to prioritized goals. Furthermore, the ability to manipulate weights within a given goal level (or to split out additional hierarchies) makes it possible to treat the two groups of points that remain unsegregated at a given stage in a nonsymmetric manner.

This leads to an approach that characteristically is able to generate a stronger set of hyperplanes, at the expense of approximately doubling the overall computational effort. The basis of this nonsymmetric approach rests on creating successive objectives to exclude a maximum segment of one group from a region that contains all of the others in a series of alternating hierarchies.

The *alternating hierarchy method* that results has the property of adapting successive hyperplanes to more closely match the distributions of the groups and generally increases the frequency with which earlier hyperplanes are permitted to be discarded as redundant. The procedure consists of solving two problems at each stage. Each of the two groups of currently unsegregated points is chosen in turn to be the one that lies completely within the region assigned to it by the current hyperplane, with the associated (subordinate) goal of excluding the maximum portion of the other group from this region.

The structure of the goals for each problem gives rise to the "alternating hierarchy" characterization of this procedure. Specifically, we adopt the conviction that the group to be completely contained in its assigned region is always designed to be Group 1. Then the problem goals are ordered as follows. At the highest level, only the external deviations of unsegregated Group 1 points are incorporated into the objective (which is equivalent to imposing the condition $A_i x \leq b$ for these points). At the next level, the external deviations of unsegregated Group 2 points are assigned corresponding lower-order weights in the objective, thus respecting the dominance of the level preceding. For the points of this second level, the b term is replaced by $b + \epsilon$ to seek strict separation. (Alternatively, a restricted β_0 variable, which appears only in the equations for the second-level points, may be incorporated with a positive weight.) At the third and fourth levels, respectively, external deviations of segregated Group 1 and Group 2 points receive weights reflecting their associated position in the hierarchy (or a single third level may treat these segregated points uniformly). Finally, two concluding levels incorporate internal deviations of both groups, first for unsegregated points and then for segregated points. These last levels are relevant to enhancing the differentiation between those groups, which are in fact separable, and may be expected to have diminished relevance after generating the first few hyperplanes.

The portion of unsegregated Group 2 points that are perfectly differentiated from unsegregated Group 1 points at a given stage, and hence that can join the set of segregated points in the stage following, may vary substantially depending on which group is chosen to be Group 1. In fact, one of the two choices for Group 1 may fail to differentiate any of the unsegregated Group 2 points (i.e., all such points may lie in the half space required to include the unsegregated Group 1 points). When the sets of points differentiated by the two choices differ significantly in size, the smaller set can be excluded form joining the segregated points on the next stage—an exclusion that, in effect, will occur automatically if the smaller set is empty. If both sets are empty, the process stops. Because of the alternating dominance of the two groups in each of the problems solved, no shifting of hyperplanes is needed in this approach. (For added refinement, after a forward pass of generating a selected set of hyperplanes, a reverse pass can be applied to improve the differentiation.)

From a practical standpoint, the hierarchical levels of this approach can be handled with greater efficiency by dividing the solution process into stages. At the first stage, attention is restricted to the objective function associated with the highest level until that objective is optimized. Then, following a process analogous to that employed by Phase 1/Phase 2 LP methods, nonbasic variables with nonzero reduced costs are fixed at their current values, and the objective appropriate to the next level is introduced and optimized. The process repeats until all levels are treated or all remaining basic variables receive fixed values (thus implicitly determining solutions for levels not yet examined). This approach requires notably less computational effort than an implementation which relies on large coefficient differences to control the treatment of hierarchies. Independent of implementation details, the approach provides an opportunity to achieve progressively improved differentiation of the original group in both the two-group and the multiple-group cases and opens up interesting research possibilities for determining the best subset of points to be segregated at each stage.

CONCLUSIONS

The LP discriminant analysis formulation (1) - (6) is susceptible to a variety of uses as a result of the ability to handle different discriminant analysis goals by varying the coefficients of the objective function. Such uses range from accommodating inherent differences in the need to classify specific points correctly to employing strategies for producing greater refinement in classification (as by the successive goal method).

Among the settings of practical relevance, situations in which there are real dollar costs for misclassifications can be modeled in a natural and highly appropriate manner by such a model. Many applications gain additional realism by an integer programming interpretation. The fact that the LP formulation employing the normalization (N) is a direct relaxation of the corresponding IP problem, and lends itself to convenient strategies for closing potential gaps between LP and IP solutions, gives further motivation for using this type of model. Related forms of postoptimizing strategies can be applied to achieve additional goals, such as diminishing the effects of outliers (whose identities are disclosed by the initial solution) without the risk of being driven to "wrong solutions" when objective function coefficients are thereby modified.

Postoptimization is also useful in the "$\in$ version" of the model to identify values of the $\in$ that yield different separation effects. In particular, this model version is equivalent to introducing a translation of the β_0 variable by the lower bound $\beta_0 \geq \in$. Thus, standard sensitivity analysis on the LP solution with β_0, included in the model can precisely determining the outcome of increasing β_0, hence $\in$, up to the point where a new optimal basis results, and a postoptimization step can then move to this new basis, allowing the analysis to repeat for larger $\in$ values. Such a mapping of the effects of different $\in$ values provides an interesting area for optimization, and has been studied in the context of international loan portfolios in Glover, Keene, and Duea, 1988.

From another perspective, the ability to weight the internal and external deviations differently for different points, and to encompass tradeoffs between such deviations and "minmax" and "maxmin" objectives, provides a direct way to handle issues that are often troubling in classical discriminant analysis. A prominent example is the type of problem in which Type I and Type II errors deserve different emphasis. As pointed out in Mahmood and Lawrence (1987), in the context of identifying firms that succumb to bankruptcy, it may be more important to be assured that a firm classed as financially strong will in fact escape bankruptcy than to be assured that a firm classed as financially weak will become insolvent.

Indeed, by the capacity to giver higher weights to firms that are dramatically successful and unsuccessful, the LP formulation will tend to position the "sure bets" more deeply inside their associated half spaces. The advantage of this is that it provides increased predictive accuracy: instead of investing in a business simply on the basis of whether discriminant analysis classifies it as financially strong or financially weak, greater confidence may be gained by investing in a firm that lies well within the financially strong region. The successive goal method provides an opportunity to additionally improve the discrimination in such cases. By the ability to remove distortion with the normalization (N), the uses of different objective function coefficients that underlie these approaches can be applied consistently and effectively.

NOTE

This chapter was prepared based on the author's earlier article, "Improved Linear Programming Models for Discriminant Analysis," in *Decision Sciences,* Volume 21, Number 4, Fall 1990, pp. 771–785, by elaborating on several aspects of the paper in further detail and adding new results on integer programming models for discriminant analysis.

REFERENCES

Bajgier, S. M., and Hill, A. V., "An Experimental Comparison of Statistical and Linear Programming Approaches to the Discriminant Problem," *Decision Sciences* 13, no. 4 (October 1982): 604-618.

Bobrowski, L., "Linear Discrimination with Symmetrical Models," *Pattern Recognition* 19, no. 1 (1986): 101-109.

Charnes, A., Cooper, W. W., and Rhodes, E., "Evaluating Program and Managerial Efficiency: An Application of Data Envelopment Analysis to Program Follow Through," *Management Science* 27 (1981): 668-687.

Freed, E. (Ned), and Glover, F., "Simple but Powerful Goal Programming Models for Discriminant Problems," *European Journal of Operational Research* 7, no. 1 (May 1981): 44-60.

Freed, E. (Ned), and Glover, F., "Resolving Certain Difficulties and Improving the Classification Power of the LP Discriminant Analysis Procedure," *Decision Sciences* 17 (1987): 589-595.

Glover, F., Gordon, K., and Palmer, M., "LP Discriminant Analysis for International Loan Portfolio Management," CAAI 89-3, University of Colorado, April 1989.

Glover, F., Keene, S., and Duea, B., "A New Class of Models for the Discriminant Problem," *Decision Sciences* 19 (1988): 269-280.

Jurs, P. C., "Pattern Recognition Used to Investigate Multivariate Data in Analytical Chemistry," *Science* 232, no. 6 (June 1986): 1219-1224.

Kazmier, L., *Statistical Analysis for Business and Economics*, McGraw Hill, New York, 1967.

Mahmood, M. A., and Lawrence, E. C., "A Performance Analysis of Parametric and Nonparametric Discriminant Approaches to Business Decision Making," *Decision Sciences* 19, no. 2 (Spring 1987): 308-326.

Markowski, E. P., and Markowski, C. A., "Some Difficulties and Improvements and Applying Linear Programming Formulations to the Discriminant Problem," *Decision Sciences* 16, no. 3 (Summer 1985): 237-247.

Spurr, W., and Bonini, C., *Statistical Analysis for Business Decision*, Richard D. Irwin, Homewood, IL, 1967.

Tou, J. T., and Gonzalez, R. C., *Pattern Recognition Principles*, Addison-Wesley, Reading, MA, 1974.

Watanabe, S. *Methodologies of Pattern Recognition*, Academic Press, New York, 1969.

17

Chance-Constrained Programming with Stochastic Processes as Parameters

Raj Jagannathan

The variables of interest in a linear programming problem are called decision variables. The problem faced by the decision maker is then to determine values of the decision variables that optimize some linear objective function. The optimal values of the decision variables are functions of parameters—namely, criterion vector c, technological coefficient matrix A, and requirement vector b—of the LP problem. In many real-world problems some of the parameters must be assumed to be random variables with known distribution functions. The stochastic decision models so obtained are classified as static models and dynamic models. In the case of static models, the values of *all* the decision variables are chosen initially, and the random parameter values ξ_t are observed later. In the case of dynamic models, however, the values of the decision variables are chosen at different points in time so that the decision x_k at time t_k depends on the historical values (ξ_t, x_t), $0 \leq t < k$.

There are two major approaches for handling uncertainty in the coefficients of an LP problem: (1) two-stage linear programming under uncertainty (Dantzig, 1955) and (2) chance constrained programming (CCP, see Charnes and Cooper, 1959; Charnes, Cooper, and Symonds, 1959).

In the case of the two-stage programming under uncertainty approach, the first-stage decision vector x is chosen initially, the random requirement vector ξ is observed later, and the second-stage recourse factor y_2 is chosen to rectify possible violation of the constraints $Ax = \xi$. The objective function is the sum of two terms: (1) $\Sigma c_j x_j$ and (2) the expected value of the penalty cost incurred in using the recourse vector y. Thus, the problem is to choose x such that the above function is minimized. The model is also called stochastic programming with recourse (see Wets, 1972). The deterministic equivalent problem is a convex program (see Dantzig, 1955; Charnes, Cooper, and Thompson, 1965; Wets, 1972; Jagannathan, 1985).

In the chance-constrained programming approach (zero-order rules), the vector x is chosen such that the constraints $\Sigma a_{ij} x_j \geq \xi_i$ are required to hold with probability α_i, $0 < \alpha_i < 1$, $i = 1, \ldots, m$ and such that the objective function $\Sigma c_j x_j$ is minimized.

Consider this chance-constrained programming problem.

$$\text{Minimize } \Sigma \, c_j x_j \tag{1}$$

$$\text{subject to} \quad P(\sum_j a_{ij} x_j \geq \xi_i) \geq \alpha_i, \, i = 1, \ldots, m \tag{2}$$

$$x_j \geq 0$$

The constraints (2) are called chance constraints. The problem is interpreted as follows: the decision vector x is chosen at time $t = 0$, and at the end of the period, when $t = t_1$, the random right-hand-side parameters $\xi_j = \hat{\xi}_j$ are observed. Then the chance constraints (2) mean that, in at least $100\alpha_i$ percent of the cases, the constraints $\Sigma a_{ij} x_i \geq \hat{\xi}_i$ are expected to be satisfied. The object is then to minimize $\Sigma c_j x_j$ subject to the chance constraints (2).

Let the known distribution function of the random variable ξ_j be $F_i(s)$, i.e., let $\Pr(\xi_i \leq s) = F_i(s)$, $i = 1, \ldots, m$.

Then the chance constraints (2) are equivalent to the constraints

$$F_i (\Sigma_j a_{ij} x_j) \geq \alpha_i, \qquad i = 1, \ldots, m$$

Then the deterministic equivalent of the chance-constrained program (1) is the linear program (Charnes and Cooper, 1959)

$$\text{Minimize } \Sigma c_j x_j \tag{3}$$

subject to

$$\sum_j a_{ij} x_j \geq F_i^{-1}(\alpha_i), \qquad\qquad i = 1, \ldots, m$$

$$x_j \geq 0, j = 1, \ldots, n$$

where $\qquad F_i^{-1}(\alpha_i) = \text{Inf } (s \mid F_i(s) \geq \alpha_i).$

Note that in constraints (2), the random variables ξ_i are assumed to be the end-of-the-period values of the requirement vectors. Consequently, possible violations of the constraints (2) *during* the period are ignored. In this chapter, the requirement-vector parameters are assumed to be stochastic processes $[\xi_i(t), t \in T]$, where $T = \{t \mid 0 \leq t \leq t_1\}$ is the planning horizon of the CCP model (1).

The CCP model (1) is modified as

$$\text{Minimize } \sum_j c_j x_j \tag{4}$$

subject to

$$P \left(\bigcap_{t \in T} (\Sigma_j a_{ij} x_j \geq \xi_i(t)) \right) \geq \alpha_i, i = 1, \ldots, m \tag{5}$$

$$x_j \geq 0, j = 1, \ldots, n$$

where constraint (5) means that the joint probability that the ith constraint will hold throughout the period is at least α_i.

In the next section, the case of finite index set T is considered. The deterministic equivalent of the above CCP model and a solution that approaches the objective function (4) are discussed. In the section that follows, similar results are obtained for the case of continuous index set T.

DISCRETE TIME MODEL

In this section, we assume that the index set $T = \{1, \ldots, k\}$, and that possible violations of constraints $\Sigma a_{ij}x_j \geq \xi_i(t)$ are checked k times during the period T at equal intervals.

We make the following assumption regarding the discrete-time stochastic process $(\xi_i(t), t \in T)$.

Assumption 1

Let $\xi_i(t) = \eta_{i1} + \ldots + \eta_{it}$, where $\eta_{i1}, \eta_{i2}, \ldots, \eta_{ik}$ are independent and identically distributed (i.i.d.) non-negative random variables such that $P(\eta_{ir} \leq s) = F_i(s)$.

The CCP model (4) becomes

$$\text{Minimize } \Sigma\, c_j x_j$$

(6)

subject to

$$P(\bigcap_{t=1}^{k} [\Sigma_j a_{ij}x_j \geq \eta_{i1} + \ldots + \eta_{it}]) \geq \alpha_i, \, i = 1, \ldots, m$$

$$x_j \geq 0, j = 1, \ldots, n$$

The constraints (6) ensure that the joint probability that constraints $\sum_j a_{ij}x_j \geq \xi_i(t)$ will hold is at least α_i.

Note that $\xi_i(t) \leq \xi_i(t')$ for $t \leq t'$ because η_{ir} are non-negative random variables.

So the CCP model reduces to

$$\text{Minimize } \Sigma c_j x_j \tag{7}$$

subject to

$$P\left[\Sigma a_{ij} x_j \geq \xi_j(k)\right] \geq \alpha_i, \, i = 1, \ldots, m$$

$$x_j \geq 0, \, j = 1, \ldots, n$$

The distribution function of $\xi_i(k)$ is $F_{ik}(s)$, where $F_{ik}(s)$ is the k-fold convolution of the common distribution $F_i(s)$.

The deterministic equivalent of model (7) is this linear program.

$$\text{Minimize } \sum_j c_j x_j \tag{8}$$

subject to

$$\Sigma a_{ij} x_j \geq F_{ik}^{-1}(\alpha_i), \, i = 1, \ldots, m$$

$$x_j \geq 0, \, j = 1, \ldots, n$$

where

$$F_{ik}^{-1}(\alpha_i) = \text{Inf } [s \mid F_{ik}(s) \geq \alpha_i].$$

Remark 1

If $\eta_{ir}, \, r = 1, \ldots, k$, are independent exponential random variables with mean $1/\mu_i$, then $\xi_i(k)$ has a Gamma distribution with parameters k and μ_i. Then $P[\xi_i(k) \leq y] = P[N_i(y) \geq k]$, where $N_i(y)$ has a Poissan distribution with mean $\mu_i y$ (Ross, 1983).

A Numerical Example

Consider this example

$$\text{Minimize } 3x_1 + 2x_2 + 7x_3 \tag{9}$$

subject to

$$P\left(\bigcap_{t \in T} (x_1 + 2x_2 + 3x_3 \geq \xi_1(t))\right) \geq .9$$

$$P\left(\bigcap_{t \in T} (2x_1 + x_2 + 5x_3 \geq \xi_2(t))\right) \geq .95$$

$$x_j \geq 0, j = 1, \ldots, 3$$

Let

$$T = (1, \ldots, 10)$$

$$\xi_1(t) = \sum_{j=1}^{t} \xi_{1j}$$

$$\xi_2(t) = \sum_{j=1}^{t} \xi_{2j}$$

Let $\eta_{11}, \eta_{12}, \ldots, \eta_{1,10}$ be i.i.d. exponential random variables with $\mu_1 = 5$, and let $\eta_{21}, \eta_{22}, \ldots, \eta_{2,10}$ be i.i.d. exponential random variables with $\mu_2 = 4$. Then $\xi_1(t) \sim$ Gamma (t, μ_1) and $\xi_2(t) \sim$ Gamma (t, μ_2). Using Remark 1 and problem (8), the deterministic equivalent of model (9) is this linear program.

$$\text{Minimize } 3x_1 + 2x_2 + 7x_3 \tag{10}$$

subject to

$$x_1 + 2x_2 + 3x_3 \geq 2.85$$

$$2x_1 + x_2 + 5x_3 \geq 3.90$$

$$x_1, x_2, x_3 \geq 0$$

CONTINUOUS-TIME MODEL

In this section, possible violations of the constraints $\Sigma a_{ij}x_j \geq \xi_i(t)$ are reviewed continuously. So $T = \{t \mid 0 \leq t \leq t_1\}$.

We make the following assumption regarding the stochastic nature of $[\xi_i(t), t \in T]$:

Assumption 2

Let $\{\xi_i(t), t \geq 0\}$ be a Brownian motion with drift coefficient $\mu_i > 0$ and variance $\sigma_i^2, i = 1, \ldots, m$.

Let $\tau_i(y)$ be the time it takes for the ith Brownian motion process with drift coefficient μ_i to hit y. Note that the event $\tau_i(y) \geq t_1$ means that the constraint $\Sigma a_{ij} x_j \geq \xi_i(t)$ is satisfied for all $t, 0 \leq t \leq t_1$.

The CCP model (4) can be recast as

$$\text{Minimize } \Sigma c_j x_j \tag{11}$$

subject to

$$P(\tau_i(y_i) \geq t_1) \geq \alpha_i, i = 1, \ldots, m$$

$$\sum_j a_{ij}x_j - y_i = 0$$

$$x_j \geq 0, j = 1, \ldots, n$$

The distribution of the random variable $\tau_i(y_i)$ is known to be an inverse normal distribution which is approximately normal with mean y_i/μ_i and variance $y_i\sigma_i^2/\mu_i^3$ (see Cox and Miller,1968, pp. 210-213; Folks and Chihikara, 1978).

Let $\Phi\,(z_{\alpha_i}) = \alpha_i$, where $\Phi\,(\bullet)$ is the distribution function of the standard normal distribution. In other words, z_{α_i} is the α_i^{th} fractile of the standard normal distribution. Then the deterministic equivalent to (11), using the approximate normal distribution of $\tau_i(y_i)$, is

$$\text{Minimize } \Sigma\, c_j x_j \qquad\qquad (12)$$

subject to

$$y_i/\mu_i - z_{\alpha_i}\sqrt{y_i}\;\;\sigma_i/\mu_i^{3/2} \geq t_1, \; i = 1, \ldots, m \qquad (13)$$

$$\sum_j a_{ij}x_j - y_i = 0$$

$$x_j \geq 0, \, j = 1, \ldots, n$$

Let $a = 1/\mu_i$, $b = \sigma_i z_{\alpha_i}/\mu_i^{3/2}$. Also let $ay_i - b\sqrt{y_i} - t_1 = a\,(\sqrt{y_i} - \gamma_{ij})$ $(\sqrt{y_i} - \gamma_{2i})$, i.e., $\sqrt{y_i} = \gamma_{1i}, \gamma_{2i}$ are the two roots of the equations $(ay_i - b\sqrt{y_i} - t_1 = 0)$. Then $\gamma_{1i} > 0$ and $\gamma_{2i} < 0$.

Consequently, constraint (13) is equivalent to $\sqrt{y_i} \geq \gamma_{1i} > 0$. So problem (12) is equivalent to this linear program:

$$\text{Minimize } \Sigma c_j x_j$$

subject to

$$\sum_j a_{ij}x_j \geq \gamma_{1i}^2, \, i = 1, \ldots, m$$

$$x_j \geq 0, \, j = 1, \ldots, n$$

where γ_{1i} is the positive root of the quadratic equation in $\sqrt{y_i}$.

$$y_i/\mu_i - (z_{\alpha_i}\,\sigma_i/\mu_i^{3/2})\,\sqrt{y_i} - t_1 = 0$$

In this chapter, we have restricted ourselves to static models (zero-order rules) of chance-constrained programming. It is possible to generalize the results to the case of random a_{ij} elements and multistage CCP models. Also, similar results can be obtained in the case of stochastic programming with recourse models or models that are combinations of the CCP and recourse approaches (see Bynes et al., 1971).

REFERENCES

Bynes, R., A. Charnes, W. W. Cooper, O. David, and D. Gilford (eds.), *Studies in Budgeting*, North Holland, Amsterdam, 1971.

Charnes, A., and W. W. Cooper, "Chance-Constrained Programming," *Management Science* 6, no. 1 (October 1959): 73-79.

Charnes, A., W. W. Cooper, and G. H. Symonds, "Cost Horizons and Certainty Equivalents: An Approach to Stochastic Programming of Heating Oil," *Management Science* 4, no. 3 (1958): 235-263.

Charnes, A., W. W. Cooper, and G. L. Thompson, "Constrained Generalized Medians and Hypermedians as Deterministic Equivalents for Two-Stage Linear Programs under Uncertainty," *Management Science* 12 (1965): 83-112.

Cox, D. R., and H. D. Miller, *The Theory of Stochastic Processes*, John Wiley, New York, 1968.

Dantzig, G. B., "Linear Programming under Uncertainty," *Management Science* 1 (3 and 4) (April-July 1955): 197-206.

Folks, J. L., and R. S. Chihikara, "The Inverse Gaussian Distribution and Its Statistical Application—A Review," *Journal of the Royal Statistical Society* 40 (3), Series B (1978): 263-275.

Jagannathan, R., "Use of Sample Information in Stochastic Recourse and Chance Constrained Programming Models," *Management Science* 31, no. 1 (1985): 96-108.

Ross, S. M., *Stochastic Processes*, John Wiley, 1983.

Wets, R. J. B., "Characterization Theorems for Stochastic Programming," *Mathematical Programming* 2 (1972): 166-175.

18

Single Machine Total Tardiness Problem Revisited

Wlodzimierz Szwarc

This chapter deals with the well-known single machine total tardiness model. The problem is to schedule n jobs to minimize $f(S) = \sum_{k \in s} \max(C_k - d_k, 0)$, where C_k is the completion time of job k, $k = 1, 2, \ldots, n$, for a given schedule S, while d_k and p_k are, respectively, the due date and the processing time of job k (if $S = 1, 2, \ldots, n$ then $c_k = \sum_{i=1}^{k} p_i$). The jobs are assumed to be processed without interruption, from the time zero, on a single machine that can handle only one job at a time.

Du and Leung (1990) recently proved that the problem was NP hard. The properties of this problem were examined in Emmons (1969), Lawler (1977), and Potts and Van Wessenhove (1982). Emmons (1969) developed dominance rules later incorporated by others in branch and bound algorithms (see Fischer, 1976; Rinnooy Kan, Lageweg and Lenstra, 1975) as well as in dynamic programming algorithms (see Baker and Schrage, 1978; Potts and Van Wassenhove, 1982; Schrage and Baker, 1978; and Srinivasan, 1971). Rinnooy Kan, Lageweg, and Lenstra (1975) extended Emmons's dominance rules for a more general objective function $f(S) = \sum_{k \in S} c_k(C_k)$. Lawler (1977) discovered that the model could be decomposed into smaller subproblems and showed how to reduce the initial list of possible partitions. This list was further reduced by Potts and Rinnooy Kan, Wassenhove (1982). Lawler's result was actually established for a special case of the weighted tardiness problem where $f(S) = \sum_{k \in S} w_k \max (C_k - d_k, 0)$ and $w_i \geq w_j$ whenever $p_i < p_j$.

This chapter presents a theory of the total tardiness problem based on a precedence relation concept that determines the ordering between adjacent jobs. We show that for each pair of jobs i and j that are adjacent in an optimal schedule there is a *critical value* t_{ij} such that i precedes j (i—>j) if processing of this pair starts at time $t \geq t_{ij}$ and j—>i if $t < t_{ij}$. Thus, the ordering of a pair of adjacent jobs depends on their start time t where $t_{min} = 0 \leq \sum_{k=1}^{n} \leq \Sigma_k\, p_i - p_j - p_k = t_{max}$. If the critical value t_{ij} is outside or on a boundary of the feasible interval (t_{min}, t_{max}), then the adjacent ordering is called *unconditional* since it does not change direction. The chapter establishes the following three basic properties of the total tardiness problem:

1. Transitivity of the unconditional adjacent orderings

2. Equivalency between unconditional adjacent and nonadjacent orderings

3. For any three jobs i_1, i_2, and i_3, inequality $p_{i_2} \geq \max(p_{i_1}, p_{i_3})$ along with unconditional orderings i_1 —> i_2 and i_2 —> i_3 implying that $d_{i_3} > \max(d_{i_1}, d_{i_2})$

The solution of the problem depends on the decomposability of the adjacent precedence matrix t_{ij}. The following sections present decomposition rules adopted from Sczwarc (1988) that prove to be very powerful in handling a single machine model with the objective function $f(S) = \sum_{k \in S} w_k c_k^2$ ($n = 50$ and 100) without making use of the second basic property (it does not hold for that model). Those rules are especially useful given the position of job n with the largest processing time in the optimal schedule. These sections examine the findings of Lawler (1977) and Potts and Van Wassenhover (1982) and derives a new condition that further reduces the list of possible positions of job n. The adjacent ordering should be computationally useful in any algorithm that uses dominance conditions since this ordering holds for every pair of jobs. The critical values t_{ij} provide additional information not included in Emmons's dominance condition.

ADJACENT AND NONADJACENT ORDERINGS

Number the jobs such that

$$p_1 \leq p_2 \leq \ldots \leq p_n \tag{1}$$

In case $p_i = p_j$, place job i in front of job j whenever $d_i < d_j$. Throughout the chapter, we assume that $i < j$.

To establish precedence relations between each pair of adjacent jobs i, j, consider two schedules $\sigma ij\pi$ and $\sigma ji\pi$ where σ and π are subsequences of jobs.

Let $\sum_{k \in S} p_k = t$.

Define an upper triangular matrix $\{t_{ij}\}$, $1 \le i < j \le n$, as follows:

$$t_{ij} = \begin{cases} \max(d_i - p_j, 0) & \text{if } d_i > d_j \\ 0 & \text{if } d_i \le d_j \end{cases} \tag{2}$$

Let $\Delta = f(\sigma ji\pi) - f(\sigma ij\pi)$ be the cost of interchanging adjacent jobs i and j. Then

$$\Delta = \max(t + p_j, d_j) + \max(t + p_i + p_j, d_i)$$

$$- \max(t + p_i, d_i) - \max(t + p_i + p_j, d_j) \tag{3}$$

Notice that $W = 0$ if $t + p_i + p_j \le \min(d_i, d_j)$. Assume that $t > \min(d_i, d_j)$. Consider cases $d_i \le d_j$ (case 1) and $d_i > d_j$ (case 2). It is easy to show that

1. $\Delta > 0$ (case 1).

2. $\Delta = 0$ for $t = t_{ij}$, $\Delta > 0$ for $t > t_{ij}$, and $\Delta < 0$ for $t < t_{ij}$ (case 2).

Thus, we have shown the following.

Property 1: $i \longrightarrow j$ for $t \ge t_{ij}$ and $j \longrightarrow i$ for $t < t_{ij} > 0$.

An adjacent ordering is unconditional (written $i \longrightarrow j$) if it maintains the same direction for every t, $t_{min} \le t \le t_{max}$, ($t_{min} = 0$, $t_{max} = \sum_{k=1}^{n} = p_k - p_i - p_j$). This is the case when $t_{ij} \le t_{min}$ or $t_{ij} \ge t_{max}$. Hence, $i \longrightarrow j$ if $t_{ij} \le t_{min}$ and $j \longrightarrow i$ for every t if $t_{ij} \ge t_{max}$.

The following two results demonstrate an unusual property that the unconditional adjacent ordering is an ordering. Let $\sigma_1 i \sigma_2 j\pi$, $\sigma_1 j \sigma_2 i\pi$, and $\sigma_1 \sigma_2 j i\pi$ be n job schedules and $t = \sum_{k \in \sigma_1} p_k$.

Property 2: If $t \geq t_{min} \geq t_{ij}$, then $f(\sigma_1 i \sigma_2 j\pi \leq f(\sigma_1 j \sigma_2 i\pi)$.

Property 3: If $t \leq t_{max} \leq t_{ij}$, then $f(\sigma_1 i \sigma_2 j\pi) \geq f(\sigma_1 \sigma_2 j i\pi)$.

Those properties can be shown by using Emmons's (1969) proofs of Theorems 1 and 2, where $W = \sum_{k \in \sigma_1 \sigma_2} p_k$ and $C = \sum_{k \in \sigma_1 \sigma_2 j} p_k$.

Next we prove the transition property. For an earlier proof, see Szwarc, Posner, and Lin (1988).

Property 4: Ordering $i \longrightarrow j$ $(j \longrightarrow i)$ is transitive.

Proof. Consider three jobs i, j, and k where $i < j < k$ (i.e., $p_i \leq p_j \leq p_k$).

There are six possible cases.

> **Case 1:** $i \longrightarrow j$ and $j \longrightarrow k$.
> $t \geq \max(d_i - p_j, 0)$ implies that $t \geq \max(d_i - p_k, 0)$.
> Hence, $i \longrightarrow k$.

> **Case 2:** $j \longrightarrow i$ and $i \longrightarrow k$.
> Then $\max(d_i > d_j, 0)$ and $t \geq \max(d_i - p_k, 0)$.
> Hence, $t \geq \max(d_j - p_k, 0)$ i.e., $j \longrightarrow k$.

> **Case 3:** $i \longrightarrow k$ and $k \longrightarrow j$.
> Then $d_j > d_k$, $t \geq \max(d_i - p_k, 0)$, and $t < d_j - p_k > 0$.
> Hence, $d_i < d_j$, which means that $i \longrightarrow j$.

> **Case 4:** $j \longrightarrow k$ and $k \longrightarrow i$.
> Then $d_i > d_k$, $t \geq \max(d_j - p_k, 0)$, and $t < d_i - p_k > 0$, which means that $d_i > d_j$. Assumption $t < d_i - p_k$ then implies $t < d_i - p_j$. Hence, $j \longrightarrow i$.

> **Case 5:** $k \longrightarrow i$ and $i \longrightarrow j$.
> This case is ruled out since inequalities $t < d_i - p_k$ and $t \geq d_i - p_j$ are inconsistent.

Case 6: $k \longrightarrow j$ and $j \longrightarrow i$.
   Then $d_i > d_j > d_k$. Assumption $t < d_j - p_k$ implies $t < d_i - p_k$
   i.e., $k \longrightarrow i$, *Q.E.D.*

The transitivity of unconditional ordering plays a crucial role in decomposing the problem into separate subproblems. This will be discussed in the next two sections.

The proofs of Cases 3 and 4 imply an important property.

Property 5: Consider three jobs i_1, i_2, and i_3 where $p_{i_2} \geq \max(p_{i_1}, p_{i_3})$. If $i_1 \longrightarrow i_2 \longrightarrow i_3$, then $d_{i_3} > \max(d_{i_1}, d_{i_2})$.

TWO BLOCK PARTITION

Mark cell (i,j) of the precedence matrix by "-" when $i \longrightarrow j$ and by "+" when $j \longrightarrow i$. If each cell is a "+" or "-", then the optimal schedule is immediately available by applying a simple rule of Szwarc (1989) for adjacent orderings.

Rule 1: Job k is first (last) in an optimal schedule if all entries are "+" ("-") in column k and "-" ("+") in row k.

The transitivity of the ordering assures that the first and last jobs of the schedule can be identified by Rule 1.

Suppose not all cells of the precedence matrix are "+" or "-". Rule 1 can still be applied. We also recommend another rule of Szwarc (1989) to decompose the problem into two subproblems. Divide the set of jobs into two disjoint subsets called blocks β_1 and $\bar{\beta}_1$. Let $\beta_1 = (1, 2, \ldots, u)$ and $\bar{\beta}_1 = (u+1, \ldots, n)$.

Rule 2: If, for some block β_1, $t_{ij} \leq t_{min}$ for each $i \in \beta_1$ and $j \in \bar{\beta}_1$, then there exists an optimal block schedule $\beta_1 \bar{\beta}_1$. The optimal arrangement of the job within each block remains to be determined.

Notice that $t_{min} = 0$ is the starting time for block β_1. Once β_1 is found, block $\bar{\beta}_1$ can be further partitioned by Rule 2 into $\beta_2 \bar{\beta}_2$ with the new $t_{min} = \sum_{k \in \beta_1} p_k$ and so on until a block schedule $\beta_1, \beta_2, \ldots, \beta_m$ is found.

Consider cells (i,j) where $t_{min} < t_{ij} < t_{max}$. Those cells may turn into "+" or "-" as a result of decomposition by Rule 2 once t_{min} increases or t_{max}

decreases. Suppose Rule 2 identifies block $\bar{\beta}_k$ with a completion time $T(\beta_k)$. Then the updated $t_{min} = T(\beta_k)$ for all jobs of β_k, and the updated $t_{max} = T(\beta_k) - p_i - p_j$ for each pair of jobs i, j, of β_k.

To illustrate Rule 2, consider the following example of Potts and Van Wassenhove (1982).

Example 1

$p_i (i = 1, \ldots, 7)$ are 12, 13, 14, 16, 26, 31, 32; d_i are 42, 33, 51, 48, 63, 88, 146. All cells of the precedence matrix are marked by "-" (since $t_{ij} \leq 0$) except $t_{12} = 29$ and $t_{34} = 35$ (see Figure 18.1).

Figure 18.1. Adjacent Precedence Matrix of Example 1

1	2	3	4	5	6	7	
•	29	–	–	–	–	–	1
	•	–	–	–	–	–	2
		•	35	–	–	–	3
			•	–	–	–	4
				•	–	–	5
					•	–	6
						•	7

The first block $\beta_1 = (1,2)$. Convert cell (i,j), i,j$\in \bar{\beta}_1 = (3,4,5,6,7)$ with positive t_{ij} into "-" whenever $t_{ij} \leq 25$. None has been converted.

Next identify $\beta_2 = (3,4)$, where $T(\beta_2) = 55$. Block $\bar{\beta}_2 = (5,6,7)$ is decomposed into $\beta_3 = (5)$, $\beta_4 = (6)$, and $\beta_5 = (7)$. The optimal block schedule is (1,2), (3,4), 5, 6, 7. To find the optimal schedule, update t_{max} for blocks β_1 and β_2. For β_1, $t_{max} = 25 - p_1 - p_2 = 0 < t_{12}$, and cell (1,2) becomes a "+". For β_2, $t_{max} = 55 - p_3 - p_4 = 25 < t_{34}$, and cell (3,4) is marked by a "+". Thus 2, 1, 4, 3, 5, 6, 7 is the optimal schedule.

Up to now all jobs of the same block β shared the same t_{min} and $t_{max} = T(\beta) - p_i - p_j$. Properties 2 and 3 allow us to update those values by defining t_{min} and t_{max} for job $i \in \beta$ as follows:

$$t^{i}_{min} = t_{min} + \sum_{k \in \sigma} p_k,$$

$$t^{i}_{max} = t_{max} - \sum_{k \in \pi} p_{k'} \tag{4}$$

where σ is a set of jobs that precede i, while π is a set of jobs that follow i.

We illustrate the application of formula (4) in the next example.

Example 2

p_i (i=1, 2, . . . , 8) are 10, 11, 12, 13, 15, 25, 28, 30; d_i are 15, 24, 22, 19, 16, 120, 35, 40.

The adjacent precedence matrix is given in Figure 18.2.

Find $\beta_1 = (1)$ by applying Rule 2 (or Rule 1 for k=1). Since $t_{min} = 10$ for block $\bar{\beta}_1$, cells (2,5), (3,4), (3,5) and (4,5) are marked by "-". Hence $\beta_2 = (2,3,4)$, $\beta_3 = (5)$, and $\beta_4 = (6,7,8)$. The optimal block schedule is 1, (2,3,4), 5, (6,7,8). Consider job 4 which is preceded by job 3. Applying formula (4) we get $t^{4}_{min} = t_{min} + p_3 = 10 + 12 = 22$. Examine the cells in column 4 that are neither "+" nor "-". There is only one cell (2,4) where $t_{24} = 11$. Since $t_{24} < t^{4}_{min}$, cell (2,4) is marked by a "-". As a result, block (2,3,4) is decomposed into (2,3), (4). Next consider block (2,3). Cell (2,3) is marked by a "+" since $t_{23} = 12 > t_{max} = T(2,3) - p_2 - p_3 = (10 + 11 + 12) - 11 - 12 = 10$. Similarly, cells (6,7) and (6,8) are marked by "+". Applying Rule 1 to blocks (2,3) and (6,7,8), we find the optimal schedule 1, 3, 2, 4, 5, 7, 8, 6.

The adjacent precedence matrix also offers computational advantages when Rules 1 and 2 cannot be initially applied. Consider the following four-job example of Du and Leung (1990).

Figure 18.2. Adjacent Precedence Matrix of Example 2

1	2	3	4	5	6	7	8	
•	–	–	–	–	–	–	–	1
	•	12	11	9	–	–	–	2
		•	9	7	–	–	–	3
			•	4	–	–	–	4
				•	–	–	–	5
					•	92	90	6
						•	–	7
							•	8

Example 3

p_i (i=1, . . . , 4) are 20, 30, 35, 45; d_i are 70, 60, 55, 50. The elements of the adjacent precedence matrix are $t_{12} = 40$, $t_{13} = 35$, $t_{14} = 25$, $t_{23} = 25$, $t_{24}=15$, and $t_{34}=10$. No decomposition is possible. Notice that if the start time were 40, all entries would be "-", and schedule 1, 2, 3, 4 would be optimal.

Looking at the first row of the precedence matrix one can see that job 1 cannot start earlier than t = 25 (it also cannot be last since after t ≥ 40 it must be followed by another job). Hence, only job 2, 3, or 4 may be first. Suppose job 2 is first. Then t_{min} = 30 for the remaining jobs. Rule 1 immediately produces an optimal "tail" 3, 1, 4. Branch 2 is ruled out since job 2 cannot directly precede job 3 for t = 0 ($t_{23} = 25$). We will learn from the next section (Properties 7a and 7b) that 1 and 4 are the only possible positions of job 4 in an optimal schedule. Rule 1 instantly generates schedules 4, 1, 2, 3 if 4 is first and 3, 2, 1, 4 if 4 is last (the second schedule is optimal).

THREE BLOCK PARTITION

This section examines a three block decomposition when the optimal block schedule is $\alpha k \beta$, $1 \leq k \leq n$. The transitivity of the ordering suggests the following.

Rule 3: If all cells of the adjacent precedence matrix are "+" or "-" in row k and column k, then the optimal block schedule is where the jobs of α precede job k and *k* precedes each job of β.

Example 4

p_i (i= 1, . . . , 6) are 2, 6, 8, 9, 11, 12; d_i are 40, 30, 50, 34, 45, 18. Examine row 4 and column 4 of the adjacent precedence matrix. Cells (2,4) and (4,5) are "-" ($t_{ij} \leq 0$), while (3,4) is "+" ($t_{ij} \geq \sum\limits_{k=1}^{6} p_k - p_i - p_j$). Using formula (4) convert cells (1,4) and (4,6) into "+". Then $\alpha = (2, 6)$, $\beta = (1, 3, 5)$. The optimal block schedule is (2,6), 4, (1,3,5).

Next we deal with an important special case when k = n. Assume that Rule 3 is applicable for this case. We will show that α and β have a unique property. Applying Property 5 for $i_2 = n$ and assuming arbitrarily two jobs $i_1 \in \alpha$ and $i_3 \in \beta$, we get

Corollary 1: $\max\limits_{k \in \alpha} d_k < \min\limits_{k \in \beta} d_k$ if $\alpha \neq \phi$ and $\beta \neq \phi$

Arrange jobs 1, 2, . . . , n in a sequence [1],[2], . . . , [n] such that

$$d_{[1]} \leq d_{[2]} \leq \ldots \leq d_{[n]} \qquad (5)$$

where jobs with the same due dates are arranged in a nondecreasing order in terms of their processing times. Assume that job n is in the rth position of sequence [1],[2], . . . , [n]. Notice that $d_n = d_{(r)} < d_{(r+1)}$ unless r = n. According to equation (1) and Property 2, condition $d_i \leq d_n$ implies that i precedes n (for every $t \geq 0$). Thus, jobs [1], [2], . . . , [r–1] precede job n.

Suppose not all cells are marked by "+" and "-" in column n of matrix $\{t_{ij}\}$ [cells ([1],n),...,([r - 1],n) are "-"]. Due to Corollary 1, sets α and β are uniquely determined given the position, s, of job n. Alas, Corollary 1 does not hold for every s. Lawler (1977) established, however, the following powerful result.

Property 6: There exists an optimal block schedule $\alpha k \beta$ where job n is in position s, for some $s \geq r$, and

$$\alpha = ((1], [2], \ldots, [r - 1], [r + 1], \ldots, [s]),$$

$$\beta = ([s + 1], \ldots, [n]).$$

(6)

Thus, for some optimal block schedule Corollary 1 does hold (as a weak inequality). Property 6 was established under the assumption that early jobs are scheduled in a nondecreasing order according to their due dates and job n, whenever late, is scheduled as late as possible.

Remark: α and β symbolize sets or sequences (if they appear in schedules).

Lawler (1977), Potts and Van Wassenhove (1982) showed that the list of possible positions of job n can be considerably reduced. To prove their findings under the same assumptions consider α and β defined by equation (6) where [r] = n.

Property 7a [Lawler (1977)]: Job n is not in position s of an optimal schedule if

$$\sum_{k \in \alpha} p_k + p_n \geq d_{[s+1]}$$

(7a)

Property 7b [Potts and Wassenhove (1982)]: Job n is not in position s + 1 of an optimal schedule if

$$\sum_{k \in \alpha} p_k + p_n < d_{[s+1]}$$

(7b)

Proof. Assume for convenience that $[s + 1] = i$. Consider element t_{in} of the adjacent precedence matrix. Since $d_i > d_n$, $t_{in} = d_i - p_n$. Let $\sum\limits_{k \in \alpha} p_k = t$.

To prove Property 7a, consider condition (7a), which can be written as $t \geq t_{in}$. According to Property 1, $f(\alpha ni \beta) \geq f(\alpha in \beta)$ which means that job i, where $p_i \leq p_n$, should precede job n. Hence, job n cannot be in position s.

Suppose $\beta' = ([s+2], \ldots, [n])$. To prove Property 7b, notice that condition (7b) is $t < t_{in}$ which implies that $f(\alpha ni \beta') = f(\alpha in \beta')$ if $t + p_i + p_n \leq d_n$ and $f(\alpha ni \beta') < f(\alpha in \beta')$ otherwise (see proof of Property 1). Thus, without loss of optimality, we can assume that job n cannot occupy position s + 1, *Q.E.D.*

Corollary 2: Properties 7a and 7b eliminate at least $\left[\dfrac{n - r + 1}{2} \right]$ positions (where [x] is an integer portion of x) from the list r, r + 1, ..., n.

Proof. Notice that for every set exactly one position is eliminated since either (7a) or (7b) holds. The same position may be eliminated twice, however. In the worst case, those conditions eliminate twice positions r + 1, r + 3, ..., n - 1 (n - r even) and r + 1, r + 3, ..., n (n - r odd), *Q.E.D.*

We will show that the list of possible positions is further reduced whenever the following property holds.

Property 8: Job n is not in position s of an optimal schedule if there exists a job $i \in \alpha$, $i \neq [s]$, $d_i > d_n$, such that

$$\sum_{k \in \alpha} p_k + p_n \leq d_i + p_i \tag{8}$$

Proof: Consider block schedule $\alpha n \beta$ where $\alpha = \alpha_1 i \alpha_2$, $\alpha_2 \neq \phi$, and job n is in position s. Since β is fixed, t_{max} for jobs i and n is $\sum\limits_{k \in \alpha} p_k + p_n - (p_i + p_n) = \sum\limits_{k \in \alpha} p_k - p_i$. Then condition (8) is $t_{max} \leq d_i - p_n = t_{in}$. According to Property 3, $f(\alpha_1 i \alpha_2 n \beta) \geq f(\alpha_1 \alpha_2 ni \beta)$ where the equality sign holds only for case $d_i > \sum\limits_{k \in \alpha} p_k + p_n \leq d_n$. Then both jobs i and n are early, and job n is scheduled first. Hence, job n cannot be in position s, *Q.E.D.*

Example 5

$p_i(i=1, \ldots, 6)$ are 7, 8, 10, 12, 15, 20; d_i are 10, 41, 52, 55, 40, 25.

Jobs 1, 6, 5, 2, 3, 4 form an increasing sequence of the due dates. Here $n = 6$, $r = 2$, and $s \geq 2$. For $s = 2$, $\alpha = (1)$, and $\beta = (5, 2, 3, 4)$, condition (7b) holds, and position 3 is eliminated. Properties 7a and 7b reduce the list to positions 2, 4, and 6. Next apply Property 8 for $s = 4$. Then $\alpha = (1, 5, 2)$. Since condition (8) is met for $i = 5$, position 4 is eliminated. Thus, only positions 2 and 6 remain in the final reduced list.

Remark: Property 7b is a special case of Property 8 if equation (8) is a strict inequality, $\alpha_2 = \phi$, $\alpha = ([1], [2], \ldots, [r - 1], [r + 1], \ldots, [s], [s + 1])$, and $i = [s + 1]$.

CONCLUSIONS

This chapter presents a theory of the single machine total tardiness problem based on an adjacent precedence relation concept. For each pair of adjacent jobs i, j, a critical start time t_{ij} exists after which the ordering changes direction. The key to solving the problem is the decomposability of matrix $\{t_{ij}\}$ and the position of job n with the largest processing time in the optimal schedule. Partition rules are presented that decompose the problem into smaller subproblems. A condition is derived that further reduces the list of possible positions of job n in the optimal schedule. This author feels that the list can be even further reduced. Notice that if job n always occupies a single position, the problem would be polynomially solvable.

REFERENCES

Baker, K.R., and L.E. Schrage, "Finding an Optimal Sequence by Dynamic Programming: An Extension to Precedence-Related Tasks," *Operations Research* 26 (1978): 111-120.

Du, J., and J.Y-T. Leung, "Minimizing Total Tardiness on One Precessor Is NP-hard," *Mathematics of Operations Research* 15, no. 3 (August 1990): 483-495.

Emmons, H., "One-Machine Sequencing to Minimize Certain Functions of Job Tardiness," *Operations Research,* 17 (1969): 701-715.

Fischer, M.L., "A Dual Algorithm for the One-Machine Scheduling Problem," *Mathematical Programming* 11 (1976): 229-251.

Lawler, E.L, "A Pseudopolynomial Algorithm for Sequencing Jobs to Minimize Total Tardiness," *Annals of Discrete Mathematics* 1 (1977): 331-342.

Potts, C.W., and L.N. Van Wassenhove, "A Decomposition Algorithm for the Single Machine Total Tardiness Problem," *Operations Research Letters* 1 (1982): 177-181.

Rinnooy Kan, A.H.G., B.J. Lageweg, and J.K. Lenstra, "Minimizing Total Costs in One-Machine Scheduling, *Operations Research* 23 (1975): 908-927.

Schrage, L., and K.R. Baker, "Dynamic Programming Solution of Sequencing Problems with Precedence Constraints," *Operations Research* 26 (1978): 444-449.

Srinivasan, V., "A Hybrid Algorithm for the One-Machine Sequencing Problem to Minimize Total Tardiness," *Naval Research Logistics Quarterly* 18, 317-327 (1971).

Szwarc, W., "Adjacent Orderings in Single Machine Scheduling with Earliest and Tardiness Penalties." Working Paper, School of Business Administration, University of Wisconsin-Milwaukee, July 1989.

Szwarc, W., M.E. Posner, and J.J. Liu, "The Single Machine Problem with a Quadratic Cost Function of Completion Times," *Management Science* 34 (1988): 1480-1488.

Part VII

Methodological Issues

Multiple Criteria Decision Making and Negotiating: Some Observations

Stanley Zionts

In this chapter we explore some of the similarities and differences between multiple criteria decision making and negotiating. Multiple criteria decision making (MCDM) has been an active area of research for almost thirty years, beginning with the work of Charnes and Cooper (1961) and evolving through the 1973 conference organized by Cochrane and Zeleny (1973) and beyond. [Recent books on the subject are Steuer (1986) and Yu (1985).] It can be argued that MCDM goes back to the work of von Neumann and Morganstern (1944) and even earlier to some welfare economists. Simply speaking, it involves making decisions in the face of multiple, conflicting objectives. Most of the work done in the area assumes a single decision maker, who chooses among a number of alternatives. The alternatives may either comprise a discrete set or be described by mathematical constraints. We further assume that the decision maker acts as if he were maximizing a utility or value function, a mathematical function of this objective, that is in turn a function of the attributes of the alternatives. [A value function is assumed in the case of certain outcomes, and a utility function is assumed in the case of uncertain outcomes. See, for example, Keeney and Raiffa (1976). We shall henceforth use the term *utility function* for either.] Some relaxations for these assumptions may be assumed, as for example discussed in Simon (1958).

Negotiating is also a long-studied phenomenon; from the work of Edgeworth (1881), and Zeuthen (1930), through the work of Pruitt (1981) and Raiffa (1982), as well as more recent work. These researchers have studied the behavior of parties involved in negotiations from the perspective of their own objectives and the pursuance of those objectives in negotiating a solution to a problem. A simple linking of the two problems can be made by observing that the negotiating problem is one not only of multiple criteria, but of *multiple decision makers* as well. The interaction of the multiple decision makers is the negotiation or bargaining. Not only do tradeoffs have to be made among objectives, but also they have to be made between decision makers.

We assume in negotiation problems that the *group* of decision makers is divided into two or more *parties* and that each party consists of one or more individuals. We assume that all parties have the same objectives (this is no restriction in practice because a given objective may have little or no influence on a party's utility function). A party is assumed to have a utility function of the objectives that it wishes to maximize, and the group a whole is assumed to have a societal utility function of the party utility functions that it wishes to maximize.

Our purpose is not to consider the methods that have been developed for approaching these two problems. Rather, we consider the two problems and explore their similarities, using appropriate concepts. Many methods have been developed to approach the two problems. They can be categorized as methods that involve the estimation of the various utility functions and those that do not.

We have organized this chapter into five sections. In the first section, we provide an overview of multiple criteria problems and negotiating. In the second section, we develop a number of considerations, including the important concepts of nondominance and Pareto optimality, as well as a number of useful geometric spaces. Then, in the third section, we explore some of the theoretical considerations concerning how we can assure that negotiations result in Pareto-optimal solutions, and in the fourth section, we explore some ways in which we can practically try to do the same. We offer conclusions in the fifth section.

MCDM: SOME GEOMETRICAL CONSIDERATIONS

We first consider some of the geometric spaces that provide useful representations for both problems, but particularly the MCDM problem.

The Decision Variable Space

The decision variables are the detailed decisions that are made, such as, for example, the number of units of product 5A4 a plant is to produce on Thursday, July 6, 199X. The level of decision variable may be coarse or fine, depending on the situation. For example, it might be the total number of sprockets produced in a month or the total production time devoted to a class of products. The decision variable variable is a familiar concept in mathematical programming where the x vector is the vector of decision variables. The space of decision variables is a graphical representation of feasible values of decision variables. For a discrete problem, the variable space would consist only of the possible solutions, defined as a set of discrete points. In a mathematical programming situation, the decision variable space would be the space of all possible solutions, with the constraints limiting the feasible solutions. For some problems it may be convenient to omit the concept of a decision variable space: for example, for a problem evaluating a number of different management strategies for a large corporation, each strategy involves so many decisions that the corresponding decision variable space would be so large as to be worthless.

Examples of two-dimensional decision variable spaces may be seen in Figure 19.1, for the discrete case (a) and the continuous case (b). (The two-dimensional examples are simpler than we would like, but they are easiest to illustrate.) Because of our choice of examples, these two decision variable spaces are very similar. The discrete space (a) consists of the points listed in Table 19.1 (the x_1 and x_2 coordinates are as given, and the objective function values u_1 and u_2 (to be discussed below) are also given, where $u_1 = x_1 + .5 x_2$, and $u_2 = .5 x_1 + x_2$.)

Figure 19.1 Discrete (a) and Continuous (b) Decision Variable Spaces

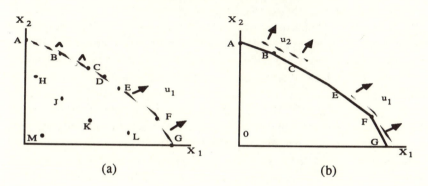

(a)   (b)

**Table 19.1. The Discrete Points Used and
Their Objective Function Values**

	x_1	x_2	u_1	u_2
A	0	44	22	44
B	10	40	30	45
C	20	34	37	44
D	26	26	39	39
E	34	20	44	37
F	40	10	45	30
G	44	0	44	22
H	4	30	19	32
J	10	20	20	25
K	20	10	25	20
L	30	4	32	19
M	4	4	6	6
O	0	0	0	0

The continuous decision variable space consists of points A, B, C, E, F, G, and O and all of the convex combinations or "blends" of those points, including all of the points in the discrete decision variable space.

The Objective Function Space

A second space to consider is the objective function space. The objective function space has one dimension for each objective, and the level of that objective achieved by a particular solution is indicated. Mathematically, the objective function space is a transformation of the decision variable space. It is usually, but not always, a space of lower dimension than the decision variable space. Any constraints are transformed into the objective function space, as well. If the objectives are linear, the transformations are linear. Let us denote the number of objectives by p. In most mathematical programming situations, the objectives might be maximized, but in a broader context, some objectives may be treated as goals (as in goal programming) in that particular values or ranges of values are most desired. Assume that all objectives are to be either maximized or minimized. Then, without loss of generality, we may assume that all objectives are to be maximized.

Examples of objective function space for our example problem are shown in Figure 19.2 for the discrete case (a) and the continuous case (b). The values given in Table 19.1 for u_1 and u_2 are plotted. (Each point in Figure 19.2 may be found by using the formulas given above and the points x_1 and x_2.) As in Figure 19.1, the objective function space for the discrete case is a subset of the continuous space.

Figure 19.2. Discrete and Continuous Objective Function Spaces

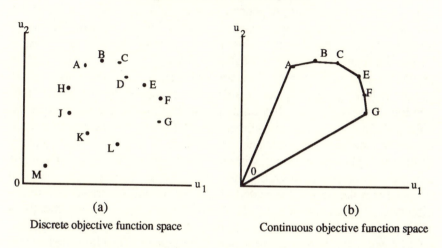

(a)
Discrete objective function space

(b)
Continuous objective function space

Assuming that all objectives are to be maximized, a nondominated solution is desirable.

Definition: A solution is nondominated (or efficient) if and only if there does not exist another solution that is at least as good as the first solution in every objective and strictly better in at least one objective.

In the various spaces we may identify the set of nondominated solutions or efficient solutions: those that are not dominated. In a two-dimensional objective function space plotted using Cartesian coordinates, the nondominated solutions are the most "northeast" solutions (solutions that have no other solutions to their northeast). The nondominated solutions are shown in Figure 19.2. In Figure 19.2(a), they are solutions, B, C, D, E, and F, and in Figure 19.2(b), they are the northeast solutions along the broken line from B to C to E to F. The nondominated solutions may also be observed in the decision variable space by considering solutions that maximize any convex combination of objective functions. (They are, of the course, the same points.)

The Weight Space

The third space that we consider is the weight space, the space of linear (strictly) positive weights (which we shall consider as non-negative, for convenience). We have one weight for each objective. We use these weights to give a linear utility function of all objectives, which is to maximize the sum of the weights times the objectives. (Using the weight spaces does not restrict us to linear utility functions in general.) For every possible set of weights, we indicate a solution (in nondegenerate cases, a unique solution) found by maximizing the linear function using that set of weights. Where everything is linear, the result is a set of mutually exclusive and collective exhaustive polyhedra, each corresponding to a nondominated solution that makes up the space. (More generally, the result is a mapping of the space into nondominated solutions.) It would appear that the weight space, like the objective function space, is p-dimensional. Though the weight space can indeed be viewed as p-dimensional, one dimension is the redundant and may be dropped. The reason is that, without loss of generality, any set of weights may be normalized by dividing them by the sum of the weights, thereby assuring that the sum of the scaled weights is unity. This transforms the p-dimensional space into a $p - 1$ dimensional space or, more specifically, a simplex bounded by the sum of the weights equalling unity. Such a set of coordinates is also known as barycentric coordinates. (The eliminated weight is simply unity minus the sum of the other weights.)

A clever approach for solving three-objective linear programming problems ($p = 3$) uses a two-dimensional weight space ($p - 1 = 2$) in a computer graphics approach for the Apple Macintosh computer titled *Trimap* (see Climaco and Antunes, 1987). Using that approach, it is only necessary to use a computer mouse to locate a desired set of weights on the screen and then have the computer determine the solution as well as the corresponding weight-space polyhedron.

We illustrate the weight space for our example in Figure 19.3. The horizontal axis gives the value of w_1, the weight on objective one, and the vertical axis gives the value of w_2, the weight on objective two. The line $w_1 + w_2 = 1$ gives the condition that allows us to reduce the weight space by one dimension. (The one-dimensional representation is simply the line segment of $w_1 + w_2 = 1$ between the two intercepts, with the positions marked for the solutions B, C, E, and F.) The three dashed lines are $w_2 = 7w_1$, $w_2 = w_1$, and $w_2 = 1/7 \ w_1$. These are the sets of weights for which solutions B and C, C and E, and E and F, respectively, have the same linear utility function value. For example, when $w_1 = w_2 = 1$, solution E has a utility of $34 + 20$ or 54, and solution C has a utility of $20 + 34$ or 54. Hence, for equal weights, the utilities of solutions E and C are equal. This is true for either the discrete or the continuous example.

Figure 19.3. Weight Space

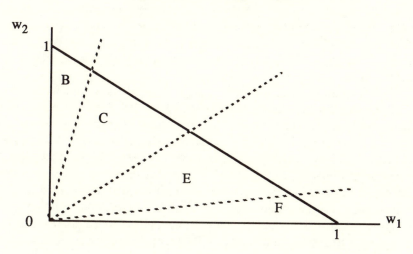

NEGOTIATING: SOME GEOMETRICAL CONSIDERATIONS

The geometrical considerations presented in the previous section are also relevant for the negotiating problem. However, in the negotiating problem, there are some additional geometrical concepts that are useful.

The Party Space

We next consider the party space. Up to this point all of the spaces defined refer to either the multiple criteria or the negotiation problem. This space and the next are defined only for the negotiation problem. The party space consists of one dimension for each party to the negotiation, that dimension indicating the utility function level achieved for the party by a given solution. Assume that we have q parties. Then the dimension of the party space is q.

There is an analogy between the objective function space and the party space. Just as we have the concept of nondominated or efficient solutions in the objective function space, we have the concept of *Pareto*-optimal solutions in the party space.

Definition: A solution is Pareto optimal if and only if there does not exist another solution for which every party is at least as well off and at least one party is strictly better off. Pareto-optimal solutions are desirable in negotiations. If a solution is not Pareto optimal, that means that one or more parties can negotiate gains at *no cost* to the other parties to the negotiations. Pareto-optimal solutions guarantee that all joint gains have been squeezed out and that no additional joint gains remain to be gleaned. Analogous to the weight space, the set of Pareto-optimal solutions may be represented in $q - 1$ dimensions.

As indicated earlier, a party's utility function is a function of his objectives. We illustrate the party space in Figure 19.4. For convenience, we consider only the continuous case. (The discrete case follows similarly.) Using the same example that we used above, assume that party 1 wishes to maximize its utility, which we assume to be $u_1 - 30 + 0\ u_2$ and that party 2 wishes to maximize its utility, which we assume to be $0\ u_1 + u_2 - 30$. We omit negative values of the utility function. They may be omitted in this example because they are not Pareto optimal. We have shown solution D in this figure to illustrate that although it is Pareto optimal in the discrete case (it is not inferior to any solutions), it is not Pareto optimal in the continuous case (it is inferior to a blend of, for example, .5 C and .5 E).

Figure 19.4. Party Space

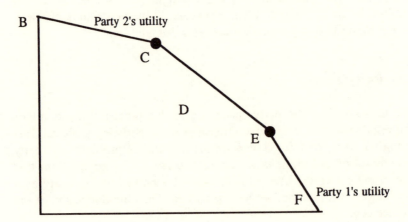

The Party Weight Space

In the party space, if we were to assume a linear societal utility function (also called a social welfare function), we could construct a weight space just as we did for the objective function space. The party weight space is q-dimensional and, as in the case of the objective function space, may be reduced to $q - 1$ dimensions. For a linear function, the space may be partitioned into mutually exclusive and collectively exhaustive polyhedra, each polyhedron indicating the set of weights for which a given Pareto-optimal solution is optimal for a linear societal function.

The party weight space is illustrated in Figure 19.5. For our example, if the weights of party 1 were four times as great as those of party 2 (e.g., w_1 = .8 and w_2 = .2), then from the party weight space we see that solution E is optimal. That can also be illustrated in Figure 19.4 by maximizing .8 (party 1's utility) + .2 (party 2's utility).

Figure 19.5. Party Weight Space

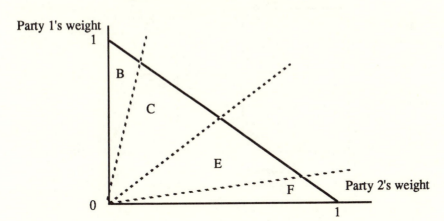

The Party Space and Unstructured Negotiation

By reference to our example, assuming the continuous decision space, consider how our two parties to the negotiation might reason, given an unstructured negotiation. We proceed from the party space and utility functions in Figure 19.4. Each party would like to get its best utility of fifteen, but because both parties 1 and 2 ask for the levels of utility achieved by points B and A, respectively, they soon learn that they cannot both achieve their desired levels. As a result, the two disputants relax their requirements until they either reach an agreement or do not, depending on the outcome of their negotiations. We suppose that in the first round of negotiations, parties 1 and 2 relax their requirements to eleven and twelve units of utility, respectively. That is, both require that they obtain that many (i.e., at least eleven or twelve) units of utility from any solution. See Figure 19.6, in which we have shown both party 1's and 2's first concessions. In order for a solution satisfying those concessions be found, we must find a solution above party 1's first concession line and to the right of party 2's first concession line that satisfies the constraints of the problem. Such a solution does not exist, and, accordingly, there can be no solution that satisfies the constraints imposed above.

Figure 19.6. An Example of a Negotiation

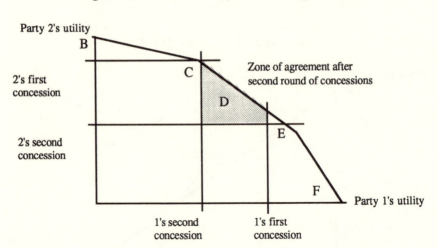

Suppose that, after further discussion, both parties agree to relax their minimum utility level further. Party 1 reduces his minimum to 8.5, and party 2 reduces his minimum to 8. We have indicated the corresponding concession lines in Figure 19.6. Now we do have a region or zone of agreement, the shaded region in the upper right of the figure. Depending on the parties' negotiating skills, they may or may not find the region, however. For example, if they negotiate only along the straight line from B to F (as is often the case), none of those solutions is in the region of agreement. In that case, the parties will not reach an agreement, and further concessions will be necessary. Further, even if the parties are able to agree on a solution, there is no assurance that their agreement will be a Pareto-optimal solution, here one of the shaded solutions on the line segment between C and E. And, for reasons described above, it is desirable that the parties find a Pareto-optimal solution.

Superimposing Objective Function Spaces: The Edgeworth Box

Let us now look at the objective function space from a different perspective. In developing our two weight spaces, we have constructed the spaces based on linear utility functions and societal utility functions. This is generally not the case, of course. Here we specifically consider the nonlinear utility function for each party. Consider the objective function space of two (in general, more) parties, and, for convenience, assume two objectives. Assume further that the two parties are generally in opposition, such as, that is, a buyer and a seller of a commodity. We assume, in our example, that one party wants to maximize both objectives, and the other wants to minimize both objectives. (To represent this in a way consistent with what we stated in the first section, we would have to have four objectives: to maximize and minimize each of the two objectives. In order to represent this in a two-dimensional Edgeworth box, we show only the original two objectives.)

We may then construct the objective function space in a special way for the two parties (see Figure 19.7), so that at the origin (point 2) we have what party 2 regards as its best possible solution and what party 1 regards as its worst possible solution. At the appropriate point (point 1), we construct party 1's best possible solution, which is also the worst solution for party 2. By reference to our previous example, the two points would be points B and F (corresponding to points 1 and 2, respectively). (There are points that are worse points for both—that is, points having negative utility.)

Further, by superimposing curves of constant utility of both parties on the graph, we may construct the set of Pareto-optimal solutions. However, here we do it in the objective function space. As a result, we have a geometric construct known as an Edgeworth box. By constructing the locus of points where the curves of constant utility for each party are tangent to each other (special changes being made in the case of degeneracy, that is, linearity or piecewise linearity), we have what is called the contract curve (curve from 1 to 7 to 6 to 4 to 2). The contract curve is the locus of Pareto-optimal solutions to the negotiation.

Though the Edgeworth box concept can be extended to higher dimensions, it has been almost exclusively used in two-party and two-objective (or issue) situations for obvious reasons. To understand how the

Edgeworth box works, consider a solution such as point 3. Party 1's utility at point 3 is on an isoutility curve going from 3 to 4 to 5 and increasing to the upper right. Party 2's utility is on an isoutility curve going from 3 to 6 to 5 and increasing to the lower left. From point 3 both parties can improve their utilities, or achieve joint gains, by moving to an interior point of the region 3 - 4 - 5 - 6. The argument may be repeated until a point on the contract curve within the region has been reached. At such a point, the two isoutility curves will be tangent, and no further joint gains are possible. (See point 7, for example.)

Figure 19.7. An Edgeworth Box

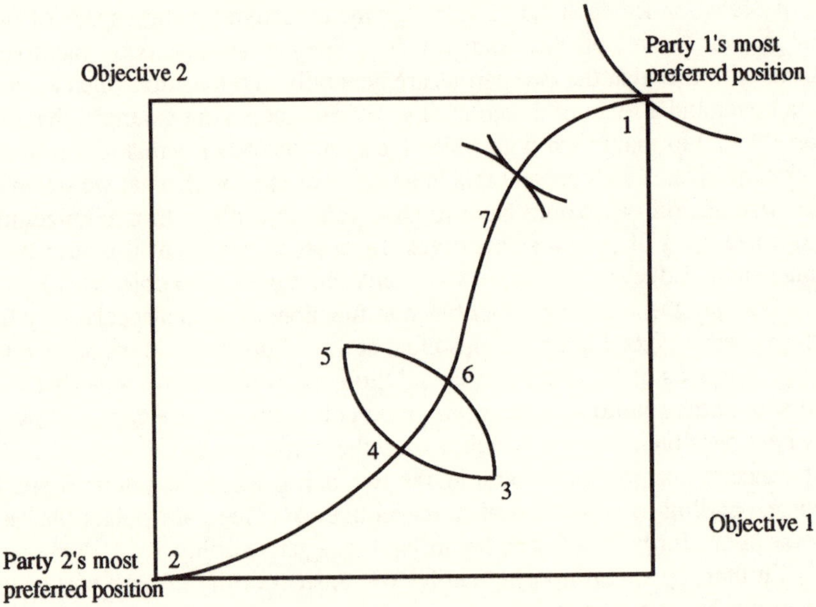

Both the party space and the Edgeworth box show the Pareto-optimal solutions; however, their representations are different. In the party space, the Pareto-optimal solutions are the northeast-most solutions. In the Edgeworth box, the Pareto-optimal solutions are on the contract curve.

ACHIEVING NONDOMINATED AND
PARETO-OPTIMAL SOLUTIONS IN THEORY

For reasons described above, it is desirable to achieve both nondominated and Pareto-optimal solutions, at least in theory. Most methods for solving MCDM problems provide nondominated solutions. Therefore, we restrict our discussion here to negotiating problems. Compared to non-Pareto-optimal solutions, Pareto-optimal solutions provide gains to parties that are not realized at the expense of others. Moving from non-Pareto-optimal solutions toward Pareto-optimal solutions is referred to as a win-win move, in that both parties win, rather than allowing one party to win at the expense of another.

Let us consider how we can assure ourselves of a Pareto-optimal solution, at least from a theoretical perspective. First, assume that we know all of the relationships of the utility functions and the decision variables. Further, maximizing the utility function is equivalent to maximizing a concave function subject to a set of constraints that constitute a convex set.

One way to find a Pareto-optimal solution is to use a positive weight for each party and to maximize the weighted sum of utilities. Different sets of weights generate different solutions, although from what we have observed about the weight spaces, more than one set of weights will often generate the same solution. For two-party negotiations, the Pareto-optimal set is one-dimensional ($q - 1 = 1$), and it is not difficult to construct, provided that we know the relationships. (We observe the one-dimensional nature of the two-party contract curve in Figure 19.7.)

Given the above assumptions, we may determine all Pareto-optimal solutions by solving a parametric linear programming problem. That problem would maximize a weighted (positive) sum of objectives, while keeping all but one objective fixed at minimum values. (In the case of two objectives, the problem would be to maximize a weighted sum (using positive weights) of objectives, subject to a minimum level of the other.)

If the set of feasible solutions does not comprise a convex set, as is the case where there is simply a set of discrete alternatives, for example, then there may be Pareto-optimal solutions that are not identified by the above procedure. Consider Figure 19.8, which shows three discrete alternative solutions. The procedure suggested above would identify solutions A and C, but not B. Nonetheless, solution B is Pareto optimal. Such a solution is inferior to a convex combination of solutions A and C (a "blend" of those solutions). However, in a discrete situation it is not possible to blend the solutions. (A similar example occurs in Figure 19.2a. Solution D is inferior to a convex combination of C and E, but is nonetheless nondominated.)

**Figure 19.8. A Convex Dominated Solution
That Is Pareto Optimal**

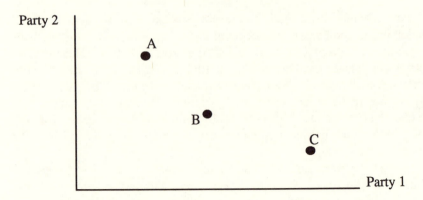

ACHIEVING PARETO-OPTIMAL SOLUTIONS IN PRACTICE

How do we achieve Pareto-optimal solutions in practice? First, let us assume that somehow or other we know which solutions are Pareto optimal. Then, if we could convince the parties that they would be better off by restricting their choice to Pareto-optimal solutions, possibly they would be willing to do so. They may not be willing, however, because of the concern that their adversary may gain at their expense, in spite of assurances we may give.

Now, let us consider the more likely reality in which we do not know which solutions are Pareto optimal. Were our functions known, then we could at least try to use the procedure identified above—namely, maximizing weight sums of the parties' utilities—to identify Pareto-optimal solutions. Different weighted sums give different Pareto-optimal solutions. Unfortunately, the functions are usually not known. In that case, we could, of course, try to use proxy functions or otherwise estimate the utility functions (e.g., using the procedure of Keeney and Raiffa, 1976), hoping that any resulting solutions were Pareto optimal.

Another way to identify Pareto-optimal solutions, in two-party negotiations as well as in larger negotiations, is to determine the contract curve of the Edgeworth box. (With more than two parties, the procedure is more complicated. With two parties, the contract curve is one-dimensional; with three or more, it is higher-dimensional. In general, with q parties, the contract function (not necessarily a curve) has $q - 1$ dimensions. Accordingly, we describe the procedure for only two parties.) The way in which this is done by economists is to find points at which the curves of constant utility of each party are tangent and to connect such points with a curve. Practically speaking, such a procedure is impossible to do.

Teich's Procedure

Jeffrey Teich, a Ph.D. student in the School of Management at the State University of New York, in work on his doctoral dissertation, has developed a way of approximating the contract curve. The idea is as follows. First, have the two parties determine their (reasonable) most desirable solution points. (Because of the gaming aspects of negotiations, having the parties state this is nontrivial also.) Such solution points would define a range on each issue. Then, partitioning the range on each issue (between their most desirable solution points) into four equal segments, determine the three intermediate levels of each issue. Use the Cartesian product of a corresponding pair of levels as an anchor point to construct a common "budget constraint" to be used by each party. Such a budget contract is arbitrary initially, in that, for example, the sum of the levels of all issues might be whatever constant is determined by the anchor point.

Then each party is asked to determine his preferred point, subject to the "budget constraint." If the preferred points of the two parties are sufficiently close, then that point is assumed to be on the contract curve. Otherwise, the "budget constraint" prices are adjusted, using a search procedure in which convergence to a common point is guaranteed, subject to mild assumptions. Once the parties agree on a point on a suitably adjusted "budget constraint," then the process is repeated for each of the other anchor points. The three points on the contract curve, together with the most preferred points of each party, give us five points for fitting an approximate contract curve. [This procedure is roughly analogous to the procedure used by Keeney and Raiffa (1976) for fitting utility functions.] Teich has evaluated some assumed linear and nonlinear utility functions using this approach and is applying it in his dissertation.

His procedure for then determining a settlement of the negotiation is to have the parties negotiate along the contract curve to come up with a final agreement.

Single Negotiating Text/Win-Win Solutions

Another approach for generating Pareto-optimal solutions in practice has been proposed by Raiffa (1982). Borrowing from Raiffa and from Fisher and Ury (1981), I call it the single negotiating text/win-win approach. The idea is that the parties should begin the negotiations at a solution that is sufficiently poor for *both* parties that it is certainly not Pareto optimal (in the Edgeworth box, for example, points from either the lower right-hand or upper left-hand corner of the box suffice). Then, together and perhaps with the aid of a mediator, they should search for joint gains whereby they both benefit. The process continues until no further joint gains can be gleaned.

CONCLUSION

In this chapter we have tried to create an awareness of the related problems of multiple criteria decision making and negotiating. The two problems have many similarities, and yet they are quite different. A great deal of work has been done on both problems, primarily on a theoretical level. There are many computer models, particularly in the MCDM area. What is needed is an increase in applications of the concepts and results of both MCDM and negotiating.

REFERENCES

Charnes, A., and W. W. Cooper, *Management Models and Industrial Applications of Linear Programming*, New York: John Wiley, 1961.

Climaco, J. C. N., and C. H. Antunes, "Trimap: An Interactive Tricriteria Linear Programming Package," *Foundations of Control and Engineering* 12 (1987).

Cochrane, J. L., and M. Zeleny, *Multiple Criteria Decision Making*, Columbia: University of South Carolina Press, 1973.

Edgeworth, F. Y., *Mathematical Psychics*, London: Kegal Paul, 1881.

Fisher, R., and W. Ury, *Getting to Yes*, Boston: Houghton Mifflin, 1981.

Keeney, R. L., and H. Raiffa, *Decisions with Multiple Objectives: Preferences and Value Tradeoffs*, New York: John Wiley, 1976.

Pruitt, D. G., *Negotiation Behavior*, New York: Academic Press, 1981.

Raiffa, H., *The Art and Science of Negotiations*, Cambridge: Harvard University Press, 1982.

Simon, H. A., *Administrative Behavior*, New York : Macmillan, 1958.

Steuer, R. E., *Multiple Criteria Optimization: Theory, Computation, and Application*, New York: John Wiley, 1986.

von Neumann, J., and O. Morganstern, *Theory of Games and Economic Behavior*, New York: John Wiley, 1944.

Yu, P. L., *Multiple Criteria Decision Making: Concepts, Techniques, and Extensions*, New York: Plenum Press, 1985.

Zeuthen, F., *Problems of Monopoly and Economic Warfare*, London: Routledge and Kegan Paul, 1930.

20

Bootstrapping: Implications for Decision Making

Sheryl E. Kimes

One of the primary goals of statistics is to try to learn what is true, or to assess the best estimate of the truth. If a statistical estimate is inaccurate, how does a researcher know, and what ills will befall the decision maker? How does a researcher determine if the answer given by a particular technique is better than an answer derived from some other method?

Bootstrapping, a computer-intensive statistical method, can be used to address these issues (Efron, 1979). Bootstrapping can be used to obtain additional information about true probability distributions, error terms and model validity. Bootstrapping is a nonparametric technique and, as such, requires no assumptions about probability distributions. Bootstrapping is thus a powerful tool for evaluating error terms and distributions that may not conform to standard distributions.

Essentially, bootstrapping employs Monte Carlo simulation to draw repeated samples with replacement for a given data set (Efron, 1979). Given a data set of size n, a probability of $1/n$ is assigned to each x_i. Simulation is used to draw a number of random samples of the same size as the original data set with each x_i drawn independently, with replacement and equal probability of selection (Figure 20.1). For example, in a data base with fifty observations, each observation would have a 1/50 chance of being selected next in a bootstrap sample. The statistic in question is calculated for each sample, and the results among samples are compared.

The bootstrap method can be used with nearly any statistic (Pari and Chatterjee, 1986). It can be used in a number of ways, including validation of models, establishment of confidence intervals, determination of overoptimism or bias, and development of decision rules. The bootstrap method is computationally intense and has only recently achieved acceptance, mainly because of its reliance on low-cost, high-power computing.

Figure 20.1. Bootstrapping Procedure

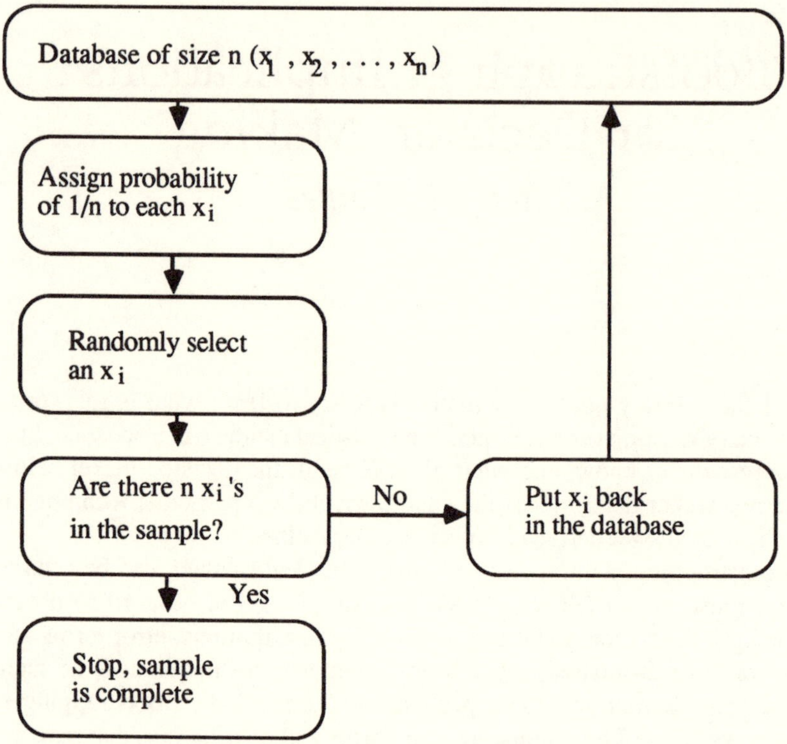

```
┌──────────────────────────────────────────────────────────────┐
│  Database of size n (x₁ , x₂ , . . . , xₙ)                     │
└──────────────────────────────────────────────────────────────┘
          │                                           ▲
          ▼                                           │
┌──────────────────────┐                              │
│ Assign probability    │                             │
│ of 1/n to each xᵢ     │                             │
└──────────────────────┘                              │
          │                                           │
          ▼                                           │
┌──────────────────────┐                              │
│ Randomly select       │                             │
│ an xᵢ                 │                             │
└──────────────────────┘                              │
          │                                           │
          ▼                                           │
┌──────────────────────┐    No    ┌──────────────────┐
│ Are there n xᵢ 's     │ ───────▶ │ Put xᵢ back       │
│ in the sample?        │          │ in the database   │
└──────────────────────┘          └──────────────────┘
          │  Yes
          ▼
┌──────────────────────┐
│ Stop, sample          │
│ is complete           │
└──────────────────────┘
```

The term *bootstrap* originated from the use of one sample to give birth to many samples (Diaconis and Efron, 1983). Efron considered other names for the bootstrap; among his favorites was the shotgun, which "can blow the head off any problem if the statistician can stand the resulting mess" (Tukey, 1979, quoted in Efron, 1979, p. 25).

Bootstrapping has two primary advantages over traditional statistical methods (Diaconis and Efron, 1983). Since bootstrapping is distribution-free, assumptions do not have to be made about a particular probability distribution. Frequently, these unverifiable assumptions involve a Gaussian distribution, which may not be appropriate for the given data. Bootstrapping can also be used to numerically explore the properties of a sample. Since statistical measures are often not available for complex estimates of a sample, bootstrapping can be used to focus on statistical measures that are not mathematically-closed.

With the absence of the limiting assumptions of normality and mathematically closed forms, bootstrapping can be used to develop more accurate estimates of error by substituting computing power for theoretical analysis. With the decrease in the cost of computer time, bootstrapping often represents a good value for accurate problem solution.

This chpater discusses three main areas of bootstrap application: true error estimation, determination of true probability distributions, and small sample sizes. Research in each of the areas will be reviewed, and the incremental benefit gained from the use of the bootstrap technique will be examined. The cost and time requirements required for bootstrapping will be discussed, and the tradeoffs between the cost and the value gained from bootstrapping will be analyzed.

BOOTSTRAP APPLICATIONS

Bootstrapping has been applied in a number of fields. Improved forecast accuracy was the goal of several studies. Peters and Freedman (1984) looked at the accuracy of a regional energy forecast model, while Bianchi et al. (1987) analyzed the error from a macroeconomic model of the French economy. Macroeconomic issues have also attracted attention from Godek (1986) in his study of trade restrictions and from Williams and Baumann (1988) in their assessment of the effectiveness of the Lucas natural rate hypothesis. Other application areas include audit population selection (Tamura and Frost, 1986), antitrust law (Williams, 1986), prediction of chronic hepatitis patient survival (Efron and Gong, 1983), maintenance of light fixtures (Grier, 1988), hotel site location (Kimes, 1987; Biemer and Kimes, 1989), sizing of electric utility capacity (Veall, 1987), selection of real estate investments (Kelley and Kuhle, 1987), and selection of criteria for law school admission (Efron, 1983). The diversity of applications demonstrates the versatility of the bootstrap and indicates the type of problems that lend themselves well to this approach. The studies to be reviewed generally address at least one of the following three issues:

1.   What is the true error of the estimate, and is the apparent error different?

2.   What is the true probability distribution of the data?

3.   Can information be gleaned from a small sample size?

True Error Estimates

Apparent error rates calculated from an original data set may under-estimate the true error since the model was built from the original data (Mosteller and Tukey, 1977). Only by testing the model on other data, whether real or simulated, can the researcher begin to understand what the actual error rates might be. The difference between the apparent error rates and the actual error rates is referred to as the model overoptimism (Efron, 1979). By knowing what the over-optimism of the model is, the decision-maker can be better informed as to the consequences of a particular decision.

Peters and Freedman (1984) used bootstrapping to find the true error in a regional energy demand forecasting method. Bootstrapping allowed them to assess the variability in the estimate without collecting additional data. Independent variables included heating degree days, cooling degree days, price of fuel, value added by manufacturing, and energy demand of the previous year. After building the model, they took bootstrap samples of the residuals (in their terminology, the "pseudo-error") and tested the model against its assumptions.

The error rate resulting from the bootstrap method was two to three times higher than that from the traditional asymptotic delta method. By demonstrating that the error estimate was overoptimistic, Peters and Freedman were able to show that the regional energy demand forecasting model was much less reliable than was traditionally thought.

Efron and Gong (1983), in a study of the means to predict survival of chronic hepatitis patients, used bootstrapping to show that the error predicted from a logistic regression model was overly optimistic. The original model misclassified 16 percent of the cases. This error estimate was considered to be overoptimistic because the model had been built for the data and might be best suited to that particular data set (Diaconis and Efron, 1983; p. 128). Sufficient bootstrap samples were taken, and the misclassification rate was recalculated and found to be 20 percent. As with the regional energy demand forecasting model (Peters and Freedman, 1984), the apparent error estimates were much lower than those resulting from testing the model on a number of bootstrap samples.

Grier (1988) studied confidence bonds resulting from application of the Kaplan-Meier estimator to the censored data problem of maintaining light fixtures in a large public building. He was trying to estimate the mean time between failures by determining the life of the light fixtures and developing several different confidence bands. He gave no comparison of the error rates calculated, but showed that bootstrapping performed on a supercomputer could greatly decrease the amount of time necessary to complete the calculations.

Kimes (1987) and Biemer and Kimes (1989) developed a regression-based decision rule to assist with the site selection procedure of a mid-sized hotel chain. The binary decision rule, either "build" or "do not build," was based on a prediction of operating margin. Independent variables included median income, market area population, and competitive room price. Bootstrapping was used to determine the true misclassification rate from applying the decision rule to 200 bootstrap samples. The error rate resulting from the original regression model was found to underestimate the true error by 5 to 7 percent. Application of the original decision rule would have resulted in twenty-two bad "build" decisions in a three-year time period, while application of the bootstrap-based decision rule would have resulted in six false "build" decisions during the same time period.

True Probability Distribution

In some situations, additional information on an entire probability distribution or a particular part of a probability distribution may be required. For example, in accounting, auditors might be interested in examining unusual cases. Obviously, finding sufficient unusual cases might be difficult in practice, but in bootstrapping, sufficient bootstrap samples could be drawn that would allow for numerous cases in the tail of the probability distribution. By studying these "unusual" cases, a researcher can learn more about the behavior of those cases.

Tamura and Frost (1986), in their study of upper bound establishment for the total error of an accounting population using dollar unit sampling (DUS), used bootstrapping to show that the traditional bound-setting methods might result in unnecessary overauditing. The traditional method of the Stringer bound was not statistically efficient, especially when a population had low taintings. Other combined attributes and variables (CAV) bounds had similar problems. If the auditor has inefficient bounds, he may conclude that the aggregate error is too large, which may result in expensive overauditing. A simple parametric approach can be used if the distribution of taintings is known, but this information is often unavailable.

Using a power-function distribution, the upper bounds resulting from a parametric bootstrap approach were compared with the Stringer bound and a simple parametric approach (Tamura and Frost, 1986). A simulation using various population error rates (.01, .02, .03, .04, .06, .08, and .10) and power function parameters was conducted, and the reliability and tightness of upper bounds resulting from each of the three methods were calculated. Bootstrapping was found to give a more conservative confidence interval and a much tighter bound than the Stringer method. The classical method of calculating the upper bound was found to be extremely unreliable. The authors recommended further research into the potential of using bootstrap applications with the audit selection procedure (Tamura and Frost, 1986).

Veall (1987) used bootstrapping to estimate the probability distribution of peak electricity demand for Ontario Hydro. The intent of the study was to estimate the entire probability distribution of peak demand so that more accurate and efficient capacity-sizing decisions could be made. If an optimal probability of shortage could be determined, the utility would make a better capacity decision. Traditional parametric techniques might lead to incorrect decisions because the assumption of normality may not be met, and independent variables may possess inherent uncertainty.

Veall (1987) built a regression model for predicting peak demand as a function of average demand per year. Average demand per year was determined in another regression model, which included the independent variables of the real average price of electricity, total real provincial income, and time. Both regression models were relatively simple because of the computational burden of the bootstrap. "Essentially, sophistication in estimation of the first moment of the forecast is being traded for improved estimation of the second moment of the error distribution" (Veall, 1987; p. 206).

The results showed that it was extremely important to allow for variability in the independent variables. The estimation of peak demand using bootstrapping was shown to be a valuable tool.

Kelley and Kuhle (1987) used bootstrapping to determine real estate investment potential for a sample of 170 observations in two cities. Investors require data to make rational real estate investment decisions, but often lack the necessary information. Assumptions about the distribution of the values of the data are difficult to make, but bootstrapping helps ameliorate this problem.

Information on property type (apartment, industrial, office and shopping center), date of sale, price, net operating income, and financing terms was collected and used to predict return. Kelley and Kuhle (1987) hypothesized that neither the return values for the different property types nor the return values for the two cities would be significantly different.

One thousand bootstrap samples for each property type were run, and return values were calculated for each city and each property type. Return values for the different property levels were found to be significantly different, as were the return values for the two cities. Unfortunately, Kelley and Kuhle (1987) did not compare the results of their bootstrap with those of a more traditional method.

Williams and Baumann (1988) concurred with a recent study (Addison et al., 1986), which disproved Lucas's natural rate hypothesis, but showed that the Addison, et al. (1986) study rested on an incorrect normality assumption. Lucas's natural rate hypothesis concerns the Phillips curve tradeoff between inflation and real output. Nominal aggregate demand changes were thought to affect real output only if suppliers of goods and services view the transmutations as changes in relative price. Addison et al. (1986) assumed that output-inflation data from thirty-four countries were normal and showed that the natural rate hypothesis was incorrect. Williams and Baumann (1988) used bootstrapping with 1000 samples and found similar results without making the normality assumption.

Bianchi et al. (1987) studied the accuracy of a macro forecasting model for the French economy. The method, Mini-DUS, was so complex that analytical investigation of the sampling distribution was not possible. They tested several different methods to see how the error terms compared. Their primary goal was to determine the amount of faith they should have in their forecasting model.

Methods tested included a simple analytical method, Monte Carlo simulation on coefficients, static parametric stochastic simulation and reestimation, dynamic parametric stochastic simulation and reestimation, static bootstrap sampling and reestimation, and dynamic bootstrap sampling and reestimation. Error terms resulting from each were similar, but the basic analytical method usually resulted in the lowest error estimate, indicating possible overoptimism.

Small Sample Size

A small sample size often prevents researchers from thoroughly analyzing possible relationships among variables. Bootstrapping can assist in this situation since many repeated samples of the original data set can be taken and tested.

Godek (1986), in his study of trade restrictions in developed countries, used bootstrapping to assess the true error present in his regression models. Since he had data on only fifteen developed countries, bootstrapping provided a convenient means of testing the validity of his original regression model. Three independent variables (gross domestic product, gross domestic product per capita, and government spending per gross national product) were used to predict three different dependent variables (index of total protection, tariff rate, and quota index). Regression models were built for 500 bootstrap samples to help assess the error estimate. The t-statistics from the bootstrap sampling were in the same confidence region as the simple regressions, demonstrating that the original model could be considered reliable.

In another instance of a small sample size, Efron (1983) studied the relationship between undergraduate grade point average and law school admission test scores for fifteen law schools. A reasonably strong correlation (r = .776) was found, but could not necessarily be trusted because of the small sample size. Efron then took 1000 bootstrap samples and calculated the correlation coefficient for each. Over two-thirds (68%) of the samples had correlation coefficients between .654 and .908. Information on the entire population of law schools was available, and the true correlation coefficient was .761, well within the bounds expected. The additional bootstrap calculations took less than one second and cost less than one dollar (Efron, 1983).

Williams (1986), in his study of the 1898 *Addyston Pipe* antitrust decision showed that a previous study of the decision (Bittlingmayer, 1982, discussed in Williams, 1986) made incorrect assumptions which led to several incorrect statistical inferences. In the *Addyston Pipe* use, the U.S. Supreme Court decided that a group of nine cast-iron manufacturers had formed a price cartel. Bittlingmayer (1982, discussed in Williams, 1986) found that the firms had stochastic demand, operated at rates of output with decreasing average and marginal costs, and had large avoidable costs. He concluded that the cooperative behavior of the firms provided a sufficient condition for market equilibrium.

Because of the small sample size, assumptions made about distribution may have been incorrect. Williams (1986) took 500 bootstrap samples to help analyze the decision. He found that six of the nine plants had constant marginal and average costs and that a competitive market equilibrium was in existence. The errors from the original work were found to be biased by a factor of two.

COST AND TIME REQUIREMENTS

One of the major problems associated with bootstrapping is the computer time and coding required. The programming might not be a particularly troublesome issue since packaged procedures are available (Williams, 1986; Efron and Tibshirani, 1986), but the issue of central processing (CPU) time is of concern. If it costs more to run the bootstrap than the value of the improved accuracy, it makes little sense to use bootstrapping. Also, since bootstrapping is ideally suited to some of the advances in parallel processing and supercomputers, the issue of program vectorization arises.

Grier (1988) discussed the potential applications of supercomputing to simulation-based modeling. In an example on bootstrapping the Kaplan-Meier estimator, he compared the amount of computer time required to complete his experiment with that required for other more traditional approaches. Essentially, the problem entailed performing forty runs of a single program and then replicating this experiment 1000 times. When running the bootstrap on a DEC-VAX 11/750, 120 hours of CPU time were required to perform one experiment. The CPU time required was similar for the Ridge workstation. Running a unvectorized program on a CRAY XMP required 11 hours of a reduced CPU time. Subsequent vectorizing of 10 percent of the program resulted in CPU time of 5.5 hours. After considerable programming time, they were able to reduce the CPU time to 1 hour.

Grier did not compare the results of his bootstrap experiment with those of a traditional "one-shot" computer program. He cautioned that rewriting a program to take advantage of supercomputing capabilities may not be worth the additional effort. The amount of time saved on program execution must be compared with the amount of time spent on optimizing the program.

Kimes (1987) ran nine experiments of 200 bootstrap samples each. The bootstrap program was written in SAS and run on an IBM 3081. Each experiment took approximately twenty-four hours to run and required nearly constant attention because of frequent computer breakdowns. The improved decision rule that was developed using the bootstrap-based decision rule resulted in a much lower error rate (six mistakes over a three-year period) than a non-bootstrap-based decision rule (twenty-two mistakes over a three-year period).

Bianchi et al. (1987), in a study of a macro forecasting model for the French economy, reported the CPU time required for each of the methods they tested. The analytical method required 2 minutes of CPU time; Monte Carlo simulation, 10 minutes; static parametric stochastic simulation and reestimation, 200 minutes; dynamic parametric stochastic simulation and reestimation, 500 minutes; static bootstrapping and reestimation, 190 minutes; and dynamic bootstrapping and reestimation, 190 minutes.

As shown above, bootstrapping can greatly improve error estimation, give more detailed information on true probability distributions, and assist in analyzing small samples. This improved information comes at a cost, primarily of computer programming time and CPU time. With the decrease in computer costs and the increase in speed, bootstrapping and other computer-intensive statistical methods may become common tools of analysis.

CONCLUSIONS

Bootstrapping is a powerful statistical tool that can lead to improved accuracy of decisions. The selection of bootstrapping as a tool for analysis becomes an issue of whether the improved accuracy results in improved decisions, and whether the improved decisions are worth the cost of the improved accuracy. In most of the studies reviewed, bootstrapping gave improved information for the decision maker in the form of better error estimates or additional information on a probability distribution. With the decrease in computer costs, bootstrapping will probably become a common analysis tool, which can lead to better decisions.

The danger with bootstrapping, as with most analytical techniques, is that researchers may not address the key issue of whether the improved accuracy results in better decision making. Mathematical exercises have their place, but may not be applicable to real problems unless they lead to more accurate and easier decisions.

REFERENCES

Addison, John T., Henry W. Chappell, and Alberto C. Castro. (1986). "Output-Inflation Tradeoffs in 34 Countries," *Journal of Economics and Business* 38 (4): 353-360.

Bianchi, Carlo, Giorgio Calzolari, and Jean-Louis Brillet. (1987). "Measuring Forecast Uncertainty: A Review with Evaluation Based on a Macro Model of the French Economy," *International Journal of Forecasting* 3: 211-227.

Biemer, Paul P., and Sheryl E. Kimes. (1989). "An Application of Bootstrapping for Determining a Decision Rule for Site Location," Working paper, Ithaca, NY: Cornell University.

Bittlingmayer, George. (1982). "Decreasing Average Cost and Competition: A New Look at the *Addyston Pipe* Case," *Journal of Law and Economics* 25: 201-229.

Diaconis, Perry, and Bradley Efron. (May 1983). "Computer-Intensive Methods in Statistics," *Scientific American* 248(5): 116-130.

Efron, Bradley. (1979). "Bootstrap Methods: Another Look at the Jackknife," *Annals of Statistics* 7(1): 1-26.

Efron, Bradley. (1983). "Estimating the Error Rate of a Prediction Rule: Improvement on Cross-Validation," *Journal of the American Statistical Association* 78: 316-331.

Efron, Bradley, and Gail Gong. (1983). "A Leisurely Look at the Bootstrap, the Jackknife and Cross-Validation," *American Statistician* 37(1): 36-48.

Efron, Bradley, and R. Tibshirani. (1986). "Bootstrap Methods for Standard Errors, Confidence Intervals and Other Measures of Statistical Accuracy," *Statistical Science* 1 (1): 54-77.

Godek, Paul E. (1986). "The Politically Optimal Tariff: Levels of Trade Restrictions across Developed Countries," *Economic Inquiry* 26: 587-592.

Grier, David Alan. (1988). "Supercomputers and Monte Carlo Experiments," *Chance* 1(2): 19-28.

Kelley, Joseph D., and James L. Kuhle. (Summer 1987). "A Bootstrap Approach to Determining Real Estate Investment Performance," *The Real Estate Appraiser and Analyst* 53 (2): 29-32.

Kimes, Sheryl E. (1987). "Location Analysis in the Lodging Industry," unpublished Ph.D. dissertation, The University of Texas at Austin.

Mosteller, Frederick, and John W. Tukey. (1977). *Data Analysis and Regression.* Reading, MA: Addison-Wesley.

Pari, Robert, and Sangit Chatterjee. (1986). "Using L_2 Estimation for L_1 Estimators: An Application to the Single-Index Model," *Decision Sciences* 17 (3): 414-423.

Peters, Stephen C., and David A. Freedman. (1984). "Using the Bootstrap to Evaluate Forecasting Equations," *Journal of Forecasting* 4(3): 253-262.

Tamura, Hirokuni and Peter A. Frost. (1986). "Tightening CAV (DUS) Bounds by Using a Parametric Model," *Journal of Accounting Research* 24(2): 364-371.

Veall, Michael R. (1987). "Bootstrapping the Probability Distribution of Peak Electricity Demand," *International Economic Review* 28(1): 203-212.

Williams, Michael A. (1986). "An Economic Application of Bootstrap Statistical Methods: *Addyston Pipe* Revisited," *American Economist* 30(2): 52-58.

Williams, Michael A., and Michael G. Baumann. (1988). "Output-Inflation Tradeoffs in 34 Countries: Comment," *Journal of Economics and Business* 40: 97-101.

21

Methodological Issues in Testing Contingency Theories: An Assessment of Alternative Approaches

Anil K. Gupta
Vijay Govindarajan

Few scholars would disagree that contingency perspectives have been adopted widely in the organizational sciences. As Venkatraman and Camillus (1984) observed, contingency theories have proven useful in explaining a variety of phenomena. That is, associations between alternative strategies and firm performance have been explained through such environmental contingencies as product life cycle, entry and exit barriers, and environmental volatility (Anderson and Zeithaml, 1984; Harrigan, 1982; Porter, 1976); similarly, associations between alternative organizational structures and firm performance have been explained through such environmental or strategic contingencies as technoeconomic uncertainty, and extent and form of corporate diversity (Chandler, 1962; Lawrence and Lorsch, 1967).

Recently, many researchers have voiced concern that most contingency studies in the organizational sciences have tended to be very imprecise regarding the exact form of the postulated relationships between the variables of interest (Dewar and Werbel, 1979; Drazin and Van de Ven, 1985; Joyce, Slocum, and Von Glinow, 1982; Schoonhoven, 1981; Tosi and Slocum, 1984). Arguably, this imprecision creates at least two major problems: (1) the risk becomes high that the analytical procedures employed might be inappropriate for the contingency relationships being tested; and (2) it becomes difficult to reconcile the findings of different studies and build an integrated body of knowledge.

In this context, the objective of this chapter is to undertake an assessment of the various approaches that have been employed for testing bivariate contingency hypotheses (i.e., those involving a predicted interactive impact of one context variable and one design variable on some performance variable). Such an undertaking is viewed as important because, even though different methods often yield different results, researchers have generally tended not to provide the reasons for selecting a specific method employed in a particular study; more critically, in many of the instances where reasons for methodological choice have been provided, they are questionable.

TESTING BIVARIATE CONTINGENCY THEORIES: BACKGROUND

Multiple Levels of Contingency Specifications

Following Drazin and Van de Ven (1985), at a broad level, contingency hypotheses can be specified at three levels of complexity (see Figure 21.1).

Level 1 contingency hypotheses (i.e., those of the bivariate causal type) include only two variables, a context variable and a design variable with no attention paid to any performance variable. The premise here is that values of the context variable cause the design variable to acquire certain specific values; a concrete example of a level 1 hypothesis would be "product-market diversification leads to decentralization." *Level 2 contingency hypotheses* (i.e., those of the bivariate interaction type) incorporate a performance variable in addition to a context and a design variable. These specifications allow for the possibility that the design variable can acquire particular values on account of factors other than the context variable, that is, the impact of the context variable on the design variable is viewed as nondeterministic. Further, the contingency relationship between the context and the design variables is hypothesized as existing in the form of their interactive impact on performance; one concrete example of a level 2 hypothesis would be "when high product-market diversification and high decentralization coexist, return on equity will be high; otherwise, return on equity will be low." Finally, *level 3 contingency hypotheses* (i.e., those of the multivariate interaction type) are even more complex because they focus simultaneously on not just one but multiple context, design, and performance variables. As an extension of level 2 specifications, the premise here is that performance is a function of interaction between not just one context and one design variable, but a whole multivariate system of context and design variables; a concrete example of a level 3 hypothesis would be "if structure and control systems are linked to both corporate and business unit strategies in certain predicted ways, then corporate sales growth rate and return on equity will be high; if not, then corporate sales growth rate and return on equity will be low."

Figure 21.1. Alternative Contingency Conceptualizations

Approach	Nature of Relationship Hypothesized	Identifying Features
Level 1		
Bivariate Causal Approach	Context Variable $\downarrow$ Design Variable	Each contingency proposition includes only two variables—a context variable and a design variable. No attention is given to any performance variables.
Level 2		
Bivariate Interaction Approach	Context Variable $\rightarrow$ Performance Variable Design Variable	Each contingency proposition includes three variables—a context variable, a design variable, and a performance variable. Performance is hypothesized to be a function of interaction between the single context variable and the single design variable.
Level 3		
Multivariate Interaction Approach	Context Variable $\rightarrow$ Performance Variable System of Multiple Design Variables	Each contingency proposition includes more than three variables—one (or more) context variable(s), multiple design variables, and a performance variable. Performance is hypothesized to be a function of interaction between the single (or multiple) context variable(s) and the system of multiple design variables.

As Drazin and Van de Ven (1985) have argued, these three levels of contingency specifications "are not mutually exclusive and can provide both unique and complementary information on the fit in a researcher's data" (p. 522). Accordingly, a comprehensive assessment of the strengths and weaknesses of methodological approaches is necessary at each of these three levels. It might be noted that the testing of level 1 hypotheses is the most straightforward and obvious (i.e., through correlations). Thus, the issue of choice among alternative methodological approaches becomes salient for contingency specifications at levels 2 and 3 only. Within this context, this chapter focuses on the testing of contingency hypotheses at level 2 (i.e., the bivariate interaction approach). Parenthetically, it might be noted that methodological clarity at level 2 also has the potential to serve as a useful platform for the pursuit of similar clarity at level 3.

Types of Bivariate Contingency Specifications

The traditional and perhaps dominant form of bivariate contingency specifications has been based on the belief that optimal performance requires a strict one-to-one match or isomorphism between the context and the design variables. A classic example of isomorphic contingency specifications would be Lawrence and Lorsch's (1967) prediction that, for every level of environmental uncertainty, there exists a uniquely optimal level of organizational differentiation. Two complementary representations of such an isomorphic contingency perspective are depicted in Figure 21.2.

Figure 21.2. Complementary Representations of an Isomorphic Contingency Relationship

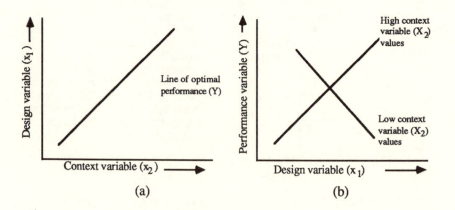

(a)   (b)

It should be noted from Figure 21.2(b) that, in the isomorphic contingency case, the design variable is predicted to have a necessarily non-monotonic impact on performance i.e., the impact of the design variable on performance is predicted to be positive for some values of the context variable and negative for the other.

More recently, Joyce, Slocum, and Von Glinow (1982) as well as Schoonhoven (1981), have argued that the isomorphic model of fit is only one of several alternative possibilities. They argue also for the possibility that, for some context, design, and performance variables, the impact of the design variable on performance may be monotonic (i.e., always positive or always negative), *while still being contingent* on values of the context variable. Representations of some alternative nonisomorphic contingency scenarios are depicted in Figure 21.3.

Figure 21.3. Alternative Representations of Non-Isomorphic Contingency Relationships

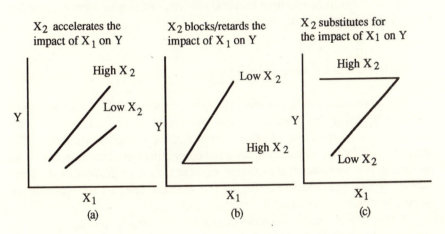

An example of a nonisomorphic contingency specification would be the joint prediction that (1) open communication within top management teams always has a positive impact on organizational performance, and (2) that this positive impact of communication openness on performance is greater when environmental turbulence is high than when it is low. By way of differentiation between isomorphic and nonisomorphic specifications, it might be noted that the graphical representation for the hypothesis just stated would be the one in Figure 21.3(a) rather than the one in Figure 21.2(b).

This identification of alternative bivariate contingency specifications is important because the strengths and weaknesses of alternative methods can be assessed only in the context of their ability to test for one or more of these contingency specifications.

Alternative Methodological Approaches

At a macrolevel, three different methodological approaches have been employed by previous contingency researchers: the split-sample approach (Khandwalla, 1974; Morrow, 1981), the residual misfit approach (Dewar and Werbel, 1979; Alexander and Randolph, 1985), and the multiplicative interaction approach (Schoonhoven, 1981; Tushman, 1979). At a micro-level, there also exist variants within each of these macro approaches. Details pertaining to the procedural steps underlying each approach are given below, along with an assessment of the strengths and weaknesses of each approach.

THE SPLIT-SAMPLE APPROACH: AN ASSESSMENT

Researchers have employed several variants of the split-sample approach for testing bivariate contingency theories.

Split Based on One Variable

As illustrated by Khandwalla (1974) and Morrow (1981), this approach involves splitting the sample into two subgroups based on high and low values of one of the three variables: context, design, and performance. The actual test of the hypothesis then involves computing correlations between the remaining two variables and assessing whether they are significantly different across the two subgroups. Generally, the variable selected for splitting the sample is either performance or context.

If the performance variable is used for splitting the sample (e.g., Khandwalla, 1974), then this becomes a test of whether the correlation between the context and the design variables is stronger for the high-performing subgroup as compared to the low-performing subgroup. If the results are significant, then support for an isomorphic (but not a nonisomorphic) contingency relationship can be inferred. If the results are not significant, then the inference would be that an isomorphic contingency relationship does not exist; however, the test would be silent on whether a nonisomorphic relationship does or does not exist. Thus, one key limitation of this approach is that it is designed to test for only isomorphic contingency theories. A second major limitation of this method arises from the fact that by converting interval scale performance data into nominal high and low categories, it forces a significant loss of information.

On the other hand, if the context variable is used for splitting the sample (e.g., Morrow, 1981), then this becomes a test of whether the correlation between the design and the performance variables is stronger for one set of context values than for another. If the two correlations are significantly different from each other and have opposite signs (i.e., one positive and the other negative), then support for a nonmonotonic, and thus isomorphic, contingency relationship can be inferred. If the two correlations are significantly different from each other and have the same signs (i.e., both positive or both negative), then support for a monotonic, and thus nonisomorphic, contingency relationship can be inferred. Finally, if the correlations are not significantly different from each other, then neither type of contingency relationship can be inferred. Given this ability to identify both isomorphic and nonisomorphic contingency relationships, it can be argued that splitting the sample on the basis of the context variable yields more information and is superior when compared to splitting the sample on the basis of the performance variable. Nonetheless, the limitation on account of information loss caused by a split sample remains. Another limitation of such a correlational approach has been pointed out by Arnold (1982); he has argued that a comparison of the subsample correlations tests only for the moderating effect of the context variable on the "degree" of the relationship between the design and the performance variables and not on the "form" of this relationship. If a researcher's interest lies in examining variations in the "form" of the relationship between the design and the performance variables, then Arnold recommends the multiplicative interaction approach discussed later in this chapter.

Split Based on Two Variables

As illustrated by Joyce, Slocum, and Von Glinow (1982) and Lawrence and Lorsch (1967), this approach involves splitting the sample into four subgroups by using the high and low values of two of the three variables. The next step involves a choice between either of the following two routes: (1) a pairwise cell comparison to assess if the mean values of the third variable differ across the four cells in predicted ways (e.g., Lawrence and Lorsch, 1967), or (2) an analysis of variance (ANOVA) to assess the main and the interaction effects of the two variables used to split the sample on the third variable (e.g., Joyce, Slocum, and Von Glinow, 1982). Depending upon the nature of the expected results, either approach can be used for testing isomorphic as well as nonisomorphic contingency theories. Despite their intuitive appeal, we argue that, when a researcher's data are interval scale, the appropriateness of both of these approaches is questionable. First, because the pairwise cell comparison does not use the pooled variance for the whole sample, it could lead to inferences not justified in light of an ANOVA;

thus, if one were to pursue a 2X2 split approach, ANOVA would be the more appropriate method to adopt. Second, as Allison (1977) and Cohen (1978) have argued, the ANOVA approach is identical to the multiplicative interaction approach, except that ANOVA requires a sample split and an accompanying loss of information, whereas the multiplicative interaction approach does not. Thus, in the presence of interval-scale data, the multiplicative interaction approach emerges as superior in every way to these split-sample approaches.

THE RESIDUAL MISFIT APPROACH: AN ASSESSMENT

This approach is aimed strictly at testing only for isomorphic forms of contingency theories. The isomorphic perspective implies that, for any given value of the context variable (e.g., environmental uncertainty), values of the design variable (e.g., decentralization) either above or below a uniquely ideal level imply a state of "misfit." Further, the greater the distance of the actual value of the design variable from the ideal value, the greater the extent of misfit. Thus, the analytical procedure reduces to (1) calculating the residual misfit (actual vs. ideal) for each observation and (2) testing for a negative correlation between this residual misfit and performance.

If one knew a priori the formula for calculating the ideal value of the design variable for any given value of the contingency variable, the analytical procedure for testing isomorphic contingency theories would be, as just outlined, quite straightforward. However, such formulas currently do not exist for any known contingency theory in the organizational sciences. In an attempt to sidestep this problem, Dewar and Werbel (1979) suggested and utilized a "regression-residual" approach, which has also been adopted by Fry and Slocum (1984) and Drazin and Van de Ven (1985).

The regression-residual approach assumes that the descriptive linear regression between the observed values of the design and the contingency variables in the sample is a close approximation of the ideal relationship (Dewar and Werbel, 1979; Drazin and Van de Ven, 1985; Fry and Slocum, 1984). Thus, in specific terms, the analytical procedure associated with the regression-residual approach becomes

1. Regress the design variable (X_1) on the contingency variable (X_2):

    $$X_1 = a + bX_2 + \varepsilon.$$

2. Assume the ideal values of the design variable to be $\hat{X}_1 = a + bX_2$.

3. Based on this assumption, calculate the value of the design misfit for each observation:

$$\text{Misfit} = |X_1 - \hat{X}_1|$$

4. Test for a negative coefficient c_3 in the following regression where the dependent variable, Y, is some appropriate measure of performance.

$$Y = c_0 + c_1 X_1 + c_2 X_2 + c_3 |X_1 - \hat{X}_1| + \varepsilon$$

Despite the intuitive appeal of the regression-residual method, we argue that several major problems render its continued use inadvisable even for isomorphic contingency specifications.

First, the results are extremely sensitive to even minor errors in estimating the "ideal" relationship between the context and the design variables. Assume that an ideal relationship between the context and the design variables does indeed exist and that X_1' represents the unknown ideal value of the design variable. In that case, the true misfit would equal $|X_1 - X_1'|$. The relationship between this true misfit and the assumed misfit, $|X_1 - \hat{X}_1|$, can now be depicted as follows:

$$|X_1 - \hat{X}_1| = |(X_1 - X_1') + (X_1' - \hat{X}_1)|$$

Thus, $|X_1 - \hat{X}_1|$ can serve as a good approximation for $|X_1 - X_1'|$ only when one is certain that the magnitude of $(X_1' - \hat{X}_1)$ is much smaller relative to that of $(X_1 - X_1')$. A priori, there is no basis whatsoever for making this assumption. In fact, for any given data, $(X_1' - \hat{X}_1)$ might even be larger than $(X_1 - X_1')$. Thus, this critical assumption—with profound implications for the test results—must be regarded as arbitrary. In fact, as the data of Dewar and Werbel (1979), Drazin and Van de Ven (1985), and Fry and Slocum (1984) indicate, there may often be no significant relationship whatsoever between X_2 and X_1 (step 1 above); in that case, to assume that the descriptive absence of relationship between X_2 and X_1 represents the "ideal" relationship, while trying to discover the presence of an "ideal" relationship, is internally contradictory and is even more likely to lead to spurious results.

Second, totally aside from the just discussed problem of presupposing the form of the "ideal" relationship, another arbitrary assumption made by the regression-residual approach is to regard $|X_1 - \hat{X}_1|$, rather than $|X_2 - \hat{X}_2|$, as the appropriate measure of misfit. Since the explicit objective of any residual misfit approach is to test only for the presence of a congruence relationship between X_1 and X_2, there is no reason to regard $|X_1 - \hat{X}_1|$, rather than $|X_2 - \hat{X}_2|$, as the appropriate measure of misfit. Analyses (not being reported here because of space constraints) undertaken by the authors with several sets of data indicate that $|X_1 - \hat{X}_1|$ and $|X_2 - \hat{X}_2|$ often have no significant correlation. Thus, to pick one of these residuals as the measure of misfit further compounds the arbitrariness of the procedure.

Third, as Johns (1981) has argued, all difference score measures—whether or not they are free from the problems of arbitrariness noted above—suffer from two additional problems: (1) the difference score is usually highly correlated with the original variables from which it was derived, thereby creating ambiguity in the interpretation of the results; such high correlations are evident also in Dewar and Werbel's (1979) results; and (2) the reliability of the difference score will often be very low because it cannot exceed the product of the reliabilities of the two original variables.

The emergent conclusion from the above discussion is that a researcher utilizing the regression-residual approach runs a major risk of reporting spurious results; accordingly, we argue that its continued use is inadvisable.

A minor variant of this approach is somewhat less problematic. Van de Ven and Ferry (1980) proposed a "modified regression residual" approach where the imputed ideal relationship between X_1 and X_2 is derived by regressing these variables not for the entire subsample, but across only a high-performing subset within the whole sample. While this approach is less arbitrary in its imputing of an "ideal" relationship between the context and the design variables, the following limitations remain: (1) the decision to regress X_1 over X_2, rather than X_2 over X_1, would still be ad hoc; (2) the researcher would still reach an impasse if it turns out that, even in the high performing subsample, there is no significant correlation between X_1 and X_2; (3) all of the problems endemic to difference score measures as outlined by Johns (1981), would still remain; and (4) the use of this approach would be feasible only for very large sample sizes.

We propose that, if a researcher must use a residual misfit method to test strictly isomorphic contingency hypotheses, the most defensible approach would be to use an "absolute difference score" method (Miller, 1980). Under this method, the imputed misfit can be calculated in a much more direct manner; that is, $|Z_1 - Z_2|$, where Z_1 and Z_2 are standardized values of X_1 and X_2, respectively. The contingency hypothesis would then be tested in the form of an expected negative correlation between $|Z_1 - Z_2|$ and performance. In using this method, the impact of "congruence" or "misfit" between the context and the design variables is tested directly without making any arbitrary assumptions or using only part of the sample. The only remaining limitations would be those pertaining to the low reliability of all difference score variables (Johns, 1981); additionally, the researcher would need to be aware that even this method cannot test for nonisomorphic forms of bivariate contingency relationships. Parenthetically, it might be noted that, in using the "absolute difference score" method, X_1 and X_2 must first be standardized in order to eliminate the arbitrary effects of scaling decisions; this has not always been done (e.g., Alexander and Randolph, 1985).

THE MULTIPLICATIVE INTERACTION APPROACH: AN ASSESSMENT

Unlike the residual misfit approach, the multiplicative interaction approach does not assume that the contingency relationship between the design and the context variables must necessarily be of the isomorphic type (it may, but it is not essential); thus, it does not require the imputing of any ideal relationship between these two variables. What it does is to test whether the impact of the design variable on performance ($\delta Y/\delta X_1$) is a function of the context variable X_2 (Blalock, 1965; Peters and Champoux, 1979; Schoonhoven, 1981; Sharma, Durand, and Gur-Arie, 1981; Zedeck, 1971). That is,

$$\delta Y/\delta X_1 = a_1 + b_1 X_2$$

When integrated over X_1, this becomes

$$Y = a_0 + a_1 X_1 + a_2 X_2 + b_1 X_1 X_2 + \varepsilon$$

where the sign and significance of b_1 are tested to confirm or disprove the contingency hypothesis. Parenthetically, it should be noted here that, in the above regression, the main variables X_1 and X_2 must *always* be entered in addition to the interaction term $X_1 X_2$; otherwise, the coefficient b_1 would also capture the variance attributable to the effect of the main variables and would become uninterpretable (for details, see Arnold and Evans, 1979; Cohen and Cohen, 1975; Stone and Hollenbeck, 1984).

Besides the fact that it does not require the making of any arbitrary assumptions, another major strength of the multiplicative interaction approach is that it is capable of testing for and differentiating among several alternative isomorphic as well as nonisomorphic contingency scenarios. This is demonstrated in Figure 21.4 and has been discussed at some length also by Schoonhoven (1981).

Figure 21.4. Multiplicative Interaction Approach: Mathematical Representation of Alternative Contingency Scenarios

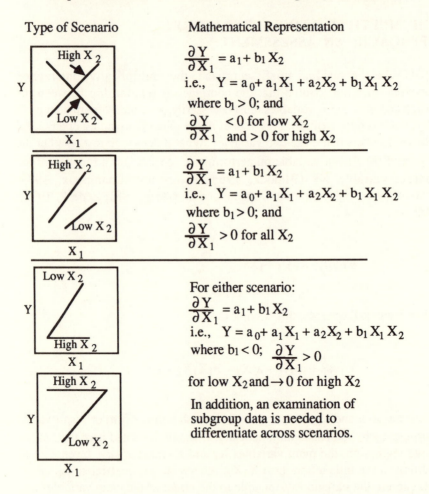

Type of Scenario   Mathematical Representation

$\frac{\partial Y}{\partial X_1} = a_1 + b_1 X_2$

i.e., $Y = a_0 + a_1 X_1 + a_2 X_2 + b_1 X_1 X_2$

where $b_1 > 0$; and

$\frac{\partial Y}{\partial X_1} < 0$ for low X_2 and > 0 for high X_2

$\frac{\partial Y}{\partial X_1} = a_1 + b_1 X_2$

i.e., $Y = a_0 + a_1 X_1 + a_2 X_2 + b_1 X_1 X_2$

where $b_1 > 0$; and

$\frac{\partial Y}{\partial X_1} > 0$ for all X_2

For either scenario:

$\frac{\partial Y}{\partial X_1} = a_1 + b_1 X_2$

i.e., $Y = a_0 + a_1 X_1 + a_2 X_2 + b_1 X_1 X_2$

where $b_1 < 0$; $\frac{\partial Y}{\partial X_1} > 0$

for low X_2 and $\to 0$ for high X_2

In addition, an examination of subgroup data is needed to differentiate across scenarios.

Notwithstanding the greater versatility and the lack of assumption arbitrariness in using the multiplicative interaction approach, many researchers have argued recently that the use of this approach is not justified because of its endemic multicollinearity problems:

> The correlations between the individual X's in the equation and the product term, X_1X_2, appear to undermine the substantive interpretation of estimated regression coefficients....It would appear, in short, that including multiplicative terms in regression models is not an appropriate way of assessing the presence of interaction among...independent variables. (Althauser, 1971, pp. 454, 466)

> Multiple regression with a multiplicative interaction term might have been a solution...were it not for the fact that the interaction term is highly correlated with the terms that compose it, leading to serious levels of multicollinearity. (Dewar and Werbel, 1979, p. 435)

> In the construction of the interaction or fit variables, the technique used by Dewar and Werbel (1979) was followed....In using this method, multicollinearity is usually less of a problem than in the standard multiple regression procedure, which uses multiplicative interaction terms. (Fry and Slocum, 1984, p. 233)

> Schoonhoven (1981) measured fit with (multiplicative) interaction terms....As Dewar and Werbel (1979) suggested, (such) interaction terms are highly correlated with the terms that compose them, which causes multicollinearity problems in regression analyses. (Alexander and Randolph, 1985, p. 847)

> Multiplicative interactions are usually correlated with the variables from which they are developed, causing multicollinearity problems in the analysis. (Drazin and Van de Ven, 1985, p. 519)

Based on this reasoning, it also has been argued by these researchers that the residual misfit method is superior to the multiplicative interaction approach. However, as the following analysis indicates, a criticism of the multiplicative interaction approach on the grounds of multicollinearity is unwarranted. In fact, through a priori linear shifts in the origin points of X_1 and X_2, the correlations between X_1X_2 and both X_1 and X_2 can *always* be reduced to zero. The mathematical proof for this counterintuitive conclusion, derived originally by the present authors and not currently available in the literature, is as follows:

Let X_1, X_2 = Main explanatory variables;

$M = X_1 X_2$ (Multiplicative interaction term);

$X_1' = X_1 + k_1$;

$X_2' = X_2 + k_2$;

$M' = X_1' X_2'$

Our objective is to derive values of k_1 and k_2 such that $r_{M'x1'} = r_{M'x2'} = 0$. We know that:

$$r_{M'x1'} = \frac{\sum_i (M_i - \bar{M}')(X_{1i}' - \bar{X}_1')}{\sqrt{\sum_i (M_i' - \bar{M}')^2} \sqrt{\sum_i (X_{1i} - \bar{X}')^2}} \qquad (1)$$

Since we are dealing with variables rather than constants here, the denominator will always be $\neq 0$. Thus, $r_{M'x1'} = 0$ when

$$\sum_i (M_i' - \bar{M}')(X_{1i}' - \bar{X}_1') = 0$$

or $\sum_i [(X_{1i} + k_1)(X_{2i} + k_2) - \overline{(X_1 + k_1)(X_2 + k_2)}]$

$\cdot [X_{1i} + k_1 - \bar{X}_1 - k_1] = 0$

or $\sum_i [(X_{1i} X_{2i} - \overline{X_1 X_2}) + k_1 (X_{2i} - \bar{X}_2) + k_2 (X_{1i} - \bar{X}_1)]$

$\cdot [X_{1i} - \bar{X}_1] = 0$

or $\sum_i [(M_i - \overline{M})(X_{1i} - X_1) + k_1(X_{1i} - X_1)(X_{2i} - X_2)$

$$+ k_2 (X_{1i} - X_1)^2] = 0$$

or $(n-1)\sigma_M\sigma_{X_1}r_{MX_1} + k_1(n-1)\sigma_{X_1}\sigma_{X_2}r_{X_1X_2}$

$$+ k_2(n-1)\sigma_{X_1}^2 = 0$$

or $\sigma_M r_{MX_1} + k_1\sigma_{X_2}r_{X_1X_2} + k_2\sigma_{X_1} = 0$ (2)

Similarly, we can derive that $r_{M'X_2'} = 0$ when

$$\sigma_M r_{MX_2} + k_1\sigma_{X_2} + k_2\sigma_{X_1}r_{X_1X_2} = 0 \tag{3}$$

The simultaneous equations (2) and (3) can now be solved to yield the following:

$$k_1 = \frac{\sigma_M}{\sigma_{X_2}}\left(\frac{r_{X_1X_2}r_{MX_1} - r_{MX_2}}{1 - r_{X_1X_2}^2}\right)$$

and

$$k_2 = \frac{\sigma_M}{\sigma_{X_1}}\left(\frac{r_{X_1X_2}r_{MX_1} - r_{MX_2}}{1 - r_{X_1X_2}^2}\right)$$

To conclude, for any given X_1 and X_2, that the substitution of X_1 by X_1 + k_1 and of X_2 by X_2 + k_2, where the values of k_1 and k_2 are derived from the above formulas, will necessarily reduce the collinearity between X_1X_2 and X_1 and between X_1X_2 and X_2 to zero. This conclusion has been cross checked empirically by the authors with several different sets of data and the results are always as mathematically predicted.

Since, for any given X_1 and X_2, k_1 and k_2 are constants, X_1' and X_2' represent mere linear shifts in the origin points of X_1 and X_2. For "interval scale" data so common in organization theory research, these linear shifts are completely innocuous. Further, as Allison (1977), Arnold (1982), and Southwood (1978) have argued, linear shifts do not in any way influence the inferential statistics yielded by the multiplicative interaction approach. Thus, in practice, there would really be no need to shift the origin points in order to remove multicollinearity. One should simply ignore it as a nonissue and focus on whether the interactive results are significant or not with the data as is.

However, what if the variables are ratio-scale (e.g., market share, industry concentration) and the origin points cannot be shifted? Here, multicollinearity, if present, must be regarded as unavoidable. Nonetheless, even here, the often overlooked implication of multicollinearity would be *not* to make the regression results useless, *but* to make the test more, rather than less, conservative. The analogy of "signal-to-noise ratio" might be helpful in understanding the impact of multicollinearity. If we treat an estimated regression coefficient as the "signal" and its standard error as the "noise," then, in the presence of high multicollinearity, the signal is likely to get swamped by the noise (Belsley, Kuh, and Welsch, 1980, p. 115; Kmenta, 1971, p. 389). Thus, given ratio scales and high multicollinearity, the primary risk would be of Type II and not Type I errors—a significantly less troublesome limitation than that resulting from the arbitrary assumptions required by the residual misfit methods that can cause both Type I and Type II errors.

CONCLUSIONS

Contingency predictions are now central to theory development in most fields of management. Yet, two critical issues—what specifically an interactive relationship between the contingency and the design variables means, and what the most appropriate method to test for such interactive relationships is—remain unresolved. Focusing on the bivariate level of complexity in contingency theorizations (i.e., those involving a single context variable, a single design variable, and a single performance variable), this chapter has compared the strengths and weaknesses of the various split-sample, residual misfit, and multiplicative interaction approaches that have (or can) be utilized to test such contingency theories. In a departure from the dominant methodological trend, which favors the split-sample approach, as well as the advice currently being offered in the literature, which favors the regression-residual approach, the conclusion of this chapter is that the multiplicative approach is significantly superior to the other approaches on several important grounds: (1) it utilizes more of the information contained in the data; (2) it does not require the making of critical, but arbitrary, assumptions; and (3) it is more powerful in its ability to identify and discriminate between various forms of isomorphic and nonisomorphic contingency relationships. Finally, contrary to the view currently prevailing in the literature, in using the multiplicative interaction approach, multicollinearity is a complete nonissue at least for interval-scale data; it is such data that are most commonly employed in organization theory research.

NOTE

We are indebted to W. W. Cooper and V. Ramanujam for their helpful comments on an earlier draft of this chapter.

REFERENCES

Alexander, J.W., and Randolph, W.A. 1985. The fit between technology and structure as a predictor of performance in nursing subunits. *Academy of Management Journal* 28: 844-859.

Allison, P.D. 1977. Testing for interaction in multiple regression. *American Journal of Sociology* 83: 144-153.

Althauser, R.P. 1971. Multicollinearity and non-additive regression models. In H.M. Blalock, Jr. (Ed.), *Causal Models in the Social Sciences,* 453-472. Chicago: Aldine Atherton.

Anderson, C.R., and Zeithaml, C.P. 1984. Stage of the product life cycle, business strategy, and business performance. *Academy of Management Journal* 27: 5-24.

Arnold, H.J. 1982. Moderator variables: A classification of conceptual, analytic, and psychometric issues. *Organizational Behavior and Human Performance* 29: 143-174.

Arnold, H.J., and Evans, M.G. 1979. Testing multiplicative models does not require ratio scales. *Organizational Behavior and Human Performance* 24: 41-59.

Belsley, D.A., Kuh, E., and Welsch, R.E. 1980. *Regression diagnostics: Identifying influential data and sources of collinearity.* New York: John Wiley.

Blalock, H.M. 1965. Theory building and the concept of interaction. *American Sociological Review* 30: 374-381.

Chandler, A.D. 1962. *Strategy and structure.* Cambridge, MA: MIT Press.

Cohen, J. 1978. Partialled products are interactions; partialled powers are curve components. *Psychological Bulletin* 85: 858-866.

Cohen, J., and Cohen, P. 1975. *Applied multiple regression/correlation analysis for the behavioral sciences.* Hillsdale, NJ: Erlbaum.

Dewar, R., and Werbel, J. 1979. Universalistic and contingency predictions of employee satisfaction and conflict. *Administrative Science Quarterly* 24: 426-448.

Drazin, R., and Van de Ven, A.H. 1985. Alternative forms of fit in contingency theory. *Administrative Science Quarterly* 30: 514-539.

Fry, L.W., and Slocum, J.W. 1984. Technology, structure, and work group effectiveness: A test of a contingency model. *Academy of Management Journal* 27: 221-246.

Gupta, A.K., and Govindarajan, V. 1986. Resource sharing among SBUs: Strategic antecedents and administrative implications. *Academy of Management Journal* 29: 695-714.

Harrigan, K.R. 1982. Exit decisions in mature industries. *Academy of Management Journal* 25: 707-732.

Johns, G. 1981. Difference score measures of organizational behavior variables: A critique. *Organizational Behavior and Human Performance* 27: 443-463.

Joyce, W.F., Slocum, J.W., and Von Glinow, M. 1982. Person-situation interaction: Competing models of fit. *Journal of Occupational Behavior* 3: 265-280.

Khandwalla, P.N. 1974. Mass output orientation of operations technology and organizational structure. *Administrative Science Quarterly* 19: 74-97.

Kmenta, J. 1971. *Elements of econometrics.* New York: Macmillan.

Lawrence, P.R., and Lorsch, J.W. 1967. *Organization and environment.* Boston: Division of Research, Harvard Graduate School of Business Administration.

Miller, J.P. 1980. Information processing in organizations: The development and test of a contingency model of ambiguity, differentiation, interdependence, communication, decision-making, conflict, and effectiveness. Unpublished dissertation. Evanston, Ill.: Northwestern University.

Morrow, P.C. 1981. Work related communication, environmental uncertainty, and subunit effectiveness: A second look at the information-processing approach to subunit communication. *Academy of Management Journal* 24: 851-858.

Peters, W.S., and Champoux, J.E. 1979. The role and analysis of moderator variables in organizational research. In R.T. Mowday and R.N. Steers (Eds.), *Research in organizations: Issues and controversies,* 239-253. Santa Monica, CA: Goodyear.

Porter, M.E. 1976. Please note location of nearest exit: Exit barriers and planning. *California Management Review* 19(2): 21-33.

Schoonhoven, C.B. 1981. Problems with contingency theory: Testing assumptions hidden within the language of contingency theory. *Administrative Science Quarterly* 26: 349-377.

Sharma, S., Durand, R.M., and Gur-Arie, O. 1981. Identification and analysis of moderator variables. *Journal of Marketing Research* 18: 291-300.

Southwood, K.E. 1978. Substantive theory and statistical interaction: Five models. *American Journal of Sociology* 83: 1154-1203.

Stone, E.F., and Hollenbeck, J.R. 1984. Some issues associated with the use of moderated regression. *Organization Behavior and Human Performance* 34: 194-213.

Tosi, H., and Slocum, J.W. 1984. Contingency theory: Some suggested directions. *Journal of Management* 10(1): 9-26.

Tushman, M.L. 1979. Work characteristics and subunit communications structure: A contingency analysis. *Administrative Science Quarterly* 24: 82-98.

Van de Ven, A.H., and Ferry, D.L. 1980. *Measuring and assessing organizations.* New York: John Wiley.

Venkatraman, N., and Camillus, J.C. 1984. Exploring the concept of "fit" in strategic management. *Academy of Management Review* 9: 513-525.

Zedeck, S. 1971. Problems with the use of moderator variables. *Psychological Bulletin* 76: 295-310.

Bibliographical Essay

This bibliographic essay has been written to provide guidance to readers who are interested in background or additional reading materials to gain further insight into the problems and issues presented in this book. The bibliographic materials discussed below are mostly chosen from the references at the end of each chapter to highlight a couple of items selectively. Since most chapters deal with an application of a model to a specific area, in many cases one item is selected for the methodology and the other for the area of application. Preference is given on widely available items. They are presented below for each of the twenty-one chapters grouped in seven parts. Section titles are in the boldface. The number in the parentheses refers to the chapter number, followed by the title of the chapter.

I. Accounting and Control: (1) "Variance Analysis and Triple-Entry Bookkeeping." *Momentum Accounting and Triple-Entry Bookkeeping,* by Y. Ijiri, published by the American Accounting Association in 1989, is the best book for those interested in the subject of triple-entry bookkeeping and the concept of momenta discussed in this chapter. On the technique of variance analysis used in this and the next chapters, there are many textbooks in management accounting that readers may refer to; in particular, *Advanced*

Management Accounting by R.S. Kaplan and A.A. Atkinson, 2nd edition, Prentice-Hall, 1989, is an excellent source.

(2) "Accounting for Productivity Gains." An article entitled "Nonparametric Analysis of Technical and Allocative Efficiencies in Production," in *Econometrica,* November 1988, pp. 1315–32 by R. Banker and A. Maindiratta discusses issues related to this chapter. The technique of data envelopment analysis (DEA) may be studied further by reading "Measuring the Efficiency of Decision Making Units," by A. Charnes, W.W. Cooper, and E. Rhodes, *European Journal of Operations Research,* 1978, pp. 429–44, which is one of the first articles written on DEA.

(3) "On Assessing Internal Controls." To understand the background and the significance of internal control discussed in this chapter, readers must pay attention to the Foreign Corrupt Practices Act of 1977, which mandated the management responsibility to maintain a system of internal control. This topic and the auditors' responsibilities in internal control are discussed in a 1978 publication by the American Institute of Certified Public Accountants, Commission on Auditors' Responsibilities, *Report, Conclusions, and Recommendations. Handbook of Internal Accounting Controls*, by W.A. Wallace, Prentice-Hall, 1984, is a good reference book on internal controls.

II. Computers and Decision Support: (4) "Qualitative and Causal Reasoning in Auditing." For further insight into the techniques used in this chapter, an article by B.J. Kuipers entitled "Qualitative Reasoning: Modeling and Simulation with Incomplete Knowledge," in *Automatica,* 25 (4), July 1989, pp. 571–85, will be helpful. An article by W.R. Kinney, Jr., and W.L. Felix, Jr., "Analytical Review Procedures," *Journal of Accountancy,* October 1980, pp. 96–103, will be useful for readers who wish to learn more about the analytical review in auditing, to which the techniques were applied.

(5) "Implementation of Decision Support Systems: An Empirical Study of Japanese Production Control Systems." An article by G.P. Huber and R.R. McDaniel, "Decision-Making Paradigm of Organizational Design," *Management Science,* 1986, pp. 572–89, is a helpful reading that discusses a strategy for the use of decision support systems in organizations. A good reference on the Japanese management and control systems appeared a few years ago; see *Japanese Management Accounting: A World Class Approach to Profit Management,* edited by Y. Monden and M. Sakurai, Productivity Press, 1989, which includes several articles on production processes in Japan as well as the use of decision support systems.

(6) "Model Representation in Information Resources Management." An article related to this chapter is "A Metadata System for Information Modeling and Integration" by C. Hsu, M. Bouziane, W.C. Cheung, J. Nogus, L. Rattner, and L. Yee, in *Proceedings of the international Conference on*

Systems Integration 1990 published by IEEE Computer Society, 1991. A two-volume publication by A. Charnes and W.W. Cooper, *Management Models and Industrial Applications of Linear Programming,* Wiley, 1961, is a classic publication, not only on linear programming, but also on management modeling generally, upon which this chapter's construction is based.

III. Resource Management: (7) "Integrated Modeling Systems for Corporate Human Resource Decisions." This chapter is centered on the issues of human resources management. *Human Resource Strategies for Organizations in Transition,* edited by R.J. Niehaus and K.F. Price, Plenum Press, 1990, offers a broader coverage of the issues. The fundamental approach to modeling illustrated in this chapter may be traced back to *Management Sciences Approaches to Manpower Planning and Organization Design* by A. Charnes, W.W. Cooper, and R.J. Niehaus, Elsevier North Holland, 1978.

(8) "Tradeoffs between Efficiency and Effectiveness in Management of Public Services." An article closely related to this chapter is "Organizational Determinants of Efficiency and Effectiveness in Mental Health Partial Care Programs," by A.P. Schinnar, E. Kamis-Gould, N. Delucia, and A.B. Rothbard, *Health Services Research,* 1990. This chapter is also related to data envelopment analysis, for which readers are referred to the Charnes-Cooper-Rhodes article cited in (2) above.

(9) "Sensitivity of DEA to Models and Variable Sets in a Hypothesis Test Setting: The Efficiency of University Operations." This chapter deals with the issues that arise in applying the data envelopment analysis, for which the Charnes-Cooper-Rhodes article has already been mentioned. For further details of the efficiency of public and private university operations discussed in this chapter, readers are referred to a doctoral dissertation by T. Ahn, "Efficiency and Related Issues in Higher Education: A Data Envelopment Analysis Approach," Graduate School of Business, University of Texas at Austin, 1987. This chapter is also methodologically based on "A Multiplicative Model for Efficiency Analysis," by A Charnes, W.W. Cooper, L. Seiford, and J. Stutz, *Socio-Economic Planning Sciences,* 1982, pp. 223-24.

IV. Organization Design: (10) "The Optimal Size of a Law Firm and the Contingency Fee Decision." This chapter extends in part an earlier article by F.K. Levy, "The Managerial Economics of Civil Litigation," *Management Science,* 1985, pp. 323-42. Also, the portfolio risk analysis discussed in this chapter is related to an article entitled, "Selecting a Portfolio of Credit Risks by Markov-Chains," by R.M. Cyert and G.L. Thompson, *Journal of Business,* 1968, pp. 39-46.

(11). "A Fractal Analysis of Capital Structure." This chapter uses fractal analysis as a tool and applies it to the capital structure of a firm, in particular in determining bankruptcy probabilities. B. Mandelbrot, who found the fractals originally, published a book in 1982, *The Fractal Geometry of Nature,* Freeman. J.M. Stern and D.H. Chew edited a book, *The Revolution in Corporate Finance,* Basil Blackwell, 1986, which is a good reference on recent developments incorporate finance, including the issue of integrated corporate financial risk, which is a subject of this chapter.

(12) "Applying the Audit Risk Model to the Organization Design of the Firm." An article closely related to this chapter, especially in dealing with organization design, is "Determining Organizational Effectiveness: Another Look, and an Agenda for Research," by A.Y. Lewin and J.W. Minton, *Management Science* 32 (5), May 1986, pp. 514-38. Issues in auditing discussed in the chapter are also elaborated on in a monograph by B.E. Cushing and J.K. Loebbecke, *Comparison of Audit Methodologies of Large Accounting Firms,* American Accounting Association, 1986.

V. Industry and Economy: (13) "Longitudinal Analysis of Industries: An Ordinal Time Series Approach." An article that is most directly related to this chapter is one by T.W. Ruefli and C.L. Wilson, "Ordinal Time Series Methodology for Industry and Competitive Analysis," *Management Science,* May 1987, pp. 640-61. There is also a book dealing with the methodology used in the chapter as well as its applications—namely, T.W. Ruefli (editor), *Ordinal Time Series Analysis: Methodology and Applications in Management Strategy and Policy,* Quorum Books, 1990.

(14) "An Analysis of the Financial Competitiveness of Defense Industry Firms." On the background of government policies and the defense industry, *The Impact of Government Policies on Defense Contractors,* published by the Financial Executives Institute, 1987, is a good reference. For further details of the data envelopment analysis applied to defense-related entities, see a doctoral dissertation by W.F. Bowlin "A Data Envelopment Analysis Approach to Performance Evaluation in Not-for-Profit Entities with an Illustrative Application to the U.S. Air Force," Graduate School of Business, University of Texas at Austin, 1984.

(15) "A Multiregional Model for India, 2000 A.D." An article closely related to the chapter is R. Dhar, M.R. Rao, and S. Goel, "An Optimizing Model for India's Eighth and Ninth Plans: With Analysis of Basic Needs," in M.R. Rao (Ed.), *Modeling and Analysis of Large Systems,* Oxford and IBH Publishing Co., 1991. For a multiregional input-output analysis using U.S.

data, see K.R. Polenske, *The U.S. Multi-Regional Input-Output Accounts and Models,* Heath/Lexington Books, 1980.

VI. Programming Models: (16) "Improved Linear and Integer Programming Models for Discriminant Analysis." A further discussion of some of the basic issues in this chapter may be seen in F. Glover, S. Keene, and B. Duea, "A New Class of Models for the Discriminant Problem," *Decision Sciences,* 1988, pp. 269–80. The issue discussed in this chapter is related to "pattern recognition," which has been a subject of study in many other fields; see, for example, P.C. Jurs, "Pattern Recognition Used to Investigate Multivariate Data in Analytical Chemistry, *Science,* June 1986, pp. 1219–24.

(17) "Chance-Constrained Programming with Stochastic Processes as Parameters." Details of the chance-constrained programming techniques are discussed by its original inventors, A. Charnes and W.W. Cooper in "Chance-Constrained Programming," *Management Science,* 1959, pp. 73–79. An article by R. Jagannathan, "Use of Sample Information in Stochastic Recourse and Chance Constrained Programming Models," *Management Science,* 1985, pp. 96-108, provides additional background materials for this chapter.

(18) "Single Machine Total Tardiness Problem Revisited." This chapter presents a new technique for a scheduling problem that further improves the results derived in earlier papers—in particular, E.L. Lawler, "A Pseudopolynomial Algorithm for Sequencing Jobs to Minimize Total Tardiness," *Annals of Discrete Mathematics,* 1977, pp. 331-42, as well as C.W. Potts and L.N. Van Wassenhove, "A Decomposition Algorithm for the Single Machine Total Tardiness Problem," *Operations Research Letters,* 1982, pp. 177-81.

VII. Methodological Issues: (19) "Multiple Criteria Decision Making and Negotiating: Some Observations." This chapter examines multiple criteria decision making and compares it with the process of negotiation. On the former topic, J.L. Cochrane and M. Zeleny, *Multiple Criteria Decision Making,* University of South Carolina Press, 1973, is a classic publication that contains many valuable articles on the subject. On the latter, H. Raiffa, *The Art and Science of Negotiations,* Harvard University Press, 1982, is an excellent reference.

(20) "Bootstrapping: Implications for Decision Making." A basic article on the subject of bootstrapping, in which one sample is used to produce many samples, is B. Efron, "Bootstrap Methods: Another Look at the Jackknife," *Annals of Statistics,* 1979, pp. 1-26. An application of the bootstrapping method in a different field may be seen in M.R. Veall,

"Bootstrapping the Probability Distribution of Peak Electricity Demand," *International Economic Review,* 1987, pp. 203-12.

(21) "Methodological Issues in Testing Contingency Theories: An Assessment of Alternative Approaches." A useful article in gaining the background for this chapter is R. Drazin and, A.H. Van de Ven, "Alternative Forms of Fit in Contingency Theory," *Administrative Science Quarterly,* 1985, pp. 514-39. On the broader subject of organizational assessment, a book by A.H. Van de Ven and K.L. Ferry, *Measuring and Assessing Organizations, Wiley,* 1980, will be helpful.

Author Index

Ackoff, R.L., 117, 132
Adaniya, Ana R., xix, 269
Addison, John T., 446, 447, 450
Aguilar, M., 166, 172
Ahn, Taesik, xviii, 191, 192, 198, 206, 475
Aigner, D.J., 32, 33, 41
Akresh, A., 68, 69, 74, 110
Alavi, M., 116, 132
Alchian, A.A., 195, 206
Aldrich, Howard E., 269, 291, 294
Alexander, J.W., 458, 463, 465, 469
Allison, J., 315, 315
Allison, P.D., 460, 468, 469
Althauser, R.P., 465, 469
Altman, E.I., 82, 108, 246
American Accounting Association, 250, 262
American Institute of Certified Public Accountants (AICPA), 57, 58, 59, 61, 68, 72, 108, 474
Anderson, C.R., 453, 469

Andrews, K., 291
Angle, H.L., 260, 265
Ansoff, H.I., 269, 291
Anthony, R.N., 56
Antunes, C.H., 428, 438
Argyris, C., 250, 262
Arnold, H.J., 459, 463, 468, 469
Arthur Andersen & Co., 60
Arthur Young (Ernst & Young), 60
Artman, J.T., 261, 264
Ashby, A.S., 121, 132
Ashton, R.H., 250, 262
Atkinson, A.A., 474
Atwater, D.M., 167, 172

Bailey, Andrew D., Jr., xvi, 61, 62, 67, 67, 74, 75, 107, 108, 109, 110
Bain, J.S., 292
Bajgier, S.M., 366, 369, 394
Baker, K.R., 407, 418, 419
Baker, S.H., 292
Banares, R., 155

Banker, R.D., xvi, 27, 34, 35, 37, 40,
    41, 42, 193, 206, 302, 303, 307,
    315, 474
Barnsley, M., 234, 246
Bartholomew, D.J., 174
Bass, F.M., 292
Basu, A., 143, 154
Baumann, Michael G., 443, 446, 447,
    451
Bean, A.S., 116, 132
Beard, D.W., 269, 270, 278, 291, 292,
    293
Bell, M.A., 70, 108
Belsley, D.A., 468, 469
Berlin, V.N., 261, 262
Berry, B.J.L., 328, 360
Bettis, R.A., 269, 292
Beyer, J.M., 260, 262
Bhatia, V.G., 328, 360
Bianchi, Carlo, 443, 447, 449, 450
Bidualt, F., 292
Biemer, Paul P., 443, 445, 450
Bittlingmayer, George, 448, 450
Bjaradwaj, R.K., 360
Blalock, H.M., 463, 469
Blanning, R.W., 143, 154
Bobrowski, L., 365, 394
Bonczek, R., 135, 136, 142, 154
Bonini, C., 365, 395
Bourgeois, L.J., III, 261, 262
Bouziane, M., 155, 474
Bowen, H.R., 197, 206
Bowlin, William F., xx, 299, 315, 316,
    476
Bowman, E.H., 269, 270, 292
Breleant, D., 108, 109
Bres, E.S., III, 160, 166, 167, 168,
    172, 175
Bridgeland, D.M., 108
Brillet, Jean-Louis, 450
Brinkman, P.T., 191, 192, 198, 206,
    207
Brockett, P.L., 271, 292
Brody, A., 361
Brown, J.S., 76, 98, 108

Bryant, D., 175
Burns, David C., 60, 168, 172
Byrnes, R., 405

Calzolari, Giorgio, 450
Camillus, J.C., 453, 471
Campbell, J.P., 260, 263
Cao-Pinna, Vera, 360
Carbozo, E., 155
Carnegie Commission on Higher
    Education, 196, 207
Carter, A.P., 361
Carter, N.M., 117, 132
Cashell, James, 60
Cass, D., 167, 173
Castro, Alberto C., 450
Cattin, P., 292
Caves, D.W., 34, 42, 195, 207
Caves, Richard E., 283, 292
Chakravarty, A., 360
Chakravathy, Balaji S., 292
Chalfan, K.M., 155
Champoux, J.E., 463, 470
Chandler, A.D., Jr., 292, 453, 469
Chappell, Henry W., 450
Charnes, A., 34, 37, 41, 42, 135, 136,
    137, 138, 140, 153, 154, 159,
    160, 164, 166, 167, 168, 169,
    171, 172, 173, 174, 175, 176,
    177, 189, 192, 193, 194, 199,
    205, 206, 207, 302, 313, 315,
    316, 365, 394, 397, 398, 405,
    423, 438, 474, 475, 477
Chatterjee, Sangit, 441, 451
Chenery, H.B., 327, 360
Cheung, W.C., 155, 474
Chew, D.H., 247, 476
Chihikara, R.S., 404, 405
Chiu, C., 107, 108, 109
Christensen, L.R., 34, 42, 195, 207
Christensen, H. Kurt, 269, 292
Clark, P.G., 360
Clarkson, K.W., 195, 207
Clelland, D.I., 117, 133
Climaco, J.C.N., 428, 438

Clinard, M.B., 263
Cochrane, J.L., 423, 438, 477
Cohen, J., 460, 463, 463, 470
Cohn, E., 198, 207
Collins, James M., 291, 292
Comanor, W., 292
Connor, Joseph, 60
Conrad, G.R., 269, 270, 292
Cook, K.S., 253, 259, 263
Cool, K.O., 288, 293
Cooper, W.W., 3, 34, 37, 41, 42, 56,
    135, 136, 137, 138, 153, 154,
    159, 160, 164, 166, 167, 168,
    169, 171, 172, 172, 173, 174,
    175, 176, 177, 189, 192, 193,
    194, 199, 205, 206, 207, 302,
    313, 315, 316, 365, 394, 397,
    398, 405, 423, 438, 474, 475, 477
Corless, J.C., 61
Courtney, J.F., 116, 134
Cox, D.R., 404, 405
Cubbin, J., 284, 293
Cullen, J.B., 265
Cushing, Barry E., 62, 258, 258, 263,
    476
Cyert, Richard M., 119, 132, 227,
    231, 254, 263, 476

Dantzig, G.B., 397, 398, 405
Davis, O., 405
Davies, D.G., 195, 207
Dearden, J., 117, 132
Defense Industry Advisory Group,
    301, 316
deKleer, J., 76, 98, 108
DeLacy, B., 261, 264
Deloitte, Haskins & Sells (Deloitte &
    Touche), 60
Delucia, N., 177, 180, 189, 475
Derry, R., 263
Desai, A., 177, 178, 189
Dess, G.G., 269, 270, 278, 291, 292,
    293
Dewar, R., 453, 458, 460, 461, 462,
    465, 470

Dhar, Ranajit, xx, 327, 328, 329, 340,
    341, 360, 476
Diaconis, Perry, 442, 444, 450
Dirsmith, M.W., 258, 263
Doktor, R.H., 116, 132
Dolk, D.R., 136, 142, 143, 154
Doll, W.J., 116, 132
Donaldson, G., 234, 236, 246
Dong, C., 150, 155
Drazin, R., 453, 454, 455, 460, 461,
    465, 470, 478
Drzycimski, E.F., 269, 270, 294
Du, J., 407, 413, 418
Duea, B., 365, 366, 367, 381, 382,
    393, 395, 477
Duke, Gordon L., 62, 108
Duncan, R., 255, 263
Durand, R.M., 463, 471
Dutta, A., 143, 154

Eden, C., 138, 154
Edgeworth, F.Y., 423, 438
Edwards, W., 250, 263
Efron, Bradley, 441, 442, 443, 444,
    448, 450, 477
Eisenhardt, K.M., 261, 262
Elam, J., 142, 154
Elliot, R.K., 258, 263
Emerson, R.M., 253, 259, 263
Emmons, H., 407, 418
Ernst & Whinney, 60
Eubanks, T., 167, 175
Evans, D.D., 313, 316
Evans, J.R., 154
Evans, M.G., 463, 469

Farrell, M.J., 302, 316
Farrow, D., 116, 134
Feder, J., 234, 246
Felix, W.K., Jr., 68, 109, 474
Ference, T.P., 116, 133
Ferguson, R., 173
Ferry, D.K., 462, 471, 478
Fichman, M., 259, 264
Figenbaum, A., 269, 270, 293

Financial Executives Institute, 301, 316, 476
Financial Executives Research Foundation, 50
Fischer, M.L., 407, 418
Fisher, R., 437
Folks, J.L., 404, 405
Forbus, K.D., 98, 108
Frank, R.G., 184, 189
Fredrickson, J.W., 291, 293
Freed, E., 365, 366, 367, 369, 370, 390, 395
Freedman, David A., 443, 444, 451
Freeman, John, 293
Friesen, P., 288, 294
Frost, Peter A., 443, 445, 446, 451
Fry, L.W., 460, 461, 465, 470

Gadh, V., 35, 42
Galbraith, J.R., 117, 119, 120, 133, 256, 263
Gale, Bradley, 270, 284, 293
Gallegos, J. Armando, xix, 269
General Accounting Office, 301, 302, 315, 316, 317
Geoffrion, A.M., 135, 136, 137, 138, 151, 154
Gerlach, James H., 62, 108
Geroski, P., 284, 293
Ghosh, A., 328, 360
Gilford, D., 405
Ginzberg, M.J., 116, 133
Glover, Fred, xx, 365, 366, 367, 369, 370, 381, 382, 390, 393, 395, 477
Godek, Paul E., 443, 447, 451
Goel, Sanjay, xx, 327, 329, 341, 360, 476
Golany, B., 168, 173, 194, 207
Gong, Gail, 443, 444, 450
Gonzalez, R.C., 365, 395
Goodman, P.S., 263
Gordon, K., 395
Gorr, W.L., 35, 42, 154
Govindarajan, Vijay, xxii, 453, 470
Green, D.O., 250, 263

Grier, David Alan, 443, 444, 448, 451
Gupta, Anil K., xxii, 453, 470
Gupta, M.C., 269, 293
Gur-Arie, O., 463, 471

Halek, B., 207
Hall, W.K., 269, 292
Hambrick, D.C., 269, 293
Hamilton, W.F., 116, 132
Hamlen, Susan S., 62
Hammond, K.R., 250, 263
Han, K.S., 74, 109
Hannan, Michael T., 293
Hansen, J.V., 75, 110
Hanushek, A.A., 191, 192, 208
Harrald, J., 154
Harrigan, K.R., 293, 453, 470
Harvey, A., 116, 133
Hashim, S.R., 328, 361
Hax, A.C., 270, 293
Heckman, J.J., 313, 316
Henderson, J.C., 116, 132, 133, 134, 154
Henderson, J.J., 328, 361
Henderson, J.M., 271, 293
Hill, A.V., 366, 369, 394
Hitt, M.A., 269, 293
Hofer, C.W., 269, 270, 293, 294
Hoffenberg, M., 327, 361
Hofstede, G.H., 249, 263
Hofstedt, T.R., 250, 263
Hollenbeck, J.R., 463, 471
Holsapple, C.W., 154
Holstrum, G.L., 258, 263
Howard, R.A., 137, 138, 155
Hsu, Cheng, xvii, 135, 148, 149, 150, 154, 155, 474
Huang, Z.M., 316
Huber, G.P., 117, 119, 122, 133, 474
Huff, A.S., 269, 294
Huysmans, J.H.B.M., 116, 133

Ijiri, Yuji, xv, 3, 25, 56, 109, 473
Ireland, R.D., 269, 293
Isard, W., 327, 361

Ishikawa, A., 62
Itami, H., 119, 123, 133

Jacob, Varghese, 61, 67, 109
Jacobs, D., 269, 294
Jaedicke, R.K., 72, 109
Jaenicke, Henry R., 60
Jagannathan, Raj, xxi, 397, 398, 405, 477
Jensen, M.C., 234, 246
Johns, G., 462, 463, 470
Johnson, Kenneth P., 60
Johnson, P.E., 110
Jondrow, J., 33, 42
Jones, S., 154
Joobbavz, A., 155
Joyce, W.F., 453, 457, 459, 470
Jurs, P.C., 367, 370, 395, 477

Kamis-Gould, E., 177, 180, 189, 475
Kaplan, R.S., 69, 109, 474
Karwan, K., 154
Kassirer, J.P., 76, 109
Kazmier, L., 365, 366, 395
Keen, P.G.W., 116, 133
Keene, S., 365, 366, 367, 381, 382, 393, 395, 477
Keeney, R.L., 423, 436, 437, 438
Kell, Walter G., 61
Kelley, Joseph D., 443, 446, 451
Kemperman, J.H.B., 271, 292
Khandwalla, P.N., 458, 470
Kiang, Yihwa, xvi, 67
Kilman, R.H., 133, 257, 261, 264
Kim, E., 116, 133
Kimes, Sheryl E., xxii, 441, 443, 445, 449, 450, 451
King, W.R., 117, 133
Kinney, W.R., Jr., 68, 74, 109, 258, 264, 474
Kitzmiller, C.T., 140, 155
Kleinbaum, D.G., 127, 133
Klingman, D., 169, 173
Klopp, B., 207
Kmenta, J., 468, 470

Kmetz, J.L., 117, 133
Ko, Chen-en, 62
Konsynski, B., 142, 154
Kotteman, J., 143, 155
Kowalik, J.S., 140, 141, 155, 156
Kozmetsky, G., 291, 294
Kuh, E., 468, 469
Kuhle, James L., 443, 446, 451
Kuipers, Benjamin, xvi, 67, 69, 70, 71, 72, 76, 77, 97, 98, 107, 108, 109, 474
Kupper, L., 127, 133
Kusbiantoro, B., 177, 178, 190

Lageweg, B.J., 407, 419
Lamb, Robert B., 292
Lawler, E.L., 407, 408, 416, 419, 477
Lawrence, E.C., 394, 395
Lawrence, P.R., 453, 456, 459, 470
Leào, L., 155
Lee, J., 116, 133
Leiferm, R., 133
Lenstra, J.K., 407, 419
Leonard-Barton, D., 260, 261, 264
Leontief, W., 327, 361
Leung, J.Y-T., 407, 413, 418
Lev, B., 82, 109
Levinthal, D.A., 259, 264
Levy, Ferdinand K., xviii, xix, 211, 218, 229, 231, 475
Lewin, Arie Y., xix, 249, 254, 257, 258, 261, 264, 476
Lewis, K.A., 166, 173, 175
Libby, R., 250, 261, 264
Lieblich, N., 174
Limb, Seong-Joon, xix, 269
Lindsay, C.M., 195, 208
Liu, J.J., 410, 419
Livingstone, John Leslie, 59
Loebbecke, James K., 60, 68, 109, 258, 263, 476
Lorsch, J.W., 120, 133, 453, 456, 459, 470
Lovegren, V., 173
Lovell, C.A.K., 32, 33, 41, 42

MAC Group, 301, 315, 316
Macaulay, S., 253, 264
Mackenzie, K.D., 257, 264
Maher, Michael W., 61
Mahmood, M.A., 394, 395
Maindiratta, A., 34, 42, 474
Majluf, N.S., 270, 293
Mandelbrot, B., 234, 246, 476
March, J.G., 119, 132, 134, 254, 263, 264
Marcus, R.I., 154, 155
Markowski, C.A., 366, 369, 395
Markowski, E.P., 366, 369, 395
Markus, M.L., 117, 134
Martin, 284
Mason, S.P., 236, 246
Materov, I.S., 33, 42
Math, P.F., 299, 317
Matheson, J.E., 138, 155
Mathur, P.N., 328, 360, 361
Matsuda, Takehiko, xvii, 115
Mautz, Robert K., 61, 62
Mayfield, W.T., 173
McAllister, J.P., 258, 263
McComas, M., 27, 42
McDaniel, R.R., 117, 119, 122, 133, 474
McKelvey, B., 269, 294
Meckling, W., 234, 246
Mensch, G., 172
Merten, Alan G., 61
Merton, R.C., 236, 246
Meservy, Rayman D., 62, 76, 108, 110
Messier, W.R., Jr., 75, 110
Midlin, S., 269, 294
Miller, D., 288, 294
Miller, H.D., 404, 405
Miller, J.P., 462, 470
Miller, L., 154
Miller, M., 233, 234, 237, 246
Ministry of International Trade and Industry, Japan, 327, 361
Minton, J.W., 254, 257, 258, 261, 264, 476

Mitchell, T.R., 291, 293
Modigliani, F., 233, 237, 246
Monden, Y., 474
Monteverde, K., 259, 264
Montgomery, C.A., 269, 270, 292, 295
Mooney, J.D., 118, 134
Morgenstern, O., 423, 438
Morrow, P.C., 458, 470
Moses, L.N., 327, 328, 361
Mosteller, Frederick, 444, 451
Mowday, R.T., 470
Myers, S.C., 234, 247

Nadler, D.A., 116, 134, 257, 264
Namiki, T., 125, 134
Narain, D., 328, 361
Näslund, Bertil, , xix, 233
Nelson, A., 166, 173
Nelson, R., 259, 264
Neter, J., 62
Niehaus, Richard J., xvii, 159, 160, 164, 166, 167, 169, 170, 171, 172, 173, 174, 175, 176, 475
Nielsen, Oswald, 109
Nightengale, J., 294
Nitterhouse, D., 167, 175
Nogus, J., 155, 474

Oosterhaven, J., 327, 361
Oota, Toshizumi, xvii, 115
Owen, D.T., 138, 155

Padalino, D., 174
Paine Webber, Inc., 301, 317
Palmer, M., 395
Pari, Robert, 441, 451
Parson, Talcott, 134
Pashigian, 195
Pennings, J.M., 254, 263, 264
Peters, Stephen C., 443, 444, 451
Peters, W.S., 463, 470
Pettigrew, A.M., 119, 134
Pfeffer, Jeffrey, 254, 264, 269, 291, 294

Pietronero, L., 247
Piper, T.R., 237, 247
Plotkin, I.H., 269, 270, 292
Polenske, K.R., 327, 361, 477
Pondy, L.R., 133
Poole, M.S., 260, 265
Porter, M.E., 269, 294, 453, 471
Posner, M.E., 410, 419
Potts, C.W., 407, 408, 412, 416, 419, 477
Price, K.F., 170, 172, 175, 176, 475
Price Waterhouse & Co., 60
Pruitt, D.G., 423, 438
Pugel, T., 283, 292

Quandt, R.E., 271, 293
Quinlan, J.R., 70, 110

Råde, L., 246, 247
Radnor, N.M., 132
Raiffa, H., 423, 436, 437, 438, 477
Randolph, W.A., 458, 463, 465, 469
Rao, M.R., xx, 327, 328, 341, 360, 476
Rapp, John, 63
Rattner, L., 155, 474
Ravenscraft, D., 284, 294
Reckers, Philip M.J., 61
Reilly, Raymond R., 61
Reilly, F.K., 269, 270, 294
Remus, W.E., 143, 155
Rhodes, E., 34, 42, 177, 189, 193, 196, 198, 207, 208, 302, 316, 365, 394, 474, 475
Ringles, M., 177, 178, 189
Rinnooy Kan, A.H.G., 407, 419
Robey, D., 116, 134
Ross, S.A., 234, 247
Ross, S.M., 401, 405
Rothbard, A.B., 177, 180, 189, 475
Rothlisberger, F.J., 56
Ruefli, Timothy W., xix, 269, 270, 272, 273, 291, 292, 294, 295, 476
Rumelt, R.P., 269, 295

Sakurai, M., 474
Salamon, G.L., 68, 74, 109
Salancik, G.R., 254, 264, 269, 294
Santos, M.C., 198, 207
Sardesai, D.B., 328, 361
Saunders, G.K., 116, 134
Saxton, M.J., 257, 261, 263
Schachter, R.D., 138, 155
Schendel, D., 270, 288, 293, 294
Schiff, M., 249, 264
Schilling, D.A., 116, 133
Schinnar, Arie P., xviii, 174, 177, 178, 180, 189, 190, 475
Schmalensee, R., 295
Schmidt, P.J., 32, 33, 41, 42
Schmitz, E., 207
Schnlan, T.J., 134
Schonberger, R.J., 116, 134
Schoonhoven, C.B., 453, 457, 458, 463, 464, 465, 471
Schrage, L.E., 407, 418, 419
Schultz, R.L., 116, 134
Scott-Morton, M.S., 116, 133
Seiford, Lawrence M., xviii, 191, 194, 207, 475
Severance, Dennis G., 61
Shapira, Z., 264
Shapiro, A.C., 236, 247
Sharkey, F.J., 166, 172
Sharma, S., 463, 471
Shepard, W.G., 269, 284, 295
Sheridan, J.A., 167, 172
Sholtz, D., 169, 174, 175, 176
Simon, H.A., 119, 134, 138, 155, 250, 264, 265, 423, 438
Sims, D., 154
Sisk, D., 196, 208
Skillman, T.L., 155
Slevin, D.P., 116, 133, 134
Slocum, J.W., 453, 457, 459, 460, 461, 465, 470, 471
Smith, G.F., 137, 155
Solla, S.A., 234, 247
Southwick, L., 196, 198, 208
Southwood, K.E., 468, 471

Spurr, W., 365, 395
Srinivasan, V., 407, 419
State of California, Department of
    Finance, 197, 207
Stedry, A., 175
Steers, R.N., 470
Steinbart, P.J., 68, 109
Steinberg, Richard M., 59
Stephens, Ray G., xvi, 43, 62
Stern, J.M., 247, 476
Steuer, R.E., 423, 438
Stone, E.F., 463, 471
Stringer, K.W., 258, 265
Strout, A.S., 327, 361
Stutz, J., 194, 207, 475
Subrahmanyam, M.G., 246
Sueyoshi, Toshiyuki, xvii, 115, 313,
    315, 316
Sun, D.B., 316
Swarts, J., 315
Symonds, G.H., 397, 405
Szilagyi, A.D., 120, 134
Szwarc, Wlodzimierz, xxi, 407, 408,
    410, 411, 419

Talukdar, S.N., 140, 155
Tamura, Hirokuni, 443, 445, 446,
    451
Tansik, D.A., 132
Taylor, Martin E., 61
Teece, D., 259, 264, 295
Thomas, D., 207, 315
Thomas, H., 269, 270, 293
Thompson, Gerald L., xviii, xix, 167,
    169, 175, 176, 211, 227, 231,
    398, 405, 476
Tibshirani, R., 448, 450
Titman, S., 236, 240, 247
Tosi, H., 453, 471
Tossatti, E., 247
Tou, J.T., 365, 395
Touche Ross & Co. (Deloitte &
    Touche), 60
Trice, H.M., 260, 262
Tukey, John W., 442, 444, 451

Tushman, M.L., 116, 134, 257, 264,
    458, 471

U.S. Department of Defense, 301,
    316, 318
U.S. Department of Education, 208
U.S. Office of Management and
    Budget, 274, 295
Ullman, J., 133
Uretsky, M., 116, 133
Urwich, L., 118, 134
Ury, W., 437

Van de Ven, A.H., 260, 265, 453,
    454, 455, 460, 461, 462, 465,
    470, 471, 478
Van Horne, J.C., 306, 317
Van Wassenhove, L.N., 407, 408, 412,
    416, 419, 477
Veall, Michael R., 443, 446, 451, 477
Venkatramaiah, P., 361
Venkatraman, N., 453, 471
Venning, R., 328, 360
Victor, B., 265
Von Glinow, M., 453, 457, 459, 470
von Neumann, J., 423, 438
von Rabenau, B., 154
Vroom, V.H., 120, 134

Waelchi, F., 315, 317
Wallace, M.J., 120, 134
Wallace, Wanda A., 60, 68, 69, 74,
    110
Wallace, William A., xvii, 135, 154,
    474
Walters, L.C., 177, 178, 190
Watanabe, S., 365, 395
Weber, C.K., 166, 172
Weber, M., 118, 134
Weber, R., 61
Weinhold, W.A., 237, 247
Weiss, W.L., 265
Welsch, R.E., 468, 469
Werbel, J., 453, 458, 460, 461, 462,
    465, 470

Wernerfelt, B., 269, 270, 295
Wessels, R., 240, 247
Westergren, B., 246, 247
Weston, J.F., 234, 247
Wets, R.J.B., 398, 405
Whinston, Andrew B., xvi, 62, 67, 108, 154
White, Bernard J., 61
Willemain, T., 138, 156
Williams, Michael A., 443, 446, 447, 448, 451
Williamson, O.E., 259, 265
Willingham, J.J., 253, 261, 264
Wilson, C.L., 270, 272, 273, 295, 476
Winter, S., 259, 264
Wittink, D.R., 292

Wolfe, M., 173
Wood, L., 177, 178, 190

Yee, L., 155, 474
Yetton, P.W., 120, 134
Yin, R.K., 260, 265
Yu, P.L., 423, 438
Yu, S., 62
Yue, P., 291, 294

Zedeck, S., 463, 471
Zeithaml, C.P., 453, 469
Zeleny, M., 423, 438, 477
Zeuthen, F., 423, 439
Zionts, Stanley, xxi, 423
Zuber, George R., 60

Subject Index

accounting, productivity, *see* productivity accounting

accounting, triple-entry, *see* triple-entry accounting

additive models of DEA, 194

aerospace defense firms versus S&P or Dow Jones industrials firms, 307

aerospace defense industry financial positions, not adversely impacted, 313

alternating hierarchy method in discriminant analysis, 391

analytical review procedures in auditing, 68

auditing and organization design, 251

auditing and qualitative simulation, xvi, 67-113, 474

  analytical review procedures, 68

  cash-flow management system, 80

  cash-flow model, 101

  causal models, 69

  expert systems, 74

  limit analysis, 94

  model-based reasoning, 69

  propagating through the cash-flow model, 92

  qualitative and causal reasoning in auditing, 98

  qualitative model, 72

  qualitative simulation program (QSIM), 77

  qualitative simulation, 69, 97

  quantitative versus qualitative reasoning, 71

  rule-based versus model-based reasoning, 70

audit risk model and organization design, xix, 249-265, 476

audit risk model, 253

audit risk, research strategies and methods, 259

audit structures, efficiency and
    effectiveness, 258
auditing and organization design,
    251
behavioral aspects of accounting,
    250
control risk and inherent risk, 252
Heinz USA case, 249
inherent risk and control risk, 252
organization design and auditing,
    251

back to the future in human resource
    management, 171
balance sheet in momentum
    accounting, 23
bankruptcy transmission in corporate
    capital structure, 238
BCC (Banker, Charnes, and Cooper)
    ratio form of DEA, 193
behavioral aspects of accounting, 250
beta normalization, 370, 374
billing ratios of a law firm, 215
bootstrapping and decision making
    implications, xxii, 441-451, 477
    bootstrap applications, 443
    bootstrapping procedure, 442
    bootstrapping, 441, 442, 443
    cost and time requirements, 448
    Monte Carlo simulation, 441
    small sample size, 447
    true error estimates, 444
    true probability distribution, 445

Cantor sets in fractal analysis, 234
capital structure and fractal analysis,
    234, see also corporate capital
    structure and fractal analysis
cardinal data, 270
cardinality-oriented representation
    (OER), 146
cash-flow management system, 80
cash-flow model, 101
causal models in auditing, 69

causal relationship in accounting
    records, 7
CCR (Charnes, Cooper, and Rhodes)
    ratio form of DEA, 193
chance constrained programming
    and stochastic processes, xxi,
    397-406, 477
    deterministic equivalent of, 399
    zero-order rules, 398
change sheet versus balance sheet, 23
Commission on Fraudulent Financial
    Reporting, 45
complementarity between efficiency
    and effectiveness, 188
contingency conceptualizations,
    alternative, 455
contingency fee decision, 218, see
    also law firm sizes and
    contingency fee decision
contingency theory testing and
    methodological issues, xxii, 453-
    471, 478
    alternative contingency
      conceptualizations, 455
    isomorphic contingency
      relationship, 456
    multiplicative interaction approach,
      463, 464
    non-isomorphic contingency
      relationship, 457
    residual misfit approach, 460
    split-sample approach, 458
    testing bivariate contingency
      theories, 454
control indices for production
    processes, 126
control risk and inherent risk in an
    organization, 252
control, defined, 44
corporate capital structure and fractal
    analysis, xix, 233-247, 476
    bankruptcy transmission, 238
    Cantor sets, 234
    capital structure, 234

critical probability of bankruptcy, 239, 240
debt ratio, 240
fractal geometry, 233, 234
grouping of projects, 235
hierarchical model, 235
Modigliani-Miller (MM) theory, 233
optimal debt ratio, 233, 242
organizational form, 244
Weibul distribution, 236
correlation measures of efficiency and effectiveness, three prior studies, 178
cost and time requirements in bootstrapping applications, 448
critical probability of bankruptcy in hierarchical capital structure, 239, 240

data envelopment analysis (DEA), 34, 299, 302, *see also* defense industry competitiveness; productivity accounting; university operations efficiency
DEA models: CCR ratio, BCC ratio, multiplicative, and additive, 192
DEA, 34, see also data envelopment analysis
debt ratio in corporate capital structure, 240
decision support systems (DSSs), 115, *see also* Japanese production control and decision support systems
decision variable space, 425
defense industries versus Dow Jones industrials financial competitiveness measures, 323
defence industries versus S&P financial competitiveness measures, 320
defense industry competitiveness, xx, 299-325, 476

aerospace defense firms and Dow Jones industrials, 307
aerospace defense firms and S&P 500 firms, 307
aerospace defense industry financial positions, not adversely impacted, 313
data envelopment analysis (DEA), 299, 302
defence industries vs. S&P financial competitiveness measures, 320
defense industries versus Dow Jones industrials financial competitiveness measures, 323
output and input variables, 305
procurement policy changes: a summary, 317
procurement policy revisions, 300
variables, 304
defense industry competitiveness analysis, key variables, 304
discriminant analysis and linear/integer programming models, xx, 365-395, 477
alternating hierarchy method, 391
beta normalization, 370, 374
discriminant analysis, 365
dual model formulation, 378
epsilon version of the model, 375
goal programming model, 368
hybrid LP discriminant model, 367
integer programming (IP) discriminant model, 370
linear programming (LP) discriminant analysis, 365, 366
LP and IP discrimination models, their links, 384
min sum LP model, 384
new normalization, 374
normalization issues, 369
normalizations in linear programming, 366
postoptimizing heuristics, 389
stability theorem, 382
successive goal method, 390, 391

domestic trade of each region in the Indian economy, 336
double-entry bookkeeping, 3
double-entry data in accounting, 7
DSS, 115, *see also* decision support systems
DSS implementation in Japanese manufacturing firms, 125
dual model formulation in the LP-model for discriminant analysis, 378

edgeworth box in negotiation, 433, 434
education system and Japanese production control, 122
effectiveness as outcomes divided by service activities, 179
effectiveness of internal controls, 53
efficiency, 28
efficiency as service activities divided by resources, 179
efficiency frontier in DEA, 37
elasticity and variance in the tradeoffs between efficiency and effectiveness, 189
entropy of ordinal statistics, 273
epsilon version of the discriminant model, 375
evaluation system and Japanese production control, 122
event flow approach in integrated human resource management systems, 161, 162
expert systems in auditing, 74
explanandum in accounting records, 7
explanans in accounting records, 7
explanations in accounting records, 7
Exxon Valdez oil spill, influence diagram, 139

factor analysis and Japanese production control, 127, 128

Foreign Corrupt Practices Act (FCPA), 44
fractal geometry and corporate capital structure, 233, 234, *see also* corporate capital structure and fractal analysis

global information resources dictionary (GIRD), 145, 149
goal programming approach in integrated human resource management systems, 161, 163
goal programming model, 368
goal-setting system and Japanese production control, 121
grouping of projects in corporate capital structure, 235
growth rate of domestic trade in India, 337

Heinz USA case and audit risk model, 249
hierarchical model of corporate capital structure, 235
human resource modeling and technology trends, 169
human resource planning, 159
human resource planning, triple-track approach, 165
human resource management, xvii, 159-176, 475
  back to the future, 171
  event flow approach in integrated systems, 161, 162
  goal programming approach in integrated systems, 161, 163
  human resource modeling and technology trends, 169
  human resource planning process, triple-track approach, 165
  human resource planning, 159
  human resources, 159
  integrated modeling systems, 164
  manpower modeling, 159

modeling during policy analysis, 161

modeling of corporate information systems, 168

hybrid LP discriminant model, 367

IHLs (institutions of higher learning), 191

impulses and momenta in accounting records, 17

incentive system and Japanese production control, 122

income momenta in triple-entry accounting, 17

income-action statement, 15

income-variance analysis, 10

Indian economy and multiregional optimizing models, xx, 327-361, 476

  analysis of results, 340

  domestic trade of each region, 336

  growth rate of domestic trade of the country, 337

  macro-economic balances, 347

  multiregional and multisectoral optimizing model for the Indian economy, 329

  multiregional optimizing model (MROM), 328, 329

  sectoral gross output for each region, 350

  sectoral per capital consumption, 351

industry longitudinal data and ordinal time series analysis, xix, 269-298, 476

  cardinal data, 270

  entropy, 273

  inter- versus intraindustry effects, 290

  interindustry ordinal behavior, 275

  intraindustry ordinal behavior, 283

  ordinal data, 270

  ordinal production functions, 271

  ordinal time series analysis, 270

R&D expenditures as the most stable dimension, 281

rank positions of industrial firms, 275

relative uncertainty, 273

risk transition, 272

SIC code, 282

total uncertainty, 273

influence diagram and model representation, 138, 139

information resources dictionary system (IRDS), 143

information resources management, xvii, 135-156, 474

  cardinality-oriented representation (OER), 146

  Exxon Valdez oil spill, 139

  global information resources dictionary (GIRD), 145, 149

  influence diagram, 138, 139

  information resources dictionary system (IRDS), 143

  information resources management, 136

  metadata representation, 145

  metadata, 144

  metadatabase, 144

  model bases, 142

  model resources management, 142

  modeling methodology, 146

  modeling processes, 136, 137

  semantics-oriented representation (SER), 146

  two-stage entity-relationship (TSER) model, 146

information system in Japanese production control, 119

information systems and control indices in Japanese production control, 129

inherent risk and control risk in audit risk model, 252

institutions of higher learning (IHLs), 191

institutions of higher learning: their
    policies, 205
integer programming (IP)
    discriminant model, 370
integrated modeling systems for
    human resource management,
    examples, 164
inter- versus intraindustry effects in
    ordinal time series data, 290
interindustry ordinal behavior, 275
internal accounting control, xvi, 43-
    64, 474
    Commission on Fraudulent
        Financial Reporting, 45
    control, 44
    effectiveness of internal controls,
        53
    Foreign Corrupt Practices Act
        (FCPA), 44
    internal accounting control, 44, 46,
        51, 53
    risk aggregation, 55
    statement by management on
        internal accounting control
        (SMIAC), 45
    Treadway Commission, 45
internal accounting control, empirical
    research on assessing, 46
internal accounting control,
    evaluation, 51
internal accounting control, guidance
    on assessing, 46, 53
intraindustry ordinal behavior, 283
isomorphic contingency relationship,
    456

Japanese production control and
    decision support systems, xvii,
    115-134, 474
    control indices, 126
    decision support systems (DSSs),
        115
    DSS implementation in Japanese
        manufacturing firms, 125
    education system, 122

evaluation system, 122
factor analysis, 127, 128
goal-setting system, 121
incentive system, 122
information system, 119
information systems and control
    indices, 129
management control systems
    (MCSs), 118
measurement system, 121
responsibily system, 120
standard-setting system, 122

law firm sizes and contingent fee
    decision, xviii, 211-231, 475
    billing ratios, 215
    contingency fee decision, 218
    expected lawyer-hour demand
        profile, 229
    expected profit of law firms, 213
    expected profits, 216
    expected returns from litigation,
        219
    expected returns from taking cases
        on contingency fee basis, 222,
        224
    load profile, 228
    models of law firm sizes, 213
    plaintiff's expected gains and
        maximum costs from litigation,
        220
    size of law firms, 212
    total cumulative lawyer-hour
        demand profile, 230
law firm's expected profit, 213
law firm's expected profits, optimal
    hires, and cost of uncertainty, 216
law firm's expected returns from
    taking cases on contingency fee
    basis, 222, 224
lawyer-hour demand profile, 229
limit analysis in qualitative
    simulation, 94
linear programming (LP)
    discriminant analysis, 365, 366,

see also discriminant analysis and linear/integer programming models

litigation's expected returns, 219

load profile of a law firm, 228

LP and IP discriminant models, their links, 384

macro-economic balances of the Indian economy, 347

management control systems (MCSs) and Japanese production control, 118

manpower modeling, 159

maximum likelihood problem in DEA, 34

means-ends analysis for accounting records, 14

measurement issues in DEA for university operations, 197

measurement system and Japanese production control, 121

metadata in information recource management, 144

metadata representation in the GIRD model, 145

metadatabase for information recource management, 144

min sum LP model in discriminant analysis, 384

model bases and information resource management, 142

model resources management, 142

model-based reasoning in auditing, 69

modeling and model representation, 136

modeling during policy analysis, 161

modeling methodology, 146

modeling of corporate information systems, 168

modeling processes, 137

models of law firm sizes, 213

Modigliani-Miller (MM) theory, 233

momenta in accounting statements, 17

momentum accounting, 17

momentum-impulse statement, 18, 19, 21

Monte Carlo simulation in bootstrapping, 441

multiple criteria decision making (MCDM), 423, *see also* negotiating and multiple criteria decision making

multiple criteria decision making (MCDM), some geometrical considerations, 424

multiplicative interaction approach in contingency theory, 463, 464

multiplicative models of DEA, 194

multiregional and multisectoral optimizing model for the Indian economy, 329

multiregional models for the Indian economy, 328

multiregional optimizing, analysis of results, 340

multiregional optimizing, models for the Indian economy, 328, 329, *see also* Indian economy and multiregional optimizing models

negotiating and multiple criteria decision making, xxi, 423-439, 477

decision variable space, 425

edgeworth box, 433, 434

multiple criteria decision making (MCDM), 423

multiple criteria decision making (MCDM), some geometrical considerations, 424

negotiating, 423

negotiating, some geometrical considerations, 429

objective function space, 426

Pareto-optimal solutions in practice, 436

Pareto-optimal solutions in theory, 435
party space, 429
party weight space, 431
unstructured negotiation, 431
weight space, 428
negotiating, some geometrical considerations, 429
Newton's first law of motion and its accounting interpretation, 20
non-isomorphic contingency relationship, 457
normalization in linear programming, 366
normalization issues, 369
normalization, new approaches, 374

objective function space and negotiating, 426
optimal debt ratio and corporate capital structure, 233, 242
ordering: adjacent and nonadjacent, 408
ordinal and industry longitudinal data, 270
ordinal production functions, 271
ordinal time series analysis, 270, *see also* industry longitudinal data and ordinal time series analysis
organization design and audit risk model, 251, *see also* audit risk model and organization design
organizational form and corporate capital structure, 244
output and input variables in defense industry competitiveness analysis, 305

Pareto-optimal solutions for negotiating, practice, 436
Pareto-optimal solutions for negotiating, theory, 435
party space in negotiating, 429
party weight space in negotiating, 431

plaintiff's expected gains and maximum costs from litigation, 220
postoptimizing heuristics for discriminant analysis, 389
private versus public universities, efficiency and effectiveness, 205
procurement policy by the Department of Defense: a summary of changes, 317
procurement policy by the Department of Defense, revisions, 300
production frontier and productivity, 29
productivity management, 189
productivity, 28
productivity accounting, xvi, 27-42, 474
data envelopment analysis (DEA), 34
DEA, 34
efficiency frontier, 37
efficiency, 28
maximum likelihood problem, 34
production frontier, 29
productivity, 28
stochastic DEA, 34
sustained productivity gains, 27, 36
transitory efficiency fluctuations, 27
variances, 30
propagation through the cash-flow model in qualitative simulation, 92
public service management, 178
public versus private universities, efficiency and effectiveness, 205
public service management, xviii, 177-190, 475
complementarity, 188
correlation measures of efficiency and effectiveness, three prior studies, 178

effectiveness as outcomes divided by service activities, 179

efficiency as service activities divided by resources, 179

elasticity and variance, 189

productivity management, 189

public management, 178

relationship between effectiveness and efficiency, 188

relationship between service amount and probability of attaining service goals, 187

tradeoffs between efficiency and effectiveness, a simple model, 185

tradeoffs, 188

qualitative and causal reasoning in auditing, 98

qualitative models in auditing, 72

qualitative simulation program (QSIM), 77

qualitative simulation, 69, and auditing, *see* auditing and qualitative simulation

qualitative simulation, using the results of, 97

quantitative versus qualitative reasoning, 71

R&D expenditures as the most stable dimension in industry longitudinal data, 281

rank positions of industrial firms, 275

relationship between effectiveness and efficiency, 188

relationship between service amount and probability of attaining service goals, 187

relative efficiences between public and private IHLs, 195

relative uncertainty in industry longitudinal data, 273

residual misfit approach in contingency theory, 460

responsibily system and Japanese production control, 120

risk aggregation in internal accounting control, 55

risk transition in industry longitudinal data, 272

rule-based versus model-based reasoning in auditing, 70

sectoral gross output for each region in the Indian economy, 350

sectoral per capita consumption in the Indial economy, 351

semantics-oriented representation (SER), 146

sensitivity to DEA model selection, 205

SIC code in industry longitudinal data, 282

single machine total tardiness model, xxi, 407-419, 477

adjacent and nonadjacent orderings, 408

single machine total tardiness model, 407

three block decomposition, 415

single-entry data in accounting, 5

size of law firms, 212

small sample size and bootstrapping, 447

split-sample approach and bootstrapping, 458

stability theorem in discriminant analysis, 382

standard-setting system and Japanese production control, 122

statement by management on internal accounting control (SMIAC), 45

stochastic DEA, 34

successive goal method in discriminant analysis, 390, 391

sustained productivity gains, 27, 36

tardiness model, *see* single-machine total tardiness model

testing bivariate contingency theories, 454

three block decomposition in single machine total tardiness problem, 415

total cumulative lawyer-hour demand profile, 230

total uncertainty in industry longitudinal data, 273

tradeoffs between efficiency and effectiveness, 188

tradeoffs between efficiency and effectiveness, a simple model, 185

transitory efficiency fluctuations in productivity accounting, 27

Treadway Commission, *see* Commission on Fraudulent Financial Reporting

triple-entry accounting, xv, 3-25, 473
  balance sheet, 23
  causal relationship, 7
  change sheet, 23
  double-entry bookkeeping, 3, 7
  explanandum-explanans, 7
  explanations, 7
  impulses, 17
  income momenta, 17
  income-action statement, 15
  income-variance analysis, 10
  means-ends analysis, 14
  momentum accounting, 17
  momentum-impulse statement, 18, 19, 21
  Newton's first law of motion, 20
  single-entry data, 5
  triple-entry bookkeeping, 3
  variance analysis, 14
  wealth-income statement, 5, 6

true error estimates in bootstrapping, 444

true probability distribution in bootstrapping, 445

two-stage entity-relationship (TSER) model and information resources management, 146

unstructured negotiation and multiple criteria decision making, 431

university operations efficiency, xviii, 191-208, 475
  additive models, 194
  BCC (Banker, Charnes, and Cooper) model, 193
  CCR (Charnes, Cooper, and Rhodes) model, 193
  DEA models, CCR ratio, 192
  findings and their use in setting IHL policy, 205
  institutions of higher learning (IHLs), 191
  measurement issues, 197
  multiplicative models, 194
  private universities, 205
  public universities, 205
  relative efficiences between public and private IHLs, 195
  sensitivity to DEA model selection, 205
  variable selections, 197

variable selections in DEA for university operations, 197

variances in productivity accounting, 30

variances in triple-entry bookkeeping, 14

wealth-income statement, 5, 6

Weibul distribution and corporate capital structure, 236

weight space in negotiating, 428

About the
Editor and Contributors

ANA R. ADANIYA is Professor, Escuela de Administracion de Negocios para Graduados (ESAN), Lima, Peru.

TAESIK AHN is Assistant Professor of Accounting, College of Business Administration, Ajou University, Suwon, Korea.

ANDREW D. BAILEY, JR., is Professor of Accounting, Department of Accounting, College of Business and Public Administration, The University of Arizona.

RAJIV D. BANKER is Arthur Andersen Professor of Accounting and Information Systems, Carlson School of Management, University of Minnesota.

WILLIAM F. BOWLIN was Lieutenant Colonel, USAF and Assistant for Business Management, Office of the Deputy Assistant Secretary of the Air Force (Cost and Economics), and, upon retirement from the Air Force joined the faculty of the Department of Accounting and Law, the School of Management, Clarkson University.

RANAJIT DHAR is Professor of Economics and Planning, Indian Institute of Management, Bangalore, India.

J. ARMANDO GALLEGOS is Professor, Escuela de Administracion de Negocios para Graduados (ESAN), Lima, Peru.

FRED GLOVER is US West Chair in Systems Science, Center for Applied Artificial Intelligence, Graduate School of Business, The University of Colorado, Boulder.

SANJAY GOEL is Reader in Policy Analysis and Quantitative Methods, Lal Bahadur Shastri National Academy of Administration, Mussorie, India.

VIJAY GOVINDARAJAN is Professor of Strategy and Control, Amos Tuck School of Business Administration, Dartmouth College.

ANIL K. GUPTA is Associate Professor of Business Administration, College of Business and Management, The University of Maryland at College Park.

CHENG HSU is Associate Professor of Decision Sciences and Engineering Systems, School of Management, Engineering and Science, Rensselaer Polytechnic Institute.

YUJI IJIRI (also Editor) is Robert M. Trueblood University Professor of Accounting and Economics, Graduate School of Industrial Administration, Carnegie Mellon University.

RAJ JAGANNATHAN is Professor of Operations Research, Department of Management Science, School of Business Administration, The University of Iowa.

YIHWA KIANG is Assistant Professor, Department of Decision and Information Systems, College of Business Administration, Arizona State University.

SHERYL E. KIMES is Assistant Professor, School of Hotel Administration, Cornell University.

BENJAMIN KUIPERS is Associate Professor of Computer Science, Department of Computer Science, School of Natural Sciences, The University of Texas at Austin.

FERDINAND K. LEVY is Professor of Economics, School of Management, Georgia Institute of Technology and Dean, City Polytechnic of Hong Kong, Hong Kong.

ARIE Y. LEWIN is Professor of Management and Organizational Behavior, Fuqua School of Business, Duke University.

SEONG-JOON LIMB is in the Department of Management, Graduate School of Business, The University of Texas at Austin.

TAKEHIKO MATSUDA is President, Sanno University, Kanagawa, Japan.

BERTIL NÄSLUND is Professor of Business Administration, Stockholm School of Economics, Stockholm, Sweden.

RICHARD J. NIEHAUS is Assistant for Human Resources Analyses, Office of Chief of Naval Operations, Department of Navy.

TOSHIZUMI OOTA is Associate Professor of Organization, Toyohashi Science and Technology University, Toyohashi, Japan.

M. R. RAO is Professor of Operations Research, Graduate School of Business Administration, New York University and Visiting Professor, Indian Institute of Management, Bangalore, India.

TIMOTHY W. RUEFLI is Director, Information Systems Management Program and Daniel B. Stuart Centennial Professor, Graduate School of Business and Frank C. Erwin, Jr. Centennial Research Fellow, IC^2 Institute, The University of Texas at Austin.

ARIE P. SCHINNAR is Director of Policy Modeling Workshop and Associate Professor of Public Policy and Management, The Wharton School, University of Pennsylvania.

LAWRENCE M. SEIFORD is Professor of Industrial Engineering and Operations Research, College of Engineering, University of Massachusetts at Amherst.

RAY G. STEPHENS is Professor of Accounting, College of Business, The Ohio State University.

TOSHIYUKI SUEYOSHI is Associate Professor of Public Policy and Management, College of Business, The Ohio State University.

WLODZIMIERZ SZWARC is Professor of Operations Research, School of Business Administration, University of Wisconsin-Milwaukee.

GERALD L. THOMPSON is IBM Professor of Systems and Operations Research, Graduate School of Industrial Administration, Carnegie Mellon University.

WILLIAM A. WALLACE is Professor of Decision Sciences and Engineering Systems, School of Management, Engineering and Science, Rensselaer Polytechnic Institute.

ANDREW B. WHINSTON is Professor of Information Systems, Computer Science and Economics, Department of Management Science and Information Systems, College of Business, The University of Texas at Austin.

STANLEY ZIONTS is Alumni Professor of Decision Support Systems and Chairman, Department of Management Science and Systems, School of Management, State University of New York at Buffalo.